SPECIAL BIOGRAPHICAL EDITION

THE WORKS OF

WILLIAM MAKEPEACE THACKERAY

WITH BIOGRAPHICAL INTRODUCTIONS BY
HIS DAUGHTER, ANNE RITCHIE

IN TWENTY-SIX VOLUMES

VOLUME VI.

THE MEMOIRS OF
MR. CHARLES J. YELLOWPLUSH
A LEGEND OF THE RHINE, ETC.

JANUARY—THE BIRTH OF THE YEAR.

Special Biographical Edition

THE MEMOIRS OF
MR. CHARLES J. YELLOWPLUSH

A LEGEND OF THE RHINE, Etc.

BY

WILLIAM MAKEPEACE THACKERAY

WITH ILLUSTRATIONS BY GEORGE CRUIKSHANK

Vol. II.

HARPER & BROTHERS PUBLISHERS

NEW YORK AND LONDON

1903

CONTENTS

THE MEMOIRS OF MR. C. J. YELLOWPLUSH

THE DIARY OF C. JEAMES DE LA PLUCHE, ESQ., WITH HIS LETTERS

A LEGEND OF THE RHINE

CONTENTS

LIST OF ILLUSTRATIONS

CHAPTER VII

THE CONSQUINSIES

THE Shevalliay did not die, for the ball came out of its own accord, in the midst of a violent fever and inflamayshn which was brot on by the wound. He was kept in bed for 6 weeks though, and did not recover for a long time after.

As for master, his lot, I'm sorry to say, was wuss than that of his advisary. Inflammation came on too ; and, to make an ugly story short, they were obliged to take off his hand at the rist.

He bore it, in cors, like a Trojin, and in a month he too was well, and his wound heel'd ; but I never see a man look so like a devvle as he used sometimes, when he looked down at the stump !

To be sure, in Miss Griffinses eyes, this only indeerd him the mor. She sent twenty noats a day to ask for him, calling him her beloved, her unfortunat, her hero, her wictim, and I dono what. I've kep some of the noats as I tell you, and curiously sentimentle they are, beating the sorrows of MacWhirter all to nothing.

Old Crabs used to come offen, and consumed a power of wine and seagars at our house. I bleave he was at Paris because there was an exycution in his own house in England ; and his son was a sure find (as they say) during his illness, and couldn't deny himself to the old genlmn. His eveninx my Lord spent reglar at Lady Griffin's ; where, as master was ill, I didn't go any more now, and where the Shevalier wasn't there to disturb him.

"You see how that woman hates you, Deuceace," says my Lord, one day, in a fit of cander, after they had been talking about Lady Griffin : "*she has not done with you yet*, I tell you fairly."

"Curse her," says master, in a fury, lifting up his maim'd arm— "curse her ! but I will be even with her one day. I am sure of Mati'da : I took care to put that beyond the reach of a failure. The girl must marry me, for her own sake."

"*For her own sake !* O ho ! Good, good !" My Lord lifted his i's, and said gravely, "I understand, my dear boy : it is an excellent plan."

"Well," says master, grinning fearcely and knowingly at his

exlent old father, "as the girl is safe, what harm can I fear from
the fiend of a stepmother ? "

My Lord only gev a long whizzle, and, soon after, taking up his
hat, walked off. I saw him sawnter down the Plas Vandome, and
go in quite calmly to the old door of Lady Griffinses hotel. Bless
his old face! such a puffickly good-natured, kind-hearted, merry,
selfish old scoundrel, I never shall see again.

His Lordship was quite right in saying to master that "Lady
Griffin hadn't done with him." No moar she had. But she never
would have thought of the nex game she was going to play, *if somebody hadn't put her up to it.* Who did? If you red the above
passidge, and saw how a venrabble old genlmn took his hat, and
sauntered down the Plas Vandome (looking hard and kind at all
the nussary-maids—*buns* they call them in France—in the way), I
leave you to guess who was the author of the nex scheam : a woman,
suttnly, never would have pitcht on it.

In the fuss payper which I wrote concerning Mr. Deuceace's ad-
venters, and his kind behayviour to Messrs. Dawkins and Blewitt,
I had the honour of laying before the public a skidewl of my master's
detts, in witch was the following itim—

"Bills of xchange and I.O.U.'s, £4963, 0s. 0d."

The I.O.U.se were trifling, saying a thowsnd pound. The bills
amountid to four thowsnd moar.

Now, the lor is in France, that if a genlmn gives these in
England, and a French genlmn gits them in any way, he can pursew
the Englishman who has drawn them, even though he should be in
France. Master did not know this fact—labouring under a very
common mistak, that, when onst out of England, he might wissle at
all the debts he left behind him.

My Lady Griffin sent over to her slissators in London, who
made arrangemints with the persons who possest the fine collection
of ortografs on stampt paper which master had left behind him;
and they were glad enuff to take any oppertunity of getting back
their money.

One fine morning, as I was looking about in the courtyard of
our hotel, talking to the servant-gals, as was my reglar custom, in
order to improve myself in the French languidge, one of them comes
up to me and says, " Tenez, Monsieur Charles, down below in the
office there is a bailiff, with a couple of gendarmes, who is asking
for your master—a-t-il des dettes par hasard ? "

I was struck all of a heap—the truth flasht on my mind's hi.
"Toinette," says I, for that was the gal's name—"Toinette," says

I, giving her a kiss, "keep them for two minnits, as you valyou my
affeckshun;" and then I gave her another kiss, and ran up stares to
our chambers. Master had now pretty well recovered of his wound,
and was aloud to drive abowt: it was lucky for him that he had
the strength to move. "Sir, sir," says I, "the bailiffs are after
you, and you must run for your life."

"Bailiffs?" says he: "nonsense! I don't, thank Heaven, owe
a shilling to any man."

"Stuff, sir," says I, forgetting my respeck; "don't you owe
money in England? I tell you the bailiffs are here, and will be on
you in a moment."

As I spoke, cling cling, ling ling, goes the bell of the anty-
shamber, and there they were sure enough!

What was to be done? Quick as litening, I throws off my livry
coat, claps my goold lace hat on master's head, and makes him put
on my livry. Then I wraps myself up in his dressing-gown, and
lolling down on the sofa, bids him open the dor.

There they were—the bailiff—two jondarms with him—Toinette, and an old waiter. When Toinette sees master, she smiles,
and says: "Dis donc, Charles! où est donc ton maître? Chez lui,
n'est-ce pas? C'est le-jeune homme à monsieur," says she, curtsying
to the bailiff.

The old waiter was just a-going to blurt out, "Mais ce n'est
pas!" when Toinette stops him, and says, "Laissez donc passer ces
messieurs, vieux bête;" and in they walk, the 2 jon d'arms taking
their post in the hall.

Master throws open the salong doar very gravely, and touching
my hat says, "Have you any orders about the cab, sir?"

"Why, no, Chawls," says I; "I shan't drive out to-day."

The old bailiff grinned, for he understood English (having had
plenty of English customers), and says in French, as master goes
out, "I think, sir, you had better let your servant get a coach, for
I am under the painful necessity of arresting you, au nom de la loi,
for the sum of ninety-eight thousand seven hundred francs, owed
by you to the Sieur Jacques François Lebrun, of Paris;" and he
pulls out a number of bills, with master's acceptances on them
sure enough.

"Take a chair, sir," says I; and down he sits; and I began to
chaff him, as well as I could, about the weather, my illness, my sad
axdent, having lost one of my hands, which was stuck into my
busum, and so on.

At last after a minnit or two, I could contane no longer, and
bust out in a horse laff.

The old fellow turned quite pail, and began to suspect somethink. "Hola!" says he; "gendarmes! à moi! à moi! Je suis floué, volé," which means, in English, that he was reglar sold.

The jondarmes jumped into the room, and so did Toinette and the waiter. Grasefly rising from my arm-chare, I took my hand from my dressing-gownd, and, flinging it open, stuck up on the chair one of the neatest legs ever seen.

I then pinted myjestickly—to what do you think?—to my PLUSH TITES! these sellabrated inigspressables which have rendered me famous in Yourope.

Taking the hint, the jondarmes and the servnts rord out laffing; and so did Charles Yellowplush, Esquire, I can tell you. Old Grippard the bailiff looked as if he would faint in his chare.

I heard a kab galloping like mad out of the hotel-gate, and knew then that my master was safe.

CHAPTER VIII

THE END OF MR. DEUCEACE'S HISTORY—LIMBO

MY tail is droring rabidly to a close : my suvvice with Mr. Deuceace didn't continyou very long after the last chapter, in which I described my admiral strattyjam, and my singlar self-devocean. There's very few servnts, I can tell you, who'd have thought of such a contrivance, and very few moar would have egg-sycuted it when thought of.

But, after all, beyond the trifling advantich to myself in selling master's roab de sham, which you, gentle reader, may remember I woar, and in dixcovering a fipun note in one of the pockets,—beyond this, I say, there was to poar master very little advantich in what had been done. It's true he had escaped. Very good. But Frans is not like Great Brittin ; a man in a livry coat, with 1 arm, is pretty easly known, and caught, too, as I can tell you.

Such was the case with master. He coodn leave Paris, moar-over, if he would. What was to become, in that case, of his bride —his unchbacked hairis ? He knew that young lady's *temprimong* (as the Parishers say) too well to let her long out of his site. She had nine thousand a yer. She'd been in love a duzn times befor, and mite be agin. The Honrabble Algernon Deuceace was a little too wide awake to trust much to the constnsy of so very inflammable a young creacher. Heavn bless us, it was a marycle she wasn't earlier married ! I do bleave (from suttn seans that past betwigst us) that she'd have married me, if she hadn't been sejuiced by the supearor rank and indianuity of the genlmn in whose survace I was.

Well, to use a commin igspreshn, the beaks were after him. How was he to manitch ? He coodn get away from his debts, and he wooden quit the fare objict of his affeckshns. He was ableejd, then, as the French say, to lie perdew,—going out at night, like a howl out of a hivy-bush, and returning in the daytime to his roast For its a maxum in France (and I wood it were followed in Ingland), that after dark no man is lible for his detts ; and in any of the Royal gardens—the Twillaries, the Pally Roil, or the Lucksimbug, for example—a man may wander from sunrise to evening, and hear nothing of the ojus dunns : they ain't admitted into these places of public enjyment and rondyvoo any more than dogs; the centuries at the garden-gate having orders to shuit all such.

Master, then, was in this uncomfrable situation—neither liking to go nor to stay! peeping out at nights to have an interview with his miss; ableagd to shuffle off her repeated questions as to the reason of all this disgeise, and to talk of his two thowsnd a year jest as if he had it and didn't owe a shilling in the world.

Of course, now, he began to grow mighty eager for the marritch.

He roat as many noats as she had done befor; swoar against delay and cerymony; talked of the pleasures of Hyming, the ardship that the ardor of two arts should be allowed to igspire, the folly of waiting for the consent of Lady Griffin. She was but a step-mother, and an unkind one. Miss was (he said) a major, might marry whom she liked; and suttnly had paid Lady G. quite as much attention as she ought, by paying her the compliment to ask her at all.

And so they went on. The curious thing was, that when master was pressed about his cause for not coming out till night-time, he was misterus; and Miss Griffin, when asked why she wooden marry, igsprest, or rather, *didn't* igspress, a similar secrasy. Wasn't it hard? the cup seemed to be at the lip of both of 'em, and yet somehow, they could not manitch to take a drink.

But one morning, in reply to a most desprat epistol wrote by my master over night, Deuceace, delighted, gits an answer from his soal's beluffd, which ran thus :—

Miss Griffin to the Hon. A. P. Deuceace.

"DEAREST,—You say you would share a cottage with me; there is no need, luckily, for that! You plead the sad sinking of your spirits at our delayed union. Beloved, do you think *my* heart rejoices at our separation? You bid me disregard the refusal of Lady Griffin, and tell me that I owe her no further duty.

"Adored Algernon! I can refuse you no more. I was willing not to lose a single chance of reconciliation with this unnatural step-mother. Respect for the memory of my sainted father bid me do all in my power to gain her consent to my union with you; nay, shall I own it? prudence dictated the measure; for to whom should she leave the share of money accorded to her by my father's will but to my father's child?

"But there are bounds beyond which no forbearance can go; and, thank Heaven, we have no need of looking to Lady Griffin for sordid wealth : we have a competency without her. Is it not so, dearest Algernon?

"Be it as you wish then, dearest, bravest, and best. Your poor

Matilda has yielded to you her heart long ago; she has no longer
need to keep back her name.   Name the hour, and I will delay no
more; but seek for refuge in your arms from the contumely and
insult which meet me ever here.   MATILDA.

"*P.S.*—Oh, Algernon! if you did but know what a noble part
your dear father has acted throughout, in doing his best endeavours
to further our plans, and to soften Lady Griffin! It is not *his* fault
that she is inexorable as she is.   I send you a note sent by her to
Lord Crabs; we will laugh at it soon, *n'est-ce pas?*"

II

"MY LORD,—In reply to your demand for Miss Griffin's hand,
in favour of your son, Mr. Algernon Deuceace, I can only repeat
what I before have been under the necessity of stating to you—that
I do not believe a union with a person of Mr. Deuceace's character
would conduce to my step-daughter's happiness, and therefore *refuse
my consent*.   I will beg you to communicate the contents of this
note to Mr. Deuceace; and implore you no more to touch upon a
subject which you must be aware is deeply painful to me.—I remain
your Lordship's most humble servant,   L. E. GRIFFIN.

"*The Right Hon. the Earl of Crabs.*"

"Hang her Ladyship!" says my master, "what care I for it?"
As for the old lord who'd been so afishous in his kindness and advice,
master recknsiled that pretty well, with thinking that his Lordship
knew he was going to marry ten thousand a year, and igspected to
get some share of it; for he roat back the following letter to his
father, as well as a flaming one to Miss:—

"Thank you, my dear father, for your kindness in that awkward business.   You know how painfully I am situated just now,
and can pretty well guess *both the causes* of my disquiet.   A
marriage with my beloved Matilda will make me the happiest of
men.   The dear girl consents, and laughs at the foolish pretensions
of her mother-in-law.   To tell you the truth, I wonder she yielded
to them so long.   Carry your kindness a step further, and find for
us a parson, a licence, and make us two into one.   We are both
major, you know; so that the ceremony of a guardian's consent is
unnecessary.—Your affectionate,   ALGERNON DEUCEACE."

"How I regret that difference between us some time back!
Matters are changed now, and shall be more still *after the marriage*."

I knew what my master meant,—that he would give the old lord the money after he was married : and as it was probble that miss would see the letter he roat, he made it such as not to let her see two clearly into his present uncomfrable situation.

I took this letter along with the tender one for Miss, reading both of 'em, in course, by the way. Miss, on getting hers, gave an inegspressable look with the white of her i's, kist the letter, and prest it to her busm. Lord Crabs read his quite calm, and then they fell a-talking together; and told me to wait awhile, and I should git an anser.

After a deal of counseltation, my Lord brought out a card, and there was simply written on it,

To-morrow, at the Ambassador's, at Twelve.

" Carry that back to your master, Chawls," says he, " and bid him not to fail."

You may be sure I stept back to him pretty quick, and gave him the card and the messinge. Master looked sattasfied with both ; but suttnly not over happy ; no man is the day before his marridge ; much more his marridge with a humpback, Harriss though she be.

Well, as he was a-going to depart this bachelor life, he did what every man in such suckmstances ought to do : he made his will,— that is, he made a dispasition of his property, and wrote letters to his creditors telling them of his lucky chance : and that after his marridge he would sutanly pay them every stiver. *Before,* they must know his povvaty well enough to be sure that paymint was out of the question.

To do him justas, he seam'd to be inclined to do the thing that was right, now that it didn't put him to any inkinvenients to do so.

" Chawls," says he, handing me over a tenpun-note, " here's your wagis, and thank you for getting me out of the scrape with the bailiffs : when we are married, you shall be my valet out of liv'ry, and I'll treble your salary."

His vallit ! praps his butler ! Yes, thought I, here's a chance —a vallit to ten thousand a year. Nothing to do but to shave him, and read his notes, and let my whiskers grow; to dress in spick and span black, and a clean shut per day; muffings every night in the housekeeper's room ; the pick of the gals in the servants' hall ; a chap to clean my boots for me, and my master's opera bone reglar once a week. *I* knew what a vallit was as well as any genlmn in service ; and this I can tell you, he's genrally a hapier, idler, handsomer, mor genlmnly man than his master. He has more money to spend, for genlmn *will* leave their silver in their waistcoat pockets; more suxess among the gals; as good dinners, and as good wine—that is, if he's friends with the butler: and friends in corse they will be if they know which way their interest lies.

But these are only cassels in the air, what the French call *shutter d'Espang.* It wasn't roat in the book of fate that I was to be Mr. Deuceace's vallit.

Days will pass at last—even days before a wedding (the longist and unpleasantist day in the whole of a man's life, I can tell you, excep, may be, the day before his hanging); and at length Aroarer dawned on the suspicious morning which was to unite in the bonds of Hyming the Honrable Algernon Percy Deuceace, Exquire, and Miss Matilda Griffin. My master's wardrobe wasn't so rich as it had been; for he'd left the whole of his nicknax and trumpry of dressing-cases and rob dy shams, his bewtifle museum of varnished boots, his curous colleckshn of Stulz and Staub coats, when he had been ableaged to quit so sudnly our pore dear lodginx at the Hôtel Mirabew; and being incog at a friend's house, ad contentid himself with ordring a coople of shoots of cloves from a common tailor, with a suffishnt quantaty of linning.

Well, he put on the best of his coats—a blue; and I thought it my duty to ask him whether he'd want his frock again: he was good-natured and said, "Take it and be hanged to you." Half-past eleven o'clock came, and I was sent to look out at the door, if there were any suspicious charicters (a precious good nose I have to find a bailiff out I can tell you, and an i which will almost see one round a corner); and presently a very modest green glass-coach droave up, and in master stept. I didn't, in corse, appear on the box; because, being known, my appearints might have compromised master. But I took a short cut, and walked as quick as posbil down to the Rue de Foburg St. Honoré, where his exlnsy the English ambasdor lives, and where marridges are always performed betwigst English folk at Paris.

   .   .   .   .

There is, almost nex door to the ambasdor's hotel, another hotel, of that lo kind which the French call cabbyrays, or wine-houses; and jest as master's green glass-coach pulled up, another coach drove off, out of which came two ladies, whom I knew pretty well,— suffiz, that one had a humpback, and the ingenious reader will know why *she* came there; the other was poor Miss Kicksey, who came to see her turned off.

Well, master's glass-coach droav up, jest as I got within a few yards of the door; our carridge, I say, droav up, and stopt. Down gits coachmin to open the door, and comes I to give Mr. Deuceace an arm, when—out of the cabaray shoot four fellows, and draw up betwigst the coach and embassy doar; two other chaps go to the other doar of the carridge, and, opening it, one says—"Rendez-vous, Monsieur Deuceace! Je vous arrête au nom de la loi!" (which means, "Get out of that, Mr. D.; you are nabbed, and no mistake"). Master turned gashly pail, and sprung to the other side of the coach, as if a serpint had stung him. He flung open the door, and was for making off that way; but he saw the four chaps standing betwigst libbarty and him. He slams down the front window, and screams out, "Fouettez, cocher!" (which means, "Go it, coachmin!") in a despert loud voice; but coachmin wooden go it, and besides was off his box.

The long and short of the matter was, that jest as I came up to the door two of the bums jumped into the carridge. I saw all; I knew my duty, and so very mornfly I got up behind.

"Tiens," says one of the chaps in the street; "c'est ce drôle qui nous a floué l'autre jour." I knew 'em, but was too melumcolly to smile.

"Où irons-nous donc?" says coachmin to the genlmn who had got inside.

A deep woice from the intearor shouted out, in reply to the coachmin, "A SAINTE PÉLAGIE!"

. . . .

And now, praps, I ot to dixcribe to you the humours of the prizn of Sainte Pelagie, which is the French for Fleat, or Queen's Bentch: but on this subject I'm rather shy of writing, partly because the admiral Boz has, in the history of Mr. Pickwick, made such a dixcripshun of a prizn, that mine wooden read very amyousingly afterwids; and, also, because, to tell you the truth, I didn't stay long in it, being not in a humer to waist my igsistance by passing away the ears of my youth in such a dull place.

My fust errint now was, as you may phansy, to carry a noat from master to his destined bride. The poar thing was sadly taken aback, as I can tell you, when she found, after remaining two hours at the Embassy, that her husband didn't make his appearance. And so, after staying on and on, and yet seeing no husband, she was forsed at last to trudge dishconslit home, where I was already waiting for her with a letter from my master.

There was no use now denying the fact of his arrest, and so he confest it at onst; but he made a cock-and-bull story of treachery of a friend, infimous fodgery, and Heaven knows what. However, it

didn't matter much ; if he had told her that he had been betrayed
by the man in the moon, she would have bleavd him.

Lady Griffin never used to appear now at any of my visits. She
kep one drawing-room, and Miss dined and lived alone in another ;
they quarld so much that praps it was best they should live apart ;
only my Lord Crabs used to see both, comforting each with that
winning and innsnt way he had. He came in as Miss, in tears, was
lisning to my account of master's seazure, and hoping that the prisn
wasn't a horrid place, with a nasty horrid dunjeon, and a dreadfle
jailer, and nasty horrid bread and water. Law bless us ! she had
borrod her ideers from the novvles she had been reading !

"O my Lord, my Lord," says she, "have you heard this fatal
story ? "

"Dearest Matilda, what ? For Heaven's sake, you alarm me !
What—yes—no—is it—no, it can't be ! Speak ! " says my Lord,
seizing me by the choler of my coat. "What has happened to
my boy ? "

"Please you, my Lord," says I, "he's at this moment in prisn,
no wuss,—having been incarserated about two hours ago."

"In prison ! Algernon in prison ! 'tis impossible ! Imprisoned,
for what sum ? Mention it, and I will pay to the utmost farthing
in my power."

"I'm sure your Lordship is very kind," says I (recklecting the
sean betwixgst him and master, whom he wanted to diddil out of a
thowsand lb.) ; "and you'll be happy to hear he's only in for a trifle.
Five thousand pound is, I think, pretty near the mark."

"Five thousand pounds !—confusion ! " says my Lord, clasping
his hands, and looking up to heaven, "and I have not five hundred !
Dearest Matilda, how shall we help him ? "

"Alas, my Lord, I have but three guineas, and you know how
Lady Griffin has the——"

"Yes, my sweet child, I know what you would say ; but be of
good cheer—Algernon, you know, has ample funds of his own."

Thinking my Lord meant Dawkins's five thousand, of which, to
be sure, a good lump was left, I held my tung ; but I cooden help
wondering at Lord Crabs' igstream compashn for his son, and Miss,
with her £10,000 a year, having only 3 guineas in her pockit.

I took home (bless us, what a home !) a long and very inflamble
letter from Miss, in which she dixscribed her own sorror at the dis
appointment ; swoar she lov'd him only the moar for his misfortns ;
made light of them ; as a pusson for a paltry sum of five thousand
pound ought never to be cast down, 'specially as he had a certain
independence in view ; and vowed that nothing, nothing should ever
injuice her to part from him, etsettler, etsettler.

21

I told master of the conversation which had passed betwigst me and my Lord, and of his handsome offers, and his horror at hearing of his son's being taken; and likewise mentioned how strange it was that Miss should only have 3 guineas, and with such a fortn : bless us, I should have thot that she would always have carried a hundred thowsnd lb. in her pockit!

At this master only said Pshaw! But the rest of the story about his father seemed to dixquiet him a good deal, and he made me repeat it over agin.

He walked up and down the room agytated, and it seam'd as if a new lite was breaking in upon him.

"Chawls," says he, "did you observe—did Miss — did my father seem *particularly intimate* with Miss Griffin?"

"How do you mean, sir?" says I.

"Did Lord Crabs appear very fond of Miss Griffin?"

"He was suttnly very kind to her."

"Come, sir, speak at once : did Miss Griffin seem very fond of his Lordship?"

"Why, to tell the truth, sir, I must say she seemed *very* fond of him."

"What did he call her?"

"He called her his dearest gal."

"Did he take her hand?"

"Yes, and he——"

"And he what?"

"He kist her, and told her not to be so wery down-hearted about the misfortn which had hapnd to you."

"I have it now!" says he, clinching his fist, and growing gashly pail—"I have it now—the infernal old hoary scoundrel! the wicked unnatural wretch! He would take her from me!" And he poured out a volley of oaves which are impossbill to be repeatid here.

I thot as much long ago : and when my Lord kem with his vizits so pretious affeckshnt at my Lady Griffinses, I expected some such game was in the wind. Indeed, I'd heard a somethink of it from the Griffinses servnts, that my Lord was mighty tender with the ladies.

One thing, however, was evident to a man of his intleckshal capassaties : he must either marry the gal at onst, or he stood very small chance of having her. He must get out of limbo immediantly, or his respectid father might be stepping into his vaykint shoes. Oh! he saw it all now—the fust attempt at arest, the marridge fixt at 12 o'clock, and the bayliffs fixt to come and intarup the marridge!—the jewel, praps, betwigst him and De l'Orge : but no, it was the *woman* who did that—a *man* don't deal such fowl blows, igspecially a father to his son : a woman may, poar thing !—she's no other means of reventch, and is used to fight with underhand wepns all her life through.

Well, whatever the pint might be, this Deuceace saw pretty clear that he'd been beat by his father at his own game—a trapp set for him onst, which had been defitted by my presnts of mind— another trap set afterwids, in which my Lord had been suxesfle. Now, my Lord, roag as he was, was much too good-natured to do an unkind ackshn, mearly for the sake of doing it. He'd got to that pich that he didn't mind injaries—they were all fair play to him—he gave 'em and reseav'd them, without a thought of mallis. If he wanted to injer his son, it was to benefick himself. And how was this to be done ? By getting the hairiss to himself, to be sure. The Honrabble Mr. D. didn't say so ; but I knew his feelinx well enough—he regretted that he had not given the old genlmn the money he askt for.

Poar fello ! he thought he had hit it ; but he was wide of the mark after all.

Well, but what was to be done ? It was clear that he must marry the gal at any rate—*cootky coot*, as the French say : that is, marry her, and hang the igspence.

To do so he must first git out of prisn—to get out of prisn he must pay his debts—and to pay his debts, he must give every shilling he was worth. Never mind : four thousand pound is a small stake to a reglar gambler, igspecially when he must play it, or rot for life in prisn ; and when, if he plays it well, it will give him ten thousand a year.

So, seeing there was no help for it, he maid up his mind, and accordingly wrote the follying letter to Miss Griffin :—

"MY ADORED MATILDA,—Your letter has indeed been a comfort to a poor fellow, who had hoped that this night would have been the most blessed in his life, and now finds himself condemned to spend it within a prison wall ! You know the accursed conspiracy which has brought these liabilities upon me, and the foolish friendship which has cost me so much. But what matters ! We have, as you say, enough, even though I must pay this shameful demand upon me ; and five thousand pounds are as nothing, compared to the happiness which I lose in being separated a night from thee ! Courage, however ! If I make a sacrifice it is for you ; and I were heartless indeed if I allowed my own losses to balance for a moment against your happiness.

"Is it not so, beloved one ? *Is* not your happiness bound up with mine, in a union with me? I am proud to think so—proud, too, to offer such a humble proof as this of the depth and purity of my affection.

"Tell me that you will still be mine; tell me that you will be mine to-morrow; and to-morrow these vile chains shall be removed, and I will be free once more—or if bound, only bound to you! My adorable Matilda! my betrothed bride! write to me ere the evening closes, for I shall never be able to shut my eyes in slumber upon my prison couch, until they have been first blessed by the sight or a few words from thee! Write to me, love! write to me! I languish for the reply which is to make or mar me for ever.—Your affectionate, A. P. D."

Having polisht off this epistol, master intrustid it to me to carry, and bade me at the same time to try and give it into Miss Griffin's hand alone. I ran with it to Lady Griffinses. I found Miss, as I desired, in a sollatary condition; and I presented her with master's pafewmed Billy.

She read it, and the number of size to which she gave vint, and the tears which she shed, beggar digscription. She wep and sighed until I thought she would bust. She even claspt my hand in her's, and said, "O Charles! is he very, very miserable?"

"He is, ma'am," says I; "very miserable indeed—nobody, upon my honour, could be miserablerer."

On hearing this pethetic remark, her mind was made up at onst: and sitting down to her eskrewtaw, she immediantly ableaged master with an answer. Here it is in black and white:—

"My prisoned bird shall pine no more, but fly home to its nest in these arms! Adored Algernon, I will meet thee to-morrow, at the same place, at the same hour. Then, then it will be impossible for aught but death to divide us. M. G."

This kind of flumry style comes, you see, of reading novvles, and cultivating littery purshuits in a small way. How much better is it to be puffickly ignorant of the hart of writing, and to trust to the writing of the heart. This is *my* style: artyfiz I despise, and trust compleatly to natur: but *revnong a no mootong*, as our continential friends remark : to that nice white sheep, Algernon Percy Deuceace, Esquire; that wenrabble old ram, my Lord Crabs his father; and that tender and dellygit young lamb, Miss Matilda Griffin.

She had just foalded up into its proper triangular shape the noat transcribed abuff, and I was just on the point of saying, according to my master's orders, "Miss, if you please, the Honrabble Mr. Deuceace would be very much ableaged to you to keep the seminary which is to take place to-morrow a profound se——," when my master's father entered, and I fell back to the door. Miss, without a word, rusht into his arms, burst into teers agin, as was her reglar way (it must be confest she was of a very mist constitution), and showing to him his son's note, cried, "Look, my dear Lord, how nobly your Algernon, *our* Algernon, writes to me. Who can doubt, after this, of the purity of his matchless affection?"

My Lord took the letter, read it, seamed a good deal amyoused, and returning it to its owner, said, very much to my surprise, "My dear Miss Griffin, he certainly does seem in earnest; and if you choose to make this match without the consent of your mother-in-law, you know the consequences, and are of course your own mistress."

"Consequences!—for shame, my Lord! A little money, more or less, what matters it to two hearts like ours?"

"Hearts are very pretty things, my sweet young lady, but Three-per-Cents. are better."

"Nay, have we not an ample income of our own, without the aid of Lady Griffin?"

My Lord shrugged his shoulders. "Be it so, my love," says he. "I'm sure I can have no other reason to prevent a union which is founded upon such disinterested affection."

And here the conversation dropt. Miss retired, clasping her hands, and making play with the whites of her i's. My Lord began trotting up and down the room, with his fat hands stuck in his britchis pockits, his countnince lighted up with igstream joy, and singing, to my inordnit igstonishment—

> "See the conquering hero comes!
> Tiddy diddy doll—tiddydoll, doll, doll."

He began singing this song, and tearing up and down the room like mad. I stood amazd—a new light broke in upon me. He wasn't going, then, to make love to Miss Griffin! Master might marry her! Had she not got the for——?

I say, I was just standing stock still, my eyes fixt, my hands puppindicklar, my mouf wide open, and these igstrordinary thoughts passing in my mind, when my Lord having got to the last "doll" of his song, just as I came to the sillible "for" of my ventriloquism, or inward speech—we had eatch jest reached the pint digscribed, when the meditations of both were sudnly stopt, by my Lord, in the midst of his singin and trottin match, coming bolt up aginst poar me, sending me up aginst one end of the room, himself flying back to the other: and it was only after considrabble agitation that we were at length restored to anything like a liquilibrium.

"What, *you* here, you infernal rascal?" says my Lord.

"Your Lordship's very kind to notus me," says I; "I am here." And I gave him a look.

He saw I knew the whole game.

And after whisling a bit, as was his habit when puzzled (I bleave he'd have only whisled if he had been told he was to be hanged in five minits), after whisling a bit, he stops sudnly, and coming up to me, says—

"Hearkye, Charles, this marriage must take place to-morrow."

"Must it, sir?" says I; "now, for my part, I don't think——"

"Stop, my good fellow; if it does not take place, what do you gain?"

This stagger'd me. If it didn't take place, I only lost a situation, for master had but just enough money to pay his detts; and it wooden soot my book to serve him in prisn or starving.

"Well," says my Lord, "you see the force of my argument. Now, look here!" and he lugs out a crisp, fluttering, snowy HUNDRED-PUN NOTE! "If my son and Miss Griffin are married to-morrow, you shall have this; and I will, moreover, take you into my service, and give you double your present wages."

Flesh and blood cooden bear it. "My Lord," says I, laying my hand upon my busm, "only give me security, and I'm yours for ever."

The old noblemin grin'd, and pattid me on the shoulder. "Right, my lad," says he, "right—you're a nice promising youth. Here is the best security." And he pulls out his pockit-book, returns the hundred-pun bill, and takes out one for fifty. "Here is half to-day; to-morrow you shall have the remainder."

My fingers trembled a little as I took the pretty fluttering bit of paper, about five times as big as any sum of money I had ever had in my life. I cast my i upon the amount: it was a fifty sure enough—a bank poss-bill, made payable to *Leonora Emilia Griffin*, and indorsed by her. The cat was out of the bag. Now, gentle reader, I spose you begin to see the game.

"Recollect, from this day you are in my service."

"My Lord, you overpoar me with your faviours."

"Go to the devil, sir," says he; "do your duty and hold your tongue."

And thus I went from the service of the Honorabble Algernon Deuceace to that of his exlnsy the Right Honorabble Earl of Crabs.

* * * * * * *

On going back to prisn, I found Deuceace locked up in that oajus place to which his igstravygansies had deservedly led him;

and felt for him, I must say, a great deal of contemp. A raskle such as he—a swindler, who had robbed poar Dawkins of the means of igsistance; who had cheated his fellow-roag, Mr. Richard Blewitt, and who was making a musnary marridge with a disgusting creacher like Miss Griffin, didn merit any compashn on my purt; and I determined quite to keep secret the suckmstansies of my privit interchew with his exlnsy my present master.

I gev him Miss Griffinses trianglar, which he read with a satasfied air. Then, turning to me, says he: "You gave this to Miss Griffin alone?"

"Yes, sir."

"You gave her my message?"

"Yes, sir."

"And you are quite sure Lord Crabs was not there when you gave either the message on the note?"

"Not there, upon my honour," says I.

"Hang your honour, sir! Brush my hat and coat, and go *call a coach*—do you hear?"

.　　.　　.　　.　　.　　.

I did as I was ordered; and on coming back found master in what's called, I think, the *greffe* of the prisn. The officer in waiting had out a great register, and was talking to master in the French tongue, in coarse; a number of poar prisners were looking eagerly on.

"Let us see, my lor," says he; "the debt is 98,700 francs; there are capture expenses, interest so much; and the whole sum amounts to a hundred thousand francs, *moins* 13."

Deuceace, in a very myjestic way, takes out of his pocket-book four thowsnd pun notes. "This is not French money, but I presume that you know it, Monsieur Greffier," says he.

The greffier turned round to old Solomon, a money-changer, who had one or two clients in the prisn, and hapnd luckily to be there. "Les billets sont bons," says he. "Je les prendrai pour cent mille deux cents francs, et j'espère, my lor, de vous revoir."

"Good," says the greffier; "I know them to be good, and I will give my lor the difference, and make out his release."

Which was done. The poar debtors gave a feeble cheer, as the great dubble iron gates swung open and clang to again, and Deuceace stept out, and me after him, to breathe the fresh hair.

He had been in the place but six hours, and was now free again—free, and to be married to ten thousand a year nex day. But, for all that, he lookt very faint and pale. He *had* put down his great stake; and when he came out of Sainte Pelagie, he had but fifty pounds left in the world!

Never mind—when onst the money's down, make your mind easy; and so Deuceace did. He drove back to the Hôtel Mirabew, where he ordered apartmince infinately more splendid than befor; and I pretty soon told Toinette, and the rest of the suvvants, how nobly he behayved, and how he valyoud four thousnd pound no more than ditch water. And such was the consquincies of my praises, and the poplarity I got for us boath, that the delighted landlady immediantly charged him dubble what she would have done, if it hadn been for my stoaries.

He ordered splendid apartmince, then, for the nex week; a carridge-and-four for Fontainebleau to-morrow at 12 precisely; and having settled all these things, went quietly to the "Roshy de Cancale," where he dined: as well he might, for it was now eight o'clock. I didn't spare the shompang neither that night, I can tell you; for when I carried the note he gave me for Miss Griffin in the evening, informing her of his freedom, that young lady remarked my hagitated manner of walking and speaking, and said, "Honest Charles! he is flusht with the events of the day. Here, Charles, is a napoleon; take it and drink to your mistress."

I pockitid it; but, I must say, I didn't like the money—it went against my stomick to take it.

CHAPTER IX

THE MARRIAGE

WELL, the nex day came: at 12 the carridge-and-four was waiting at the ambasdor's doar; and Miss Griffin and the faithfle Kicksey were punctial to the apintment. I don't wish to digscribe the marridge seminary—how the embasy chapling jined the hands of this loving young couple—how one of the embasy footmin was called in to witness the marridge—how Miss wep and fainted, as usial—and how Deuceace carried her, fainting, to the brisky, and drove off to Fontingblo, where they were to pass the fust weak of the honeymoon. They took no servnts, because they wisht, they said, to be privit. And so, when I had shut up the steps, and bid the postilion drive on, I bid ajew to the Honrabble Algernon, and went off strait to his exlent father.

" Is it all over, Chawls ? " said he.

" I saw them turned off at igsackly a quarter past 12, my Lord," says I.

" Did you give Miss Griffin the paper, as I told you, before her marriage ? "

" I did, my Lord, in the presents of Mr. Brown, Lord Bobtail's man ; who can swear to her having had it."

I must tell you that my Lord had made me read a paper which Lady Griffin had written, and which I was comishnd to give in the manner menshnd abuff. It ran to this effect :—

" According to the authority given me by the will of my lato dear husband, I forbid the marriage of Miss Griffin with the Honourable Algernon Percy Deuceace. If Miss Griffin persists in the union, I warn her that she must abide by the consequences of her act.

" LEONORA EMILIA GRIFFIN.

" RUE DE RIVOLI : *May* 8, 1818."

When I gave this to Miss as she entered the cortyard, a minnit before my master's arrivle, she only read it contemptiously, and said, " I laugh at the threats of Lady Griffin ; " and she toar the paper in two, and walked on, leaning on the arm of the faithful and obleaging Miss Kicksey.

I picked up the paper for fear of axdents, and brot it to my Lord. Not that there was any necessaty; for he'd kep a copy, and made me and another witniss (my Lady Griffin's solissator) read them both, before he sent either away.

"Good!" says he; and he projuiced from his potfolio the fello of that bewchus fifty-pun note, which he'd given me yesterday. "I keep my promise, you see, Charles," says he. "You are now in Lady Griffin's service, in the place of Mr. Fitzclarence, who retires. Go to Frojé's, and get a livery."

"But, my Lord," says I, "I was not to go into Lady Griffinses service, according to the bargain, but into——"

"It's all the same thing," says he; and he walked off. I went to Mr. Frojé's, and ordered a new livry; and found, likwise, that our coachmin and Munseer Mortimer had been there too. My Lady's livery was changed, and was now of the same color as my old coat at Mr. Deuceace's; and I'm blest if there wasn't a tremenjióus great earl's corronit on the butins, instid of the Griffin rampint, which was worn befoar.

I asked no questions, however, but had myself measured; and slep that night at the Plas Vandome. I didn't go out with the carridge for a day or two, though; my Lady only taking one footmin, she said, until *her new carridge* was turned out.

I think you can guess what's in the wind *now!*

I bot myself a dressing-case, a box of Ody colong, a few duzen lawn sherts and neckcloths, and other things which were necessary for a genlmn in my rank. Silk stockings was provided by the rules of the house. And I completed the bisniss by writing the follying ginteel letter to my late master :—

Charles Yellowplush, Esquire, to the Honourable A. P. Deuceace.

"Sur,—Suckmstansies have acurd sins I last had the honner of wating on you, which render it impossbil that I should remane any longer in your suvvice. I'll thank you to leave out my thinx, when they come home on Sattady from the wash.—Your obeajnt servnt,

"Charles Yellowplush.

"Plas Vendôme."

The athography of the abuv noat, I confess, is atrocious; but *ke voolyvoo?* I was only eighteen, and hadn then the expearance in writing which I've enjide sins.

Having thus done my jewty in evry way, I shall prosead, in the nex chapter, to say what hapnd in my new place.

CHAPTER X

THE HONEYMOON

THE weak at Fontingblow past quickly away ; and at the end of it, our son and daughter-in-law—a pare of nice young tuttle-duvs—returned to their nest, at the Hôtel Mirabew. I suspeck that the *cock* turtle-dove was preshos sick of his barging.

When they arriv'd, the fust thing they found on their table was a large parsle wrapt up in silver paper, and a newspaper, and a couple of cards, tied up with a peace of white ribbing. In the parsle was a hansume piece of plum-cake, with a deal of sugar. On the cards was wrote, in Goffick characters,

> 𝔈𝔞𝔯𝔩 𝔬𝔣 ℭ𝔯𝔞𝔟𝔰.

And, in very small Italian,

> *Countess of Crabs.*

And in the paper was the following parrowgraff :—

"MARRIAGE IN HIGH LIFE.—Yesterday, at the British Embassy, the Right Honourable John Augustus Altamont Plantagenet, Earl of Crabs, to Leonora Emilia, widow of the late Lieutenant-General Sir George Griffin, K.C.B. An elegant *déjeuner* was given to the happy couple by his Excellency Lord Bobtail, who gave away the bride. The *élite* of the foreign diplomacy, the Prince Talleyrand and Marshal the Duke of Dalmatia on behalf of H.M. the King of France, honoured the banquet and the marriage ceremony. Lord and Lady Crabs intend passing a few weeks at Saint Cloud."

The above dockyments, along with my own triffling billy, of which I have also givn a copy, greated Mr. and Mrs. Deuceace on their arrivle from Fontingblo. Not being present, I can't say what Deuceace said; but I can fancy how he *lookt*, and how poor Mrs. Deuceace lookt. They weren't much inclined to rest after the fiteeg of the junny; for, in ½ an hour after their arrival at Paris, the hosses were put to the carridge agen, and down they came thundering to our country-house at St. Cloud (pronounst by those absud Frenchmin Sing Kloo), to interrup our chaste loves and delishs marridge injyments.

My Lord was sittn in a crimson satan dressing-gown, lolling on a sofa at an open windy, smoaking seagars, as ushle; her Ladyship, who, to du her justice, didn mind the smell, occupied another end of the room, and was working, in wusted, a pare of slippers, or an umbrellore case, or a coal-skittle, or some such nonsints. You would have thought to have sean 'em that they had been married a sentry, at least. Well, I bust in upon this conjugal *tator-tator*, and said, very much alarmed, " My Lord, here's your son and daughter-in-law."

" Well," says my Lord, quite calm, " and what then ? "

" Mr. Deuceace ! " says my Lady, starting up, and looking fritened.

" Yes, my love, my son ; but you need not be alarmed. Pray, Charles, say that Lady Crabs and I will be very happy to see Mr. and Mrs. Deuceace ; and that they must excuse us receiving them *en famille*. Sit still, my blessing—take things coolly. Have you got the box with the papers ? "

My Lady pointed to a great green box—the same from which she had taken the papers, when Deuceace fust saw them,—and handed over to my Lord a fine gold key. I went out, met Deuceace and his wife on the stepps, gave my messinge, and bowed them palitely in.

My Lord didn't rise, but smoaked away as usual (praps a little quicker, but I can't say); my Lady sat upright, looking handsum and strong. Deuceace walked in, his left arm tied to his breast, his wife and hat on the other. He looked very pale and frightened; his wife, poar thing! had her head berried in her handkerchief, and sobd fit to break her heart.

Miss Kicksey, who was in the room (but I didn't mention her, she was less than nothink in our house), went up to Mrs. Deuceace at onst, and held out her arms—she had a heart, that old Kicksey, and I respect her for it. The poor hunchback flung herself into Miss's arms, with a kind of whooping screech, and kep there for some time, sobbing in quite a historical manner. I saw there was going to be a sean, and so, in cors, left the door ajar.

" Welcome to Saint Cloud, Algy, my boy ! " says my Lord, in a loud hearty voice. "You thought you would give us the slip, eh, you rogue? But we knew it, my dear fellow : we knew the whole affair—did we not, my soul?—and, you see, kept our secret better than you did yours."

"I must confess, sir," says Deuceace, bowing, "that I had no idea of the happiness which awaited me in the shape of a mother-in-law."

"No, you dog; no, no," says my Lord, giggling : "old birds, you know, not to be caught with chaff, like young ones. But here we are, all spliced and happy, at last. Sit down, Algernon ; let us smoke a segar, and talk over the perils and adventures of the last month. My love," says my Lord, turning to his lady, "you have no malice against poor Algernon, I trust? Pray shake *his hand.*" (A grin.)

But my Lady rose and said, "I have told Mr. Deuceace, that I never wished to see him, or speak to him more. I see no reason, now, to change my opinion." And herewith she sailed out of the room, by the door through which Kicksey had carried poor Mrs. Deuceace.

"Well, well," says my Lord, as Lady Crabs swept by, "I was in hopes she had forgiven you ; but I know the whole story, and I must confess you used her cruelly ill. Two strings to your bow !—that was your game, was it, you rogue?"

"Do you mean, my Lord, that you know all that past between me and Lady Grif—— Lady Crabs, before our quarrel?"

"Perfectly—you made love to her, and she was almost in love with you ; you jilted her for money, she got a man to shoot your hand off in revenge : no more dice-boxes, now, Deuceace ; no more *sauter la coup.* I can't think how the deuce you will manage to live without them."

"Your lordship is very kind ; but I have given up play altogether," says Deuceace, looking mighty black and uneasy.

"Oh, indeed! Benedick has turned a moral man, has he? This is better and better. Are you thinking of going into the Church, Deuceace?"

"My Lord, may I ask you to be a little more serious?"

"Serious! *à quoi bon?* I am serious—serious in my surprise that, when you might have had either of these women, you should have preferred that hideous wife of yours."

"May I ask you, in turn, how you came to be so little squeamish about a wife, as to choose a woman who had just been making love to your own son?" says Deuceace, growing fierce.

"How can you ask such a question? I owe forty thousand pounds—there is an execution at Sizes Hall—every acre I have is in the hands of my creditors; and that's why I married her. Do you think there was any love? Lady Crabs is a dev'lish fine woman, but she's not a fool—she married me for my coronet, and I married her for her money."

"Well, my Lord, you need not ask me, I think, why I married the daughter-in-law."

"Yes, but I *do*, my dear boy. How the deuce are you to live? Dawkins's five thousand pounds won't last for ever. And afterwards?"

"You don't mean, my Lord—you don't—I mean, you can't—— D——!" says he, starting up, and losing all patience, "you don't dare to say that Miss Griffin had not a fortune of ten thousand a year?"

My Lord was rolling up, and wetting betwigst his lips, another segar; he lookt up, after he had lighted it, and said quietly—

"Certainly, Miss Griffin had a fortune of ten thousand a year."

"Well, sir, and has she not got it now? Has she spent it in a week?"

"*She has not got a sixpence now: she married without her mother's consent!*"

Deuceace sank down in a chair; and I never see such a dreadful picture of despair as there was in the face of that retchid man!—he writhed, and nasht his teeth, he tore open his coat, and wriggled madly the stump of his left hand, until, fairly beat, he threw it over his livid pale face, and sinking backwards, fairly wept alowd.

Bah! it's a dreddfle thing to hear a man crying! his pashn torn up from the very roots of his heart, as it must be before it can git such a vent. My Lord, meanwhile, rolled his segar, lighted it, and went on.

"My dear boy, the girl has not a shilling. I wished to have left you alone in peace, with your four thousand pounds; you might have lived decently upon it in Germany, where money is at 5 per cent., where your duns would not find you, and a couple of hundred a year would have kept you and your wife in comfort. But, you see, Lady Crabs would not listen to it. You had injured her; and, after she had tried to kill you and failed, she determined to ruin you, and succeeded. I must own to you that I directed the arresting business, and put her up to buying your protested bills: she got them for a trifle, and as you have paid them, has made a good two thousand pounds by her bargain. It was a painful thing, to be sure, for a father to get his son arrested; but *que voulez-vous?* I did not appear in the transaction: she would have you ruined; and it was absolutely necessary that *you* should marry before I could, so I pleaded your cause with Miss Griffin, and made you the happy man you are. You rogue, you rogue! you thought to match your old father, did you? But, never mind; lunch will be ready soon. In the meantime, have a segar, and drink a glass of Sauterne."

Deuceace, who had been listening to this speech, sprung up wildly.

"I'll not believe it," he said: "it's a lie, an infernal lie! forged by you, you hoary villain, and by the murderess and strumpet you have married. I'll not believe it: show me the will. Matilda! Matilda!" shouted he, screaming hoarsely, and flinging open the door by which she had gone out.

"Keep your temper, my boy. You *are* vexed, and I feel for you: but don't use such bad language: it is quite needless, believe me."

"Matilda!" shouted out Deuceace again; and the poor crooked thing came trembling in, followed by Miss Kicksey.

"Is this true, woman?" says he, clutching hold of her hand.

"What, dear Algernon?" says she.

"What?" screams out Deuceace,—"what? Why, that you are a beggar, for marrying without your mother's consent—that you basely lied to me, in order to bring about this match—that you are a swindler, in conspiracy with that old fiend yonder and the she-devil his wife?"

"It is true," sobbed the poor woman, "that I have nothing; but——"

"Nothing but what? Why don't you speak, you drivelling fool?"

"I have nothing!—but you, dearest, have two thousand a year. Is that not enough for us? You love me for myself, don't you, Algernon? You have told me so a thousand times—say so again, dear husband; and do not, do not be so unkind." And here she sank on her knees, and clung to him, and tried to catch his hand, and kiss it.

"How much did you say?" says my Lord.

"Two thousand a year, sir; he has told us so a thousand times."

"*Two thousand!* Two thou—ho, ho, ho!—haw! haw! haw!" roars my Lord. "That is, I vow, the best thing I ever heard in my life. My dear creature, he has not a shilling—not a single maravedi, by all the gods and goddesses." And this exlnt noblemin began laffin louder than ever: a very kind and feeling genlmn he was, as all must confess.

There was a paws: and Mrs. Deuceace didn begin cussing and swearing at her husband as he had done at her: she only said, "Oh Algernon! is this true?" and got up, and went to a chair, and wep in quiet.

My Lord opened the great box. "If you or your lawyers would like to examine Sir George's will, it is quite at your service; you will see here the proviso which I mentioned, that gives the entire fortune to Lady Griffin—Lady Crabs that is: and here, my dear boy, you see the danger of hasty conclusions. Her Ladyship only showed you the *first page of the will*, of course; she wanted to try you. You thought you made a great stroke in at once proposing to Miss Griffin—do not mind it, my love, he really loves you now very sincerely!—when, in fact, you would have done much better to have read the rest of the will. You were completely bitten, my boy—humbugged, bamboozled—ay, and by your old father, you dog. I told you I would, you know, when you refused to lend me a portion of your Dawkins money. I told you I would; and I *did*. I had you the very next day. Let this be a lesson to you, Percy, my boy; don't try your luck again against such old hands: look deuced well before you leap; *audi alteram partem*, my lad, which means, read both sides of the will. I think lunch is ready; but I see you don't smoke. Shall we go in?"

"Stop, my Lord," says Mr. Deuceace, very humble: "I shall not share your hospitality—but—but you know my condition; I am penniless—you know the manner in which my wife has been brought up——"

"The Honourable Mrs. Deuceace, sir, shall always find a home here, as if nothing had occurred to interrupt the friendship between her dear mother and herself."

"And for me, sir," says Deuceace, speaking faint, and very slow; "I hope—I trust—I think, my Lord, you will not forget me?"

"Forget you, sir; certainly not."

"And that you will make some provision——?"

"Algernon Deuceace," says my Lord, getting up from the sophy, and looking at him with sich a jolly malignity, as *I* never see, "I declare, before Heaven, that I will not give you a penny!"

Hereupon my Lord held out his hand to Mrs. Deuceace, and said, "My dear, will you join your mother and me? We shall always, as I said, have a home for you."

"My Lord," said the poar thing, dropping a curtsey, "my home is with *him!*"

.   .   .   .

.   .   .   .

.   .   .   .   .   .

About three months after, when the season was beginning at Paris, and the autumn leafs was on the ground, my Lord, my

Lady, me and Mortimer, were taking a stroal in the Boddy Balong, the carridge driving on slowly ahead, and us as happy as possbill, admiring the pleasant woods and the goldn sunset.

My Lord was expayshating to my Lady upon the exquizit beauty of the sean, and pouring forth a host of butifle and virtuous sentaments sootable to the hour.   It was dalitefle to hear him.   "Ah!" said he, "black must be the heart, my love, which does not feel the influence of a scene like this ; gathering, as it were, from those sunlit skies, a portion of their celestial gold, and gaining somewhat of heaven with each pure draught of this delicious air!"

Lady Crabs did not speak, but prest his arm and looked upwards. Mortimer and I, too, felt some of the infliwents of the sean, and lent on our goold sticks in silence.   The carriage drew up close to us, and my Lord and my Lady sauntered slowly tords it.

Jest at the place was a bench, and on the bench sate a poorly drest woman, and by her, leaning against a tree, was a man whom I thought I'd sean befor.   He was drest in a shabby blew coat, with white seems and copper buttons ; a torn hat was on his head, and great quantaties of matted hair and whiskers disfiggared his countnints.   He was not shaved, and as pale as stone.

My Lord and Lady didn tak the slightest notice of him, but past on to the carridge.   Me and Mortimer lickwise took *our* places. As we past, the man had got a grip of the woman's shoulder, who was holding down her head, sobbing bitterly.

No sooner were my Lord and Lady seated, than they both, with igstream dellixy and good natur, bust into a ror of lafter, peal upon peal, whooping and screaching enough to frighten the evening silents.

DEUCEACE turned round.   I see his face now—the face of a devvle of hell!   Fust, he lookt towards the carridge, and pinted to it with his maimed arm ; then he raised the other, *and struck the woman by his side*.   She fell, screaming.

Poor thing !   Poor thing !

22

MR. YELLOWPLUSH'S AJEW

THE end of Mr. Deuceace's history is going to be the end of my corrispondince. I wish the public was as sory to part with me as I am with the public; becaws I fansy reely that we've become frends, and feal for my part a becoming greaf at saying ajew.

It's imposbill for me to continyow, however, a-writin, as I have done—violetting the rules of authography, and trampling upon the fust princepills of English grammar. When I began, I knew no better : when I'd carrid on these papers a little further, and grew accustmd to writin, I began to smel out somethink quear in my style. Within the last sex weaks I have been learning to spell : and when all the world was rejoicing at the festivvaties of our youthful Quean *—when all i's were fixt upon her long sweet of ambasdors and princes, following the splendid carridge of Marshle the Duke of Damlatiar, and blinking at the pearls and dimince of Prince Oystereasy—Yellowplush was in his loanly pantry—*his* eyes were fixt upon the spelling-book—his heart was bent upon mastring the difickleties of the littery professhn. I have been, in fact, *convertid.*

You shall here how. Ours, you know, is a Wig house ; and ever sins his third son has got a place in the Treasury, his secknd a captingsy in the Guards, his fust, the secretary of embasy at Pekin, with a prospick of being appinted ambasdor at Loo Choo —ever sins master's sons have reseaved these attentions, and master himself has had the promis of a pearitch, he has been the most reglar, consistnt, honrabble Libbaral, in or out of the House of Commins.

Well, being a Whig, it's the fashn, as you know, to reseave littery pipple ; and accordingly, at dinner, tother day, whose name do you think I had to hollar out on the fust landing-place about a wick ago ? After several dukes and markises had been enounced, a very gentell fly drives up to our doar, and out steps two gentlemen. One was pail, and wor spektickles, a wig, and a white neckcloth.

* This was written in 1838.

The other was slim with a hook nose, a pail fase, a small waist, a
pare of falling shoulders, a tight coat, and a catarack of black
satting tumbling out of his busm, and falling into a gilt velvet
weskit. The little genlmn settled his wigg, and pulled out his
ribbins; the younger one fluffed the dust of his shoos, looked at his
wiskers in a little pockit-glas, settled his crevatt; and they both
mounted upstairs.

"What name, sir?" says I, to the old genlmn.

"Name!—a! now, you thief o' the wurrld," says he, "do you
pretind nat to know *me*? Say it's the Cabinet Cyclopa—no, I
mane the Litherary Chran—psha!—bluthanowns!—say it's DOCTHOR
DIOCLESIAN LARNER—I think he'll know me now—ay, Nid?"
But the genlmn called Nid was at the botm of the stare, and pretended to be very busy with his shoo-string. So the little genlmn
went upstares alone.

"DOCTOR DIOLESIUS LARNER!" says I.

"DOCTOR ATHANASIUS LARDNER!" says Greville Fitz-Roy,
our secknd footman, on the fust landing-place.

"𝔇octor 𝔈gnatius 𝔏oyola!" says the groom of the chambers,
who pretends to be a schollar; and in the little genlmn went.
When safely housed, the other chap came; and when I asked him
his name, said, in a thick, gobbling kind of voice—

"Sawedwadgeorgeearllittnbulwig."

"Sir what?" says I, quite agast at the name.

"Sawedwad—no, I mean *Mistaw*edwad Lyttn Bulwig."

My neas trembled under me, my i's fild with tiers, my voice
shook, as I past up the venrabble name to the other footman, and
saw this fust of English writers go up to the drawing-room!

It's needless to mention the names of the rest of the compny,
or to dixcribe the suckmstansies of the dinner. Suffiz to say that
the two littery genlmn behaved very well, and seamed to have
good appytights; igspecially the little Irishman in the whig, who
et, drunk, and talked as much as ½ a duzn. He told how he'd
been presented at cort by his friend, Mr. Bulwig, and how the
Quean had received 'em both, with a dignity undigscribable; and
how her blessid Majisty asked what was the bony fidy sale of the
Cabinit Cyclopædy, and how he (Doctor Larner) told her that, on
his honner, it was under ten thowsnd.

You may guess that the Doctor, when he made this speach, was
pretty far gone. The fact is, that whether it was the coronation,
or the goodness of the wine (cappitle it is in our house, *I* can tell
you), or the natral propensaties of the gests assembled, which made
them so igspecially jolly, I don't know; but they had kep up the
meating pretty late, and our poar butler was quite tired with the

perpechual baskits of clarrit which he'd been called upon to bring up. So that about 11 o'clock, if I were to say they were merry, I should use a mild term; if I wer to say they were intawsicated, I should use an igspresshn more near to the truth, but less rispeckful in one of my situashn.

The cumpany reseaved this annountsmint with mute extonishment.

" Pray, Doctor Larnder," says a spiteful genlmn, willing to keep up the littery conversation, " what is the Cabinet Cyclopædia ? '

" It's the littherary wontherr of the wurrld," says he ; " and sure your Lordship must have seen it ; the latther numbers ispicially —cheap as durrt, bound in gleezed calico, six shillings a vollum. The illusthrious neems of Walther Scott, Thomas Moore, Docther Southey, Sir James Mackintosh, Docther Donovan, and meself, are to be found in the list of conthributors. It's the Phaynix of Cyclopajies—a litherary Bacon."

" A what ? " says the genlmn nex to him.

" A Bacon, shining in the darkness of our age ; fild wid the pure end lambent flame of science, burning with the gorrgeous scintillations of divine litherature—a *monumintum* in fact, *are perinnius*, bound in pink calico, six shillings a vollum."

" This wigmawole," said Mr. Bulwig (who seemed rather disgusted that his friend should take up so much of the convassation), " this wigmawole is all vewy well ; but it's cuwious that you don't wemember, in chawactewising the litewawy mewits of the vawious magazines, cwonicles, weviews, and encyclopædias, the existence of a cwitical weview and litewawy chwonicle, which, though the æwa of its appeawance is dated only at a vewy few months pwevious to the pwesent pewiod, is, nevertheless, so wemarkable for its intwinsic mewits as to be wead, not in the metwopolis alone, but in the countwy—not in Fwance merely, but in the west of Euwope—whewever our pure Wenglish is spoken, it stwetches its peaceful sceptre—pewused in Amewica, fwom New York to Niagawa—wepwinted in Canada, from Montweal to Towonto—and, as I am gwatified to hear fwom my fwend the governor of Cape Coast Castle, wegularly weceived in Afwica, and twanslated into the Mandingo language by the missionawies and the bushwangers. I need not say, gentlemen—sir—that is, Mr. Speaker—I mean, Sir John— that I allude to the Litewawy Chwonicle, of which I have the honour to be pwincipal contwibutor."

" Very true, my dear Mr. Bullwig," says my master : " you and I being Whigs, must of course stand by our own friends ; and I will agree, without a moment's hesitation, that the Literary what-d'ye-call-'em is the prince of periodicals."

"The Pwince of pewiodicals?" says Bullwig; "my dear Sir John, it's the empewow of the pwess."

"*Soit*,—let it be the emperor of the press, as you poetically call it : but, between ourselves, confess it,—Do not the Tory writers beat your Whigs hollow? You talk about magazines. Look at——"

"Look at hwat?" shouts out Larder. "There's none, Sir Jan, compared to ourrs."

"Pardon me, I think that——"

"It is ' Bentley's Mislany' you mane?" says Ignatius, as sharp as a niddle.

"Why, no ; but——"

"O thin, it's Co'burn, sure ; and that divvle Thayodor—a pretty paper, sir, but light—thrashy, milk-and-wathery—not sthrong, like the Litherary Chran—good luck to it."

"Why, Doctor Larnder, I was going to tell at once the name of the periodical,—it is FRASER'S MAGAZINE."

"FRESER!" says the Doctor. "O thunder and turf!"

"FWASER!" says Bullwig. "O—ah—hum—haw—yes—no— why,—that is weally—no, weally, upon my weputation, I never before heard the name of the pewiodical. By-the-bye, Sir John, what wemarkable good clawet this is ; is it Lawose or Laff——?"

Laff, indeed ! he cooden git beyond laff ; and I'm blest if I could kip it neither,—for hearing him pretend ignurnts, and being behind the skreend, settlin sumthink for the genlmn, I bust into such a raw of laffing as never was igseeded.

"Hullo !" says Bullwig, turning red. "Have I said anything impwobable, aw widiculous? for, weally, I never befaw wecollect to have heard in society such a twemendous peal of cachinnation—that which the twagic bard who fought at Mawathon has called an *anë-withmon gelasma*."

"Why, be the holy piper," says Larder, "I think you are dthrawing a little on your imagination. Not read *Fraser!* Don't believe him, my Lord Duke ; he reads every word of it, the rogue ! The boys about that magazine baste him as if he was a sack of oat-male. My reason for crying out, Sir Jan, was because you mintioned *Fraser* at all. Bullwig has every syllable of it be heart—from the paillitix down to the ' Yellowplush Correspondence.'"

"Ha, ha !" says Bullwig, affecting to laff (you may be sure my years prickt up when I heard the name of the "Yellowplush Correspondence"). "Ha, ha ! why, to tell twuth, I *have* wead the cowespondence to which you allude : it's a gweat favowite at Court. I was talking with Spwing Wice and John Wussel about it the other day."

"Well, and what do you think of it?" says Sir John, looking mity waggish—for he knew it was me who roat it.

"Why, weally and twuly, there's considewable cleverness about the cweature; but it's low, disgustingly low : it violates pwobability, and the orthogwaphy is so carefully inaccuwate, that it requires a positive study to compwehend it."

"Yes, faith," says Larner; "the arthagraphy is detestible; it's as bad for a man to write bad spillin as it is for 'em to speak wid a brrogue. Iducation furst, and ganius afterwards. Your health, my Lord, and good luck to you."

"Yaw wemark," says Bullwig, "is very appwopwiate. You will wecollect, Sir John, in Hewodotus (as for you, Doctor, you know more about Iwish than about Gweek),—you will wecollect, without doubt, a stowy nawwated by that cwedulous though fascinating chwonicler, of a certain kind of sheep which is known only in a certain distwict of Awabia, and of which the tail is so enormous, that it either dwaggles on the gwound, or is bound up by the shepherds of the country into a small wheelbawwow, or cart, which makes the chwonicler sneewingly wemark that thus 'the sheep of Awabia have their own chawiots.' I have often thought, sir (this clawet is weally nectaweous)—I have often, I say, thought that the wace of man may be compawed to these Awabian sheep—genius is our tail, education our wheelbawwow. Without art and education to pwop it, this genius dwops on the gwound, and is polluted by the mud, or injured by the wocks upon the way : with the wheelbawwow it is stwengthened, incweased, and supported—a pwide to the owner, a blessing to mankind."

"A very appropriate simile," says Sir John; "and I am afraid that the genius of our friend Yellowplush has need of some such support."

"A propos," said Bullwig, "who is Yellowplush? I was given to understand that the name was only a fictitious one, and that the papers were written by the author of the 'Diary of a Physician;' if so, the man has wonderfully improved in style, and there is some hope of him."

"Bah!" says the Duke of Doublejowl; "everybody knows it's Barnard, the celebrated author of 'Sam Slick.'"

"Pardon, my dear duke," says Lord Bagwig; "it's the authoress of 'High Life,' 'Almack's,' and other fashionable novels."

"Fiddlestick's end!" says Doctor Larner; "don't be blushing and pretinding to ask questions : don't we know yo··, Bullwig? It's you yourself, you thief of the world: we smoked y ·u from the very beginning."

Bullwig was about indignantly to reply, when Sir John inter

rupted them, and said,—"I must correct you all, gentlemen; Mr. Yellowplush is no other than Mr. Yellowplush: he gave you, my dear Bullwig, your last glass of champagne at dinner, and is now an inmate of my house, and an ornament of my kitchen!"

"Gad!" says Doublejowl, "let's have him up."

"Hear, hear!" says Bagwig.

"Ah, now," says Larner, "your Grace is not going to call up and talk to a footman, sure? Is it gintale?"

"To say the least of it," says Bullwig, "the pwactice is iwwegular, and indecowous; and I weally don't see how the interview can be in any way pwofitable."

But the vices of the company went against the two littery men, and everybody excep them was for having up poor me. The bell was wrung; butler came. "Send up Charles," says master; and Charles, who was standing behind the skreand, was persnly abliged to come in.

"Charles," says master, "I have been telling these gentlemen who is the author of the 'Yellowplush Correspondence' in *Fraser's Magazine*."

"It's the best magazine in Europe," says the Duke.

"And no mistake," says my Lord.

"Hwhat!" says Larner; "and where's the Litherary Chran?"

I said myself nothink, but made a bough, and blusht like picklecabbitch.

"Mr. Yellowplush," says his Grace, "will you, in the first place, drink a glass of wine?"

I boughed agin.

"And what wine do you prefer, sir,—humble port or imperial burgundy?"

"Why, your Grace," says I, "I know my place, and ain't above kitchin wines. I will take a glass of port, and drink it to the health of this honrabble compny."

When I'd swigged off the bumper, which his Grace himself did me the honour to pour out for me, there was a silints for a minnit; when my master said:—

"Charles Yellowplush, I have perused your memoirs in *Fraser's Magazine* with so much curiosity, and have so high an opinion of your talents as a writer, that I really cannot keep you as a footman any longer, or allow you to discharge duties for which you are now quite unfit. With all my admiration for your talents, Mr. Yellowplush, I still am confident that many of your friends in the servants' hall will clean my boots a great deal better than a gentleman of your genius can ever be expected to do—it is for this purpose I employ footmen, and not that they may be writing articles in magazines. But—you need not look so red, my good fellow, and had better take another glass of port—I don't wish to throw you upon the wide world without the means of a livelihood, and have made interest for a little place which you will have under Government, and which will give you an income of eighty pounds per annum; which you can double, I presume, by your literary labours."

"Sir," says I, clasping my hands, and busting into tears, "do not—for Heaven's sake, do not!—think of any such think, or drive me from your suvvice, because I have been fool enough to write in magaseens. Glans but one moment at your honour's plate—every spoon is as bright as a mirror; condysend to igsamine your shoes—your honour may see reflected in them the fases of every one in the company. *I* blacked them shoes, *I* cleaned that there plate. If occasionally I've forgot the footman in the litterary man, and committed to paper my remindicences of fashnabble life, it was from a sincere desire to do good, and promote nollitch: and I appeal to your honour,—I lay my hand on my busm, and in the fase of this noble company beg you to say, When you rung your bell, who came to you fust? When you stopt out at Brooks's till morning, who sat up for you? When you was ill, who forgot the natral dignities of his station, and answered the two-pair bell? Oh, sir," says I, "I know what's what; don't send me away. I know them littery chaps, and, beleave me, I'd rather be a footman. The work's not so hard—the pay is better: the vittels incompyrably supearor. I have but to clean my things, and run my errints, and you put clothes on my back, and meat in my mouth. Sir! Mr. Bullwig! ain't I right? shall I quit *my* station and sink—that is to say, rise—to *yours*?"

Bullwig was violently affected; a tear stood in his glistening i. "Yellowplush," says he, seizing my hand, "you *are* right. Quit not your present occupation; black boots, clean knives, wear plush all your life, but don't turn literary man. Look at me. I am the first novelist in Europe. I have ranged with eagle wing over the wide regions of literature, and perched on every eminence in its turn. I have gazed with eagle eyes on the sun of philosophy, and fathomed the mysterious depths of the human mind. All languages are familiar to me, all thoughts are known to me, all men understood by me. I have gathered wisdom from the honeyed lips of Plato, as we wandered in the gardens of Academes—wisdom, too, from the mouth of Job Johnson, as we smoked our 'backy in Seven Dials. Such must be the studies, and such is the mission, in this world, of the Poet-Philosopher. But the knowledge is only emptiness; the initiation is but misery; the initiated, a man shunned and bann'd by his fellows. Oh," said Bullwig, clasping his hands, and throwing his fine i's up to the chandelier, "the curse of

Pwometheus descends upon his wace. Wath and punishment pursue them from genewation to genewation! Wo to genius, the heaven-scaler, the fire-stealer! Wo and thrice bitter desolation! Earth is the wock on which Zeus, wemorseless, stwetches his withing victim —men, the vultures that feed and fatten on him. Ai, Ai! it is agony eternal—gwoaning and solitawy despair! And you, Yellow-plush, would penetwate these mystewies: you would waise the awful veil, and stand in the twemendous Pwesence. Beware; as you value your peace, beware! Withdwaw, wash Neophyte! For Heaven's sake—O for Heaven's sake!"—here he looked round with agony—" give me a glass of bwandy-and-water, for this clawet is beginning to disagwee with me."

Bullwig having concluded this spitch, very much to his own sattasfackshn, looked round to the compny for aplaws, and then swigged off the glass of brandy-and-water, giving a sollum sigh as he took the last gulph; and then Doctor Ignatius, who longed for a chans, and, in order to show his independence, began flatly contradicting his friend, addressed me, and the rest of the genlmn present, in the following manner:—

"Hark ye," says he, "my gossoon, doan't be led asthray by the nonsinse of that divil of a Bullwig. He's jillous of ye, my bhoy: that's the rale undoubted thruth; and it's only to keep you out of litherary life that he's palavering you in this way. I'll tell you what—Plush, ye blackguard,—my honourable frind the mimber there has told me a hunder times by the smallest computation, of his intense admiration of your talents, and the wonderful sthir they were making in the world. He can't bear a rival. He's mad with envy, hatred, oncharatableness. Look at him, Plush, and look at me. My father was not a juke exactly, nor aven a markis, and see, neverthe-liss, to what a pitch I am come. I spare no ixpinse; I'm the iditor of a cople of pariodicals; I dthrive about in me carridge; I dine wid the lords of the land; and why—in the name of the piper that pleed before Mosus, hwy? Because I'm a litherary man. Because I know how to play me cards. Because I'm Docther Larner, in fact, and mimber of every society in and out of Europe. I might have re-mained all my life in Thrinity Colledge, and never made such an incom as that offered you by Sir Jan; but I came to London—to London, my boy, and now see! Look again at me friend Bullwig. He *is* a gentleman, to be sure, and bad luck to 'im, say I; and what has been the result of his litherary labour? I'll tell you what; and I'll tell this gintale society, by the shade of Saint Patrick, they're going to make him a BARINET!"

"A BARNET, Doctor!" says I; "you don't mean to say they're going to make him a barnet!"

"As sure as I've made meself a docthor," says Larner.

"What, a baronet, like Sir John?"

"The divle a bit else."

"And pray what for?"

"What faw?" says Bullwig.   "Ask the histowy of litwatuwe what faw?   Ask Colburn, ask Bentley, ask Saunders and Otley, ask the gweat Bwitish nation, what faw?   The blood in my veins comes puwified thwough ten thousand years of chivalwous ancestwy ; but that is neither here nor there : my political pwinciples—the equal wights which I have advocated—the gweat cause of fweedom that I have celebwated, are known to all.   But this, I confess, has nothing to do with the question.   No, the question is this—on the thwone of litewature I stand unwivalled, pwe-eminent ; and the Bwitish government, honowing genius in me, compliments the Bwitish nation by lifting into the bosom of the heweditawy nobility the most gifted member of the democwacy."   (The honrabble genlmn here sunk down amidst repeated cheers.)

"Sir John," says I, "and my Lord Duke, the words of my rivrint frend Ignatius, and the remarks of the honrabble genlmn who has just sate down, have made me change the detummination which I had the honor of igspressing just now.

"I igsept the eighty pound a year ; knowing that I shall have plenty of time for pursuing my littery career, and hoping some day to set on that same bentch of barranites, which is deckarated by the presnts of my honrabble friend.

"Why shooden I?   It's trew I ain't done anythink as *yet* to deserve such an honour ; and it's very probable that I never shall. But what then?—*quaw dong*, as our friends say?   I'd much rayther have a coat-of-arms than a coat of livry.   I'd much rayther have my blud-red hand spralink in the middle of a shield, than underneath a tea-tray.   A barranit I will be ; and, in consiquints, must cease to be a footmin.

"As to my politticle princepills, these, I confess, ain't settled : they are, I know, necessary ; but they ain't necessary *until askt for ;* besides, I reglar read the *Sattarist* newspaper, and so ignirince on this pint would be inigscusable.

"But if one man can git to be a doctor, and another a barranit, and another a capting in the navy, and another *a* countess, and another the wife of a governor of the Cape of Good Hope, I begin to perseave that the littery trade ain't such a very bad un ; igspecially if you're up to snough, and know what's o'clock.   I'll learn to make myself usefle, in the fust place ; then I'll larn to spell ; and, I trust, by reading the novvles of the honrabble member, and the scientafick treatiseses of the reverend doctor, I may find the secrit of suxess, and git a litell for my own share. I've sevral frends in the press, having paid for many of those chaps' drink, and given them other treets; and so I think I've got all the emilents of suxess; therefore, I am detummined, as I said, to igsept your kind offer, and beg to withdraw the wuds which I made yous of when I refyoused your hoxpatable offer. I must, however——"

"I wish you'd withdraw yourself" said Sir John, bursting into a most igstrorinary rage, "and not interrupt the company with your infernal talk! Go down, and get us coffee: and, heark ye! hold your impertinent tongue, or I'll break every bone in your body. You shall have the place as I said; and while you're in my service, you shall be my servant; but you don't stay in my service after to-morrow. Go downstairs, sir; and don't stand staring here!"

.   .   .   .

In this abrupt way, my evening ended: it's with a melancholy regret that I think what came of it. I don't wear plush any more. I am an altered, a wiser, and, I trust, a better man.

I'm about a novvle (having made great progriss in spelling), in the style of my friend Bullwig; and preparing for publigation, in the Doctor's Cyclopedear, "The Lives of Eminent Brittish and Foring Wosherwomen."

SKIMMINGS FROM "THE DAIRY OF GEORGE IV."

CHARLES YELLOWPLUSH, ESQ., TO OLIVER YORKE, ESQ.*

DEAR WHY,—Takin advantage of the Crismiss holydays, Sir John and me (who is a member of parlyment) had gone down to our place in Yorkshire for six wicks, to shoot grows and woodcox, and enjoy old English hospitalaty. This ugly Canady bisniss unluckaly put an end to our sports in the country, and brot us up to Buckly Square as fast as four posterses could gallip. When there, I found your parcel, containing the two vollumes of a new book ; witch, as I have been away from the literary world, and emplied solely in athlatic exorcises, have been laying neglected in my pantry, among my knife-cloaths, and dekanters, and blacking-bottles, and bedroom candles, and things.

This will, I'm sure, account for my delay in notussing the work. I see sefral of the papers and magazeens have been befoarhand with me, and have given their apinions concerning it : specially the *Quotly Revew*, which has most mussilessly cut to peases the author of this *Dairy of the Times of George IV.*†

That it's a woman who wrote it is evydent from the style of the writing, as well as from certain proofs in the book itself. Most suttnly a femail wrote this *Dairy ;* but who this *Dairy-maid* may be, I, in coarse, can't conjecter : and indeed, common galliantry forbids me to ask. I can only judge of the book itself ; which, it appears to me, is clearly trenching upon my ground and favrite

---

* These Memoirs were originally published in *Fraser's Magazine,* and it may be stated for the benefit of the unlearned in such matters that " Oliver Yorke " is the assumed name of the editor of that periodical.

† *Diary illustrative of the Times of George the Fourth, interspersed with Original Letters from the late Queen Caroline, and from various other distinguished Persons.*

" Tôt ou tard, tout se sçait."—MAINTENON.

In 2 vols. London, 1838. Henry Colburn.

subjicks, viz. fashnabble life, as igsibited in the houses of the nobility, gentry, and rile fammly.

But I bare no mallis—infamation is infamation, and it doesn't matter where the infamy comes from; and whether the *Dairy* be from that distinguished pen to witch it is ornarily attributed—whether, I say, it comes from a lady of honour to the late Quean, or a scullion to that diffunct majisty, no matter: all we ask is nollidge; never mind how we have it. Nollidge, as our cook says, is like trikel-possit—it's always good, though you was to drink it out of an old shoo.

Well, then, although this *Dairy* is likely searusly to injur my pussonal intrests, by fourstalling a deal of what I had to say in my private memoars—though many many guineas is taken from my pockit, by cuttin short the tail of my narratif—though much that I had to say in souperior languidge, greased with all the ellygance of my orytory, the benefick of my classcle reading, the chawms of my agreble wit, is thus abruply brot befor the world by an inferior genus, neither knowing nor writing English; yet I say, that nevertheless I must say, what I am puffickly prepaired to say, to gainsay which no man can say a word—yet I say, that I say I consider this publication welkom. Far from viewing it with enfy, I greet it with applaws; because it increases that most exlent specious of nollidge, I mean "FASHNABBLE NOLLIDGE:" compayred to witch all other nollidge is nonsince—a bag of goold to a pare of snuffers.

Could Lord Broom, on the Canady question, say moar? or say what he had tu say better? We are marters, both of us, to prinsple; and everybody who knows eather knows that we would sacrafice anythink rather than that. Fashion is the goddiss I adoar. This delightful work is an offring on her srine; and as sich all her wushippers are bound to hail it. Here is not a question of trumpry lords and honrabbles, generals and barronites, but the crown itself, and the king and queen's actions; witch may be considered as the crown jewels. Here's princes, and grand-dukes, and airsparent, and Heaven knows what; all with blood-royal in their veins, and their names mentioned in the very fust page of the peeridge. In this book you become so intmate with the Prince of Wales, that you may follow him, if you please, to his marridge-bed; or, if you prefer the Princiss Charlotte, you may have with her an hour's tator-tator.*

Now, though most of the remarkable extrax from this book have been given already (the cream of the *Dairy*, as I wittily say),

---

* Our estimable correspondent means, we presume, *tête-à-tête.*—O. Y.

I shall trouble you, nevertheless, with a few; partly because they can't be repeated too often, and because the toan of obsyvation with which they have been genrally received by the press, is not igsackly such as I think they merit. How, indeed, can these common magaseen and newspaper pipple know anythink of fashnabble life, let alone ryal?

Conseaving, then, that the publication of the *Dairy* has done reel good on this scoar, and may probly do a deal moor, I shall look through it, for the porpus of selecting the most ellygant passidges, and which I think may be peculiarly adapted to the reader's benefick.

For you see, my dear Mr. Yorke, in the fust place, that this is no common catchpny book, like that of most authors and authoresses who write for the base looker of gain. Heaven bless you! the Dairymaid is above anything musnary. She is a woman of rank, and no mistake; and is as much above doin a common or vulgar action as I am superaor to taking beer after dinner with my cheese. She proves that most satisfackarily, as we see in the following passidge :—

"Her Royal Highness came to me, and having spoken a few phrases on different subjects, produced all the papers she wishes to have published : her whole correspondence with the Prince relative to Lady J——'s dismissal; his subsequent neglect of the Princess ; and, finally, the acquittal of her supposed guilt, signed by the Duke of Portland, &c., at the time of the secret inquiry : when, if proof could have been brought against her, it certainly would have been done ; and which acquittal, to the disgrace of all parties concerned, as well as to the justice of the nation in general, was not made public at the time. A common criminal is publicly condemned or acquitted. Her Royal Highness commanded me to have these letters published forthwith, saying, 'You may sell them for a great sum.' At first (for she had spoken to me before concerning this business), I thought of availing myself of the opportunity ; but, upon second thoughts, I turned from this idea with detestation : for, if I do wrong by obeying her wishes and endeavouring to serve her, I will do so at least from good and disinterested motives, not from any sordid views. The Princess commands me, and I will obey her, whatever may be the issue ; but not for fare or fee. I own I tremble, not so much for myself, as for the idea that she is not taking the best and most dignified way of having these papers published. Why make a secret of it at all? If wrong, it should not be done ; if right, it should be done openly, and in the face of her enemies. In Her Royal Highness's case, as in that of wronged princes in general, why do they shrink from straightforward dealings, and rather have recourse to crooked policy?

I wish, in this particular instance, I could make Her Royal Highness feel thus: but she is naturally indignant at being falsely accused, and will not condescend to an avowed explanation."

Can anythink be more just and honrabble than this? The Dairy-lady is quite fair and abovebored. A clear stage, says she, and no faviour! "I won't do behind my back what I am ashamed of before my face: not I!" No more she does; for you see that, though she was offered this manyscrip by the Princess *for nothink*, though she knew that she could actially get for it a large sum of money, she was above it, like an honest, noble, grateful, fashnabble woman, as she was. She aboars secrecy, and never will have recors to disguise or crookid polacy. This ought to be an ansure to them *Radicle sneerers*, who pretend that they are the equals of fashnabble pepple; whereas it's a well-known fact, that the vulgar roagues have no notion of honour.

And after this positif declaration, which reflex honor on her Ladyship (long life to her! I've often waited behind her chair!)— after this positif declaration, that, even for the porpus of *defending* her missis, she was so hi-minded as to refuse anythink like a peculiarly consideration, it is actially asserted in the public prints by a booxeller, that he has given her *a thousand pound* for the *Dairy*. A thousand pound! nonsince!—it's a phigment! a base lible! This woman take a thousand pound, in a matter where her dear mistriss, friend, and benyfactriss was concerned! Never! A thousand baggonits would be more prefrabble to a woman of her xqizzit feelins and fashion.

But to proseed. It's been objected to me, when I wrote some of my expearunces in fashnabble life, that my languidge was occasionally vulgar, and not such as is generally used in those exquizzit famlies which I frequent. Now, I'll lay a wager that there is in this book, wrote as all the world knows by a rele lady, and speakin of kings and queens as if they were as common as sand-boys—there is in this book more wulgarity than ever I displayed, more nastiness than ever I would dare to *think on*, and more bad grammar than ever I wrote since I was a boy at school. As for authografy, evry genlmn has his own: never mind spellin, I say, so long as the sence is right.

Let me here quot a letter from a corryspondent of this charming lady of honour; and a very nice corryspondent he is, too, without any mistake :—

"Lady O——, poor Lady O——! knows the rules of prudence, I fear me, as imperfectly as she doth those of the Greek and Latin

Grammars: or she hath let her brother, who is a sad swine, become master of her secrets, and then contrived to quarrel with him. You would see the outline of the *mélange* in the newspapers; but not the report that Mr. S—— is about to publish a pamphlet, as an addition to the Harleian Tracts, setting forth the amatory adventures of his sister. We shall break our necks in haste to buy it, of course crying ' Shameful ' all the while; and it is said that Lady O—— is to be cut, which I cannot entirely believe. Let her tell two or three old women about town that they are young and handsome, and give some well-timed parties, and she may still keep the society which she hath been used to. The times are not so hard as they once were, when a woman could not construe Magna Charta with anything like impunity. People were full as gallant many years ago. But the days are gone by wherein my lord-protector of the commonwealth of England was wont to go a love-making to Mrs. Fleetwood, with the Bible under his arm.

"And so Miss Jacky Gordon is really clothed with a husband at last, and Miss Laura Manners left without a mate ! She and Lord Stair should marry and have children, in mere revenge. As to Miss Gordon, she's a Venus well suited for such a Vulcan,— whom nothing but money and a title could have rendered tolerable, even to a kitchen wench. It is said that the matrimonial correspondence between this couple is to be published, full of sad scandalous relations, of which you may be sure scarcely a word is true. In former times, the Duchess of St. A——s made use of these elegant epistles in order to intimidate Lady Johnstone: but that *ruse* would not avail; so in spite, they are to be printed. What a cargo of amiable creatures ! Yet will some people scarcely believe in the existence of Pandemonium.

"*Tuesday Morning.*—You are perfectly right respecting the hot rooms here, which we all cry out against, and all find very comfortable—much more so than the cold sands and bleak neighbourhood of the sea; which looks vastly well in one of Van der Velde's pictures hung upon crimson damask, but hideous and shocking in reality. H—— and his ' *elle* ' (talking of parties) were last night at Cholmondeley House, but seem not to ripen in their love. He is certainly good-humoured, and, I believe, good-hearted, so deserves a good wife; but his *cara* seems a genuine London miss, made up of many affectations. Will she form a comfortable helpmate? For me, I like not her origin, and deem many strange things to run in blood, besides madness and the Hanoverian evil.

"*Thursday.*—I verily do believe that I shall never get to the end of this small sheet of paper, so many unheard-of interruptions have I had; and now I have been to Vauxhall, and caught the

toothache. I was of Lady E. B——m and H——'s party : very
dull—the Lady giving us all a supper after our promenade—

> ' Much ado was there, God wot
> She would love, but he would not.'

He ate a great deal of ice, although he did not seem to require it ;
and she '*faisoit les yeux doux*' enough not only to have melted
all the ice which he swallowed, but his own hard heart into the
bargain. The thing will not do.   In the meantime, Miss Long
hath become quite cruel to Wellesley Pole, and divides her favour
equally between Lords Killeen and Kilworth, two as simple Irishmen as ever gave birth to a bull.   I wish to Hymen that she were
fairly married, for all this pother gives one a disgusting picture of
human nature."

A disgusting pictur of human nature, indeed—and isn't he who
moralises about it, and she to whom he writes, a couple of pretty
heads in the same piece ?   Which, Mr. Yorke, is the wust, the
scandle or the scandle-mongers ?   See what it is to be a moral man
of fashn.   Fust, he scrapes togither all the bad stoaries about all
the people of his accuentance—he goes to a ball, and laffs or snears
at everybody there—he is asked to a dinner, and brings away,
along with meat and wine to his heart's content, a sour stomick
filled with nasty stories of all the people present there.   He has
such a squeamish appytite, that all the world seems to *disagree*
with him.   And what has he got to say to his dellicate female
frend ?   Why that—

Fust Mr. S. is going to publish indescent stoaries about Lady
O——, his sister, which everybody's goin to by.

Nex. That Miss Gordon is going to be cloathed with an usband ;
and that all their matrimonial corryspondins is to be published too.

3. That Lord H. is going to be married ; but there's something
rong in his wife's blood.

4. Miss Long has cut Mr. Wellesley, and is gone after two
Irish lords.

Wooden you phancy, now, that the author of such a letter,
instead of writin about pipple of tip-top qualaty, was describin
Vinegar Yard ?   Would you beleave that the lady he was a-ritin
to was a chased, modist lady of honour, and mother of a family ?
O trumpery !   O morris ! as Homer says : this is a higeous pictur
of manners, such as I weap to think of, as evry morl man must
weap.

The above is one pritty pictur of mearly fashnabble life : what
follows is about families even higher situated than the most fash-

23

nabble. Here we have the Princessregient, her daughter the Princess Sharlot, her grandmamma the old Quean, and Her Madjisty's daughters the two princesses. If this is not high life, I don't know where it is to be found; and it's pleasing to see what affeckshn and harmny rains in such an exolted spear.

"*Sunday* 24*th.*—Yesterday the Princess went to meet the Princess Charlotte at Kensington. Lady —— told me that, when the latter arrived, she rushed up to her mother, and said, 'For God's sake, be civil to her,' meaning the Duchess of Leeds, who followed her. Lady —— said she felt sorry for the latter; but when the Princess of Wales talked to her, she soon became so free and easy, that one could not have any *feeling* about her *feelings*. Princess Charlotte, I was told, was looking handsome, very pale, but her head more becomingly dressed—that is to say, less dressed than usual. Her figure is of that full round shape which is now in its prime; but she disfigures herself by wearing her bodice so short, that she literally has no waist. Her feet are very pretty; and so are her hands and arms, and her ears, and the shape of her head. Her countenance is expressive, when she allows her passions to play upon it; and I never saw any face, with so little shade, express so many powerful and varied emotions. Lady —— told me that the Princess Charlotte talked to her about her situation, and said, in a very quiet, but determined way, she *would not bear it*, and that as soon as Parliament met, she intended to come to Warwick House, and remain there; that she was also determined not to consider the Duchess of Leeds as her *governess*, but only as her *first lady.* She made many observations on other persons and subjects; and appears to be very quick, very penetrating, but imperious and wilful. There is a tone of romance, too, in her character, which will only serve to mislead her.

"She told her mother that there had been a great battle at Windsor between the Queen and the Prince, the former refusing to give up Miss Knight from her own person to attend on Princess Charlotte as sub-governess. But the Prince-Regent had gone to Windsor himself, and insisted on her doing so; and the 'old Beguin' was forced to submit, but has been ill ever since: and Sir Henry Halford declared it was a complete breaking up of her constitution—to the great delight of the two princesses, who were talking about this affair. Miss Knight was the very person they wished to have; they think they can do as they like with her. It has been ordered that the Princess Charlotte should not see her mother alone for a single moment; but the latter went into her room, stuffed a pair of large shoes full of papers, and having given them to her daughter, she went home. Lady —— told me everything was written down and sent to Mr. Brougham *next day*."

See what discord will creap even into the best regulated famlies. Here are six of 'em—viz., the Quean and her two daughters, her son, and his wife and daughter ; and the manner in which they hate one another is a compleat puzzle.

The Prince hates . . . . $\left\{\begin{array}{l}\text{his mother.}\\\text{his wife.}\\\text{his daughter.}\end{array}\right.$

Princess Charlotte hates her father.
Princess of Wales hates her husband.

The old Quean, by their squobbles, is on the pint of death ; and her two jewtiful daughters are delighted at the news. What a happy, fashnabble, Christian famly ! O Mr. Yorke, Mr. Yorke, if this is the way in the drawin-rooms, I'm quite content to live below, in pease and charaty with all men ; writin, as I am now, in my pantry, or els havin a quite game at cards in the servants-all. With *us* there's no bitter wicked quarling of this sort. *We* don't hate our children, or bully our mothers, or wish 'em ded when they're sick, as this Dairy-woman says kings and queens do. When we're writing to our friends or sweethearts, *we* don't fill our letters with nasty stoaries, takin away the carricter of our fellow-servants, as this maid of honour's amusin' moral frend does. But, in coarse, it's not for us to judge of our betters ;—these great people are a supeerur race, and we can't comprehend their ways.

Do you recklect—it's twenty years ago now—how a bewtiffle princess died in givin buth to a poar baby, and how the whole nation of Hengland wep, as though it was one man, over that sweet woman and child, in which were sentered the hopes of every one of us, and of which each was as proud as of his own wife or infnt ? Do you recklet how pore fellows spent their last shillin to buy a black crape for their hats, and clergymen cried in the pulpit, and the whole country through was no better than a great dismal funeral ? Do you recklect, Mr. Yorke, who was the person that we all took on so about ? We called her the Princis Sharlot of Wales ; and we valyoud a single drop of her blood more than the whole heartless body of her father. Well, we looked up to her as a kind of saint or angle, and blest God (such foolish loyal English pipple as we ware in those days) who had sent this sweet lady to rule over us. But Heaven bless you ! it was only souperstition. She was no better than she should be, as it turns out—or at least the Dairymaid says so. No better?—if my daughters or yours was ½ so bad, we'd as leaf be dead ourselves, and they hanged. But listen to this pritty charritable story, and a truce to reflexshuns :—

"*Sunday, January* 9, 1814.—Yesterday, according to appointment, I went to Princess Charlotte. Found at Warwick House the harp-player, Dizzi; was asked to remain and listen to his performance, but was talked to during the whole time, which completely prevented all possibility of listening to the music. The Duchess of Leeds and her daughter were in the room, but left it soon. Next arrived Miss Knight, who remained all the time I was there. Princess Charlotte was very gracious—showed me all her *bonny dyes*, as B—— would have called them—pictures, and cases, and jewels, &c. She talked in a very desultory way, and it would be difficult to say of what. She observed her mother was in very low spirits. I asked her how she supposed she could be otherwise? This *questioning* answer saves a great deal of trouble, and serves two purposes—*i.e.* avoids committing oneself, or giving offence by silence. There was hung in the apartment one portrait, amongst others, that very much resembled the Duke of D——. I asked Miss Knight whom it represented. She said that was not known; it had been supposed a likeness of the Pretender, when young. This answer suited my thoughts so comically I could have laughed, if one ever did at Courts anything but the contrary of what one was inclined to do.

"Princess Charlotte has a very great variety of expression in her countenance—a play of features, and a force of muscle, rarely seen in connection with such soft and shadeless colouring. Her hands and arms are beautiful; but I think her figure is already gone, and will soon be precisely like her mother's : in short it is the very picture of her, and *not in miniature.* I could not help analysing my own sensations during the time I was with her, and thought more of them than I did of her. Why was I at all flattered, at all more amused, at all more supple to this young princess, than to her who is only the same sort of person set in the shade of circumstances and of years? It is that youth, and the approach of power, and the latent views of self-interest, sway the heart and dazzle the understanding. If this is so with a heart not, I trust, corrupt, and a head not particularly formed for interested calculations, what effect must not the same causes produce on the generality of mankind?

"In the course of the conversation, the Princess Charlotte contrived to edge in a good deal of *tum-de-dy,* and would, if I had entered into the thing, have gone on with it, while looking at a little picture of herself, which had about thirty or forty different dresses to put over it, done on *isinglass*, and which allowed the general colouring of the picture to be seen through its transparency. It was, I thought, a pretty enough conceit, though rather like dressing up a doll. 'Ah!' said Miss Knight, 'I am not content though, madame—for I yet should have liked one more dress—that of the favourite Sultana.'

"'No, no!' said the Princess, 'I never was a favourite, and never can be one'—looking at a picture which she said was her father's, but which I do not believe was done for the Regent any more than for me, but represented a young man in a hussar's dress —probably a former favourite.

"The Princess Charlotte seemed much hurt at the little notice that was taken of her birthday. After keeping me for two hours and a half she dismissed me; and I am sure I could not say what she said, except that it was an *olio* of *décousus* and heterogeneous things, partaking of the characteristics of her mother grafted on a younger scion. I dined *tête-à-tête* with my dear old aunt: hers is always a sweet and soothing society to me."

There's a pleasing, lady-like, moral extract for you! An innocent young thing of fifteen has pictures of *two* lovers in her room, and expex a good number more. This dellygate young creature *edges* in a good deal of *tumdedy* (I can't find it in Johnson's Dixonary), and would have *gone on with the thing* (ellygence of languidge), if the dairy-lady would have let her.

Now, to tell you the truth, Mr. Yorke, I doan't beleave a single syllible of this story. This lady of honner says, in the fust place, that the Princess would have talked a good deal of *tumdedy*: which means, I suppose, indeasnsy, if she, the lady of honner, *would have let her*. This *is* a good one! Why, she lets everybody else talk tumdedy to their hearts' content; she lets her friends *write* tumdedy, and, after keeping it for a quarter of a sentry, she *prints* it. Why then be so squeamish about *hearing* a little! And, then, there's the stoary of the two portricks. This woman has the honner to be received in the frendlyest manner by a British princess; and what does the grateful loyal creature do? 2 pictures of the Princess's relations are hanging in her room, and the Dairy-woman swears away the poor young Princess's carrickter, by swearing they are picturs of her *lovers*. For shame, oh, for shame! you slanderin backbitin dairy-woman you! If you told all them things to your "dear old aunt," on going to dine with her, you must have had very "sweet and soothing society" indeed.

I had marked out many more extrax, which I intended to write about ; but I think I have said enough about this Dairy : in fack, the butler, and the gals in the servants'-hall are not well pleased that I should go on reading this naughty book ; so we'll have no more of it, only one passidge about Pollytics, witch is sertnly quite new :—

" No one was so likely to be able to defeat Bonaparte as the Crown Prince, from the intimate knowledge he possessed of his character.   Bernadotte was also instigated against Bonaparte by one who not only owed him a personal hatred, but who possessed a mind equal to his, and who gave the Crown Prince both information and advice how to act.   This was no less a person than Madame de Staël.   It was not, as some have asserted, *that she was in love with Bernadotte ;* for, at the time of their intimacy, *Madame de Staël was in love with Rocca.*   But she used her influence (which was not small) with the Crown Prince, to make him fight against Bonaparte, and to her wisdom may be attributed much of the success which accompanied his attack upon him.   Bernadotte has raised the flame of liberty, which seems fortunately to blaze all around.   May it liberate Europe ; and from the ashes of the laurel may olive branches spring up, and overshadow the earth ! "

There's a discuvery ! that the overthrow of Boneypart is owing to *Madame de Staël !*   What nonsince for Colonel Southey or Doctor Napier to write histories of the war with that Capsican hupstart and murderer, when here we have the whole affair explaned by the lady of honour !

" *Sunday, April* 10, 1814.—The incidents which take place every hour are miraculous.   Bonaparte is deposed, but alive ; subdued, but allowed to choose his place of residence.   The island of Elba is the spot he has selected for his ignominious retreat.   France is holding forth repentant arms to her banished sovereign.   The Poissardes who dragged Louis XVI. to the scaffold are presenting flowers to the Emperor of Russia, the restorer of their legitimate king !   What a stupendous field for philosophy to expatiate in !   What an endless material for thought !   What humiliation to the pride of mere human greatness !   How are the mighty fallen !   Of all that was great in Napoleon, what remains ?   Despoiled of his usurped power, he sinks to insignificance.   There was no moral greatness in the man.   The meteor dazzled, scorched, is put out—utterly, and for ever.   But the power which rests in those who have delivered the nations from bondage, is a power that is delegated to them from Heaven ; and the manner in which they have used it is a guarantee for its continuance.   The Duke of Wellington has gained laurels un-stained by any useless flow of blood.   He has done more than conquer others—he has conquered himself: and in the midst of the blaze and flush of victory, surrounded by the homage of nations, he has not been betrayed into the commission of any act of cruelty or wanton offence.   He was as cool and self-possessed under the blaze and dazzle of fame as a common man would be under the shade of his garden-tree, or by the hearth of his home.   But the tyrant who kept Europe in awe is now a pitiable object for scorn to point the finger of derision at : and humanity shudders as it remembers the scourge with which this man's ambition was permitted to devastate every home tie, and every heartfelt joy."

And now, after this sublime passidge, as full of awfle reflections and pious sentyments as those of Mrs. Cole in the play, I shall only quot one little extrak more :—

" All goes gloomily with the poor Princess.   Lady Charlotte Campbell told me she regrets not seeing all these curious personages ; but she says, the more the Princess is forsaken, the more happy she is at having offered to attend her at this time.   *This is very ami-able in her,* and cannot fail to be gratifying to the Princess."

So it is—wery amiable, wery kind and considerate in her, indeed. Poor Princess ! how lucky you was to find a frend who loved you for your own sake, and when all the rest of the wuld turned its back kep steady to you.   As for believing that Lady Sharlot had any hand in this book,* Heaven forbid ! she is all gratitude, pure grati-tude, depend upon it.   *She* would not go for to blacken her old frend and patron's carrickter, after having been so outrageously faithful to her ; *she* wouldn't do it, at no price, depend upon it.   How sorry she must be that others an't quite so squemish, and show up in this indesent way the follies of her kind, genrus, foolish bennyfactris !

---

* The "authorised" announcement, in the *John Bull* newspaper, sets this question at rest.   It is declared that her Ladyship is not the writer of the *Diary.*—O. Y.

EPISTLES TO THE LITERATI

Ch–s Y–ll–wpl–sh, Esq., to Sir Edward Lytton Bulwer, Bt.

John Thomas Smith, Esq., to C—s Y——h, Esq.

NOTUS

THE suckmstansies of the following harticle are as follos :—Me and my friend, the sellabrated Mr. Smith, reckonised each other in the Haymarket Theatre, during the performints of the new play. I was settn in the gallery, and sung out to him (he was in the pit), to jine us after the play, over a glass of bear and a cold hoyster, in my pantry, the family being out.

Smith came as appinted. We descorsed on the subjick of the comady ; and, after sefral glases, we each of us agreed to write a letter to the other, giving our notiums of the pease. Paper was brought that momint ; and Smith writing his harticle across the knife-bord, I dasht off mine on the dresser.

Our agreement was, that I (being remarkabble for my style of riting) should cretasize the languidge, whilst he should take up with the plot of the play ; and the candied reader will parding me for having holtered the original address of my letter, and directed it to Sir Edward himself ; and for having incopperated Smith's remarks in the midst of my own :—

Mayfair: *Nov.* 30, 1839. *Midnite.*

Honrabble Barnet !—Retired from the littery world a year or moar, I didn't think anythink would injuice me to come forrards again ; for I was content with my share of reputation, and propoas'd to add nothink to those immortial wux which have rendered this Magaseen so sallybrated.

Shall I tell you the reazn of my re-appearants ?—a desire for the benefick of my fellow-creatures ? Fiddlestick ! A mighty truth with which my busm laboured, and which I must bring forth or die ? Nonsince—stuff : money's the secret, my dear Barnet,—

money—*l'argong, gelt, spicunia.* Here's quarter-day coming, and I'm blest if I can pay my landlud, unless I can ad hartificially to my inkum.

This is, however, betwigst you and me. There's no need to blacard the streets with it, or to tell the British public that Fitzroy Y–ll–wpl–sh is short of money, or that the sallybrated hauthor of the Y—— Papers is in peskewniary difficklties, or is fiteagued by his superhuman littery labors, or by his famly suckmstansies, or by any other pusnal matter : my maxim, dear B, is on these pints to be as quiet as posbile. What the juice does the public care for you or me ? Why must we always, in prefizzes and what not, be a-talking about ourselves and our igstrodnary merrats, woas, and injaries ? It is on this subjick that I porpies, my dear Barnet, to speak to you in a frendly way ; and praps you'll find my advise tolrabbly holesum.

Well, then,—if you care about the apinions, fur good or evil, of us poor suvvants, I tell you, in the most candied way, I like you, Barnet. I've had my fling at you in my day (for, *entry nou,* that last stoary I roat about you and Larnder was as big a bownsir as ever was)—I've had my fling at you ; but I like you. One may objeck to an immence deal of your writings, which, betwigst you and me, contain more sham scentiment, sham morallaty, sham poatry, than you'd like to own ; but, in spite of this, there's the *stuff* in you : you've a kind and loyal heart in you, Barnet—a trifle deboshed, perhaps ; a kean i, igspecially for what's comic (as for your tradgady, it's mighty flatchulent), and a ready plesnt pen. The man who says you are an As is an As himself. Don't believe him, Barnet ! not that I suppose you wil,—for, if I've formed a correck apinion of you from your wucks, you think your small-beear as good as most men's : every man does,—and why not ? We brew, and we love our own tap—amen ; but the pint betwigst us, is this stewpid, absudd way of crying out, because the public don't like it too. Why shood they, my dear Barnet ? You may vow that they are fools ; or that the critix are your enemies ; or that the wuld should judge your poams by your critticle rules, and not their own : you may beat your breast, and vow you are a marter, and you won't mend the matter. Take heart, man ! you're not so misrabble after all : your spirits need not be so *very* cast down ; you are not so *very* badly paid. I'd lay a wager that you make, with one thing or another—plays, novvles, pamphlicks, and little odd jobbs here and there—your three thowsnd a year. There's many a man, dear Bullwig, that works for less, and lives content. Why shouldn't you ? Three thowsnd a year is no such bad thing, —let alone the barnetcy : it must be a great comfort to have that bloody hand in your skitching.

But don't you sea, that in a wuld naturally envius, wickid, and fond of a joak, this very barnetcy, these very cumplaints,—this ceaseless groning, and moning, and wining of yours, is igsackly the thing which makes people laff and snear more ? If you were ever at a great school, you must recklect who was the boy most bullid, and buffitid, and purshewd—he who minded it most. He who could take a basting got but few ; he who rord and wep because the knotty boys called him nicknames, was nicknamed wuss and wuss. I recklect there was at our school, in Smithfield, a chap of this milksop spoony sort, who appeared among the romping, ragged fellers in a fine flanning dressing-gownd, that his mama had given him. That pore boy was beaten in a way that his dear ma and aunts didn't know him ; his fine flanning dressing-gownd was torn all to ribbings, and he got no pease in the school ever after, but was abliged to be taken to some other saminary, where, I make no doubt, he was paid off igsactly in the same way.

Do you take the halligory, my dear Barnet ? *Mutayto nominy* —you know what I mean. You are the boy, and your barnetcy is the dressing-gownd. You dress yourself out finer than other chaps and they all begin to sault and hustle you ; it's human nature, Barnet. You show weakness, think of your dear ma, mayhap, and begin to cry : it's all over with you ; the whole school is at you— upper boys and under, big and little ; the dirtiest little fag in the place will pipe out blaggerd names at you, and take his pewny tug at your tail.

The only way to avoid such consperracies is to put a pair of stowt shoalders forrards, and bust through the crowd of raggy-muffins. A good bold fellow dubls his fistt, and cries, " Wha dares meddle wi' me ? " When Scott got *his* barnetcy, for instans, did any one of us cry out ? No, by the laws, he was our master ; and wo betide the chap that say neigh to him ! But there's barnets and barnets. Do you recklect that fine chapter in " Squintin Durward," about the too fellos and cups, at the siege of the bishop's castle ? One of them was a brave warrier, and kep *his* cup ; they strangled the other chap—strangled him, and laffed at him too.

With respeck, then, to the barnetcy pint, this is my advice : brazen it out. Us littery men I take to be like a pack of school-boys—childish, greedy, envius, holding by our friends, and always ready to fight. What must be a man's conduck among such ? He must either take no notis, and pass on myjastick, or else turn round and pummle soundly—one, two, right and left, ding dong over the face and eyes ; above all, never acknowledge that he is hurt. Years ago, for instans (we've no ill-blood, but only mention this by way of igsample), you began a sparring with this Magaseen. Law bless

you, such a ridicklus gaym I never see : a man so belaybord, be-
flustered, bewolloped, was never known ; it was the laff of the whole
town.   Your intelackshal natur, respected Barnet, is not fizzickly
adapted, so to speak, for encounters of this sort.   You must not
indulge in combats with us course bullies of the press : you have
not the *staminy* for a reglar set-to.   What, then, is your plan ?   In
the midst of the mob to pass as quiet as you can : you won't be
undistubbed.   Who is ?   Some stray kix and buffits will fall to
you—mortial man is subjick to such ; but if you begin to wins and
cry out, and set up for a marter, wo betide you !

These remarks, pusnal as I confess them to be, are yet, I assure
you, written in perfick good-natur, and have been inspired by your
play of the " Sea Capting," and prefiz to it ; which latter is on
matters intirely pusnal, and will, therefore, I trust, igscuse this kind
of *ad hominam* (as they say) diskcushion.   I propose, honrabble
Barnit, to cumsider calmly this play and prephiz, and to speak of
both with that honisty which, in the pantry or studdy, I've been
always phamous for.   Let us, in the first place, listen to the opening
of the " Preface to the Fourth Edition : "—

" No one can be more sensible than I am of the many faults
and deficiencies to be found in this play ; but, perhaps, when it is
considered how very rarely it has happened in the history of our
dramatic literature that good acting plays have been produced, except
by those who have either been actors themselves, or formed their
habits of literature, almost of life, behind the scenes, I might have
looked for a criticism more generous, and less exacting and rigorous,
than that by which the attempts of an author accustomed to another
class of composition have been received by a large proportion of the
periodical press.

" It is scarcely possible, indeed, that this play should not contain faults of two kinds : first, the faults of one who has necessarily
much to learn in the mechanism of his art ; and, secondly, of one
who, having written largely in the narrative style of fiction, may
not unfrequently mistake the effects of a novel for the effects of a
drama.   I may add to these, perhaps, the deficiencies that arise
from uncertain health and broken spirits, which render the author
more susceptible than he might have been some years since to that
spirit of depreciation and hostility which it has been his misfortune
to excite amongst the general contributors to the periodical press ;
for the consciousness that every endeavour will be made to cavil, to
distort, to misrepresent, and, in fine, if possible, to *run down*, will
occasionally haunt even the hours of composition, to check the inspira-
tion, and damp the ardour.

"Having confessed thus much frankly and fairly, and with a hope that I may ultimately do better, should I continue to write for the stage (which nothing but an assurance that, with all my defects, I may yet bring some little aid to the drama, at a time when any aid, however humble, ought to be welcome to the lovers of the art, could induce me to do), may I be permitted to say a few words as to some of the objections which have been made against this play?"

Now, my dear sir, look what a pretty number of please you put forrards here, why your play shouldn't be good.

First. Good plays are almost always written by actors.

Secknd. You are a novice to the style of composition.

Third. You *may* be mistaken in your effects, being a novelist by trade, and not a play-writer.

Fourthly. Your in such bad helth and sperrits.

Fifthly. Your so afraid of the critix, that they damp your arder.

For shame, for shame, man! What confeshns is these,—what painful pewling and piping! Your not a babby. I take you to be some seven or eight and thutty years old—"in the morning of youth," as the flosofer says. Don't let any such nonsince take your reazn prisoner. What you, an old hand amongst us,—an old soljer of our sovring quean the press,—you, who have had the best pay, have held the topmost rank (ay, and *deserved* them too!—I gif you lef to quot me in sasiaty, and say, "I *am* a man of genius: Y–ll–wpl–sh says so"),—you to lose heart, and cry pickavy, and begin to howl, because little boys fling stones at you! Fie, man! take courage; and, bearing the terrows of your blood-red hand, as the poet says, punish us, if we've ofended you: punish us like a man, or bear your own punishment like a man. Don't try to come off with such misrabble lodgic as that above.

What do you? You give four satisfackary reazns that the play is bad (the secknd is naught,—for your no such chicking at play-writing, this being the forth). You show that the play must be bad, and *then* begin to deal with the critix for finding folt!

Was there ever wuss generalship? The play *is* bad,—your right,—a wuss I never see or read. But why kneed *you* say so? If it was so *very* bad, why publish it? *Because you wish to serve the drama!* O fie! don't lay that flattering function to your sole as Milton observes. Do you believe that this "Sea Capting" can serve the drama? Did you never intend that it should serve anything, or anybody *else*? Of cors you did! You wrote it for money,—money from the maniger, money from the bookseller,—for the same reason that I write this. Sir, Shakspeare wrote for the very same reasons, and I never heard that he bragged about serving the drama. Away with this canting about great motifs! Let us not be too prowd, my dear Barnet, and fansy ourselves marters of the truth, marters or apostels. We are but tradesmen, working for bread, and not for righteousness' sake. Let's try and work honestly ; but don't let us be prayting pompisly about our "sacred calling." The taylor who makes your coats (and very well they are made too, with the best of velvit collars)—I say Stulze, or Nugee, might cry out that *their* motifs were but to assert the eturnle truth of tayloring, with just as much reazn; and who would believe them ?

Well ; after this acknollitchment that the play is bad, come sefral pages of attack on the critix, and the folt those gentry have found with it. With these I shan't middle for the presnt. You defend all the characters 1 by 1, and conclude your remarks as follows :—

"I must be pardoned for this disquisition on my own designs. When every means is employed to misrepresent, it becomes, perhaps, allowable to explain. And if I do not think that my faults as a dramatic author are to be found in the study and delineation of character, it is precisely because *that* is the point on which all my previous pursuits in literature and actual life would be most likely to preserve me from the errors I own elsewhere, whether of misjudgment or inexperience.

"I have now only to add my thanks to the actors for the zeal and talent with which they have embodied the characters entrusted to them. The sweetness and grace with which Miss Faucit embellished the part of Violet—which, though only a sketch, is most necessary to the colouring and harmony of the play—were perhaps the more pleasing to the audience from the generosity, rare with actors, which induced her to take a part so far inferior to her powers. The applause which attends the performance of Mrs. Warner and Mr. Strickland attests their success in characters of unusual difficulty ; while the singular beauty and nobleness, whether of conception or execution, with which the greatest of living actors has elevated the part of Norman (so totally different from his ordinary range of character), is a new proof of his versatility and accomplishment in all that belongs to his art. It would be scarcely gracious to conclude these remarks without expressing my acknowledgment of that generous and indulgent sense of justice which, forgetting all political differences in a literary arena, has enabled me to appeal to approving audiences—from hostile critics. And it is this which alone encourages me to hope that, sooner or later, I may add to the dramatic literature of my country something that may find, perhaps, almost as many friends in the next age as it has been the fate of the author to find enemies in this."

See, now, what a good comfrabble vanaty is! Pepple have quarld with the dramatic characters of your play. "No," says you; "if I *am* remarkabble for anythink, it's for my study and delineation of character; *that* is presizely the pint to which my littery purshuits have led me." Have you read "Jil Blaw," my dear sir? Have you pirouzed that exlent tragady, the "Critic"? There's something so like this in Sir Fretful Plaguy, and the Archbishop of Granadiers, that I'm blest if I can't laff till my sides ake. Think of the critix fixing on the very pint for which you are famus!—the roags! And spose they had said the plot was absudd, or the langwitch absudder still, don't you think you would have had a word in defens of them too—you who hope to find frends for your dramatic wux in the nex age? Poo! I tell thee, Barnet, that the nex age will be wiser and better than this; and do you think that it will imply itself a reading of your trajadies? This is misantrofy, Barnet—reglar Byronism; and you ot to have a better apinian of human natur.

Your apinion about the actors I shan't here meddle with. They all acted exlently as far as my humbile judgement goes, and your write in giving them all possible prays. But let's consider the last sentence of the prefiz, my dear Barnet, and see what a pretty set of apiniuns you lay down.

1. The critix are your inymies in this age.
2. In the nex, however, you hope to find newmrous frends.
3. And it's a satisfackshn to think that, in spite of politticle diffrances, you have found frendly aujences here.

Now, my dear Barnet, for a man who begins so humbly with what my friend Father Prout calls an *argamantum ad misericorjam* who ignowledges that his play is bad, that his pore dear helth is bad, and those cussid critix have played the juice with him—I say, for a man who beginns in such a humbill toan, it's rayther *rich* to see how you end.

My dear Barnet, *do* you suppose that *politticle diffrances* prejudice pepple against *you*? What *are* your politix? Wig, I presume—so are mine, *ontry noo*. And what if they *are* Wig, or Raddiccle, or Cumsuvvative? Does any mortial man in England care a phig for your politix? Do you think yourself such a mity man in parlymint, that critix are to be angry with you, and aujences to be cumsidered magnanamous because they treat you fairly? There, now, was Sherridn, he who roat the "Rifles" and

"School for Scandle" (I saw the "Rifles" after your play, and, O Barnet, if you *knew* what a relief it was!)—there, I say, was Sherridn—he *was* a politticle character, if you please—he *could* make a spitch or two—do you spose that Pitt, Purseyvall, Castlerag, old George the Third himself, wooden go to see the "Rivles"— ay, and clap hands too, and laff and ror, for all Sherry's Wiggery? Do you spose the critix wouldn't applaud too? For shame, Barnet! what ninnis, what hartless raskles, you must beleave them to be,— in the fust plase, to fancy that you are a politticle genus; in the secknd, to let your politix interfear with their notiums about littery merits!

"Put that nonsince out of your head," as Fox said to Bonypart. Wasn't it that great genus, Dennis, that wrote in Swiff and Poop's time, who fansid that the French king wooden make pease unless Dennis was delivered up to him? Upon my wud, I doan't think he carrid his diddlusion much further than a serting honrabble barnet of my aquentance.

And then for the nex age. Respected sir, this is another diddlusion; a gross misteak on your part, or my name is not Y——sh. These plays immortial? Ah, *parrysampe*, as the French say, this is too strong—the small-beer of the "Sea Capting," or of any suxessor of the "Sea Capting," to keep sweet for sentries and sentries! Barnet, Barnet! do you know the natur of bear? Six weeks is not past, and here your last casque is sour—the public won't even now drink it; and I lay a wager that, betwigst this day (the thuttieth November) and the end of the year, the barl will be off the stox altogether, never never to return.

I've notted down a few frazes here and there, which you will do well to igsamin :—

NORMAN.

"The eternal Flora
Woos to her odorous haunts the western wind;
While circling round and upwards from the boughs,
Golden with fruits that lure the joyous birds,
Melody, like a happy soul released,
Hangs in the air, and from invisible plumes
Shakes sweetness down!"

NORMAN.

"And these the lips
Where, till this hour, the sad and holy kiss
Of parting linger'd, as the fragrance left
By *angels* when they touch the earth and vanish."

NORMAN.

" Hark ! she has blessed her son ! I bid ye witness,
Ye listening heavens—thou circumambient air :
The ocean sighs it back—and with the murmur
Rustle the happy leaves.   All nature breathes
Aloud—aloft—to the Great Parent's ear,
The blessing of the mother on her child."

NORMAN.

" I dream of love, enduring faith, a heart
Mingled with mine—a deathless heritage,
Which I can take unsullied to the *stars*,
When.the Great Father calls his children home."

NORMAN.

" The blue air, breathless in the *starry* peace,
After long silence hushed as heaven, but filled
With happy thoughts as heaven with *angels.*"

NORMAN.

" Till one calm night, when over earth and wave
Heaven looked its love from all its numberless *stars.*"

NORMAN.

' Those eyes, the guiding *stars* by which I steered."

NORMAN.

                       " That great mother
(The only parent I have known), whose face
Is bright with gazing ever on the *stars*—
The mother-sea."

NORMAN.

               " My bark shall be our home ;
The *stars* that light the *angel* palaces
Of air, our lamps."

NORMAN.

" A name that glitters, like a *star*, amidst
The galaxy of England's loftiest born."

LADY ARUNDEL.

" And see him princeliest of the lion tribe,
Whose swords and coronals gleam around the throne,
The guardian *stars* of the imperial isle."

The fust spissymen has been going the round of all the papers, as real reglar poatry. Those wicked critix! they must have been laffing in their sleafs when they quoted it. Malody, suckling round and uppards from the bows, like a happy soul released, hangs in the air, and from invizable plumes shakes sweetness down. Mighty fine, truly! but let mortial man tell the meanink of the passidge. Is it *musickle* sweetniss that Malody shakes down from its plumes—its wings, that is, or tail—or some pekewliar scent that proceeds from happy souls released, and which they shake down from the trees when they are suckling round and uppards? *Is* this poatry, Barnet? Lay your hand on your busm, and speak out boldly: Is it poatry, or sheer windy humbugg, that sounds a little melojous, and won't bear the commanest test of comman sence?

In passidge number 2, the same bisniss is going on, though in a more comprehensable way: the air, the leaves, the otion, are fild with emocean at Capting Norman's happiness. Pore Nature is dragged in to partisapate in his joys, just as she has been befor. Once in a poem, this universle simfithy is very well; but once is enuff, my dear Barnet; and that once should be in some great suckmstans, surely,—such as the meeting of Adam and Eve, in "Paradice Lost," or Jewpeter and Jewno, in Hoamer, where there seems, as it were, a reasn for it. But sea-captings should not be eternly spowting and invoking gods, hevns, starrs, angels, and other silestial influences. We can all do it, Barnet; nothing in life is esier. I can compare my livry buttons to the stars, or the clouds of my backopipe to the dark vollums that ishew from Mount Hetna; or I can say that angels are looking down from them, and the tobacco silf, like a happy sole released, is circling round and upwards, and shaking sweetness down. All this is as esy as drink; but it's not poatry, Barnet, nor natural. People, when their mothers reckonise them, don't howl about the suckumambient air, and paws to think of the happy leaves a-rustling—at least, one mistrusts them if they do. Take another instans out of your own play. Capting Norman (with his eternll *slack-jaw!*) meets the gal of his art :—

> " Look up, look up, my Violet—weeping? fie!
> And trembling too—yet leaning on my breast.
> In truth, thou art too soft for such rude shelter.
> Look up! I come to woo thee to the seas,
> My sailor's bride! Hast thou no voice but blushes?
> Nay—From those roses let me, like the bee,
> Drag forth the secret sweetness!"

VIOLET.

" Oh what thoughts
Were kept for *speech* when we once more should meet,
Now blotted from the *page ;* and all I feel
Is—*thou* art with me ! "

Very right, Miss Violet—the scentiment is natral, affeckshnit, pleasing, simple (it might have been in more grammaticle languidge, and no harm done) ; but never mind, the feeling is pritty ; and I can fancy, my dear Barnet, a pritty, smiling, weeping lass, looking up in a man's face and saying it. But the capting !—oh, this capting !— this windy spouting captain, with his prittinesses, and conseated apollogies for the hardness of his busm, and his old, stale, vapid simalies, and his wishes to be a bee ! Pish ! Men don't make love in this finniking way. It's the part of a sentymentle, poeticle taylor, not a galliant gentleman, in command of one of Her Madjisty's vessels of war.

Look at the remaining extrac, honored Barnet, and acknollidge that Capting Norman is eturnly repeating himself, with his endless jabber about stars and angels. Look at the neat grammaticle twist of Lady Arundel's spitch, too, who, in the corse of three lines, has made her son a prince, a lion, with a sword and coronal, and a star. Why jumble and sheak up metafors in this way ? Barnet, one simily is quite enuff in the best of sentenses (and I preshume I kneedn't tell you that it's as well to have it *like*, when you are about it). Take my advice, honrabble sir—listen to a humble footmin : it's genrally best in poatry to understand puffickly what you mean yourself, and to igspress your meaning clearly afterwoods —in the simpler words the better, praps. You may, for instans, call a coronet a coronal (an "ancestral coronal," p. 74) if you like, as you might call a hat a "swart sombrero," "a glossy four-and-nine," "a silken helm, to storm impermeable, and lightsome as the breezy gossamer ;" but, in the long run, it's as well to call it a hat. It *is* a hat ; and that name is quite as poetticle as another. I think it's Playto, or els Harrystottle, who observes that what we call a rose by any other name would smell as sweet. Confess, now, dear Barnet, don't you long to call it a Polyanthus ?

I never see a play more carelessly written. In such a hurry you seem to have bean, that you have actially in some sentences forgot to put in the sence. What is this, for instance ?—

" This thrice precious one
Smiled to my eyes—drew being from my breast—
Slept in my arms ;—the very tears I shed
Above my treasures were to men and angels
Alike such holy sweetness ! "

In the name of all the angels that ever you invoked—Raphael, Gabriel, Uriel, Zadkiel, Azrael—what does this "holy sweetness" mean? We're not spinxes to read such dark conandrums. If you knew my state sins I came upon this passidg—I've neither slep nor eton; I've neglected my pantry; I've been wandring from house to house with this riddl in my hand, and nobody can understand it. All Mr. Frazier's men are wild, looking gloomy at one another, and asking what this may be. All the cumtributors have been spoak to. The Doctor, who knows every languitch, has tried and giv'n up; we've sent to Docter Pettigruel, who reads horyglifics a deal ezier than my way of spellin'—no anser. Quick! quick with a fifth edition, honored Barnet, and set us at rest! While your about it, please, too, to igsplain the two last lines :—

> "His merry bark with England's flag to crown her."

See what dellexy of igspreshn, "a flag to crown her!"

> "His merry bark with England's flag to crown her,
> Fame for my hopes, and woman in my cares."

Likewise the following :—

> "Girl, beware,
> THE LOVE THAT TRIFLES ROUND THE CHARMS IT GILDS
> OFT RUINS WHILE IT SHINES."

Igsplane this, men and angels! I've tried every way; backards, forards, and in all sorts of trancepositions, as thus :—

> The love that ruins round the charms it shines,
> Gilds while it trifles oft;

Or,

> The charm that gilds around the love it ruins,
> Oft trifles while it shines;

Or,

> The ruins that love gilds and shines around,
> Oft trifles where it charms;

Or,

> Love, while it charms, shines round, and ruins oft,
> The trifles that it gilds;

Or,

> The love that trifles, gilds and ruins oft,
> While round the charms it shines.

All which are as sensable as the fust passidge.

And with this I'll alow my friend Smith, who has been silent all this time, to say a few words. He has not written near so much as me (being an infearor genus, betwigst ourselves), but he says he never had such mortial difficklty with anything as with the dixcripshn of the plott of your pease. Here his letter :—

To Ch–rl–s F–tzr–y Pl–nt–g–n–t Y–ll–wpl–sh, Esq., &c. &c.

30th Nov., 1839.

My dear and honoured Sir,—I have the pleasure of laying before you the following description of the plot, and a few remarks upon the style of the piece called "The Sea Captain."

Five-and-twenty years back, a certain Lord Arundel had a daughter, heiress of his estates and property: a poor cousin, Sir Maurice Beevor (being next in succession); and a page, Arthur Le Mesnil by name.

The daughter took a fancy for the page, and the young persons were married unknown to his Lordship.

Three days before her confinement (thinking, no doubt, that period favourable for travelling), the young couple had agreed to run away together, and had reached a chapel near on the sea-coast from which they were to embark, when Lord Arundel abruptly put a stop to their proceedings by causing one Gaussen, a pirate, to murder the page.

His daughter was carried back to Arundel House, and, in three days, gave birth to a son. Whether his Lordship knew of this birth I cannot say; the infant, however, was never acknowledged, but carried by Sir Maurice Beevor to a priest, Onslow by name, who educated the lad and kept him for twelve years in profound ignorance of his birth. The boy went by the name of Norman.

Lady Arundel meanwhile married again, again became a widow, but had a second son, who was the acknowledged heir, and called Lord Ashdale. Old Lord Arundel died, and her Ladyship became countess in her own right.

When Norman was about twelve years of age, his mother, who wished to "*waft* young Arthur to a distant land," had him sent on board ship. Who should the captain of the ship be but Gaussen, who received a smart bribe from Sir Maurice Beevor to kill the lad. Accordingly, Gaussen tied him to a plank, and pitched him overboard.

.   .   .   .

About thirteen years after these circumstances, Violet, an orphan niece of Lady Arundel's second husband, came to pass a few weeks with her Ladyship. She had just come from a sea-voyage, and had been saved from a wicked Algerine by an English sea captain. This sea captain was no other than Norman, who had been picked up off his plank, and fell in love with, and was loved by, Miss Violet.

A short time after Violet's arrival at her aunt's the captain came to pay her a visit, his ship anchoring off the coast, near Lady Arundel's residence. By a singular coincidence, that rogue Gaussen's ship anchored in the harbour too. Gaussen at once knew his man, for he had "tracked" him (after drowning him), and he informed Sir Maurice Beevor that young Norman was alive.

Sir Maurice Beevor informed her Ladyship. How should she get rid of him? In this wise. He was in love with Violet, let him marry her and be off; for Lord Ashdale was in love with his cousin too; and, of course, could not marry a young woman in her station of life. "You have a chaplain on board," says her Ladyship to Captain Norman; "let him attend to-night in the ruined chapel, marry Violet, and away with you to sea." By this means she hoped to be quit of him for ever.

But unfortunately the conversation had been overheard by Beevor, and reported to Ashdale. Ashdale determined to be at the chapel and carry off Violet; as for Beevor, he sent Gaussen to the chapel to kill both Ashdale and Norman: thus there would only be Lady Arundel between him and the title.

Norman, in the meanwhile, who had been walking near the chapel, had just seen his worthy old friend, the priest, most barbarously murdered there. Sir Maurice Beevor had set Gaussen upon him; his reverence was coming with the papers concerning Norman's birth, which Beevor wanted in order to extort money from the Countess. Gaussen, was, however, obliged to run before he got the papers; and the clergyman had time, before he died, to tell Norman the story, and give him the documents, with which Norman sped off to the castle to have an interview with his mother.

He lays his white cloak and hat on the table, and begs to be left alone with her Ladyship. Lord Ashdale, who is in the room, surlily quits it; but, going out, cunningly puts on Norman's cloak. "It will be dark," says he, "down at the chapel; Violet won't know me; and, egad! I'll run off with her."

Norman has his interview. Her Ladyship acknowledges him, for she cannot help it; but will not embrace him, love him, or have anything to do with him.

Away he goes to the chapel. His chaplain was there waiting to marry him to Violet, his boat was there to carry him on board his ship, and Violet was there, too.

"Norman," says she, in the dark, "dear Norman, I knew you by your white cloak; here I am." And she and the man in a cloak go off to the inner chapel to be married.

There waits Master Gaussen; he has seized the chaplain and the boat's crew, and is just about to murder the man in the cloak, when—

Norman rushes in and cuts him down, much to the surprise of Miss, for she never suspected it was sly Ashdale who had come, as we have seen, disguised, and very nearly paid for his masquerading.

Ashdale is very grateful; but, when Norman persists in marrying Violet, he says—no, he shan't. He shall fight; he is a coward if he doesn't fight. Norman flings down his sword, and says he *won't* fight; and—

Lady Arundel, who has been at prayers all this time, rushing in, says, "Hold! this is your brother, Percy—your elder brother!" Here is some restiveness on Ashdale's part, but he finishes by embracing his brother.

Norman burns all the papers; vows he will never peach; reconciles himself with his mother; says he will go loser; but, having ordered his ship to "veer" round to the chapel, orders it to veer back again, for he will pass the honeymoon at Arundel Castle.

As you have been pleased to ask my opinion, it strikes me that there are one or two very good notions in this plot. But the author does not fail, as he would modestly have us believe, from ignorance of stage business; he seems to know too much, rather than too little, about the stage; to be too anxious to cram in effects, incidents, perplexities. There is the perplexity concerning Ashdale's murder, and Norman's murder, and the priest's murder, and the page's murder, and Gaussen's murder. There is the perplexity about the papers, and that about the hat and cloak (a silly foolish obstacle), which only tantalise the spectator, and retard the march of the drama's action: it is as if the author had said, "I must have a new incident in every act, I must keep tickling the spectator perpetually, and never let him off until the fall of the curtain."

The same disagreeable bustle and petty complication of intrigue you may remark in the author's drama of "Richelieu." "The Lady of Lyons" was a much simpler and better wrought plot; the incidents following each other not too swiftly or startingly. In "Richelieu," it always seemed to me as if one heard doors perpetually clapping and banging; one was puzzled to follow the train of conversation, in the midst of the perpetual small noises that distracted one right and left.

Nor is the list of characters of "The Sea Captain" to be despised. The outlines of all of them are good. A mother, for whom one feels a proper tragic mixture of hatred and pity; a gallant single-hearted son, whom she disdains, and who conquers her at last by his noble conduct; a dashing haughty Tybalt of a brother; a wicked poor cousin, a pretty maid, and a fierce buccanier. These people might pass three hours very well on the stage, and interest the audience hugely; but the author fails in filling up the outlines. His language is absurdly stilted, frequently careless; the reader or spectator hears a number of loud speeches, but scarce a dozen lines that seem to belong of nature to the speakers.

Nothing can be more fulsome or loathsome to my mind than the continual sham-religious claptraps which the author has put into the mouth of his hero; nothing more unsailorlike than his namby-pamby starlit descriptions, which my ingenious colleague has, I see, alluded to. "Thy faith my anchor, and thine eyes my haven," cries the gallant captain to his lady. See how loosely the sentence is constructed, like a thousand others in the book. The captain is to cast anchor with the girl's faith in her own eyes: either image might pass by itself, but together, like the quadrupeds of Kilkenny, they devour each other. The captain tells his lieutenant *to bid his bark veer round* to a point in the harbour. Was ever such language My Lady gives Sir Maurice a thousand pounds to *waft* him (her son) to some distant shore. Nonsense, sheer nonsense; and, what is worse, affected nonsense!

Look at the comedy of the poor cousin. "There is a great deal of game on the estate—partridges, hares, wild-geese, snipes, and plovers (*smacking his lips*)—besides a magnificent preserve of sparrows, which I can sell *to the little blackguards* in the streets at a penny a hundred. But I am very poor—a very poor old knight!"

Is this wit or nature? It is a kind of sham wit: it reads as if it were wit, but it is not. What poor, poor stuff, about the little blackguard boys! what flimsy ecstasies and silly "smacking of lips" about the plovers! Is this the man who writes for the next age? O fie! Here is another joke:—

SIR MAURICE.

"Mice! zounds, how can I
Keep mice! I can't afford it! They were starved
To death an age ago. The last was found
Come Christmas three years, stretched beside a bone
In that same larder, so consumed and worn
By pious fast, 'twas awful to behold it!
I canonised its corpse in spirits of wine,
And set it in the porch—a solemn warning
To thieves and beggars!"

Is not this rare wit? "Zounds! how can I keep mice?" is well enough for a miser; not too new, or brilliant either; but this miserable dilution of a thin joke, this wretched hunting down of the poor mouse! It is humiliating to think of a man of *esprit* harping so long on such a mean pitiful string. A man who aspires to immortality, too! I doubt whether it is to be gained thus; whether our author's words are not too loosely built to make "starry-pointing pyramids" of. Horace clipped and squared his blocks more carefully before he laid the monument which *imber edax*, or *aquila impotens*, or *fuga temporum* might assail in vain. Even old Ovid, when he raised his stately shining heathen temple, had placed some columns in it, and hewn out a statue or two which deserved the immortality that he prophesied (somewhat arrogantly) for himself. But let not all be looking forward to a future, and fancying that, "*incerti spatium dum finiat ævi*," our books are to be immortal. Alas! the way to immortality is not so easy, nor will our "Sea Captain" be permitted such an unconscionable cruise. If all the immortalities were really to have their wish, what a work would our descendants have to study them all!

Not yet, in my humble opinion, has the honourable baronet achieved this deathless consummation. There will come a day (may it be long distant!) when the very best of his novels will be forgotten; and it is reasonable to suppose that his dramas will pass out of existence, some time or other, in the lapse of the *secula seculorum*. In the meantime, my dear Plush, if you ask me what the great obstacle is towards the dramatic fame and merit of our friend, I would say that it does not lie so much in hostile critics or feeble health, as in a careless habit of writing, and a peevish vanity which causes him to shut his eyes to his faults. The question of original capacity I will not moot; one may think very highly of the honourable baronet's talent, without rating it quite so high as he seems disposed to do.

And to conclude: as he has chosen to combat the critics in person, the critics are surely justified in being allowed to address him directly.

With best compliments to Mrs. Yellowplush, I have the honour to be, dear Sir, your most faithful and obliged humble servant,

JOHN THOMAS SMITH.

And now, Smith having finisht his letter, I think I can't do better than clothes mine lickwise; for though I should never be tired of talking, praps the public may of hearing, and therefore it's best to shut up shopp.

What I've said, respected Barnit, I hoap you woan't take un-kind. A play, you see, is public property for every one to say his say on ; and I think, if you read your prefez over agin, you'll see that it ax as a direct incouridgment to us critix to come forrard and notice you. But don't fansy, I besitch you, that we are actiated by hostillaty : fust write a good play, and you'll see we'll prays it fast enuff. Waiting which, *Agray, Munseer le Chevaleer, l'ashur-ance de ma hot cumsideratun. Voter distangy,*   **Y.**

THE DIARY OF

C. JEAMES DE LA PLUCHE, Esq.

WITH HIS LETTERS

THE DIARY OF

C. JEAMES DE LA PLUCHE, Esq.

A LUCKY SPECULATOR

CONSIDERABLE sensation has been excited in the upper and lower circles in the West End, by a startling piece of good fortune which has befallen James Plush, Esq., lately footman in a respected family in Berkeley Square.

"One day last week, Mr. James waited upon his master, who is a banker in the City; and after a little blushing and hesitation, said he had saved a little money in service, was anxious to retire, and to invest his savings to advantage.

"His master (we believe we may mention, without offending delicacy, the well-known name of Sir George Flimsy, of the house of Flimsy, Diddler, and Flash) smilingly asked Mr. James what was the amount of his savings, wondering considerably how, out of an income of thirty guineas—the main part of which he spent in bouquets, silk stockings, and perfumery—Mr. Plush could have managed to lay by anything.

"Mr. Plush, with some hesitation, said he had been *speculating in railroads*, and stated his winnings to have been thirty thousand pounds. He had commenced his speculations with twenty, borrowed from a fellow-servant. He had dated his letters from the house in Berkeley Square, and humbly begged pardon of his master for not having instructed the Railway Secretaries who answered his applications to apply at the area-bell.

"Sir George, who was at breakfast, instantly rose, and shook Mr. P. by the hand; Lady Flimsy begged him to be seated, and partake of the breakfast which he had laid on the table; and has subsequently invited him to her grand *déjeuner* at Richmond, where it was observed that Miss Emily Flimsy, her beautiful and accomplished seventh daughter, paid the lucky gentleman *marked attention*.

"We hear it stated that Mr. P. is of a very ancient family (Hugo de la Pluche came over with the Conqueror); and the new brougham which he has started bears the ancient coat of his race.

"He has taken apartments in the Albany, and is a director of thirty-three railroads. He proposes to stand for Parliament at the next general election on decidedly Conservative principles, which have always been the politics of his family.

"Report says, that even in his humble capacity Miss Emily Flimsy had remarked his high demeanour. Well, 'None but the brave,' say we, 'deserve the fair.'"—*Morning Paper.*

This announcement will explain the following lines, which have been put into our box * with a West End post-mark. If, as we believe, they are written by the young woman from whom the millionaire borrowed the sum on which he raised his fortune, what heart will not melt with sympathy at her tale, and pity the sorrows which she expresses in such artless language?

If it be not too late; if wealth have not rendered its possessor callous: if poor Maryanne *be still alive;* we trust, we trust, Mr. Plush will do her justice.

"JEAMES OF BUCKLEY SQUARE.

"A HELIGY.

"Come all ye gents vot cleans the plate,
   Come all ye ladies maids so fair—
Vile I a story vill relate
   Of cruel Jeames of Buckley Square.
A tighter lad, it is confest,
   Ne'er valked with powder in his air,
Or vore a nosegay in his breast,
   Than andsum Jeames of Buckley Square.

O Evns! it vas the best of sights,
   Behind his Master's coach and pair,
To see our Jeames in red plush tights,
   A driving hoff from Buckley Square.
He vel became his hagwilletts,
   He cocked his at with *such* a hair;
His calves and viskers *vas* such pets,
   That hall loved Jeames of Buckley Square.

---

* The letter-box of *Mr. Punch,* in whose columns these papers were first published.

He pleased the hup-stairs folks as vell,
　And o ! I vithered with despair,
Missis *vould* ring the parler bell,
　And call up Jeames in Buckley Square.
Both beer and sperrits he abhord
　(Sperrits and beer I can't a bear),
You would have thought he vas a lord
　Down in our All in Buckley Square.

Last year he visper'd, ' Mary Ann,
　Ven I've an under'd pound to spare,
To take a public is my plan,
　And leave this hojous Buckley Square.'
O how my gentle heart did bound,
　To think that I his name should bear.
' Dear Jeames,' says I, ' I've twenty pound,'
　And gev them him in Buckley Square.

Our master vas a City gent,
　His name's in railroads everywhere,
And lord, vot lots of letters vent
　Betwigst his brokers and Buckley Square !
My Jeames it was the letters took,
　And read them all (I think it's fair),
And took a leaf from Master's book,
　As *hothers* do in Buckley Square.

Encouraged with my twenty pound,
　Of which poor *I* was unavare,
He wrote the Companies all round,
　And signed hisself from Buckley Square.
And how John Porter used to grin,
　As day by day, share after share,
Came railvay letters pouring in,
　' J. Plush, Esquire, in Buckley Square.'

Our servants' All was in a rage—
　Scrip, stock, curves, gradients, bull and bear,
Vith butler, coachman, groom and page,
　Vas all the talk in Buckley Square.
But O ! imagine vot I felt
　Last Vensday veek as ever were ;
I gits a letter, which I spelt
　' Miss M. A. Hoggins, Buckley Square.'

He sent me back my money true—
　He sent me back my lock of air,
And said, ' My dear, I bid ajew
　To Mary Hann and Buckley Square.

> Think not to marry, foolish Hann,
>   With people who your betters are ;
> James Plush is now a gentleman,
>   And you—a cook in Buckley Square.
>
> ' I've thirty thousand guineas won,
>   In six short months, by genus rare ;
> You little thought what Jeames was on,
>   Poor Mary Hann, in Buckley Square.
> I've thirty thousand guineas net,
>   Powder and plush I scorn to vear ;
> And so, Miss Mary Hann, forget
>   For hever Jeames, of Buckley Square.' "

     •   •   •   •   •

The rest of the MS. is illegible, being literally washed away in a flood of tears.

A LETTER FROM "JEAMES, OF BUCKLEY SQUARE."

ALBANY, LETTER X. *August* 10, 1845.

" SIR,—Has a reglar suscriber to your emusing paper, I beg leaf to state that I should never have done so, had I supposed that it was your abbit to igspose the mistaries of privit life, and to hinjer the delligit feelings of umble individyouals like myself, who have *no ideer* of being made the subject of newspaper criticism.

" I elude, Sir, to the unjustafiable use which has been made of my name in your Journal, where both my muccantile speclations and the *hinmost pashns of my art* have been brot forrards in a ridicklus way for the public emusemint.

" What call, Sir, has the public to inquire into the suckmstansies of my engagements with Miss Mary Hann Oggins, or to meddle with their rupsher ? Why am I to be maid the hobjick of your *redicule in a doggril ballit* impewted to her ? I say *impewted*, because, in *my* time at least, Mary Hann could only sign her + mark (has I've hoften witnist it for her when she paid hin at the Savings Bank), and has for *sacrificing to the Mewses* and making *poatry*, she was as *hincapible* as Mr. Wakley himself.

" With respect to the ballit, my baleaf is, that it is wrote by a footman in a low famly, a pore retch who attempted to rivle me in my affections to Mary Hann—a feller not five foot six, and with no more calves to his legs than a donkey—who was always a-ritin (having been a doctor's boy) and who I nockt down with a pint of porter (as he well recklex) at the 3 Tuns Jerming Street, for daring to try to make a but of me. He has signed Miss H's name to his *nonsince and lies :* and you lay yourself hopen to a haction for lible for insutting them in your paper.

"It is false that I have treated Miss H. hill in *hany* way. That I borrowed 20lb of her is *trew.* But she confesses I paid it back. Can hall people say as much of the money *they've* lent or borrowed? No. And I not only paid it back, but giv her the andsomest pres'nts : *which I never should have eluded to,* but for this attack. Fust, a silver thimble (which I found in Missus's work-box) ; secknd, a vollom of Byrom's poems ; third, I halways brought her a glas of Curasore, when we ad a party, of which she was remarkable fond. I treated her to Hashley's twice (and halways a srimp-or a hoyster by the way), and a *thowsnd deligit attentions,* which I sapose count for *nothink.*

"Has for marrigge. Haltered suckmstancies rendered it him-possable. I was gone into a new spear of life—mingling with my native aristoxy. I breathe no sallible of blame against Miss H., but his a hilliterit cookmaid fit to set at a fashnable table? Do young fellers of rank genrally marry out of the Kitching? If we cast our i's upon a low-born gal, I needn say it's only a tempory distraction, *pore passy le tong.* So much for *her* claims upon me. Has for *that beest of a Doctor's boy* he's unwuthy the notas of a Gentleman.

"That I've one thirty thousand lb, *and praps more,* I dont deny. Ow much has the Kilossus of Railroads one, I should like to know, and what was his cappitle? I hentered the market with 20lb, specklated Jewdicious, and ham what I ham. So may you be (if you have 20lb, and praps you haven't—So may you be : if you choose to go in & win.

"I for my part am jusly *proud* of my suxess, and could give you a hundred instances of my gratatude. For igsample, the fust pair of hosses I bought (and a better pair of steppers I dafy you to see in hany curracle) I crisn'd Hull and Selby, in grateful elusion to my transackshns in that railroad. My riding Cob I called very unhaptly my Dublin and Galway. He came down with me the other day, and I've jest sold him at $\frac{1}{4}$ discount.

"At fust with prudence and modration I only kep two grooms for my stables, one of whom lickwise waited on me at table. I have now a confidenshle servant, a vally de shamber—He curls my air ; inspex my accounts, and hansers my hinvitations to dinner. I call this Vally my *Trent Vally,* for it was the prophit I got from that exlent line, which injuiced me to ingage him.

"Besides my North British Plate and Breakfast equipidge—I have two handsom suvvices for dinner—the goold plate for Sundays, and the silver for common use. When I ave a great party, 'Trent,' I say to my man, 'we will have the London and Bummingham plate to-day (the goold), or else the Manchester and Leeds (the silver).' I bought them after realising on the abuf lines, and if people suppose that the companys made me a presnt of the plate, how can I help it?

"In the sam way I say, 'Trent, bring us a bottle of Bristol and Hexeter!' or, 'Put some Heastern Counties in hice!' *He* knows what I mean; it's the wines I bought upon the hospicious tummination of my connexshn with those two railroads.

"So strong, indeed, as this abbit become, that being asked to stand Godfather to the youngest Miss Diddle last weak, I had her christened (provisionally) Rosamell—from the French line of which I am Director; and only the other day, finding myself rayther unwell, 'Doctor,' says I to Sir Jeames Clark, "Ive sent to consult you because my Midlands are out of horder; and I want you to send them up to a premium.' The Doctor lafd, and I beleave told the story subsquintly at Buckinum P–ll–s.

"But I will trouble you no father. My sole objict in writing has been to *clear my carrater*—to show that I came by my money in a honrable way: that I'm not ashaymd of the manner in which I gayned it, and ham indeed grateful for my good fortune.

"To conclude, I have ad my podigree maid out at the Erald Hoffis (I don't mean the *Morning Erald*), and have took for my arms a Stagg. You are corrict in stating that I am of hancient Normin famly. This is more than Peal can say, to whomb I applied for a barnetcy; but the primmier being of low igstraction, natrally stickles for his horder. Consurvative though I be, *I may change my opinions* before the next Election, when I intend to hoffer myself as a Candydick for Parlymint. Meanwhile, I have the honor to be, Sir, your most obeajnt Survnt,

"Fitz-James de la Pluche."

THE DIARY

ONE day in the panic week, our friend Jeames called at our office, evidently in great perturbation of mind and disorder of dress. He had no flower in his button-hole; his yellow kid gloves were certainly two days old. He had not above three of the ten chains he usually sports, and his great coarse knotty-knuckled old hands were deprived of some dozen of the rubies, emeralds, and other cameos with which, since his elevation to fortune, the poor fellow has thought fit to adorn himself.

"How's scrip, Mr. Jeames?" said we pleasantly, greeting our esteemed contributor.

"Scrip be ——," replied he, with an expression we cannot repeat, and a look of agony it is impossible to describe in print, and walked about the parlour whistling, humming, rattling his keys and coppers, and showing other signs of agitation. At last, "*Mr. Punch,*" says he, after a moment's hesitation, "I wish to speak to you on a pint of businiss. I wish to be paid for my contribewtions to your paper. Suckmstances is altered with me. I—I—in a word, *can* you lend me £—— for the account?"

He named the sum. It was one so great that we don't care to mention it here; but on receiving a cheque for the amount (on Messrs. Pump and Aldgate, our bankers), tears came into the honest fellow's eyes. He squeezed our hand until he nearly wrung it off, and shouting to a cab, he plunged into it at our office-door, and was off to the City.

Returning to our study, we found he had left on our table an open pocket-book, of the contents of which (for the sake of safety) we took an inventory. It contained—three tavern-bills, paid; a tailor's ditto, unsettled; forty-nine allotments in different companies, twenty-six thousand seven hundred shares in all, of which the market value we take, on an average, to be $\frac{1}{4}$ discount; and in an old bit of paper tied with pink riband a lock of chestnut hair, with the initials M. A. H.

In the diary of the pocket-book was a journal, jotted down by the proprietor from time to time. At first the entries are insignificant.

as, for instance :—" *3rd January*—Our beer in the Suvnts' Hall so *precious* small at this Christmas time that I reely *muss* give warning, & wood, but for my dear Mary Hann." " *February* 7—That broot Screw, the Butler, wanted to kis her, but my dear Mary Hann boxt his hold hears, & served him right. *I datest* Screw,"—and so forth. Then the diary relates to Stock Exchange operations, until we come to the time when, having achieved his successes, Mr. James quitted Berkeley Square and his livery, and began his life as a speculator and a gentleman upon town. It is from the latter part of his diary that we make the following

EXTRAX :—

" Wen I anounced in the Servnts All my axeshn of forting, and that by the exasizè of my own talince and ingianiuty I had reerlized a summ of 20,000 lb. (it was only 5, but what's the use of a mann depreshiating the qualaty of his own mackyrel ?)—wen I enounced my abrup intention to cut—you should have sean the sensation among hall the people !—Cook wanted to know whether I woodn like a sweatbred, or the slise of the breast of a Cold Tucky. Screw, the butler (womb I always detested as a hinsalant hoverbaring beest), begged me to walk into the *Hupper* Servnts All, and try a glass of Shuperior Shatto Margo. Heven Visp, the coachmin, eld out his and, & said, ' Jeames, I hopes theres no quarraling betwigst you & me, & I'll stand a pot of beer with pleasure.'

" The sickofnts !—that wery Cook had split on me to the House-keeper ony last week (catchin me priggin some cold tuttle soop, of which I'm remarkable fond). Has for the butler, I always *ebommi-nated* him for his precious snears and imperence to all us Gents who woar livry (he never would sit in our parlour, fasooth, nor drink out of our mugs) ; and in regard of Visp—why, it was ony the day before the wulgar beest hoffered to fite me, and thretnd to give me a good iding if I refused. ' Gentlemen and ladies,' says I, as haughty as may be, ' there's nothink that I want for that I can't go for to buy with my hown money, and take at my lodgins in the Halbany, letter Hex ; if I'm ungry I've no need to refresh myself in the *kitching.*' And so saying, I took a dignified ajew of these minnial domestics ; and ascending to my epartment in the 4 pair back, brushed the powder out of my air, and taking off those hojous livries for hever, put on a new soot, made for me by Cullin of St. Jeames Street, and which fitted my manly figger as tight as whacks.

" There was *one* pusson in the house with womb I was rayther anxious to evoid a persnal leave-taking—Mary Hann Oggins, I mean—for my art is natural tender, and I can't abide seeing a pore gal in pane. I'd given her previous the infamation of my departure

—doing the ansom thing by her at the same time—paying her back 20lb., which she'd lent me 6 months before : and paying her back not only the interest, but I gave her an andsome pair of scissars and a silver thimbil, by way of boanus. 'Mary Hann,' says I, 'suckimstancies has haltered our rellatif positions in life. I quit the Servnts Hall for ever (for has for your marrying a person in my rank, that, my dear, is hall gammin), and so I wish you a good-by, my good gal, and if you want to better yourself, halways refer to me.'

"Mary Hann didn't hanser my speech (which I think was remarkable kind), but looked at me in the face quite wild like, and bust into somethink betwigst a laugh & a cry, and fell down with her ed on the kitching dresser, where she lay until her young Missis rang the dressing-room bell. Would you bleave it ? She left the thimbil & things, & my check for 20lb. 10s., on the tabil when she went to hanser the bell. And now I heard her sobbing and vimpering in her own room nex but one to mine, vith the dore open, peraps expecting I should come in and say good-by. But, as soon as I was dressed, I cut downstairs, hony desiring Frederick my fellow-servnt, to fetch me a cabb, and requesting permission to take leaf of my lady & the famly before my departure."

.   .   .   .   .   .

"How Miss Hemly did hogle me to be sure! Her Ladyship told me what a sweet gal she was—hamiable, fond of poetry, plays the gitter. Then she hasked me if I liked blond bewties and haubin hair. Haubin, indeed ! I don't like carrits ! as it must be confest Miss Hemly's his—and has for a *blond buty*, she has pink I's like a Halbino, and her face looks as if it were dipt in a brann mash. How she squeeged my & as she went away !

"Mary Hann now *has* haubin air, and a cumplexion like roses and hivory, and I's as blew as Evin.

"I gev Frederick two and six for fetchin the cabb—been resolved to hact the gentleman in hall things. How he stared ! "

"25th.—I am now director of forty-seven hadvantageous lines, and have past hall day in the Citty. Although I've hate or nine new soots of close, and Mr. Cullin fits me heligant, yet I fansy they hall reckonise me. Conshns whispers to me, 'Jeams, you'r hony a footman in disguise hafter all.' "

"28th.—Been to the Hopra. Music tol lol. That Lablash is a wopper at singing. I coodn make out why some people called out 'Bravo,' some 'Bravar,' and some 'Bravee.' 'Bravee, Lablash,' says I, at which heverybody laft.

"I'm in my new stall. I've had new cushings put in, and my harms in goold on the back. I'm dressed hall in black, excep a gold waistcoat and dimind studds in the embriderd busom of my shameese. I wear a Camallia Jiponiky in my button-ole, and have a double-barreld opera-glas, so big, that I make Timmins, my secnd man, bring it in the other cabb.

"What an igstronry exabishn that Pawdy Carter is! If those four gals are faries, Tellioni is sutnly the fairy Queend. She can do all that they can do, and somethink they can't. There's an indiscrible grace about her, and Carlotty, my sweet Carlotty, she sets my art in flams.

"Ow that Miss Hemly was noddin and winkin at me out of their box on the fourth tear?

"What linx i's she must av. As if I could mount up there!

"*P.S.*—Talking of *mounting hup!* the St. Helena's walked up 4 per cent. this very day."

"*2nd July.*—Rode my bay oss Desperation in the park. There was me, Lord George Ringwood (Lord Cinqbars' son), Lord Bally-bunnion, Honorable Capting Trap, & sevral hother young swells. Sir John's carridge there in coarse. Miss Hemly lets fall her booky as I pass, and I'm obleged to get hoff and pick it hup, & get splashed up to the his. The gettin on hossback agin is halways the juice & hall. Just as I was hon, Desperation begins a porring the hair with his 4 feet, and sinks down so on his anches, that I'm blest if I didn't slip hoff agin over his tail; at which Ballybunnion & the hother chaps rord with lafter.

"As Bally has istates in Queen's County, I've put him on the St. Helena direction. We call it the 'Great St. Helena Napoleon Junction,' from Jamestown to Longwood. The French are taking it hup heagerly."

"*6th July.*—Dined to-day at the London Tavin with one of the Welsh bords of Direction I'm hon. The Cwrwmwrw & Plmwyddlywm, with tunnils through Snowding and Plinlimming.

"Great nashnallity of course. Ap Shinkin in the chair, Ap Llwydd in the vice; Welsh mutton for dinner; Welsh iron knives and forks; Welsh rabbit after dinner; and a Welsh harper, be hanged to him: he went strummint on his hojous hinstrument, and played a toon piguliarly disagreeble to me.

" It was *Pore Mary Hann.* The clarrit holmost choaked me as
I tried it, and I very nearly wep myself as I thought of her bewtifle
blue i's. Why *ham* I always thinkin about that gal ? Sasiety is
sasiety, it's lors is irresistabl. Has a man of rank I can't marry a
serving-made. What would Cinqbars and Ballybunnion say ?

" *P.S.*—I don't like the way that Cinqbars has of borroing
money, & halways making me pay the bill. Seven pound six at
the 'Shipp,' Grinnidge, which I dont't grudge it, for Derbyshire's
brown Ock is the best in Urup ; nine pound three at the 'Trafflygar,'
and seventeen pound sixteen and nine at the 'Star and Garter,'
Richmond, with the Countess St. Emilion & the Baroness Fron-
tignac. Not one word of French could I speak, and in consquince
had nothink to do but to make myself halmost sick with heating
hices and desert, while the hothers were chattering and parlyvooing.

" Ha ! I remember going to Grinnidge once with Mary Hann,
when we were more happy (after a walk in the park, where we ad
one gingy-beer betwigst us), more appy with tea and a simple srimp
than with hall this splender ! "——

" *July* 24.—My first-floor apartmince in the Halbiny is now
kimpletely and chasely furnished — the droring-room with yellow
satting and silver for the chairs and sophies—hemrall green tabbinet
curtings with pink velvet and goold borders & fringes ; a light blue
Haxminster Carpit, embroydered with tulips ; tables, secritaires,
cunsoles, &c., as handsome as goold can make them, and candle-
sticks and shandalers of the purest Hormolew.

" The Dining-room furniture is all *hoak,* British Hoak ; round
igspanding table, like a trick in a Pantimime, iccommadating any
number from 8 to 24—to which it is my wish to restrict my parties.
Curtings crimsing damask, Chairs crimsing myrocky. Portricks of
my favorite great men decorats the wall—namely, the Duke of
Wellington. There's four of his Grace. For I've remarked that if
you wish to pass for a man of weight and considdration you should
holways praise and quote him. I have a valluble one lickwise of
my Queend, and 2 of Prince Halbert—has a Field Martial, and
halso as a privat Gent. I despise the vulgar *snears* that are daily
hullered aginst that Igsolted Pottentat. Betwigxt the Prins &
the Duke hangs me, in the Uniform of the Cinqbar Malitia, of
which Cinqbars has made me Capting.

" The Libery is not yet done.

" But the Bedd-roomb is the Jem of the whole. If you could

but see it ! such a Bedworr ! Ive a Shyval Dressing Glass festooned
with Walanseens Lace, and lighted up of evenings with rose-coloured
tapers. Goold dressing-case and twilet of Dresding Cheny. My
bed white and gold with curtings of pink and silver brocayd held up
a top by a goold Qpid who seems always a smilin angillicly hon me,
has I lay with my Ed on my piller hall sarounded with the finest
Mechlin. I have a own man, a yuth under him, 2 groombs, and a
fimmale for the House. I've 7 osses : in cors if I hunt this winter
I must increase my ixtablishment.

"*N.B.*—Heverythink looking well in the City. Saint Helenas
12 pm. ; Madagascars, 9⅝ ; Saffron Hill and Rookery Junction,
24 ; and the new lines in prospick equily incouraging."

"People phansy it's hall gaiety and pleasure the life of us
fashnabble gents about townd—But I can tell 'em it's not hall goold
that glitters. They dont know our momints of hagony, hour ours
of studdy and reflecshun. They little think when they see Jeames
de la Pluche, Exquire, worling round in a walce at Halmax with
Lady Hann, or lazaly stepping a kidrill with Lady Jane, poring
helegant nothinx into the Countess's hear at dinner, or gallopin his
hoss Desperation hover the exorcisin ground in the Park,—they
little think that leader of the tong, seaminkly so reckliss, is a
careworn mann ! and yet so it is.

"Imprymus. I've been ableged to get up all the ecomplish-
ments at double quick, & to apply myself with treemenjuous energy.

" First,—in horder to give myself a hideer of what a gentleman
reely is, I've read the novvle of ' Pelham ' six times, and am to go
through it 4 times mor.

" I practis ridin and the acquirement of ' a steady and & a sure
seat across Country ' assijuously 4 times a week, at the Hippydrum
Riding Grounds. Many's the tumbil I've ad, and the aking boans
I've suffered from, though I was grinnin in the Park or laffin at
the Opra.

" Every morning from 6 till 9, the innabitance of Halbany may
have been surprised to hear the sounds of music ishuing from the
apartmince of Jeames de la Pluche, Exquire, Letter Hex. It's my
dancing-master. From six to nine we have walces and polkies—at
nine 'mangtiang & depotment,' as he calls it ; & the manner of
hentering a room, complimenting the ost and ostess & compotting
yourself at table. At nine I henter from my dressing-room (has to
a party), I make my bow—my master (he's a Marquis in France,

and ad misfortins, being connected with young Lewy Nepoleum) reseaves me—I hadwance—speak abowt the weather & the toppix of the day in an elegant & cussory manner. Brekfst is enounced by Fitzwarren, my mann—we precede to the festive bord—complimence is igschanged with the manner of drinking wind, adressing your neighbour, employing your napking & finger-glas, &c. And then we fall to brekfst, when I prommiss you the Marquis don't eat like a commoner. He says I'm gettn on very well—soon I shall be able to inwite people to brekfst, like Mr. Mills, my rivle in Halbany ; Mr. Macauly (who wrote that sweet book of ballets, ' The Lays of Hancient Rum ') ; & the great Mr. Rodgers himself."

" The above was wrote some weeks back. I *have* given brekfsts sins then, reglar *Deshunys.* I have ad Earls and Ycounts—Barnits as many as I chose : and the pick of the Railway world, of which I form a member. Last Sunday was a grand *Fate.* I had the *Eleet* of my friends : the display was sumptious ; the company *reshershy.* Everything that Dellixy could suggest was provided by Gunter. I had a Countiss on my right & (the Countess of Wigglesbury, that loveliest and most dashing of Staggs, who may be called the Railway Queend, as my friend George H—— is the Railway King) on my left the Lady Blanche Bluenose, Prince Towrowski, the great Sir Huddlestone Fuddlestone from the North, and a skoar of the fust of the fashn. I was in my *gloary*—the dear Countess and Lady Blanche was dying with laffing at my joax and fun—I was keeping the whole table in a roar—when there came a ring at my door-bell, and sudnly Fitzwarren, my man, henters with an air of constanation. ' Theres somebody at the door,' says he, in a visper.

" ' Oh, it's that dear Lady Hemily,' says I, ' and that lazy raskle of a husband of hers. Trot them in, Fitzwarren ' (for you see, by this time I had adopted quite the manners and hease of the arristoxy).—And so, going out, with a look of wonder he returned presently enouncing Mr. & Mrs. Blodder.

" I turned gashly pail. The table—the guests—the Countiss—Towrouski, and the rest, weald round & round before my hagitated I's. *It was my Grandmother and* Huncle Bill. She is a washerwoman at Healing Common, and he—he keeps a wegetable donkey-cart.

" Y, Y hadn't John, the tiger, igscluded them ? He had tried. But the unconscious, though worthy creeters, adwanced in spite of him, Huncle Bill bringing in the old lady grinning on his harm !

" Phansy my feelinx."

"Immagin when these unfortnat members of my famly hentered the room : you may phansy the ixtonnishment of the nobil company presnt. Old Grann looked round the room quite estounded by its horientle splender, and huncle Bill (pulling off his phantail, & seluting the company as respeckfly as his wulgar natur would alow) says—'Crikey, Jeames, you've got a better birth here than you ad where you where in the plush and powder line.' 'Try a few of them plovers hegs, sir,' I says, whishing, I'm asheamed to say, that somethink would choke huncle B——; 'and I hope, mam, now you've ad the kindniss to wisit me, a little refreshment won't be out of your way.'

"This I said, detummind to put a good fase on the matter ; and because in herly times I'd reseaved a great deal of kindniss from the hold lady, which I should be a roag to forgit. She paid for my schooling ; she got up my fine linning gratis ; shes given me many & many a lb ; and manys the time in appy appy days when me and Maryhann has taken tea. But never mind *that*. 'Mam,' says I, 'you must be tired hafter your walk.'

"'Walk? Nonsince, Jeames,' says she ; 'it's Sunday, & I came in, in *the cart*.' 'Black or green tea, ma'am?' says Fitzwarren, intarupting her. And I will say the feller showed his nouce & good breeding in this difficklt momink ! for he'd halready silenced huncle Bill, who mouth was now full of muffinx, am, Blowny sausag, Perrigole pie, and other dellixies.

"'Wouldn't you like a little *somethink* in your tea, Mam,' says that sly wagg Cinqbars. '*He* knows what I likes,' replies the hawfle hold Lady, pinting to me (which I knew it very well, having often seen her take a glass of hojous gin along with her Bohee), and so I was ableeged to horder Fitzwarren to bring round the licures, and to help my unfortnit rellatif to a bumper of Ollands. She tost it hoff to the elth of the company, giving a smack with her lipps after she'd emtied the glas, which very nearly caused me to phaint with hagny. But, luckaly for me, she didn't igspose herself much farther : for when Cinqbars was pressing her to take another glas, I cried out, 'Don't, my Lord,' on which old Grann hearing him edressed by his title, cried out, 'A Lord ! o law !' and got up and made him a cutsy, and coodnt be peswaded to speak another word. The presents of the noble gent heavidently made her uneezy.

"The Countiss on my right and had shownt symtms of ixtream disgust at the beayviour of my relations, and having called for her carridge, got up to leave the room, with the most dignified hair. I, of coarse, rose to conduct her to her weakle. Ah, what a contrast it was ! There it stood, with stars and garters hall hover the

pannels; the footmin in peach-coloured tites; the hosses worth 3
hundred a-piece;—and there stood the horrid *linnen-cart*, with
'Mary Blodder, Laundress, Ealing, Middlesex,' wrote on the bord,
and waiting till my abandind old parint should come out.

"Cinqbars insisted upon helping her in. Sir Huddlestone
Fuddlestone, the great barnet from the North, who, great as he
is, is as stewpid as a howl, looked on, hardly trusting his goggle
I's as they witnessed the sean. But little lively good naterd Lady
Kitty Quickset, who was going away with the Countiss, held her
little & out of the carridge to me and said, 'Mr. De la Pluche, you
are a much better man than I took you to be. Though her Ladyship *is* horrified, & though your Grandmother *did* take gin for
breakfast, don't give her up. No one ever came to harm yet for
honoring their father & mother.'

" And this was a sort of consolation to me, and I observed that
all the good fellers thought none the wuss of me. Cinqbars said
I was a trump for sticking up for the old washerwoman; Lord
George Gills said she should have his linning; and so they cut
their joax, and I let them. But it was a great releaf to my mind
when the cart drove hoff.

"There was one pint which my Grandmother observed, and
which, I muss say, I thought lickwise : 'Ho, Jeames,' says she,
'hall those fine ladies in sattns and velvets is very well, but there's
not one of em can hold a candle to Mary Hann.' "

" Railway Spec is going on phamusly. You should see how
polite they har at my bankers now ! Sir Paul Pump Aldgate, &
Company. They bow me out of the bank parlor as if I was a
Nybobb. Every body says I'm worth half a millium. The number
of lines they're putting me upon, is inkumseavable. I've put Fitzwarren, my man, upon several. Reginald Fitzwarren, Esquire, looks
splendid in a perspectus ; and the raskle owns that he has made two
thowsnd.

"How the ladies, & men too, foller and flatter me ! If I go
into Lady Binsis hopra box, she makes room for me, who ever is
there, and cries out, 'O do make room for that dear creature !'
And she compliments me on my taste in musick, or my new Broom-oss,
or the phansy of my weskit, and always ends by asking me for some
shares. Old Lord Bareacres, as stiff as a poaker, as prowd as Loosyfer,
as poor as Joab—even he condysends to be sivvle to the great De
la Pluche, and begged me at Harthur's, lately, in his sollom pompus
way, 'to faver him with five minutes' conversation.' I knew what

was coming—application for shares—put him down on my private list. Wouldn't mind the Scrag End Junction passing through Bareacres—hoped I'd come down and shoot there.

"I gave the old humbugg a few shares out of my own pocket. 'There, old Pride,' says I, 'I like to see you down on your knees to a footman. There, old Pompossaty! Take fifty pound; I like to see you come cringing and begging for it.' Whenever I see him in a *very* public place, I take my change for my money. I digg him in the ribbs, or slap his padded old shoulders. I call him, 'Bareacres, my old buck!' and I see him wince. It does my art good.

"I'm in low sperits. A disagreeable insadent has just occurred. Lady Pump, the banker's wife, asked me to dinner. I sat on her right, of course, with an uncommon gal ner me, with whom I was getting on in my fassanating way—full of lacy ally (as the Marquis says) and easy plesntry. Old Pump, from the end of the table, asked me to drink shampane; and on turning to tak the glass I saw Charles Wackles (with womb I'd been imployed at Colonel Spurrier's house) grinning over his shoulder at the butler.

"The beest reckonised me. Has I was putting on my palto in the hall, he came up again: '*How dy doo*, Jeames?' says he, in a findish visper. 'Just come out here, Chawles,' says I, 'I've a word for you, my old boy.' So I beckoned him into Portland Place, with my pus in my hand, as if I was going to give him a sovaring.

"'I think you said "Jeames,".Chawles,' says I, 'and grind at me at dinner?'

"'Why, sir,' says he, 'we're old friends, you know.'

"'Take that for old friendship then,' says I, and I gave him just one on the noas, which sent him down on the pavemint as if he'd been shot. And mounting myjesticly into my cabb, I left the rest of the grinning scoundrills to pick him up, & droav to the Clubb."

"Have this day kimpleated a little efair with my friend George, Earl Bareacres, which I trust will be to the advantidge both of self & that noble gent. Adjining the Bareacre proppaty is a small piece of land of about 100 acres, called Squallop Hill, igseeding advantageous for the cultivation of sheep, which have been found to have a pickewlear fine flaviour from the natur of the grass, tyme, heather, and other hodarefarus plants which grows on that mounting in the places where the rox and stones don't prevent them. Thistles here s also remarkable fine, and the land is also devided hoff by luxurient Stone Hedges—much more usefle and ickonomicle than your quickse, or any of that rubbishing sort of timber: indeed the sile is of that fine natur, that timber refuses to grow there altogether. I gave Bareacres £50 an acre for this land (the igsact premium of my St. Helena Shares)—a very handsom price for land which never yielded two shillings an acre; and very convenient to his Lordship I know, who had a bill coming due at his Bankers which he had given them. James de la Pluche, Esquire, is thus for the fust time a landed propriator—or rayther, I should say, is about to reshume the rank & dignity in the country which his Hancestors so long occupied."

"I have caused one of our inginears to make me a plann of the Squallop Estate, Diddlesexshire, the property of &c. &c., bordered on the North by Lord Bareacres's Country; on the West by Sir Granby Growler; on the South by the Hotion. An Arkytect & Survare, a young feller of great emagination, womb we have employed to make a survey of the Great Caffrarian line, has built me a beautiful Villar (on paper), Plushton Hall, Diddlesex, the seat of I. de la P., Esquire. The house is reprasented a handsome Itallian Structer, imbusmd in woods, and circumwented by beautiful gardings. Theres a lake in front with boatsful of nobillaty and musitions floting on its placid sufface—and a curricle is a driving up to the grand hentrance, and me in it, with Mrs., or perhaps Lady Hangelana de la Pluche. I speak adwisedly. I *may* be going to form a noble kinexion. I may be (by marridge) going to unight my family once more with Harrystoxy, from which misfortn has for some sentries separated us. I have dreams of that sort.

"I've sean sevral times in a dalitifle vishn *a serting Erl*, standing in a hattitude of bennydiction, and rattafying my union with a serting butifle young lady, his daughter. Phansy Mr. or Sir Jeames and Lady Hangelina de la Pluche! Ho! what will the old washywoman, my grandmother, say? She may sell her mangle then, and shall too by my honour as a Gent."

───────

"As for Squallop Hill, its not to be emadgind that I was going to give 5000 lb. for a bleak mounting like that, unless I had some ideer in vew. Ham I not a Director of the Grand Diddlesex? Don't Squallop lie ameadiately betwigst Old Bone House, Single Gloster, and Scrag End, through which cities our line passes? I will have 400,000 lb. for that mounting, or my name is not Jeames. I have arranged a little barging too for my friend the Erl. The line will pass through a hangle of Bareacre Park. He shall have a good compensation I promis you; and then I shall get back the 3000 I lent him. His banker's account, I fear, is in a horrid state."

───────

[The Diary now for several days contains particulars of no interest to the public :—Memoranda of City dinners— meetings of Directors—fashionable parties in which Mr. Jeames figures, and nearly always by the side of his new friend, Lord Bareacres, whose " pompossaty," as previously described, seems to have almost entirely subsided.]

We then come to the following :—

" With a prowd and thankfle Art, I copy off this morning's *Gyzett* the folloing news :—

" ' Commission signed by the Lord Lieutenant of the County of Diddlesex.
" ' JAMES AUGUSTUS DE LA PLUCHE, Esquire, to be Deputy Lieutenant.' "

" ' North Diddlesex Regiment of Yeomanry Cavalry.
" ' James Augustus de la Pluche, Esquire, to be Captain, *vice* Blowhard, promoted.' "

" And his it so ? Ham I indeed a landed propriator—a Deppaty Leftnant—a Capting ? May I hatend the Cort of my Sovring ? and dror a sayber in my country's defens ? I wish the French *wood* land, and me at the head of my squadring on my hoss Desparation. How I'd extonish 'em ! How the gals will stare when they see me in youniform ! How Mary Hann would—but nonsince ! I'm halways thinking of that pore gal. She's left Sir John's. She couldn't abear to stay after I went, I've heerd say. I hope she's got a good place. Any summ of money that would sett her up in bisniss, or make her comfarable, I'd come down with like a mann. I told my granmother so, who sees her, and rode down to Healing on porpose on Desparation to leave a five lb noat in an anvylope. But she's sent it back, sealed with a thimbill."

" *Tuesday*.—Reseavd the following letter from Lord B——, rellatiff to my presntation at Cort and the Youniform I shall wear on that hospicious seramony :—

" ' MY DEAR DE LA PLUCHE,—I think you had better be presented as a Deputy Lieutenant. As for the Diddlesex Yeomanry, I hardly know what the uniform is now. The last time we were out was in 1803, when the Prince of Wales reviewed us, and when we wore French grey jackets, leathers, red morocco boots, crimson pelisses, brass helmets with leopard-skin and a white plume, and the regulation pig-tail of eighteen inches. That dress will hardly answer at present, and must be modified, of course. We were called the White Feathers, in those days. For my part, I decidedly recommend the Deputy Lieutenant.

"'I shall be happy to present you at the Levée and at the Drawing-room. Lady Bareacres will be in town for the 13th, with Angelina, who will be presented on that day. My wife has heard much of you, and is anxious to make your acquaintance.

"'All my people are backward with their rents : for Heaven's sake, my dear fellow, lend me five hundred and oblige yours, very gratefully, "'BAREACRES.'

"*Note.*—Bareacres may press me about the Depity Leftnant; but *I'm* for the cavvlery."

"Jewly will always be a sacrid anniwussary with me. It was in that month that I became persnally ecquaintid with my Prins and my gracious Sovarink.

"Long before the hospitious event acurd, you may imadgin that my busm was in no triffling flutter. Sleaplis of nights, I past them thinking of the great ewent—or if igsosted natur *did* clothes my highlids—the eyedear of my waking thoughts pevaded my slummers. Corts, Erls, presntations, Goldstix, gracious Sovarinx mengling in my dreembs unceasnly. I blush to say it (for humin prisumpshn never surely igseeded that of my wicked wickid vishn), one night I actially dremt that Her R. H. the Princess Hallis was grown up, and that there was a Cabinit Counsel to detummin whether her & was to be bestoad on me or the Prins of Sax-Muffinhausen-Pumpenstein, a young Prooshn or Germing zion of nobillaty. I ask umly parding for this hordacious ideer.

"I said, in my fommer remarx, that I had detummined to be presented to the notus of my reveared Sovaring in a melintary coschewm. The Court-shoots in which Sivillians attend a Levy are so uncomming like the—the—livries (ojous wud! I 8 to put it down) I used to wear before entering sosiaty, that I couldn't abide the notium of wearing one. My detummination was fumly fixt to apeer as a Yominry Cavilry Hoffiser, in the galleant youniform of the North Diddlesex Huzzas.

"Has that redgmint had not been out sins 1803, I thought myself quite hotherized to make such halterations in the youniform

as shuited the presnt time and my metured and elygint taste.
Pig-tales was out of the question. Tites I was detummined to
mintain. My legg is praps the finist pint about me, and I was
risolved not to hide it under a booshle.

"I phixt on scarlit tites, then, imbridered with goold, as I
have seen Widdicomb wear them at Hashleys when me and Mary
Hann used to go there. Ninety-six guineas worth of rich goold
lace and cord did I have myhandering hall hover those shoperb
inagspressables.

"Yellow marocky Heshn boots, red eels, goold spurs and goold
tassles as bigg as belpulls.

"Jackit—French gray and silver oringe fasings & cuphs, according to the old patn ; belt, green and goold, tight round my pusn, &
settin hoff the cemetry of my figgar *not disadvintajusly.*

"A huzza paleese of pupple velvit & sable fir. A sayber of
Demaskus steal, and a sabertash (in which I kep my Odiclone and
imbridered pocket ankercher), kimpleat my acooterments, which,
without vannaty, was, I flatter myself, *uneak.*

"But the crownding triumph was my hat. I couldnt wear a
cock At. The huzzahs dont use 'em. I wouldnt wear the hojous
old brass Elmet & Leppardskin. I choas a hat which is dear to
the memry of hevery Brittn ; an at which was inwented by my
Feeld Marshle and adord Prins ; an At which *vulgar prejidis &
Joaking* has in vane etempted to run down. I chose the HALBERT
AT. I didn't tell Bareacres of this egsabishn of loilty, intending to
surprise him. The white ploom of the West Diddlesex Yomingry
I fixt on the topp of this Shacko, where it spread hout like a
shaving-brush.

"You may be sure that befor the fatle day arrived, I didnt
niglect to practus my part well ; and had sevral *rehustles,* as
they say.

"This was the way. I used to dress myself in my full togs.
I made Fitzwarren, my boddy servant, stand at the dor, and figger
as the Lord in Waiting. I put Mrs. Bloker, my laundress, in my
grand harm chair to reprasent the horgust pusn of my Sovring ;
Frederick, my secknd man, standing on her left, in the hattatude
of an illustrus Prins Consort. Hall the Candles were lighted.
'*Captain de la Pluche, presented by Herl Bareacres,*' Fitzwarren,
my man, igsclaimed, as adwancing I made obasins to the Thrown.
Nealin on one nee, I cast a glans of unhuttarable loilty towards the
British Crownd, then stepping gracefully hup (my Dimascus Simiter
would git betwigst my ligs, in so doink, which at fust was wery
disagreeble)—rising hup grasefly, I say, I flung a look of manly
but respeckfl hommitch tords my Prins, and then ellygntly ritreated

backards out of the Roil Presents. I kep my 4 suvnts hup for 4 hours at this gaym the night before my presntation, and yet I was the fust to be hup with the sunrice. I *coodnt* sleep that night. By abowt six o'clock in the morning, I was drest in my full uniform; and I didnt know how to pass the interveaning hours.

"'My Granmother hasnt seen me in full phigg,' says I. 'It will rejoice that pore old sole to behold one of her race so suxesfle in life. Has I ave read in the novle of "Kennleworth," that the Herl goes down in Cort dress and extoneshes *Hamy Robsart,* I will go down in all my splender and astownd my old washywoman of a Granmother.' To make this detummination; to horder my Broom; to knock down Frederick the groomb for delaying to bring it; was with me the wuck of a momint. The next sor as galliant a cavyleer as hever rode in a cabb, skowering the road to Healing.

"I arrived at the well-known cottich. My huncle was habsent with the cart; but the dor of the humble eboad stood hopen, and I passed through the little garding where the close was hanging out to dry. My snowy ploom was ableeged to bend under the lowly porch, as I hentered the apartmint.

"There was a smell of tea there—there's always a smell of tea there—the old lady was at her Bohee as usual. I advanced tords her; but ha! phansy my extonishment when I sor Mary Hann!

"I halmost faintid with himotion. 'Ho, Jeames!' (she has said to me subsquintly) 'mortial mann never looked so bewtifle as you did when you arrived on the day of the Levy. You were no longer mortial, you were diwine.

"R! what little Justas the Hartist has done to my mannly etractions in the groce carriketure he's made of me."

.   .   .   .

"Nothing, perhaps, ever created so great a sensashun as my hentrance to St. Jeames's, on the day of the Levy. The Tuckish Hambasdor himself was not so much remarked as my shuperb turn out.

"As a Millentary man, and a North Diddlesex Huzza, I was resolved to come to the ground on *hossback.* I had Desparation phigd out as a charger, and got 4 Melentery dresses from Ollywell Street, in which I drest my 2 men (Fitzwarren, hout of livry, woodnt stand it) and 2 fellers from Rimles, where my hosses stand at livry. I rode up St. Jeames's Street, with my 4 Hadycongs—the people huzzaying—the gals waving their handkerchers, as if I were a Foring Prins—hall the winders crowdid to see me pass.

27

"The guard must have taken me for a Hempror at least, when I came, for the drums beat, and the guard turned out and seluted me with presented harms.

"What a momink of triumth it was! I sprung myjestickly from Desperation. I gav the rains to one of my horderlies, and, salewting the crowd, I past into the presnts of my Most Gracious Mrs.

"You, peraps, may igspect that I should narrait at lenth the suckmstanzas of my hawjince with the British Crown. But I am not one who would gratafy *imputtnint curaiosaty*. Rispect for our reckonized instatewtions is my fust quallaty. I, for one, will dye rallying round my Thrown.

"Suffise it to say, when I stood in the Horgust Presnts,—when I sor on the right & of my Himperial Sovring that Most Gracious Prins, to admire womb has been the chief Objick of my life, my busum was seased with an imotium which my Penn rifewses to dixcribe—my trembling knees halmost rifused their hoffis—I reckleck nothing mor until I was found phainting in the harms of the Lord Chamberling. Sir Robert Peal apnd to be standing by (I knew our wuthy Primmier by *Punch's* pictures of him, igspecially his ligs), and he was conwussing with a man of womb I shall say nothink, but that he is a Hero of 100 fites, *and hevery fite he fit he one.* Nead I say that I elude to Harthur of Wellingting? I introjuiced myself to these Jents, and intend to improve the equaintance, and peraps ast Guvmint for a Barnetcy.

"But there was *another* pusn womb on this droring-room I fust had the inagspressable dalite to beold. This was that Star of fashing, that Sinecure of neighbouring i's, as Milting observes, the ecomplisht Lady Hangelina Thistlewood, daughter of my exlent frend, John George Godfrey de Bullion Thistlewood, Earl of Bareacres, Baron Southdown, in the Peeridge of the United Kingdom, Baron Haggismore, in Scotland, K.T., Lord Leftnant of the County of Diddlesex, &c. &c. This young lady was with her Noble Ma, when I was kinducted tords her. And surely never lighted on this hearth a more delightfle vishn. In that gallixy of Bewty the Lady Hangelina was the fairest Star—in that reath of Loveliness the sweetest Rosebud! Pore Mary Hann, my Art's young affeckshns had been senterd on thee; but like water through a sivv, her immidge disapeared in a momink, and left me intransd in the presnts of Hangelina.

"Lady Bareacres made me a myjestick bow—a grand and hawffle pusnage her Ladyship is, with a Roming Nose, and an enawmus ploom of Hostridge phethers; the fare Hangelina smiled with a sweetness perfickly bewhildring, and said, 'O, Mr. De la

Pluche, I'm so delighted to make your acquaintance. I have often heard of you.'

"'Who,' says I, 'has mentioned my insiggnificknt igsistance to the fair Lady Hangelina? *kel bonure igstrame poor mwaw!*' (For you see I've not studdied 'Pelham' for nothink, and have lunt a few French phraces, without which no Gent of fashn speaks now.)

"'O,' replies my Lady, 'it was papa first; and then a very *very* old friend of yours.'

"'Whose name is,' says I, pusht on by my stoopid curawsaty——

"'Hoggins—Mary Ann Hoggins'—ansurred my Lady (laffing phit to splitt her little sides). 'She is my maid, Mr. De la Pluche, and I'm afraid you are a very sad sad person.'

"'A mere baggytell,' says I. 'In fommer days I *was* equainted with that young woman : but haltered suckmstancies have sepparated us for hever, and *mong cure* is irratreevably *perdew* elsewhere.'

"'Do tell me all about it. Who is it? When was it? We are all dying to know.'

"'Since about two minnits, and the Ladys name begins with a *Ha*,' says I, looking her tendarly in the face, and conjring up hall the fassanations of my smile.

"'Mr. De la Pluche,' here said a gentleman in whiskers and mistaches standing by, 'hadn't you better take your spurs out of the Countess of Bareacres's train?'—'Never mind mamma's train' (said Lady Hangelina) : 'this is the great Mr. De la Pluche, who is to make all our fortunes—yours too. Mr. De la Pluche, let me present you to Captain George Silvertop.'—The Capting bent just one jint of his back very slitely; I retund his stare with equill hottiness. 'Go and see for Lady Bareacres's carridge, George,' says his Lordship; and vispers to me, 'a cousin of ours—a poor relation.' So I took no notis of the feller when he came back, nor in my subsquint visits to Hill Street, where it seems a knife and fork was laid reglar for this shabby Capting."

"*Thusday Night.*—O Hangelina, Hangelina, my pashn for you hogments daily! I've bean with her to the Hopra. I sent her a bewtifle Camellia Jyponiky from Covn Garding, with a request she would wear it in her raving Air. I woar another in my butnole. Evns, what was my sattusfackshn as I leant hover her chair, and igsammined the house with my glas!

"She was as sulky and silent as pawsble, however—would

scarcely speek; although I kijoled her with a thowsnd little plesntries. I spose it was because that wulgar raskle Silvertop *wood* stay in the box. As if he didn't know (Lady B.'s as deaf as a poast and counts for nothink) that people *sometimes* like a *tatytaty*."

"*Friday.*—I was sleeples all night.   I gave went to my feelings in the folloring lines—there's a hair out of Balfe's Hopera that she's fond of.   I edapted them to that mellady.

"She was in the droring-room alone with Lady B.   She was wobbling at the pyanna as I hentered.   I flung the convasation upon mewsick; said I sung myself (I've ad lesns lately of Signor Twankydillo); and, on her rekwesting me to faver her with some-think, I bust out with my pom:

"'WHEN MOONLIKE OER THE HAZURE SEAS.

"' When moonlike ore the hazure seas
   In soft effulgence swells,
When silver jews and balmy breaze
   Bend down the Lily's bells;
When calm and deap, the rosy sleap
   Has lapt your soal in dreems,
R Hangeline! R lady mine!
   Dost thou remember Jeames?

I mark thee in the Marble All,
   Where Englands loveliest shine-
I say the fairest of them hall
   Is Lady Hangeline.
My soul, in desolate eclipse,
   With recollection teems—
And then I hask, with weeping lips,
   Dost thou remember Jeames?

Away! I may not tell thee hall
   This soughring heart endures
There is a lonely sperrit-call
   That Sorrow never cures;
There is a little little Star,
   That still above me beams;
It is the Star of Hope—but ar!
   Dost thou remember Jeames?'

"When I came to the last words, "Dost thou remember Je-e-e-ams?' I threw such an igspresshn of unuttrable tenderniss into the shake at the hend, that Hangelina could bare it no more.

A bust of uncumtrollable emotium seized her.   She put her anker.
cher to her face and left the room.   I heard her laffing and sobbing
histerickly in the bedwor.
   " O Hangelina—My adored one, My Arts joy ! " . . .

   " Bareacres, me, the ladies of the famly, with their sweet
Southdown, B's eldest son, and George Silvertop, the shabby
Capting (who seems to git leaf from his ridgmint whenhever he
likes), have beene down into Diddlesex for a few days, enjying the
spawts of the feald there.
   " Never having done much in the gunning line (since when a
hinnasent boy, me and Jim Cox used to go out at Healing, and
shoot sparrers in the Edges with a pistle)—I was reyther dowtfle as
to my suxes as a shot, and practusd for some days at a stoughd
bird in a shooting gallery, which a chap histed up and down with a
string.   I sugseaded in itting the hannimle pretty well.   I bought
Awker's 'Shooting-Guide,' two double guns at Mantings, and salected
from the French prints of fashn the most gawjus and ellygant
sportting ebillyment.   A lite blue velvet and goold cap, woar very
much on one hear, a cravatt of yaller & green imbroidered satting,
a weskit of the McGrigger plaid, & a jacket of the McWhirter tartn
(with large motherapurl butns, engraved with coaches & osses, and
sporting subjix), high leather gayters, and marocky shooting shoes,
was the simple hellymence of my costewm, and I flatter myself
set hoff my figger in rayther a fayverable way.   I took down none
of my own pusnal istablishmint except Fitzwarren, my hone mann,
and my grooms, with Desparation and my curricle osses, and the
Fourgong containing my dressing-case and close.
   " I was heverywhere introjuiced in the county as the great Railroad Cappitlist, who was to make Diddlesex the most prawsperous
districk of the hempire.   The squires prest forrards to welcome
the new comer amongst 'em ; and we had a Hagricultural Meating
of the Bareacres tenantry, where I made a speech droring tears from
heavery i.   It was in compliment to a layborer who had brought
up sixteen children, and lived sixty years on the istate on seven
bobb a week.   I am not prowd, though I know my station.   I
shook hands with that mann in lavinder kidd gloves.   I told
him that the purshuit of hagriculture was the noblist hockupa-
tions of humannaty : I spoke of the yoming of Hengland, who
(under the command of my hancisters) had conquered at Hadjin-
court & Cressy ; and I gave him a pair of new velveteen inagspressables, with two and six in each pocket, as a reward for three score

years of labor. Fitzwarren, my man, brought them forrards on a satting cushing. Has I sat down defning chears selewted the horator; the band struck up 'The Good Old English Gentleman.' I looked to the ladies galry; my Hangelina waived her ankasher and kissd her &; and I sor in the distans that pore Mary Hann efected evidently to tears by my ellaquints."

"What an adwance that gal has made since she's been in Lady Hangelina's company! Sins she wears her young lady's igsploded gownds and retired caps and ribbings, there's an ellygance abowt her which is puffickly admarable; and which, haddid to her own natral bewty & sweetniss, creates in my boozum serting sensatiums . . . Shor! I *mustn't* give way to fealinx unwuthy of a member of the aristoxy. What can she be to me but a mear recklection—a vishn of former ears?

"I'm blest if I didn mistake her for Hangelina herself yesterday. I met her in the grand Collydore of Bareacres Castle. I sor a lady in a melumcolly hattatude gacing outawinder at the setting sun, which was eluminating the fair parx and gardings of the hancient demean.

"'Bewchus Lady Hangelina,' says I—'A penny for your Ladyship's thought,' says I.

"'Ho, Jeames! Ho, Mr. De la Pluche!' hansered a well-known vice, with a haxnt of sadnis which went to my art. '*You* know what my thoughts are, well enough. I was thinking of happy happy old times, when both of us were poo—poo—oor,' says Mary Hann, busting out in a phit of crying, a thing I can't ebide. I took her and and tried to cumft her: I pinted out the diffrents of our sitawashns; igsplained to her that proppaty has its jewties as well as its previletches, and that *my* juty clearly was to marry into a noble famly. I kep on talking to her (she sobbing and going hon hall the time) till Lady Hangelina herself came up—'The real Siming Pewer,' as they say in the play.

"There they stood together—them two young women. I don't know which is the ansamest. I coodn help comparing them; and I coodnt help comparing myself to a certing Hannimle I've read of, that found it difficklt to make a choice betwigst 2 Bundles of A."

"That ungrateful beest Fitzwarren—my oan man—a feller I've maid a fortune for—a feller I give 100 lb. per hannum to!—a low bred Wallydyshamber! *He* must be thinking of falling in love too! and treating me to his imperence.

"He's a great big athlatic feller—six foot i, with a pair of black whiskers like air-brushes—with a look of a Colonel in the harmy—a dangerous pawmpus-spoken raskle I warrunt you. I was coming ome from shuiting this hafternoon—and passing through Lady Hangelina's flour-garding, who should I see in the summer-ouse, but Mary Hann pretending to em an ankyshr and Mr. Fitz-warren paying his court to her?

"'You may as well have me, Mary Hann,' says he. 'I've saved money. We'll take a public-house and I'll make a lady of you. I'm not a purse-proud ungrateful fellow like Jeames—who's such a snob ('such a SNOBB' was his very words!) that I'm ashamed to wait on him—who's the laughing stock of all the gentry and the housekeeper's room too—try a *man*,' says he—'don't be taking on about such a humbug as Jeames.'

"Here young Joe the keeper's sun, who was carrying my bagg, bust out a laffing—thereby causing Mr. Fitzwarren to turn round and intarupt this polite convasation.

"I was in such a rayge. 'Quit the building, Mary Hann,' says I to the young woman; 'and you, Mr. Fitzwarren, have the good-ness to remain.'

"'I give you warning,' roars he, looking black, blue, yaller—all the colours of the ranebo.

"'Take off your coat, you imperent hungrateful scoundrl,' says I.

"'It's not your livery,' says he.

"'Peraps you'll understand me, when I take off my own,' says I, unbuttoning the motherapurls of the MacWhirter tartn. 'Take my jackit, Joe,' says I to the boy,—and put myself in a hattitude about which there was *no mistayk.*"

. . . . . .

"He's 2 stone heavier than me—and knows the use of his ands as well as most men; but in a fite, *blood's everythink ;* the Snobb can't stand before the gentleman; and I should have killed him, I've little doubt, but they came and stopt the fite betwigst us before we'd had more than 2 rounds.

"I punisht the raskle tremenjusly in that time, though; and I'm writing this in my own sittn-room, not being able to come down to dinner on account of a black-eye I've got, which is sweld up and disfiggrs me dreadfl."

———

"On account of the hoffle black i which I reseaved in my rangcounter with the hinfimus Fitzwarren, I kep my roomb for sevral days, with the rose-coloured curtings of the apartmint closed, so as to form an agreeable twilike ; and a light-bloo sattin shayd over the injard pheacher. My woons was thus made to become me as much as pawsable ; and (has the Poick well observes ' Nun but the Brayv desuvs the Fare ') I cumsoled myself in the sasiaty of the ladies for my tempory disfiggarment.

" It was Mary Hann who summind the House and put an end to my phistycoughs with Fitzwarren. I licked him and bare him no mallis : but of corse I dismist the imperent scoundrill from my suvvis, apinting Adolphus, my page, to his post of confidenshle Valley.

" Mary Hann and her young and lovely Mrs. kep paying me continyoul visits during my retiremint. Lady Hangelina was halways sending me messidges by her : while my exlent friend, Lady Bare-acres (on the contry), was always sending me toakns of affeckshn by Hangelina.   Now it was a coolin hi-lotium, inwented by herself, that her Ladyship would perscribe—then, agin, it would be a booky of flowers (my favrit polly hanthuses, pellagoniums, and jyponikys), which none but the fair &s of Hangelina could dispose about the chamber of the hinvyleed.   Ho ! those dear mothers ! when they wish to find a chans for a galliant young feller, or to ixtablish their dear gals in life, what awpertunities they *will* give a man !   You'd have phansied I was so hill (on account of my black hi) that I couldnt live exsep upon chicking and spoon-meat, and jellies, and blemonges, and that I couldnt eat the latter dellixies (which I ebomminate onternoo, prefurring a cut of beaf or muttn to hall the kickpshaws of France) unless Hangelina brought them.   I et 'em, and sacrafised myself for her dear sayk.

" I may stayt here that in privit convasations with old Lord B. and his son, I had mayd my proposals for Hangelina, and was axepted, and hoped soon to be made the appiest gent in Hengland.

" ' You must break the matter gently to her,' said her hexlant father.   ' You have my warmest wishes, my dear Mr. De la Pluche, and those of my Lady Bareacres ; but I am not—not quite certain about Lady Angelina's feelings.   Girls are wild and romantic. They do not see the necessity of prudent establishments, and I have never yet been able to make Angelina understand the embar-rassments of her family.   These silly creatures prate about love and a cottage, and despise advantages which wiser heads than theirs know how to estimate.'

" ' Do you mean that she aint fassanated by me ? ' says I, burst-ing out at this outrayjus ideer.

" ' She *will* be, my dear sir. You have already pleased her, —your admirable manners must succeed in captivating her, and a fond father's wishes will be crowned on the day in which you enter our family.'

" 'Recklect, gents,' says I to the 2 lords,—'a barging's a barging —I'll pay hoff Southdown's Jews, when I'm his brother. As a *straynger*'—(this I said in a sarcastickle toan)—'I wouldnt take such a *libbaty*. When I'm your suninlor I'll treble the valyou of your estayt. I'll make your incumbrinces as right as a trivit, and restor the ouse of Bareacres to its herly splender. But a pig in a poak is not the way of transacting bisniss imployed by Jeames De la Pluche, Esquire.'

"And I had a right to speak in this way. I was one of the greatest scrip-holders in Hengland; and calclated on a kilossle fortune. All my shares was rising immence. Every poast brot me noose that I was sevral thowsands richer than the day befor. I was detummind not to reerlize till the proper time, and then to buy istates; to found a new family of Delapluches, and to alie myself with the aristoxy of my country.

"These pints I reprasented to pore Mary Hann hover and hover agin. 'If you'd been Lady Hangelina, my dear gal,' says I, 'I would have married you: and why don't I? Because my dooty prewents me. I'm a marter to dooty; and you, my pore gal, must cumsole yorself with that ideer.'

"There seemed to be a consperracy, too, between that Silvertop and Lady Hangelina to drive me to the same pint. 'What a plucky fellow you were, Pluche,' says he (he was rayther more familliar than I liked), 'in your fight with Fitzwarren!—to engage a man of twice your strength and science, though you were sure to be beaten' (this is an etroashous folsood: I should have finnisht Fitz in 10 minnits), 'for the sake of pore Mary Hann! That's a generous fellow. I like to see a man risen to eminence like you, having his heart in the right place. When is to be the marriage, my boy?'

" 'Capting S.,' says I, 'my marridge consunns your most umble servnt a precious sight more than you;'—and I gev him to understand I didn't want him to put in *his* ore—I wasn't afrayd of his whiskers, I prommis you, Capting as he was. I'm a British Lion, I am: as brayv as Bonypert, Hannible, or Holiver Crummle, and would face bagnits as well as any Evy drigoon of 'em all.

"Lady Hangelina, too, igspawstulated in her hartfl way. 'Mr. De la Pluche (seshee), why, why press this point? You can't suppose that you will be happy with a person like me?'

" 'I adoar you, charming gal!' says I. 'Never, never go to say any such thing.'

" 'You adored Mary Ann first,' answers her Ladyship; 'you

can't keep your eyes off her now.   If any man courts her you
grow so jealous that you begin beating him.   You will break the
girl's heart if you don't marry her, and perhaps some one else's—
but you don't mind *that*.'

"'Break yours, you adoarible creature !   I'd die first !   And as
for Mary Hann, she will git over it ; people's arts ain't broakn so
easy.   Once for all, suckmstances is changed betwigst me and er.
It's a pang to part with her' (says I, my fine hi's filling with tears),
' but part from her I must.'

"It was curius to remark abowt that singlar gal, Lady
Hangelina, that melumcolly as she was when she was talking to
me, and ever so disml—yet she kep on laffing every minute like the
juice and all.

"'What a sacrifice !' says she ; 'it's like Napoleon giving up
Josephine.   What anguish it must cause to your susceptible heart!'

"'It does,' says I—'Hagnies !'   (Another laff.)

"'And if—if I don't accept you—you will invade the States
of the Emperor my papa, and I am to be made the sacrifice and
the occasion of peace between you !'

"'I don't know what you're eluding to about Joseyfeen and
Hemperors your Pas ; but I know that your Pa's estate is over
hedaneers morgidged ; that if some one don't elp him, he's no better
than an old pawper ; that he owes me a lot of money ; and that I'm
the man that can sell him up hoss & foot : or set him up agen—
that's what I know, Lady Hangelina,' says I, with a hair as much
as to say, ' Put *that* in your Ladyship's pipe and smoke it.'

"And so I left her, and nex day a serting fashnable paper
enounced—

"'MARRIAGE IN HIGH LIFE.—We hear that a matrimonial
union is on the *tapis* between a gentleman who has made a colossal
fortune in the Railway World, and the only daughter of a noble
earl, whose estates are situated in D–ddles–x.   An early day is
fixed for this interesting event.' "

"Contry to my expigtations (but when or ow can we reckn
upon the fealinx of wimming ?) Mary Hann didn't seem to be much
efected by the hideer of my marridge with Hangelinar.   I was
rayther disapinted peraps that the fickle young gal reckumsiled
herself so easy to give me hup, for we Gents are creechers of
vannaty after all, as well as those of the hopsit secks : and betwigst
you and me there *was* mominx when I almost whisht that I'd

been borne a Myommidn or Turk, when the Lor would have permitted me to marry both these sweet beinx, wherehas I was now condemd to be appy with ony one.

"Meanwild everythink went on very agreeable betwigst me and my defianced bride. When we came back to town I kemishnd Mr. Showery the great Hoctionear to look out for a town manshing sootable for a gent of my quallaty. I got from the Erald Hoffis (not the *Mawning Erald*—no no, I'm not such a Mough as to go there for ackrit infamation) an account of my famly, my harms and pedigry.

"I hordered in Long Hacre, three splendid equipidges, on which my arms and my adored wife's was drawn & quartered; and I got portricks of me and her paynted by the sellabrated Mr. Shalloon, being resolved to be the gentleman in all things, and knowing that my character as a man of fashn wasn't compleat unless I sat to that dixtinguished Hartist. My likenis I presented to Hangelina. It's not considered flattring—and though *she* parted with it, as you will hear, mighty willingly, there's *one* young lady (a thousand times handsomer) that values it as the happle of her hi.

"Would any man beleave that this picture was soald at my sale for about a twenty-fifth part of what it cost me? It was bought in by Maryhann, though: 'O dear Jeames,' says she, often (kissing of it & pressing it to her art), 'it isn't $\frac{1}{4}$ ansum enough for you, and hasn't got your angellick smile and the igspreshn of your dear dear i's.'

"Hangelina's pictur was kindly presented to me by Countess B., her mamma, though of coarse I paid for it. It was engraved for the 'Book of Bewty' the same year.

"With such a perfusion of ringlits I should scarcely have known her—but the ands, feat, and i's, was very like. She was painted in a gitar supposed to be singing one of my little melladies; and her brother Southdown, who is one of the New England poits, wrote the follering stanzys about her:—

"LINES UPON MY SISTER'S PORTRAIT.

"BY THE LORD SOUTHDOWN.

" The castle towers of Bareacres are fair upon the lea,
Where the cliffs of bonny Diddlesex rise up from out the sea:
I stood upon the donjon keep and view'd the country o'er,
I saw the lands of Bareacres for fifty miles or more.
I stood upon the donjon keep—it is a sacred place,—
Where floated for eight hundred years the banner of my race;
Argent, a dexter sinople, and gules an azure field,
There ne'er was nobler cognisance on knightly warrior's shield.

The first time England saw the shield 'twas round a Norman neck,
On board a ship from Valery, King William was on deck.
A Norman lance the colours wore, in Hastings' fatal fray—
St. Willibald for Bareacres! 'twas double gules that day!
O Heaven and sweet St. Willibald! in many a battle since
A loyal-hearted Bareacres has ridden by his Prince!
At Acre with Plantagenet, with Edward at Poitiers,
The pennon of the Bareacres was foremost on the spears!

'Twas pleasant in the battle-shock to hear our war-cry ringing:
O grant me, sweet St. Willibald, to listen to such singing!
Three hundred steel-clad gentlemen, we drove the foe before us,
And thirty score of British bows kept twanging to the chorus!
O knights, my noble ancestors, and shall I never hear
Saint Willibald for Bareacres through battle ringing clear?
I'd cut me off this strong right hand a single hour to ride,
And strike a blow for Bareacres, my fathers, at your side!

Dash down, dash down, yon Mandolin, beloved sister mine!
Those blushing lips may never sing the glories of our line:
Our ancient castles echo to the clumsy feet of churls,
The spinning Jenny houses in the mansion of our Earls.
Sing not, sing not, my Angeline! in days so base and vile,
'Twere sinful to be happy, 'twere sacrilege to smile.
I'll hie me to my lonely hall, and by its cheerless hob
I'll muse on other days, and wish—and wish I were—A SNOB."

"All young Hengland, I'm told, considers the poim bewtifle. They're always writing about battleaxis and shivvlery, these young chaps; but the ideer of Southdown in a shoot of armer, and his cuttin hoff his ' strong right hand,' is rayther too good; the feller is about 5 fit hi,—as ricketty as a babby, with a vaist like a gal; and though he may have the art and curridge of a Bengal tyger, I'd back my smallest cab-boy to lick him,—that is if I *ad* a cab-boy. But io! *my* cab-days is over.

"Be still my hagnizing Art! I now am about to hunfoald the dark payges of the Istry of my life!"

"My friends! you've seen me ither2 in the full kerear of Fortn, prawsprus but not hover prowd of my prawsperraty; not dizzy though mounted on the haypix of Good Luck—feasting hall the great (like the Good Old Henglish Gent in the song, which he has been my moddle and igsample through life), but not forgitting the small—No, my beayviour to my granmother at Healing shows that. I bot her a new donkey cart (what the French call a cart-blansh) and a handsome set of peggs for anging up her linning, and treated

Huncle Bill to a new shoot of close, which he ordered in St. Jeames's Street, much to the estonishment of my Snyder there, namely an olliff-green velvyteen jackit and smalclose, and a crimsn plush weskoat with glas-buttns. These pints of genarawsity in my disposishn I never should have eluded to, but to show that I am naturally of a noble sort, and have that kind of galliant carridge which is equel to either good or bad forting.

"What was the substns of my last chapter? In that everythink was prepayred for my marridge—the consent of the parents of my Hangelina was gaynd, the lovely gal herself was ready (as I thought) to be led to Himing's halter—the trooso was hordered—the weddin dressis were being phitted hon—a weddinkake weighing half a tunn was a gettn reddy by Mesurs Gunter, of Buckley Square; there was such an account for Shantilly and Honiton laces as would have staggerd hennyboddy (I know they did the Commissioner when I came hup for my Stiffikit), and has for Injar-shawls I bawt a dozen sich fine ones as never was given away—no not by Hiss Iness the Injan Prins Juggernaut Tygore. The juils (a pearl and dimind shoot) were from the establishmint of Mysurs Storr and Mortimer. The honey-moon I intended to pass in a continentle excussion, and was in treaty for the ouse at Halberd-gate (hopsit Mr. Hudson's) as my town-house. I waited to cumclude the putchis untle the Share-Markit which was rayther deprest (oing I think not so much to the atax of the misrabble *Times*, as to the prodidjus flams of the *Morning Erald*) was restored to its elthy toan. I wasn't going to part with scrip which was 20 primmium at 2 or 3 ; and bein confidnt that the Markit would rally, had bought very largely for the two or three new accounts.

"This will explane to those unfortnight traydsmen to womb I gayv orders for a large igstent ow it was that I couldn't pay their accounts. *I* am the soal of onour—but no gent can pay when he has no money :—it's not *my* fault if that old screw Lady Bareacres cabbidged three hundred yards of lace, and kep back 4 of the biggest diminds and seven of the largist Injar Shawls—it's not *my* fault if the tradespeople didn git their goods back, and that Lady B. declared they were *lost*. I began the world afresh with the close on my back, and thirteen and six in money, concealing nothink, giving up heverythink, Onist and undismayed, and though beat, with pluck in me still, and ready to begin agin.

"Well—it was the day before that apinted for my Unium. The *Ringdove* steamer was lying at Dover ready to carry us hoff. The Bridle apartmince had been hordered at Salt Hill, and subsquintly at Balong sur Mare—the very table cloth was laid for the weddn brexfst in Ill Street, and the Bride's Right Reverend Huncle, the

Lord Bishop of Bullocksmithy, had arrived to sellabrayt our unium. All the papers were full of it.   Crowds of the fashnable world went to see the trooso, and admire the Carridges in Long Hacre.   Our travleng charrat (light bloo lined with pink satting, and vermillium and goold weals) was the hadmaration of all for quiet ellygns.   We were to travel only 4, viz., me, my Lady, my vally, and Mary Hann as famdyshamber to my Hangelina.   Far from oposing our match, this worthy gal had quite givn into it of late, and laught and joakt, and enjoyd our plans for the fewter igseedinkly.

"I'd left my lovely Bride very gay the night before—aving a multachewd of bisniss on, and Stockbrokers' and bankers' accounts to settle: atsettrey atsettrey.   It was layt before I got these in horder: my sleap was feavrish, as most mens is when they are going to be marrid or to be hanged.   I took my chocklit in bed about one: tried on my wedding close, and found as ushle that they became me exceedingly.

"One thing distubbed my mind—two weskts had been sent home.   A blush-white satting and gold, and a kinary coloured tabbinet imbridered in silver: which should I wear on the hospicious day?   This hadgitated and perplext me a good deal.   I detummined to go down to Hill Street and cumsult the Lady whose wishis were henceforth to be my *hallinall;* and wear whichever *she* phixt on.

"There was a great bussel and distubbans in the Hall in Ill Street which I etribyouted to the eproaching event.   The old porter stared most uncommon when I kem in—the footman who was to enounce me laft I thought—I was going upstairs—

" 'Her Ladyship's not—not at *home,*' says the man; 'and my Lady's hill in bed.'

" 'Git lunch,' says I, 'I'll wait till Lady Hangelina returns.'

"At this the feller loox at me for a momint with his cheex blown out like a bladder, and then busts out in a reglar gaffau! the porter jined in it, the impident old raskle: and Thomas says, slapping his and on his thy, without the least respect—'*I say, Huffy, old boy! Isn't this a good un?*'

" 'Wadyermean, you infunnle scoundrel,' says I, 'hollaring and laffing at me?'

" 'Oh, here's Miss Mary Hann coming up,' says Thomas, 'ask *her*'—and indeed there came my little Mary Hann tripping down the stairs—her &s in her pockits; and when she saw me, *she* began to blush and look hod & then to grin too.

" 'In the name of Imperence,' says I, rushing on Thomas, and collaring him fit to throttle him—'no raskle of a flunky shall insult *me*,' and I sent him staggerin up against the porter, and both of 'em into

the hall-chair with a flopp—when Mary Hann, jumping down, says,
'O James! O Mr. Plush! read this'—and she pulled out a billy doo.
"I reckanized the and-writing of Hangelina."

"Deseatful Hangelina's billy ran as follows :—

"'I had all along hoped that you would have relinquished pretensions which you must have seen were so disagreeable to me ; and
have spared me the painful necessity of the step which I am compelled to take. For a long time I could not believe my parents were
serious in wishing to sacrifice me, but have in vain entreated them
to spare me. I cannot undergo the shame and misery of a union
with you. To the very last hour I remonstrated in vain, and only
now anticipate, by a few hours, my departure from a home from
which they themselves were about to expel me.

"'When you receive this, I shall be united to the person to
whom, as you are aware, my heart was given long ago. My parents
are already informed of the step I have taken. And I have my
own honour to consult, even before their benefit : they will forgive
me, I hope and feel, before long.

"'As for yourself, may I not hope that time will calm your
exquisite feelings too? I leave Mary Ann behind me to console
you. She admires you as you deserve to be admired, and with a
constancy which I entreat you to try and imitate. Do, my dear Mr.
Plush, try—for the sake of your sincere friend and admirer,   A.

"'*P.S.*—I leave the wedding-dresses behind for her : the
diamonds are beautiful, and will become Mrs. Plush admirably.'

"This was hall!—Confewshn! And there stood the footmen snig-
gerin, and that hojus Mary Hann half a cryin, half a laffing at me !
'Who has she gone hoff with?' rors I; and Mary Hann (smiling with
one hi) just touched the top of one of the Johns' canes who was goin
out with the noats to put hoff the brekfst. It was Silvertop then !

"I bust out of the house in a stayt of diamoniacal igsitement !

"The stoary of that ilorpmint *I* have no art to tell. Here it is
from the *Morning Tatler* newspaper :—

"ELOPEMENT IN HIGH LIFE.

"THE ONLY AUTHENTIC ACCOUNT.

"The neighbourhood of Berkeley Square, and the whole fashionable world, has been thrown into a state of the most painful excite-

ment by an event which has just placed a noble family in great perplexity and affliction.

"It has long been known among the select nobility and gentry that a marriage was on the *tapis* between the only daughter of a Noble Earl, and a Gentleman whose rapid fortunes in the railway world have been the theme of general remark. Yesterday's paper, it was supposed, in all human probability would have contained an account of the marriage of James De la Pl–che, Esq., and the Lady Angelina ——, daughter of the Right Honourable the Earl of B–re–cres. The preparations for this ceremony were complete: we had the pleasure of inspecting the rich *trousseau* (prepared by Miss Twiddler, of Pall Mall); the magnificent jewels from the establishment of Messrs. Storr and Mortimer; the elegant marriage cake, which, already cut up and portioned, is, alas! not destined to be eaten by the friends of Mr. De la Pl–che; the superb carriages, and magnificent liveries, which had been provided in a style of the most lavish yet tasteful sumptuosity. The Right Reverend the Lord Bishop of Bullocksmithy had arrived in town to celebrate the nuptials, and is staying at Mivart's. What must have been the feelings of that venerable prelate, what those of the agonised and noble parents of the Lady Angelina—when it was discovered, on the day previous to the wedding, that her Ladyship had fled the paternal mansion! To the venerable Bishop the news of his noble niece's departure might have been fatal: we have it from the waiters of Mivart's that his Lordship was about to indulge in the refreshment of turtle soup when the news was brought to him; immediate apoplexy was apprehended; but Mr. Macann, the celebrated surgeon of Westminster, was luckily passing through Bond Street at the time, and being promptly called in, bled and relieved the exemplary patient. His Lordship will return to the Palace, Bullocksmithy, to-morrow.

"The frantic agonies of the Right Honourable the Earl of Bareacres can be imagined by every paternal heart. Far be it from us to disturb—impossible is it for us to describe their noble sorrow. Our reporters have made inquiries every ten minutes at the Earl's mansion in Hill Street, regarding the health of the Noble Peer and his incomparable Countess. They have been received with a rudeness which we deplore but pardon. One was threatened with a cane; another, in the pursuit of his official inquiries, was saluted with a pail of water; a third gentleman was menaced in a pugilistic manner by his Lordship's porter; but being of an Irish nation, a man of spirit and sinew, and Master of Arts of Trinity College, Dublin, the gentleman of our establishment confronted the menial, and having severely beaten him, retired to a neighbouring hotel much frequented by the domestics of the surrounding nobility, and there obtained what we believe to be the most accurate particulars of this extraordinary occurrence.

"George Frederick Jennings, third footman in the establishment of Lord Bareacres, stated to our *employé* as follows :—Lady Angelina had been promised to Mr. De la Pluche for near six weeks. She never could abide that gentleman. He was the laughter of all the servants' hall. Previous to his elevation he had himself been engaged in a domestic capacity. At that period he had offered marriage to Mary Ann Hoggins, who was living in the quality of ladies'-maid in the family where Mr. De la P. was employed. Miss Hoggins became subsequently lady's-maid to Lady Angelina—the elopement was arranged between those two. It was Miss Hoggins who delivered the note which informed the bereaved Mr. Plush of his loss.

"Samuel Buttons, page to the Right Honourable the Earl of Bareacres, was ordered on Friday afternoon at eleven o'clock to fetch a cabriolet from the stand in Davies Street. He selected the cab No. 19,796, driven by George Gregory Macarty, a one-eyed man from Clonakilty, in the neighbourhood of Cork, Ireland (*of whom more anon*), and waited, according to his instructions, at the corner of Berkeley Square, with his vehicle. His young lady, accompanied by her maid, Miss Mary Ann Hoggins, carrying a bandbox, presently arrived, and entered the cab with the box : what were the contents of that box we have never been able to ascertain. On asking her Ladyship whether he should order the cab to drive in any particular direction, he was told to drive to Madame Crinoline's, the eminent milliner in Cavendish Square. On requesting to know whether he should accompany her Ladyship, Buttons was peremptorily ordered by Miss Hoggins to go about his business.

" Having now his clue, our reporter instantly went in search of cab 19,796, or rather the driver of that vehicle, who was discovered with no small difficulty at his residence, Whetstone Park, Lincoln's Inn Fields, where he lives with his family of nine children. Having received two sovereigns, instead doubtless of two shillings (his regular fare, by the way, would have been only one-and-eightpence), Macarty had not gone out with the cab for the two last days, passing them in a state of almost ceaseless intoxication. His replies were very incoherent in answer to the queries of our reporter ; and, had not that gentleman himself been a compatriot, it is probable he would have refused altogether to satisfy the curiosity of the public.

" At Madame Crinoline's, Miss Hoggins quitted the carriage, and *a gentleman* entered it. Macarty describes him as a very *clever* gentleman (meaning tall) with black moustaches, Oxford-grey

27

trousers, and black hat and a pea coat.   He drove the couple *to the
Euston Square Station,* and there left them.   How he employed
his time subsequently we have stated.

"At the Euston Square Station, the gentleman of our establishment learned from Frederick Corduroy, a porter there, that a
gentleman answering the above description had taken places to
Derby.   We have despatched a confidential gentleman thither, by
a special train, and shall give his report in a second edition.

"SECOND EDITION.

"(FROM OUR REPORTER.)

"NEWCASTLE : *Monday.*

" I am just arrived at this ancient town, at the ' Elephant and
Cucumber Hotel.'   A party travelling under the name of *Mr. and
Mrs. Jones,* the gentleman wearing moustaches, and having with
them a blue bandbox, arrived by the train two hours before me,
and have posted onwards to *Scotland.*   I have ordered four horses,
and write this on the hind boot, as they are putting to.

"THIRD EDITION.

" GRETNA GREEN : *Monday Evening.*

"The mystery is at length solved.   This afternoon, at four
o'clock, the Hymeneal Blacksmith, of Gretna Green, celebrated the
marriage between George Granby Silvertop, Esq., a Lieutenant in
the 150th Hussars, third son of General John Silvertop, of Silvertop
Hall, Yorkshire, and Lady Emily Silvertop, daughter of the late
sister of the present Earl of Bareacres, and the Lady Angelina
Amelia Arethusa Anaconda Alexandrina Alicompania Annemaria
Antoinetta, daughter of the last-named Earl Bareacres."

*(Here follows a long extract from the Marriage Service in the
Book of Common Prayer, which was not read on the occasion,
and need not be repeated here.)*

" After the ceremony, the young couple partook of a slight
refreshment of sherry and water—the former the Captain pronounced to be execrable ; and, having myself tasted some glasses
from the *very same bottle* with which the young and noble pair
were served, I must say I think the Captain was rather hard upon
mine host of the ' Bagpipes Hotel and Posting-House,' whence they
instantly proceeded.   I follow them as soon as the horses have fed.

"FOURTH EDITION.

"SHAMEFUL TREATMENT OF OUR REPORTER.

"WHISTLEBINKIE, N.B. : *Monday, midnight.*

" I arrived at this romantic little villa about two hours after the newly-married couple, whose progress I have the honour to trace, reached Whistlebinkie. They have taken up their residence at the ' Cairngorm Arms '—mine is at the other hostelry, the ' Clachan of Whistlebinkie.'

" On driving up to the ' Cairngorm Arms,' I found a gentleman of military appearance standing at the door, and occupied seemingly in smoking a cigar. It was very dark as I descended from my carriage, and the gentleman in question exclaimed, 'Is it you, Southdown, my boy ? You have come too late ; unless you are come to have some supper ;' or words to that effect. I explained that I was not the Lord Viscount Southdown, and politely apprised Captain Silvertop (for I justly concluded the individual before me could be no other) of his mistake.

" ' Who the deuce ' (the Captain used a stronger term) ' are you, then ? " said Mr. Silvertop. ' Are you Baggs and Tapewell, my uncle's attorneys ? If you are, you have come too late for the fair.'

" I briefly explained that I was not Baggs and Tapewell, but that my name was J–ms, and that I was a gentleman connected with the establishment of the *Morning Tatler* newspaper.

" ' And what has brought you here, Mr. Morning Tatler ? ' asked my interlocutor, rather roughly. My answer was frank— that the disappearance of a noble lady from the house of her friends had caused the greatest excitement in the metropolis, and that my employers were anxious to give the public every particular regarding an event so singular.

" ' And do you mean to say, sir, that you have dogged me all the way from London, and that my family affairs are to be published for the readers of the *Morning Tatler* newspaper ? The *Morning Tatler* be ——' (the Captain here gave utterance to an oath which I shall not repeat), 'and you too, sir; you impudent meddling scoundrel.'

" ' Scoundrel, sir ! ' said I. ' Yes,' replied the irate gentleman, seizing me rudely by the collar—and he would have choked me, but that my blue satin stock and false collar gave way, and were left in the hands of this *gentleman*. ' Help, landlord ! ' I loudly exclaimed, adding, I believe, ' murder,' and other exclamations of alarm. In vain I appealed to the crowd, which by this time was pretty considerable; and the unfeeling post-boys only burst into laughter, and called out, 'Give it him, Captain.' A struggle ensued, in which I have no doubt I should have had the better, but that the Captain, joining suddenly in the general and indecent hilarity, which was doubled when I fell down, stopped and said, 'Well, Jims, I won't fight on my marriage-day. Go into the tap, Jims, and order a glass of brandy-and-water at my expense—and mind I don't see your face to-morrow morning, or I'll make it more ugly than it is.'

"With these gross expressions and a cheer from the crowd, Mr. Silvertop entered the inn. I need not say that I did not partake of his hospitality, and that personally I despise his insults. I make them known that they may call down the indignation of the body of which I am a member, and throw myself on the sympathy of the public, as a gentleman shamefully assaulted and insulted in the discharge of a public duty."

"Thus you've sean how the flower of my affeckshns was tawn out of my busm, and my art was left bleading. Hangelina! I forgive thee. Mace thou be appy! If ever artfelt prayer for others wheel awailed on i, the beink on womb you trampled addresses those subblygations to Evn in your be$\frac{1}{2}$!

"I went home like a maniack, after hearing the announcement of Hangelina's departer. She'd been gone twenty hours when I heard the fatle noose. Purshoot was vain. Suppose I *did* kitch her up, they were married, and what could we do? This sensable remark I made to Earl Bareacres, when that distragted nobleman igspawstulated with me. Er who was to have been my mother-in-lor, the Countiss, I never from that momink sor agin. My presnts, troosoes, juels, &c., were sent back—with the igsepshn of the diminds and Cashmear shawl, which her Ladyship *coodn't find*. Ony it was wispered that at the nex buthday she was seen with a shawl *igsackly of the same pattn*. Let er keep it.

"Southdown was phurius. He came to me hafter the ewent, and wanted me to adwance 50 lb., so that he might purshew his fewgitif sister—but I wasn't to be ad with that sort of chaugh—there was no more money for *that* famly. So he went away, and gave huttrance to his feelinx in a poem, which appeared (price 2 guineas) in the *Bel Asombly*.

"All the juilers, manchumakers, lacemen, coch bilders, apolstrers, hors dealers, and weddencake makers came pawring in with their bills, haggravating feelings already woondid beyond enjurants. That madniss didn't seaze me that night was a mussy. Fever, fewry, and rayge rack'd my hagnized braind, and drove sleap from my throbbink ilids. Hall night I follered Hangelinar in imadganation along the North Road. I wented cusses & mallydickshuns on the hinfamus Silvertop. I kickd and rord in my unhuttarable whoe! I seazd my pillar: I pitcht into it: pummld it, strangled it. Ha har! I thought it was Silvertop writhing in my Jint grasp; and taw the hordayshis villing lim from lim in the terrible strenth of my despare! . . . Let me drop a cutting over the memries of that night. When my boddy-suvnt came with my ot water in the mawning, the livid copse in the charnill was not payler than the gashly De la Pluche!

"'Give me the Share-list, Mandeville,' I micanickly igsclaimed. I had not perused it for the past 3 days, my etention being engayged elseware. Hevns & huth!—what was it I red there? What was it that made me spring outabed as if sumbady had given me cold pig?—I red Rewin in that Share-list—the Pannick was in full hoparation!"

.   .   .   .

"Shall I describe that kitastrafy with which hall Hengland is familliar? My & rifewses to cronnicle the misfortns which lassarated my bleeding art in Hoctober last. On the fust of Hawgust where was I? Director of twenty-three Companies; older of scrip hall at a primmium, and worth at least a quarter of a millium. On Lord Mare's day, my Saint Helenas quotid at 14 pm, were down at $\frac{1}{2}$ discount; my Central Ichaboes at $\frac{3}{8}$ discount; my Table Mounting & Hottentot Grand Trunk, no where; my Bathershins and Derrynane Beg, of which I'd bought 2000 for the account at 17 primmium, down to nix; my Juan Fernandez, my Great Central Oregons, prostrit. There was a momint when I thought I shouldn't be alive to write my own tail!"

(Here follow in Mr. Plush's MS. about twenty-four pages of railroad calculations, which we pretermit.)

"Those beests, Pump & Aldgate, once so cringing and umble, wrote me a threatnen letter because I overdrew my account three-and-sixpence: woodn't advance me five thousand on 25,000 worth of scrip; kep me waiting 2 hours when I asked to see the house; and then sent out Spout, the jewnior partner, saying they wouldn't discount my paper, and implawed me to clothes my account. I did: I paid the three-and-six balliance, and never sor 'em mor.

"The market fell daily. The Rewin grew wusser and wusser. Hagnies, Hagnies! It wasn't in the city aloan my misfortns came upon me. They beerded me in my own ome. The biddle who

kips watch at the Halbany wodn keep misfortn out of my chambers ;
and Mrs. Twiddler, of Pall Mall, and Mr. Hunx, of Long Acre, put
egsicution into my apartmince, and swep off every stick of my
furniture. 'Wardrobe & furniture of a man of fashion.' What an
adwertisement George Robins *did* make of it ; and what a crowd
was collected to laff at the prospick of my ruing ! My chice plait ;
my seller of wine ; my picturs—that of myself included (it was
Maryhann, bless her ! that bought it, unbeknown to me) ; all—
all went to the ammer. That brootle Fitzwarren, my exvally,
womb I met, fimilliarly slapt me on the sholder, and said, 'Jeames,
my boy, you'd best go into suvvis aginn.'

"I *did* go into suvvis—the wust of all suvvices—I went into
the Queen's Bench Prison, and lay there a misrabble captif for 6
mortial weeks. Misrabble shall I say? no, not misrabble altogether ;
there was sunlike in the dunjing of the pore prisner. I had visitors.
A cart used to drive hup to the prizn gates of Saturdays ; a washywoman's cart, with a fat old lady in it, and a young one. Who
was that young one? Everyone who has an art can gess, it was
my blue-eyed blushing hangel of a Mary Hann ! 'Shall we take
him out in the linnen-basket, Grandmamma?' Mary Hann said.
Bless her, she'd already learned to say grandmamma quite natral ;
but I didn't go out that way ; I went out by the door a white-
washed man. Ho, what a feast there was at Healing the day I
came out ! I'd thirteen shillings left when I'd bought the gold
ring. I wasn't prowd. I turned the mangle for three weeks ; and
then Uncle Bill said, 'Well, there *is* some good in the feller ;' and
it was agreed that we should marry."

The Plush manuscript finishes here ; it is many weeks since we
saw the accomplished writer, and we have only just learned his
fate. We are happy to state that it is a comfortable and almost a
prosperous one.

The Honourable and Right Reverend Lionel Thistlewood, Lord
Bishop of Bullocksmithy, was mentioned as the uncle of Lady
Angelina Silvertop. Her elopement with her cousin caused deep
emotion to the venerable prelate : he returned to the palace at
Bullocksmithy, of which he had been for thirty years the episcopal
ornament, and where he married three wives, who lie buried in his
Cathedral Church of St. Boniface, Bullocksmithy.

The admirable man has rejoined those whom he loved. As he
was preparing a charge to his clergy in his study after dinner, the
Lord Bishop fell suddenly down in a fit of apoplexy ; his butler,
bringing in his accustomed dish of devilled kidneys for supper, discovered the venerable form extended on the Turkey carpet with a

glass of Madeira in his hand ; but life was extinct : and surgical aid was therefore not particularly useful.

All the late prelate's wives had fortunes, which the admirable man increased by thrift, the judicious sale of leases which fell in during his episcopacy, &c.   He left three hundred thousand pounds —divided between his nephew and niece—not a greater sum than has been left by several deceased Irish prelates.

What Lord Southdown has done with his share we are not called upon to state.   He has composed an epitaph to the Martyr of Bullocksmithy, which does him infinite credit.   But we are happy to state that Lady Angelina Silvertop presented five hundred pounds to her faithful and affectionate servant, Mary Ann Hoggins, on her marriage with Mr. James Plush, to whom her Ladyship also made a handsome present—namely, the lease, good-will, and fixtures of the "Wheel of Fortune" public-house, near Shepherd's Market, Mayfair : a house greatly frequented by all the nobility's footmen, doing a genteel stroke of business in the neighbourhood, and where, as we have heard, the "Butlers' Club" is held.

Here Mr. Plush lives, happy in a blooming and interesting wife : reconciled to a middle sphere of life, as he was to a humbler and a higher one before.   He has shaved off his whiskers, and accommodates himself to an apron with perfect good-humour.   A gentleman connected with this establishment dined at the "Wheel of Fortune' the other day, and collected the above particulars.   Mr. Plush blushed rather, as he brought in the first dish, and told his story very modestly over a pint of excellent port.   He had only one thing in life to complain of, he said—that a witless version of his adventures had been produced at the Princess's Theatre, "without with your leaf or by your leaf," as he expressed it.   "Has for the rest," the worthy fellow said, "I'm appy—praps betwixt you and me I'm in my proper spear.   I enjy my glass of beer or port (with your elth & my suvvice to you, sir) quite as much as my clarrit in my prawsprus days.   I've a good busniss, which is likely to be better.   If a man can't be appy with such a wife as my Mary Hann, he's a beest : and when a christening takes place in our famly, will you give my complments to *Mr. Punch*, and ask him to be godfather."

LETTERS OF JEAMES

JEAMES ON TIME BARGINGS

PERAPS at this present momink of Railway Hagetation and unsafety the follying little istory of a young friend of mine may hact as an olesome warning to hother weak and hirresolute young gents.

"Young Frederick Timmins was the horphan son of a respectable cludgyman in the West of Hengland. Hadopted by his uncle, Colonel T——, of the Hoss-Mareens, and regardless of expence, this young man was sent to Heaton Collidge, and subsiquintly to Hoxford, where he was very nearly being Senior Rangler. He came to London to study for the lor. His prospix was bright indead; and He lived in a secknd flore in Jerming Street, having a ginteal inkum of two hundred lbs. per hannum.

"With this andsum enuity it may be supposed that Frederick wanted for nothink. Nor did he. He was a moral and well-educated young man, who took care of his close; pollisht his hone tea-party boots; cleaned his kidd-gloves with injer rubber; and, when not invited to dine out, took his meals reglar at the Hoxford and Cambridge Club—where (unless somebody treated him) he was never known to igseed his alf-pint of Marsally Wine.

"Merrits and vuttues such as his coodnt long pass unperseavd in the world. Admitted to the most fashnabble parties, it wasn't long before sevral of the young ladies viewed him with a favorable i; one, ixpecially, the lovely Miss Hemily Mulligatawney, daughter of the Heast-Injar Derector of that name. As she was the richest gal of all the season, of corse Frederick fell in love with her. His haspirations were on the pint of being crowndid with success; and it was agreed that as soon as he was called to the bar, when he would sutnly be apinted a Judge, or a revising barrister, or Lord Chanslor, he should lead her to the halter.

"What life could be more desirable than Frederick's? He gave up his mornings to perfeshnl studdy, under Mr. Bluebag, the heminent pleader; he devoted his hevenings to helegant sosiaty at his Clubb, or with his hadord Hemily. He had no cares ; no detts ; no egstravigancies ; he never was known to ride in a cabb, unless one of his tip-top friends lent it him ; to go to a theayter unless he got a horder ; or to henter a tavern or smoke a cigar. If prosperraty was hever chocked out, it was for that young man.

" But *suckmstances* arose. Fatle suckmstances for pore Frederick Timmins. The Railway Hoperations began.

" For some time, immerst in lor and love, in the hardent hoccupations of his cheembers, or the sweet sosiaty of his Hemily, Frederick took no note of railroads. He did not reckonize the jigantic revalution which with hiron strides was a walkin over the country. But they began to be talked of even in *his* quiat haunts. Heven in the Hoxford and Cambridge Clubb, fellers were a speculatin. Tom Thumper (of Brasen Nose) cleared four thousand lb. ; Bob Bullock (of Hexeter), who had lost all his proppaty gambling, had set himself up again ; and Jack Deuceace, who had won it, had won a small istate besides by lucky specklations in the Share Markit.

" *Hevery body won.* ' Why shouldn't I ? ' thought pore Fred ; and having saved 100 lb., he began a writin for shares—using, like an ickonominicle feller as he was, the Clubb paper to a prodigious igstent. All the Railroad directors, his friends, helped him to shares —the allottments came tumbling in—he took the primmiums by fifties and hundreds a day. His desk was cramd full of bank notes : his brane world with igsitement.

" He gave up going to the Temple, and might now be seen hall day about Capel Court. He took no more hinterest in lor ; but his whole talk was of railroad lines. His desk at Mr. Bluebag's was filled full of prospectisises, and that legal gent wrote to Fred's uncle, to say he feared he was neglectin his bisniss.

" Alass ! he *was* neglectin it, and all his sober and industerous habits. He begann to give dinners, and thought nothin of partys to Greenwich or Richmond. He didn't see his Hemily near so often : although the hawdacious and misguided young man might have done so much more heasily now than before : for now he kep a Broom !

" But there's a tumminus to hevery Railway. Fred's was approachin : in an evil hour he began making *time-bargings*. Let this be a warning to all young fellers, and Fred's huntimely hend hoperate on them in a moral pint of vu !

" You all know under what favrabble suckemstanses the Great Hafrican Line, the Grand Niger Junction, or Gold Coast and Timbuctoo (Provishnal) Hatmospheric Railway came out four weeks ago : deposit ninepence per share of 20*l.* (six elephant's teeth, twelve tons of palm-oil, or four healthy niggers, African currency) —the shares of this helegeble investment rose to 1, 2, 3, in the Markit. A happy man was Fred when, after paying down 100 ninepences (3*l.*, 15*s.*), he sold his shares for 250*l.* He gave a dinner at the 'Star and Garter' that very day. I promise you there was no Marsally *there*.

"Nex day they were up at 3¼. This put Fred in a rage: they rose to 5, he was in a fewry. 'What an ass I was to sell,' said he, 'when all this money was to be won!'

"'And so you *were* an Ass,' said his partiklar friend, Colonel Claw, K.X.R., a director of the line, 'a double-eared Ass. My dear fellow, the shares will be at 15 next week. Will you give me your solemn word of honour not to breathe to mortal man what I am going to tell you?'

"'Honour bright,' says Fred.

"'HUDSON HAS JOINED THE LINE.' Fred didn't say a word more, but went tumbling down to the City in his Broom. You know the state of the streats. Claw *went by water.*

"'Buy me one thousand Hafricans for the 30th,' cries Fred, busting into his broker's; and they were done for him at 4⅞."

. . . . . .

"Can't you guess the rest? Haven't you seen the Share List? which says:—

"'Great Africans, paid 9*d.*; price ¼ par.'

"And that's what came of my pore dear friend Timmins's timebarging.

"What'll become of him I can't say; for nobody has seen him since. His lodgins in Jerming Street is to let. His brokers in vain deplores his absence. His Uncle has declared his marriage with his housekeeper; and the *Morning Erald* (that emusing print) has a paragraf yesterday in the fashnabble news, headed 'Marriage in High Life.—The rich and beautiful Miss Mulligatawney, of Portland Place, is to be speedily united to Colonel Claw, K.X.R.'

"JEAMES."

JEAMES ON THE GAUGE QUESTION

"You will scarcely praps reckonize in this little skitch the haltered linimints of 1, with woos face the reders of your valluble mislny were once fimiliar,—the unfortnt Jeames de la Pluche, fomly so selabrated in the fashnabble suckles, now the pore Jeames Plush, landlord of the 'Wheel of Fortune' public house. Yes, that is me! that is my haypun which I wear as becomes a publican—those is the checkers which hornyment the pillows of my dor. I am like the Romin Genral, St. Cenatus, equal to any emudgency of Fortun. I, who have drunk Shampang in my time, aint now abov droring a ½ pint of Small Bier. As for my wife—that Angel—-I've not ventured to depigt *her*. Fansy her a sittn in the Bar, smiln like a sunflower—and, ho, dear *Punch!* happy in nussing a deer little darlint totsy-wotsy of a Jeames, with my air to a curl, and my i's to a T!

"I never thought I should have been injuiced to write anything but a Bill agin, much less to edress you on Railway Subjix—which with all my sole I *abaw*. Railway letters, obbligations to pay hup, ginteal inquirys as to my Salissator's name, &c. &c., I dispize and scorn artily. But as a man, an usbnd, a father, and a freebon Brittn, my jewty compels me to come forwoods, and igspress my opinion upon that *nashnal newsance*—the break of Gage.

" An interesting ewent in a noble family with which I once very nearly had the honor of being kinected, acurd a few weex sins, when the Lady Angelina S——, daughter of the Earl of B——cres, presented the gallant Capting, her usband, with a Son & hair. Nothink would satasfy her Ladyship but that her old and attacht famdy-shamber, my wife Mary Hann Plush, should be presnt upon this hospicious occasion. Capting S—— was not jellus of me on account of my former attachment to his Lady. I cunsented that my Mary Hann should attend her, and me, my wife, and our dear babby acawdingly set out for our noable frend's residence, Honeymoon Lodge, near Cheltenham.

" Sick of all Railroads myself, I wisht to poast it in a Chay and 4, but Mary Hann, with the hobstenacy of her Sex, was bent upon Railroad travelling, and I yealded, like all husbinds. We set out by the Great Westn, in an eavle Hour.

" We didn't take much luggitch—my wife's things in the ushal bandboxes—mine in a potmancho. Our dear little James Angelo's (called so in complament to his noble Godmamma) craddle, and a small supply of a few 100 weight of Topsanbawtems, Farinashious food, and Lady's fingers, for that dear child, who is now 6 months old, with a *perdidgus appatite*. Likewise we were charged with a bran new Medsan chest for my Lady, from Skivary & Morris, containing enough rewbub, Daffy's Alixir, Godfrey's cawdle, with a few score of parsles for Lady Hangelina's family and owsehold; about 2000 spessymins of Babby linning from Mrs. Flummary's, in Regent Street, a Chayny Cresning bowl from old Lady Bareacres (big enough to immus a Halderman), & a case marked 'Glass,' from her Ladyship's meddicle man, which were stowed away together;

had to this an ormylew Cradle, with rose-coloured Satting & Pink lace hangings, held up by a gold tuttle-dove, &c. We had, ingluding James Hangelo's rattle & my umbrellow, 73 packidges in all.

" We got on very well as far as Swindon, where, in the Splendid Refreshment room, there was a galaxy of lovely gals in cottn velvet spencers, who serves out the soop, and 1 of whom maid an impresshn upon this Art which I shoodn't like Mary Hann to know —and here, to our infanit disgust, we changed carridges. I forgot to say that we were in the secknd class, having with us James Hangelo, and 23 other light harticles.

" Fust inconveniance ; and almost as bad as break of gage. I cast my hi upon the gal in cottn velvet, and wanted some soop, of coarse ; but seasing up James Hangelo (who was layin his dear little pors on an Am Sangwidg) and seeing my igspresshn of hi— ' James,' says Mary Hann, ' instead of looking at that young lady —and not so *very* young, neither—be pleased to look to our packidges, & place them in the other carridge.' I did so with an evy Art. I eranged them 23 articles in the opsit carridg, only missing my umberella & baby's rattle ; and jest as I came back for my baysn of soop, the beast of a bell rings, the whizzling injians proclayms the time of our departure,—& farewell soop and cottn velvet. Mary Hann was sulky. She said it was my losing the umberella. If it had been a *cotton velvet umberella* I could have understood. James Hangelo sittn on my knee was evidently unwell ; without his coral : & for 20 miles that blessid babby kep up a rawring, which caused all the passingers to simpithize with him igseedingly.

" We arrive at Gloster, and there fansy my disgust at bein ableeged to undergo another change of carridges ! Fansy me holding up moughs, tippits, cloaks, and baskits, and James Hangelo rawring still like mad, and pretending to shuperintend the carrying over of our luggage from the broad gage to the narrow gage. ' Mary Hann,' says I, rot to desperation, ' I shall throttle this darling if he goes on.' ' Do,' says she—' and *go into the refreshment room*,' says she—a snatchin the babby out of my arms. ' Do go,' says she, ' youre not fit to look after luggage,' and she began lulling James Hangelo to sleep with one hi, while she looked after the packets with the other. ' Now, sir ! if you please, mind that packet !—pretty darling—easy with that box, sir, it's glass— pooooty poppet—where's the deal case, marked arrowroot, No. 24 ? ' she cried, reading out of a list she had.—And poor little James went to sleep. The porters were bundling and carting the various harticles with no more ceremony than if each package had been of cannon-ball.

"At last—bang goes a package marked 'Glass,' and containing the Chayny bowl and Lady Bareacres' mixture, into a large white bandbox, with a crash and a smash. 'It's My Lady's box from Crinoline's!' cries Mary Hann; and she puts down the child on the bench, and rushes forward to inspeck the dammidge. You could hear the Chayny bowls clinking inside; and Lady B.'s mixture (which had the igsack smell of cherry brandy) was dribbling out over the smashed bandbox containing a white child's cloak, trimmed with Blown lace and lined with white satting.

"As James was asleep, and I was by this time uncommon hungry, I thought I *would* go into the Refreshment Room and just take a little soup; so I wrapped him up in his cloak and laid him by his mamma, and went off. There's not near such good attendance as at Swindon."

.   .   .   .

"We took our places in the carriage in the dark, both of us covered with a pile of packages, and Mary Hann so sulky that she would not speak for some minutes. At last she spoke out—

" 'Have you all the small parcels?'

" 'Twenty-three in all,' says I.

" 'Then give me baby.'

" 'Give you what?' says I.

" 'Give me baby.'

" 'What, haven't y-y-yoooo got him?' says I.

.   .   .   .

"O Mussy! You should have heard her sreak! *We'd left him on the ledge at Gloster.*

"It all came of the break of gage."

MR. JEAMES AGAIN

"DEAR MR. PUNCH,—As newmarus inquiries have been maid both at my privit ressddence, 'The Wheel of Fortune Otel,' and at your Hoffis, regarding the fate of that dear babby, James Hangelo, whose primmiture dissappearnts caused such hagnies to his distracted parents, I must begg, dear Sir, the permission to ockupy a part of your valuble collams once more, and hease the public mind about my blessid boy.

"Wictims of that nashnal cuss, the Broken Gage, me and Mrs.

Plush was left in the train to Cheltenham, soughring from that most disagreeble of complaints, a halmost *broken Art.* The skreems of Mrs. Jeames might be said almost to out-Y the squeel of the dying, as we rusht into that fashnable Spaw, and my pore Mary Hann found it was not Baby, but Bundles I had in my lapp.

"When the Old Dowidger Lady Bareacres, who was waiting heagerly at the train, herd that owing to that abawminable brake of Gage the luggitch, her Ladyship's Cherrybrandy box, the cradle for Lady Hangelina's baby, the lace, crockary and chany, was rejuiced to one immortial smash; the old cat howld at me and pore dear Mary Hann, as if it was huss, and not the infunnle Brake of Gage, was to blame; and as if we ad no misfortns of our hown to deplaw. She bust out about my stupid imparence; called Mary Hann a good for nothink creecher, and wep, and abewsd, and took on about her broken Chayny Bowl, a great deal mor than she did about a dear little Christian child. 'Don't talk to me abowt your bratt of a babby' (seshe); 'where's my bowl?—where's my medsan?—where's my bewtiffle Pint lace?—All in rewins through your stupiddaty, you brute, you!'

"'Bring your haction aginst the Great Western, Maam,' says I, quite riled by this crewel and unfealing hold wixen. 'Ask the pawters at Gloster, why your goods is spiled—it's not the fust time they've been asked the question. Git the gage haltered aginst the nex time you send for *medsan*—and meanwild buy some at the "Plow"—they keep it very good and strong there, I'll be bound. Has for us, *we're* a going back to the cussid station at Gloster, in such of our blessid child.'

"'You don't mean to say, young woman,' seshe, 'that you're not going to Lady Hangelina: what's her dear boy to do? who's to nuss it?'

"'*You* nuss it, Maam,' says I. 'Me and Mary Hann return this momint by the Fly.' And so (whishing her a suckastic ajew) Mrs. Jeames and I lep into a one oss weakle, and told the driver to go like mad back to Gloster.

"I can't describe my pore gals hagny juring our ride. She sat in the carridge as silent as a milestone, and as madd as a march Air. When we got to Gloster she sprang hout of it as wild as a Tigris, and rusht to the station, up to the fatle Bench.

"'My child, my child,' shreex she, in a hoss hot voice. 'Where's my infant? a little bewtifle child, with blue eyes,—dear Mr. Policeman, give it me—a thousand guineas for it.'

"'Faix, Mam,' says the man, a Hirishman, 'and the divvle a babby have I seen this day except thirteen of my own—and you're welcome to any one of *them*, and kindly.'

"'As if *his* babby was equal to ours,' as my darling Mary Hann said, afterwards.   All the station was scrouging round us by this time—pawters & clarx and refreshmint people and all.   'What's this year row about that there babby?' at last says the Inspector, stepping hup.   I thought my wife was going to jump into his harms. 'Have you got him?' says she.

"'Was it a child in a blue cloak?' says he.

"'And blue eyes!' says my wife.

"'I put a label on him and sent him on to Bristol; he's there by this time.   The Guard of the Mail took him and put him into a letter-box,' says he: 'he went 20 minutes ago.   We found him on the broad gauge line, and sent him on by it, in course,' says he. 'And it'll be a caution to you, young woman, for the future, to label your children along with the rest of your luggage.'

"If my piguniary means had been such as *once* they was, you may emadgine I'd have ad a speshle train and been hoff like smoak.   As it was, we was obliged to wait 4 mortial hours for the next train (4 ears they seemed to us), and then away we went.

"'My boy! my little boy!' says poor choking Mary Hann, when we got there.   'A parcel in a blue cloak?' says the man.   'No body claimed him here, and so we sent him back by the mail.   An rish nurse here gave him some supper, and he's at Paddington by his time.   Yes,' says he, looking at the clock, 'he's been there these ten minutes.'

"But seeing my poor wife's distracted histarricle state, this good-naterd man says, 'I think, my dear, there's a way to ease your mind.   We'll know in five minutes how he is.'

"'Sir,' says she, 'don't make sport of me.'

"'No, my dear, we'll *telegraph* him.'

"And he began hopparating on that singular and ingenus elecktricle inwention, which aniliates time, and carries intellagence in the twinkling of a peg-post.

"'I'll ask,' says he, for child marked G. W. 273.'

"Back comes the telegraph with the sign 'All right.'

"'Ask what he's doing, sir,' says my wife, quite amazed.   Back comes the answer in a Jiffy—

" C.R.Y.I.N.G.'

"This caused all the bystanders to laugh excep my pore Mary Hann, who pull'd a very sad face.

"The good-naterd feller presently said, 'he'd have another trile;' and what d'ye think was the answer?   I'm blest if it wasn't—

"'P.A.P.'

"He was eating pap!   There's for you—there's a rogue for

you—there's a March of Intaleck ! Mary Hann smiled now for the fust time. ' He'll sleep now,' says she. And she sat down with a full hart.

.　　.　　.　　.　　.　　.　　.

" If hever that good-naterd Shooperintendent comes to London, *he* need never ask for his skore at the ' Wheel of Fortune Otel,' I promise you—where me and my wife and James Hangelo now is ; and where only yesterday a gent came in and drew a pictur of us in our bar.

" And if they go on breaking gages ; and if the child, the most precious luggidge of the Henglishman, is to be bundled about this year way, why it won't be for want of warning, both from Professor Harris, the Commission, and from my dear *Mr. Punch's* obeajent servant,　　　　　　　　　　　　　JEAMES PLUSH."

A LEGEND OF THE RHINE

A

LEGEND OF THE RHINE

CHAPTER 1

SIR LUDWIG OF HOMBOURG

IT was in the good old days of chivalry, when every mountain
that bathes its shadow in the Rhine had its castle: not inhabited, as now, by a few rats and owls, nor covered with moss
and wallflowers, and funguses, and creeping ivy. No, no! where
the ivy now clusters there grew strong portcullis and bars of steel;
where the wallflower now quivers on the rampart there were silken
banners embroidered with wonderful heraldry; men-at-arms marched
where now you shall only see a bank of moss or a hideous black
champignon; and in place of the rats and owlets, I warrant me
there were ladies and knights to revel in the great halls, and to
feast, and to dance, and to make love there. They are passed
away:—those old knights and ladies: their golden hair first changed
to silver, and then the silver dropped off and disappeared for ever;
their elegant legs, so slim and active in the dance, became swollen
and gouty, and then, from being swollen and gouty, dwindled down
to bare bone-shanks; the roses left their cheeks, and then their
cheeks disappeared, and left their skulls, and then their skulls
powdered into dust, and all sign of them was gone. And as it was
with them, so shall it be with us. Ho, seneschal! fill me a cup of
liquor! put sugar in it, good fellow—yea, and a little hot water; a
very little, for my soul is sad, as I think of those days and knights
of old.

They, too, have revelled and feasted, and where are they?—
gone?—nay, not altogether gone; for doth not the eye catch glimpses
of them as they walk yonder in the grey limbo of romance, shining
faintly in their coats of steel, wandering by the side of long-haired
ladies, with long-tailed gowns that little pages carry? Yes! one
sees them: the poet sees them still in the far-off Cloudland, and
hears the ring of their clarions as they hasten to battle or tourney—

and the dim echoes of their lutes chanting of love and fair ladies!
Gracious privilege of poesy! It is as the Dervish's collyrium to the
eyes, and causes them to see treasures that to the sight of donkeys
are invisible. Blessed treasures of fancy! I would not change ye
—no, not for many donkey-loads of gold. . . . Fill again, jolly
seneschal, thou brave wag; chalk me up the produce on the hostel
door—surely the spirits of old are mixed up in the wondrous liquor,
and gentle visions of bygone princes and princesses look blandly
down on us from the cloudy perfume of the pipe. Do you know in
what year the fairies left the Rhine?—long before Murray's "Guide-
Book" was wrote—long before squat steamboats, with snorting
funnels, came paddling down the stream. Do you not know that
once upon a time the appearance of eleven thousand British virgins
was considered at Cologne as a wonder? Now there come twenty
thousand such annually, accompanied by their ladies'-maids. But
of them we will say no more—let us back to those who went before
them.

Many many hundred thousand years ago, and at the exact period
when chivalry was in full bloom, there occurred a little history upon
the banks of the Rhine, which has been already written in a book,
and hence must be positively true. 'Tis a story of knights and
ladies—of love and battle, and virtue rewarded; a story of princes
and noble lords, moreover: the best of company. Gentles, an ye
will, ye shall hear it. Fair dames and damsels, may your loves be
as happy as those of the heroine of this romaunt.

On the cold and rainy evening of Thursday, the 26th of October,
in the year previously indicated, such travellers as might have chanced
to be abroad in that bitter night, might have remarked a fellow-
wayfarer journeying on the road from Oberwinter to Godesberg. He
was a man not tall in stature, but of the most athletic proportions,
and Time, which had browned and furrowed his cheek and sprinkled
his locks with grey, declared pretty clearly that He must have been
acquainted with the warrior for some fifty good years. He was armed
in mail, and rode a powerful and active battle-horse, which (though
the way the pair had come that day was long and weary indeed)
yet supported the warrior, his armour and luggage, with seeming
ease. As it was in a friend's country, the knight did not think fit
to wear his heavy *destrier*, or helmet, which hung at his saddle-bow
over his portmanteau. Both were marked with the coronet of a
count; and from the crown which surmounted the helmet, rose the
crest of his knightly race, an arm proper lifting a naked sword.

At his right hand, and convenient to the warrior's grasp, hung his
mangonel or mace—a terrific weapon which had shattered the brains
of many a turbaned soldan: while over his broad and ample chest

there fell the triangular shield of the period, whereon were emblazoned his arms—argent, a gules wavy, on a saltire reversed of the second : the latter device was awarded for a daring exploit before Ascalon, by the Emperor Maximilian, and a reference to the German Peerage of that day, or a knowledge of high families which every gentleman then possessed, would have sufficed to show at once that the rider we have described was of the noble house of Hombourg. It was, in fact, the gallant knight Sir Ludwig of Hombourg : his rank as a count, and chamberlain of the Emperor of Austria, was marked by the cap of maintenance with the peacock's feather which he wore (when not armed for battle), and his princely blood was denoted by the oiled silk umbrella which he carried (a very meet protection against the pitiless storm), and which, as it is known, in the middle ages, none but princes were justified in using. A bag, fastened with a brazen padlock, and made of the costly produce of the Persian looms (then extremely rare in Europe), told that he had travelled in Eastern climes. This, too, was evident from the inscription writ on card or parchment, and sewed on the bag. It first ran, "Count Ludwig de Hombourg, Jerusalem ; " but the name of the Holy City had been dashed out with the pen, and that of " Godesberg " substituted. So far indeed had the cavalier travelled !—and it is needless to state that the bag in question contained such remaining articles of the toilet as the high-born noble deemed unnecessary to place in his valise.

"By Saint Bugo of Katzenellenbogen ! " said the good knight, shivering, " 'tis colder here than at Damascus ! Marry, I am so hungry I could eat one of Saladin's camels. Shall I be at Godesberg in time for dinner ? " And taking out his horologe (which hung in a small side-pocket of his embroidered surcoat), the crusader consoled himself by finding that it was but seven of the night, and that he would reach Godesberg ere the warder had sounded the second gong.

His opinion was borne out by the result. His good steed, which could trot at a pinch fourteen leagues in the hour, brought him to this famous castle, just as the warder was giving the first welcome signal which told that the princely family of Count Karl, Margrave of Godesberg, were about to prepare for their usual repast at eight o'clock. Crowds of pages and horsekeepers were in the court, when, the portcullis being raised, and amidst the respectful salutes of the sentinels, the most ancient friend of the house of Godesberg entered into its castle-yard. The under-butler stepped forward to take his bridle-rein. " Welcome, Sir Count, from the Holy Land ! " exclaimed the faithful old man. " Welcome, Sir Count, from the Holy Land ! " cried the rest of the servants in the hall. A stable was speedily found for the Count's horse, Streithengst, and it was not before the gallant soldier had seen that true animal well cared for, that he entered the castle itself, and was conducted to his chamber. Wax candles burning bright on the mantel, flowers in china vases, every variety of soap, and a flask of the precious essence manufactured at the neighbouring city of Cologne, were displayed on his toilet-table ; a cheering fire "crackled on the hearth," and showed that the good knight's coming had been looked and cared for. The serving-maidens, bringing him hot water for his ablutions, smiling asked, "Would he have his couch warmed at eve?" One might have been sure from their blushes that the tough old soldier made an arch reply. The family tonsor came to know whether the noble Count had need of his skill. "By Saint Bugo," said the knight, as seated in an easy settle by the fire, the tonsor rid his chin of its stubbly growth, and lightly passed the tongs and pomatum through "the sable silver" of his hair,—"By Saint Bugo, this is better than my dungeon at Grand Cairo. How is my godson Otto, master barber ; and the Lady Countess, his mother ; and the noble Count Karl, my dear brother-in-arms?"

"They are well," said the tonsor, with a sigh.

"By Saint Bugo, I'm glad on't ; but why that sigh?"

"Things are not as they have been with my good lord," answered the hairdresser, "ever since Count Gottfried's arrival."

"He here!" roared Sir Ludwig. "Good never came where Gottfried was!" and the while he donned a pair of silken hose, that showed admirably the proportions of his lower limbs, and exchanged his coat of mail for the spotless vest and black surcoat collared with velvet of Genoa, which was the fitting costume for "knight in ladye's bower,"—the knight entered into a conversation with the barber, who explained to him, with the usual garrulousness of his tribe, what was the present position of the noble family of Godesberg.

This will be narrated in the next chapter.

CHAPTER II

THE GODESBERGERS

'TIS needless to state that the gallant warrior Ludwig of Hombourg found in the bosom of his friend's family a cordial welcome. The brother-in-arms of the Margrave Karl, he was the esteemed friend of the Margravine, the exalted and beautiful Theodora of Boppum, and (albeit no theologian, and although the first princes of Christendom coveted such an honour) he was selected to stand as sponsor for the Margrave's son Otto, the only child of his house.

It was now seventeen years since the Count and Countess had been united : and although Heaven had not blessed their couch with more than one child, it may be said of that one that it was a prize, and that surely never lighted on the earth a more delightful vision. When Count Ludwig, hastening to the holy wars, had quitted his beloved godchild, he had left him a boy ; he now found him, as the latter rushed into his arms, grown to be one of the finest young men in Germany : tall and excessively graceful in proportion, with the blush of health mantling upon his cheek, that was likewise adorned with the first down of manhood, and with magnificent golden ringlets, such as a Rowland might envy, curling over his brow and his shoulders. His eyes alternately beamed with the fire of daring, or melted with the moist glance of benevolence. Well might a mother be proud of such a boy. Well might the brave Ludwig exclaim, as he clasped the youth to his breast, " By Saint Bugo of Katzenellenbogen, Otto, thou art fit to be one of Cœur de Lion's grenadiers ! " and it was the fact : the " Childe " of Godesberg measured six feet three.

He was habited for the evening meal in the costly though simple attire of the nobleman of the period—and his costume a good deal resembled that of the old knight whose toilet we have just described ; with the difference of colour, however. The *pourpoint* worn by young Otto of Godesberg was of blue, handsomely decorated with buttons of carved and embossed gold ; his *haut-de-chausses*, or leggings, were of the stuff of Nanquin, then brought by the Lombard argosies at an immense price from China. The neighbouring country of Holland had supplied his wrists and bosom with the most costly laces; and thus attired, with an opera-hat placed on one side of his head, ornamented with a single flower (that brilliant one, the tulip), the boy rushed into his godfather's dressing-room, and warned him that the banquet was ready.

It was indeed: a frown had gathered on the dark brows of the Lady Theodora, and her bosom heaved with an emotion akin to indignation; for she feared lest the soups in the refectory and the splendid fish now smoking there were getting cold: she feared not for herself, but for her lord's sake. "Godesberg," whispered she to Count Ludwig, as trembling on his arm they descended from the drawing-room, "Godesberg is sadly changed of late."

"By Saint Bugo!" said the burly knight, starting, "these are the very words the barber spake."

The lady heaved a sigh, and placed herself before the soup-tureen. For some time the good Knight Ludwig of Hombourg was too much occupied in ladling out the forcemeat balls and rich calves' head of which the delicious pottage was formed (in ladling them out, did we say? ay, marry, and in eating them, too) to look at his brother-in-arms at the bottom of the table, where he sat with his son on his left hand, and the Baron Gottfried on his right.

The Margrave was *indeed* changed. "By Saint Bugo," whispered Ludwig to the Countess, "your husband is as surly as a bear that hath been wounded o' the head." Tears falling into her soup-plate were her only reply. The soup, the turbot, the haunch of mutton, Count Ludwig remarked that the Margrave sent all away untasted.

"The boteler will serve ye with wine, Hombourg," said the Margrave gloomily from the end of the table. Not even an invitation to drink: how different was this from the old times!

But when, in compliance with this order, the boteler proceeded to hand round the mantling vintage of the Cape to the assembled party, and to fill young Otto's goblet (which the latter held up with the eagerness of youth), the Margrave's rage knew no bounds. He rushed at his son; he dashed the wine-cup over his spotless vest; and giving him three or four heavy blows which would have knocked down a bonassus, but only caused the young Childe to blush: "*You* take wine!" roared out the Margrave; "*you* dare to help yourself! Who the d–v–l gave *you* leave to help yourself?" and the terrible blows were reiterated over the delicate ears of the boy.

"Ludwig! Ludwig!" shrieked the Margravine.

"Hold your prate, madam," roared the Prince. "By Saint Buffo, mayn't a father beat his own child?"

"His own child!" repeated the Margrave with a burst, almost a shriek, of indescribable agony. "Ah, what did I say?"

Sir Ludwig looked about him in amaze; Sir Gottfried (at the Margrave's right hand) smiled ghastlily; the young Otto was too much agitated by the recent conflict to wear any expression but that of extreme discomfiture; but the poor Margravine turned her head aside and blushed, red almost as the lobster which flanked the turbot before her.

In those rude old times, 'tis known such table quarrels were by no means unusual amongst gallant knights; and Ludwig, who had oft seen the Margrave cast a leg of mutton at an offending servitor, or empty a sauce-boat in the direction of the Margravine, thought this was but one of the usual outbreaks of his worthy though irascible friend, and wisely determined to change the converse.

"How is my friend," said he, "the good knight, Sir Hildebrandt?"

"By Saint Buffo, this is too much!" screamed the Margrave, and actually rushed from the room.

"By Saint Bugo," said his friend, "gallant knights, gentle sirs, what ails my good Lord Margrave?"

"Perhaps his nose bleeds," said Gottfried with a sneer.

"Ah, my kind friend," said the Margravine with uncontrollable emotion, "I fear some of you have passed from the frying-pan into the fire." And making the signal of departure to the ladies, they rose and retired to coffee in the drawing-room.

The Margrave presently came back again, somewhat more collected than he had been. "Otto," he said sternly, "go join the ladies: it becomes not a young boy to remain in the company of gallant knights after dinner." The noble Childe with manifest unwillingness quitted the room, and the Margrave, taking his lady's place at the head of the table, whispered to Sir Ludwig, "Hildebrandt will be here to-night to an evening party, given in honour of your return from Palestine. My good friend—my true friend—my old companion in arms, Sir Gottfried! you had best see that the fiddlers be not drunk, and that the crumpets be gotten ready." Sir Gottfried, obsequiously taking his patron's hint, bowed and left the room.

"You shall know all soon, dear Ludwig," said the Margrave with a heartrending look. "You marked Gottfried, who left the room anon?"

"I did."

"You look incredulous concerning his worth; but I tell thee, Ludwig, that yonder Gottfried is a good fellow, and my fast friend. Why should he not be? He is my near relation, heir to my property : should I " (here the Margrave's countenance assumed its former expression of excruciating agony),—" *should I have no son.*"

"But I never saw the boy in better health," replied Sir Ludwig.

"Nevertheless,—ha ! ha !—it may chance that I shall soon have no son."

The Margrave had crushed many a cup of wine during dinner, and Sir Ludwig thought naturally that his gallant friend had drunken rather deeply. He proceeded in this respect to imitate him ; for the stern soldier of those days neither shrunk before the Paynim nor the punch-bowl : and many a rousing night had our crusader enjoyed in Syria with lion-hearted Richard ; with his coadjutor, Godfrey of Bouillon ; nay, with the dauntless Saladin himself.

"You knew Gottfried in Palestine ? " asked the Margrave.

"I did."

"Why did ye not greet him then, as ancient comrades should, with the warm grasp of friendship ? It is not because Sir Gottfried is poor ? You know well that he is of race as noble as thine own, my early friend ! "

"I care not for his race nor for his poverty," replied the blunt crusader. "What says the Minnesinger ? Marry, the rank is but the stamp of the guinea ; the man is the gold.' And I tell thee, Karl of Godesberg, that yonder Gottfried is base metal."

"By Saint Buffo, thou beliest him, dear Ludwig."

"By Saint Bugo, dear Karl, I say sooth. The fellow was known i' the camp of the crusaders—disreputably known. Ere he joined us in Palestine, he had sojourned in Constantinople, and learned the arts of the Greek. He is a cogger of dice, I tell thee— a chanter of horseflesh. He won five thousand marks from bluff Richard of England the night before the storming of Ascalon, and I caught him with false trumps in his pocket. He warranted a bay mare to Conrad of Mont Serrat, and the rogue had fired her."

"Ha ! mean ye that Sir Gottfried is a *leg ?*" cried Sir Karl, knitting his brows. "Now, by my blessed patron, Saint Buffo of Bonn, had any other but Ludwig of Hombourg so said, I would have cloven him from skull to chine."

"By Saint Bugo of Katzenellenbogen, I will prove my words on Sir Gottfried's body—not on thine, old brother-in-arms. And to do the knave justice, he is a good lance. Holy Bugo ! but he did good service at Acre ! But his character was such that, spite of his bravery, he was dismissed the army ; nor even allowed to sell his captain's commission."

"I have heard of it," said the Margrave ; "Gottfried hath told

me of it. 'Twas about some silly quarrel over the wine-cup—a mere
silly jape, believe me. Hugo de Brodenel would have no black bottle
on the board. Gottfried was wroth, and, to say sooth, flung the black
bottle at the Count's head. Hence his dismission and abrupt return.
But you know not," continued the Margrave, with a heavy sigh, " of
what use that worthy Gottfried has been to me. He has uncloaked
a traitor to me."

" Not *yet*," answered Hombourg satirically.

" By Saint Buffo ! a deep-dyed dastard ! a dangerous damnable
traitor !—a nest of traitors. Hildebrandt is a traitor—Otto is a
traitor—and Theodora (O Heaven !) she—she is *another*." The old
Prince burst into tears at the word, and was almost choked with
emotion.

" What means this passion, dear friend?" cried Sir Ludwig,
seriously alarmed.

" Mark, Ludwig ! mark Hildebrandt and Theodora together :
mark Hildebrandt and *Otto* together. Like, like I tell thee as two
peas. O holy saints, that I should be born to suffer this !—to have
all my affections wrenched out of my bosom, and to be left alone in
my old age ! But, hark ! the guests are arriving. An ye will not
empty another flask of claret, let us join the ladyes i' the withdraw-
ing chamber. When there, mark *Hildebrandt and Otto !* "

CHAPTER III

THE FESTIVAL

THE festival was indeed begun. Coming on horseback, or in their caroches, knights and ladies of the highest rank were assembled in the grand saloon of Godesberg, which was splendidly illuminated to receive them. Servitors, in rich liveries (they were attired in doublets of the sky-blue broadcloth of Ypres, and hose of the richest yellow sammit—the colours of the house of Godesberg), bore about various refreshments on trays of silver— cakes, baked in the oven, and swimming in melted butter; munchets of bread, smeared with the same delicious condiment, and carved so thin that you might have expected them to take wing and fly to the ceiling; coffee, introduced by Peter the Hermit, after his excursion into Arabia, and tea such as only Bohemia could produce, circulated amidst the festive throng, and were eagerly devoured by the guests. The Margrave's gloom was unheeded by them—how little indeed is the smiling crowd aware of the pangs that are lurking in the breasts of those who bid them to the feast! The Margravine was pale; but woman knows how to deceive; she was more than ordinarily courteous to her friends, and laughed, though the laugh was hollow; and talked, though the talk was loathsome to her.

"The two are together," said the Margrave, clutching his friend's shoulder. "*Now look!*"

Sir Ludwig turned towards a quadrille, and there, sure enough, were Sir Hildebrandt and young Otto standing side by side in the dance. Two eggs were not more like! The reason of the Margrave's horrid suspicion at once flashed across his friend's mind.

"'Tis clear as the staff of a pike," said the poor Margrave mournfully. "Come, brother, away from the scene; let us go play a game at cribbage!" and retiring to the Margravine's *boudoir*, the two warriors sat down to the game.

But though 'tis an interesting one, and though the Margrave won, yet he could not keep his attention on the cards: so agitated was his mind by the dreadful secret which weighed upon it. In the midst of their play, the obsequious Gottfried came to whisper a word in his patron's ear, which threw the latter into such a fury, that apoplexy was apprehended by the two lookers-on. But the Margrave mastered his emotion. "*At what time,* did you say?" said he to Gottfried.

"At daybreak, at the outer gate."

"I will be there."

"*And so will I too,*" thought Count Ludwig, the good Knight of Hombourg.

CHAPTER IV

THE FLIGHT

HOW often does man, proud man, make calculations for the future, and think he can bend stern fate to his will! Alas, we are but creatures in its hands! How many a slip between the lip and the lifted wine-cup! How often, though seemingly with a choice of couches to repose upon, do we find ourselves dashed to earth; and then we are fain to say the grapes are sour, because we cannot attain them; or worse, to yield to anger in consequence of our own fault. Sir Ludwig, the Hombourger, was *not at the outer gate* at daybreak.

He slept until ten of the clock. The previous night's potations had been heavy, the day's journey had been long and rough. The knight slept as a soldier would, to whom a feather bed is a rarity, and who wakes not till he hears the blast of the réveillé.

He looked up as he woke. At his bedside sat the Margrave. He had been there for hours watching his slumbering comrade. Watching?—no, not watching, but awake by his side, brooding over thoughts unutterably bitter—over feelings inexpressibly wretched.

"What's o'clock?" was the first natural exclamation of the Hombourger.

"I believe it is five o'clock," said his friend. It was ten. It might have been twelve, two, half-past four, twenty minutes to six, the Margrave would still have said, "*I believe it is five o'clock.*" The wretched take no count of time: it flies with unequal pinions, indeed, for *them.*

"Is breakfast over?" inquired the crusader.

"Ask the butler," said the Margrave, nodding his head wildly, rolling his eyes wildly, smiling wildly.

"Gracious Bugo!" said the Knight of Hombourg, "what has ailed thee, my friend? It is ten o'clock by my horologe. Your regular hour is nine. You are not—no, by heavens! you are not shaved! You wear the tights and silken hose of last evening's banquet. Your collar is all rumpled—'tis that of yesterday. *You have not been to bed!* What has chanced, brother of mine: what has chanced?"

"A common chance, Louis of Hombourg," said the Margrave: "one that chances every day. A false woman, a false friend, a broken heart. *This* has chanced. I have not been to bed."

"What mean ye?" cried Count Ludwig, deeply affected. "A false friend? *I* am not a false friend. A false woman? Surely the lovely Theodora, your wife——"

"I have no wife, Louis, now; I have no wife and no son."

.   .   .   .

In accents broken by grief, the Margrave explained what had occurred. Gottfried's information was but too correct. There was *a cause* for the likeness between Otto and Sir Hildebrandt: a fatal cause! Hildebrandt and Theodora had met at dawn at the outer gate. The Margrave had seen them. They walked along together; they embraced. Ah! how the husband's, the father's, feelings were harrowed at that embrace! They parted; and then the Margrave, coming forward, coldly signified to his lady that she was to retire to a convent for life, and gave orders that the boy should be sent too, to take the vows at a monastery.

Both sentences had been executed. Otto, in a boat, and guarded by a company of his father's men-at-arms, was on the river going towards Cologne, to the monastery of Saint Buffo there. The Lady Theodora, under the guard of Sir Gottfried and an attendant, were on their way to the convent of Nonnenwerth, which many of our readers have seen—the beautiful Green Island Convent, laved by the bright waters of the Rhine!

"What road did Gottfried take?" asked the Knight of Hombourg, grinding his teeth.

"You cannot overtake him," said the Margrave. "My good Gottfried, he is my only comfort now: he is my kinsman, and shall be my heir. He will be back anon."

"Will he so?" thought Sir Ludwig. "I will ask him a few questions ere he return." And springing from his couch, he began forthwith to put on his usual morning dress of complete armour; and, after a hasty ablution, donned, not his cap of maintenance, but his helmet of battle. He rang the bell violently.

"A cup of coffee, straight," said he, to the servitor who answered the summons; "bid the cook pack me a sausage and bread in paper, and the groom saddle Streithengst: we have far to ride."

The various orders were obeyed. The horse was brought; the refreshments disposed of; the clattering steps of the departing steed were heard in the courtyard; but the Margrave took no notice of his friend, and sat, plunged in silent grief, quite motionless by the empty bedside.

CHAPTER V

THE TRAITOR'S DOOM

THE Hombourger led his horse down the winding path which conducts from the hill and castle of Godesberg into the beautiful green plain below. Who has not seen that lovely plain, and who that has seen it has not loved it? A thousand sunny vineyards and cornfields stretch around in peaceful luxuriance; the mighty Rhine floats by it in silver magnificence, and on the opposite bank rise the seven mountains robed in majestic purple, the monarchs of the royal scene.

A pleasing poet, Lord Byron, in describing this very scene, has mentioned that " peasant girls, with dark blue eyes, and hands that offer cake and wine," are perpetually crowding round the traveller in this delicious district, and proffering to him their rustic presents. This was no doubt the case in former days, when the noble bard wrote his elegant poems—in the happy ancient days! when maidens were as yet generous, and men kindly! Now the degenerate peasantry of the district are much more inclined to ask than to give, and their blue eyes seem to have disappeared with their generosity.

But as it was a long time ago that the events of our story occurred, 'tis probable that the good Knight Ludwig of Hombourg was greeted upon his path by this fascinating peasantry; though we know not how he accepted their welcome. He continued his ride across the flat green country until he came to Rolandseck, whence he could command the Island of Nonnenwerth (that lies in the Rhine opposite that place), and all who went to it or passed from it.

Over the entrance of a little cavern in one of the rocks hanging above the Rhine-stream at Rolandseck, and covered with odoriferous cactuses and silvery magnolias, the traveller of the present day may perceive a rude broken image of a saint: that image represented the venerable Saint Buffo of Bonn, the patron of the Margrave; and Sir Ludwig, kneeling on the greensward, and reciting a censer, an ave, and a couple of acolytes before it, felt encouraged to think that the deed he meditated was about to be performed under the very eyes of his friend's sanctified patron. His devotion done (and the knight of those days was as pious as he was brave), Sir Ludwig, the gallant Hombourger, exclaimed with a loud voice :—

"Ho! hermit! holy hermit, art thou in thy cell?"

"Who calls the poor servant of Heaven and Saint Buffo?" exclaimed a voice from the cavern; and presently, from beneath the wreaths of geranium and magnolia, appeared an intensely venerable, ancient, and majestic head—'twas that, we need not say, of Saint Buffo's solitary. A silver beard hanging to his knees gave his person an appearance of great respectability; his body was robed in simple brown serge, and girt with a knotted cord; his ancient feet were only defended from the prickles and stones by the rudest sandals, and his bald and polished head was bare.

"Holy hermit," said the knight in a grave voice, "make ready thy ministry, for there is some one about to die."

"Where, son?"

"Here, father."

"Is he here, now?"

"Perhaps," said the stout warrior, crossing himself; "but not so if right prevail." At this moment he caught sight of a ferry-boat putting off from Nonnenwerth, with a knight on board. Ludwig knew at once, by the sinople reversed and the truncated gules on his surcoat, that it was Sir Gottfried of Godesberg.

"Be ready, father," said the good knight, pointing towards the advancing boat; and waving his hand by way of respect to the reverend hermit, without a further word he vaulted into his saddle, and rode back for a few score of paces, when he wheeled round, and remained steady. His great lance and pennon rose in the air. His armour glistened in the sun; the chest and head of his battle-horse were similarly covered with steel. As Sir Gottfried, likewise armed and mounted (for his horse had been left at the ferry hard by), advanced up the road, he almost started at the figure before him— a glistening tower of steel.

"Are you the lord of this pass, Sir Knight?" said Sir Gottfried haughtily, "or do you hold it against all comers, in honour of your lady-love?"

"I am not the lord of this pass. I do not hold it against all comers. I hold it but against one, and he is a liar and a traitor."

"As the matter concerns me not, I pray you let me pass," said Gottfried.

"The matter *does* concern thee, Gottfried of Godesberg. Liar and traitor! art thou coward, too?"

"Holy Saint Buffo! 'tis a fight!" exclaimed the old hermit (who, too, had been a gallant warrior in his day); and like the old war-horse that hears the trumpet's sound, and spite of his clerical

29

profession, he prepared to look on at the combat with no ordinary eagerness, and sat down on the overhanging ledge of the rock, lighting his pipe, and affecting unconcern, but in reality most deeply interested in the event which was about to ensue.

As soon as the word "coward" had been pronounced by Sir Ludwig, his opponent, uttering a curse far too horrible to be inscribed here, had wheeled back his powerful piebald, and brought his lance to the rest.

"Ha! Beauséant!" cried he. "Allah humdillah!" 'Twas the battle-cry in Palestine of the irresistible Knights Hospitallers. "Look to thyself, Sir Knight, and for mercy from Heaven. *I* will give thee none."

"A Bugo for Katzenellenbogen!" exclaimed Sir Ludwig piously: that, too, was the well-known war-cry of his princely race.

"I will give the signal," said the old hermit, waving his pipe. "Knights, are you ready? One, two, three. *Los !*" (Let go).

At the signal, the two steeds tore up the ground like whirlwinds; the two knights, two flashing perpendicular masses of steel, rapidly converged; the two lances met upon the two shields of either, and shivered, splintered, shattered into ten hundred thousand pieces, which whirled through the air here and there, among the rocks, or in the trees, or in the river. The two horses fell back trembling on their haunches, where they remained for half a minute or so.

"Holy Buffo! a brave stroke!" said the old hermit. "Marry, but a splinter well-nigh took off my nose!" The honest hermit waved his pipe in delight, not perceiving that one of the splinters had carried off the head of it, and rendered his favourite amusement impossible. "Ha! they are to it again! O my! how they go to it with their great swords! Well stricken, grey! Well parried, piebald! Ha, that was a slicer! Go it, piebald! go it, grey!—go it, grey! go it, pie—— Peccavi! peccavi!" said the old man, here suddenly closing his eyes, and falling down on his knees. "I forgot I was a man of peace." And the next moment, uttering a hasty matin, he sprang down the ledge of rock, and was by the side of the combatants.

The battle was over. Good knight as Sir Gottfried was, his strength and skill had not been able to overcome Sir Ludwig the Hombourger, with RIGHT on his side. He was bleeding at every point of his armour: he had been run through the body several times, and a cut in tierce, delivered with tremendous dexterity, had cloven the crown of his helmet of Damascus steel, and passing through the cerebellum and sensorium, had split his nose almost in twain.

His mouth foaming—his face almost green—his eyes full of blood—his brains spattered over his forehead, and several of his teeth knocked out—the discomfited warrior presented a ghastly spectacle, as, reeling under the effects of the last tremendous blow which the Knight of Hombourg dealt, Sir Gottfried fell heavily from the saddle of his piebald charger; the frightened animal whisked his tail wildly with a shriek and a snort, plunged out his hind legs, trampling for one moment upon the feet of the prostrate Gottfried, thereby causing him to shriek with agony, and then galloped away riderless.

Away! ay, away!—away amid the green vineyards and golden cornfields; away up the steep mountains, where he frightened the eagles in their eyries; away down the clattering ravines, where the flashing cataracts tumble; away through the dark pine-forests, where the hungry wolves are howling; away over the dreary wolds, where the wild wind walks alone; away through the plashing quagmires, where the will-o'-the-wisp slunk frightened among the reeds; away through light and darkness, storm and sunshine; away by tower and town, highroad and hamlet. Once a turnpike-man would have detained him; but, ha! ha! he charged the pike, and cleared it at a bound. Once the Cologne Diligence stopped the way: he charged the Diligence, he knocked off the cap of the conductor on the roof, and yet galloped wildly, madly, furiously, irresistibly on! Brave horse! gallant steed! snorting child of Araby! On went the horse, over mountains, rivers, turnpikes, apple-women; and never stopped until he reached a livery-stable in Cologne where his master was accustomed to put him up.

CHAPTER VI

THE CONFESSION

BUT we have forgotten, meanwhile, the prostrate individual. Having examined the wounds in his side, legs, head, and throat, the old hermit (a skilful leech) knelt down by the side of the vanquished one and said, " Sir Knight, it is my painful duty to state to you that you are in an exceedingly dangerous condition, and will not probably survive."

" Say you so, Sir Priest ? then 'tis time I make my confession. Hearken you, Priest, and you, Sir Knight, whoever you be."

Sir Ludwig (who, much affected by the scene, had been tying his horse up to a tree) lifted his visor and said, " Gottfried of Godesberg ! I am the friend of thy kinsman, Margrave Karl, whose happiness thou hast ruined ; I am the friend of his chaste and virtuous lady, whose fair fame thou hast belied ; I am the godfather of young Count Otto, whose heritage thou wouldst have appropriated. Therefore I met thee in deadly fight, and overcame thee, and have well-nigh finished thee. Speak on."

" I have done all this," said the dying man, " and here, in my last hour, repent me. The Lady Theodora is a spotless lady ; the youthful Otto the true son of his father—Sir Hildebrandt is not his father, but his *uncle*."

" Gracious Buffo ! " " Celestial Bugo ! " here said the hermit and the Knight of Hombourg simultaneously, clasping their hands.

" Yes, his uncle ; but with the *bar-sinister* in his 'scutcheon. Hence he could never be acknowledged by the family ; hence, too, the Lady Theodora's spotless purity (though the young people had been brought up together) could never be brought to own the relationship."

" May I repeat your confession ? " asked the hermit.

" With the greatest pleasure in life : carry my confession to the Margrave, and pray him give me pardon. Were there—a notary-public present," slowly gasped the knight, the film of dissolution glazing over his eyes, " I would ask—you—two—gentlemen to witness it. I would gladly—sign the deposition—that is, if I could wr-wr-wr-wr-ite ! " A faint shuddering smile—a quiver, a gasp, a gurgle — the blood gushed from his mouth in black volumes. . . .

"He will never sin more," said the hermit solemnly.

"May Heaven assoilzie him!" said Sir Ludwig. "Hermit, he was a gallant knight. He died with harness on his back, and with truth on his lips: Ludwig of Hombourg would ask no other death. . . ."

An hour afterwards the principal servants at the Castle of Godesberg were rather surprised to see the noble Lord Louis trot into the courtyard of the castle, with a companion on the crupper of his saddle. 'Twas the venerable Hermit of Rolandseck, who, for the sake of greater celerity, had adopted this undignified conveyance, and whose appearance and little dumpy legs might well create hilarity among the "pampered menials" who are always found lounging about the houses of the great. He skipped off the saddle with considerable lightness, however; and Sir Ludwig, taking the reverend man by the arm, and frowning the jeering servitors into awe, bade one of them lead him to the presence of His Highness the Margrave.

"What has chanced?" said the inquisitive servitor. "The riderless horse of Sir Gottfried was seen to gallop by the outer wall anon. The Margrave's Grace has never quitted your Lordship's chamber, and sits as one distraught."

"Hold thy prate, knave, and lead us on!" And so saying, the Knight and his Reverence moved into the well-known apartment, where, according to the servitor's description, the wretched Margrave sat like a stone.

Ludwig took one of the kind broken-hearted man's hands, the hermit seized the other, and began (but on account of his great age, with a prolixity which we shall not endeavour to imitate) to narrate the events which we have already described. Let the dear reader fancy, the while his Reverence speaks, the glazed eyes of the Margrave gradually lighting up with attention; the flush of joy which mantles in his countenance—the start—the throb—the almost delirious outburst of hysteric exultation with which, when the whole truth was made known, he clasped the two messengers of glad tidings to his breast, with an energy that almost choked the aged recluse! "Ride, ride this instant to the Margravine—say I have wronged her, that it is all right, that she may come back—that I forgive her—that I apologise, if you will"—and a secretary forthwith despatched a note to that effect, which was carried off by a fleet messenger.

"Now write to the Superior of the monastery at Cologne, and bid him send me back my boy, my darling, my Otto—my Otto of roses!" said the fond father, making the first play upon words he had ever attempted in his life. But what will not paternal love effect? The secretary (smiling at the joke) wrote another letter, and another fleet messenger was despatched on another horse.

"And now," said Sir Ludwig playfully, "let us to lunch. Holy hermit, are you for a snack?"

The hermit could not say nay on an occasion so festive, and the three gentles seated themselves to a plenteous repast; for which the remains of the feast of yesterday offered, it need not be said, ample means.

"They will be home by dinner-time," said the exulting father. "Ludwig! reverend hermit! we will carry on till then." And the cup passed gaily round, and the laugh and jest circulated, while the three happy friends sat confidently awaiting the return of the Margravine and her son.

But alas! said we not rightly at the commencement of a former chapter, that betwixt the lip and the raised wine-cup there is often many a spill? that our hopes are high, and often, too often, vain? About three hours after the departure of the first messenger, he returned, and with an exceedingly long face knelt down and presented to the Margrave a billet to the following effect:—

"CONVENT OF NONNENWERTH: *Friday Afternoon.*

"SIR,—I have submitted too long to your ill-usage, and am disposed to bear it no more. I will no longer be made the butt of your ribald satire, and the object of your coarse abuse. Last week you threatened me with your cane! On Tuesday last you threw a wine-decanter at me, which hit the butler, it is true, but the intention was evident. This morning, in the presence of all the servants, you called me by the most vile abominable name, which Heaven forbid I should repeat! You dismissed me from your house under a false accusation. You sent me to this odious convent to be immured for life. Be it so! I will not come back, because, forsooth, you relent. Anything is better than a residence with a wicked, coarse, violent, intoxicated, brutal monster like yourself. I remain here for ever, and blush to be obliged to sign myself

"THEODORA VON GODESBERG.

"*P.S.*—I hope you do not intend to keep all my best gowns, jewels, and wearing-apparel; and make no doubt you dismissed me from your house in order to make way for some vile hussy, whose eyes I would like to tear out,   T. V. G."

CHAPTER VII

THE SENTENCE

THIS singular document, illustrative of the passions of women at all times, and particularly of the manners of the early ages, struck dismay into the heart of the Margrave.

"Are her Ladyship's insinuations correct?" asked the hermit in a severe tone. "To correct a wife with a cane is a venial, I may say a justifiable practice; but to fling a bottle at her is ruin, both to the liquor and to her."

"But she sent a carving-knife at me first," said the heart-broken husband. "O jealousy, cursed jealousy, why, why did I ever listen to thy green and yellow tongue?"

"They quarrelled; but they loved each other sincerely," whispered Sir Ludwig to the hermit; who began to deliver forthwith a lecture upon family discord and marital authority, which would have sent his two hearers to sleep, but for the arrival of the second messenger, whom the Margrave had despatched to Cologne for his son. This herald wore a still longer face than that of his comrade who preceded him.

"Where is my darling?" roared the agonised parent. "Have ye brought him with ye?"

"N—no," said the man, hesitating.

"I will flog the knave soundly when he comes," cried the father, vainly endeavouring, under an appearance of sternness, to hide his inward emotion and tenderness.

"Please, your Highness," said the messenger, making a desperate effort, "Count Otto is not at the convent."

"Know ye, knave, where he is?"

The swain solemnly said, "I do. He is *there.*" He pointed as he spake to the broad Rhine, that was seen from the casement, lighted up by the magnificent hues of sunset.

"*There!* How mean ye *there?*" gasped the Margrave, wrought to a pitch of nervous fury.

"Alas! my good lord, when he was in the boat which was to conduct him to the convent, he—he jumped suddenly from it, and is dr-dr-owned."

"Carry that knave out and hang him!" said the Margrave, with a calmness more dreadful than any outburst of rage. "Let every man of the boat's crew be blown from the mouth of the cannon on the tower—except the coxswain, and let him be——"

What was to be done with the coxswain, no one knows; for at that moment, and overcome by his emotion, the Margrave sank down lifeless on the floor.

CHAPTER VIII

THE CHILDE OF GODESBERG

IT must be clear to the dullest intellect (if amongst our readers we dare venture to presume that a dull intellect should be found) that the cause of the Margrave's fainting fit, described in the last chapter, was a groundless apprehension on the part of that too solicitous and credulous nobleman regarding the fate of his beloved child. No, young Otto was *not* drowned. Was ever hero of romantic story done to death so early in the tale? Young Otto was *not* drowned. Had such been the case, the Lord Margrave would infallibly have died at the close of the last chapter; and a few gloomy sentences at its close would have denoted how the lovely Lady Theodora became insane in the convent, and how Sir Ludwig determined, upon the demise of the old hermit (consequent upon the shock of hearing the news), to retire to the vacant hermitage, and assume the robe, the beard, the mortifications of the late venerable and solitary ecclesiastic. Otto was *not* drowned, and all those personages of our history are consequently alive and well.

The boat containing the amazed young Count—for he knew not the cause of his father's anger, and hence rebelled against the unjust sentence which the Margrave had uttered—had not rowed many miles, when the gallant boy rallied from his temporary surprise and despondency, and determined not to be a slave in any convent of any order: determined to make a desperate effort for escape. At a moment when the men were pulling hard against the tide, and Kuno, the coxswain, was looking carefully to steer the barge between some dangerous rocks and quicksands, which are frequently met with in the majestic though dangerous river, Otto gave a sudden spring from the boat, and with one single flounce was in the boiling, frothing, swirling eddy of the stream.

Fancy the agony of the crew at the disappearance of their young lord! All loved him; all would have given their lives for him; but as they did not know how to swim, of course they declined to make any useless plunges in search of him, and stood on their oars in mute wonder and grief. *Once,* his fair head and golden ringlets were seen to arise from the water; *twice,* puffing and panting, it appeared for an instant again ; *thrice*, it rose but for one single moment : it was the last chance, and it sunk, sunk, sunk. Knowing the reception they would meet with from their liege lord, the men naturally did not go home to Godesberg, but, putting in at the first creek on the opposite bank, fled into the Duke of Nassau's territory ; where, as they have little to do with our tale, we will leave them.

But they little knew how expert a swimmer was young Otto. He had disappeared, it is true : but why ? because he *had dived*. He calculated that his conductors would consider him drowned, and the desire of liberty lending him wings (or we had rather say *fins*, in this instance), the gallant boy swam on beneath the water, never lifting his head for a single moment between Godesberg and Cologne —the distance being twenty-five or thirty miles.

Escaping from observation, he landed on the *Deutz* side of the river, repaired to a comfortable and quiet hostel there, saying he had had an accident from a boat, and thus accounting for the moisture of his habiliments, and while these were drying before a fire in his chamber, went snugly to bed, where he mused, not without amaze, on the strange events of the day. " This morning," thought he, " a noble, and heir to a princely estate—this evening an outcast, with but a few bank-notes which my mamma luckily gave me on my birthday.   What a strange entry into life is this for a young man of my family !   Well, I have courage and resolution : my first attempt in life has been a gallant and successful one ; other dangers will be conquered by similar bravery."   And recommending himself, his unhappy mother, and his mistaken father to the care of their patron saint, Saint Buffo, the gallant-hearted boy fell presently into such a sleep, as only the young, the healthy, the innocent, and the extremely fatigued, can enjoy.

The fatigues of the day (and very few men but would be fatigued after swimming well-nigh thirty miles under water) caused young Otto to sleep so profoundly, that he did not remark how, after Friday's sunset, as a natural consequence, Saturday's Phœbus illumined the world, ay, and sunk at his appointed hour.   The serving-maidens of the hostel, peeping in, marked him sleeping, and blessing him for a pretty youth, tripped lightly from the chamber ; the boots tried haply twice or thrice to call him (as boots will fain), but the lovely boy, giving another snore, turned on his side, and was quite unconscious of the interruption.   In a word, the youth slept for six-and-thirty hours at an elongation ; and the Sunday sun was shining, and the bells of the hundred churches of Cologne were clinking and tolling in pious festivity, and the burghers and burgheresses of the town were trooping to vespers and morning service when Otto awoke.

As he donned his clothes of the richest Genoa velvet, the astonished boy could not at first account for his difficulty in putting them on. "Marry," said he, "these breeches that my blessed mother" (tears filled his fine eyes as he thought of her)—"that my blessed mother had made long on purpose, are now ten inches too short for me. Whir-r-r! my coat cracks i' the back, as in vain I try to buckle it round me ; and the sleeves reach no farther than my elbows! What is this mystery? Am I grown fat and tall in a single night? Ah! ah! ah! ah! I have it."

The young and good-humoured Childe laughed merrily. He bethought him of the reason of his mistake : his garments had shrunk from being five-and-twenty miles under water.

But one remedy presented itself to his mind ; and that we need not say was to purchase new ones. Inquiring the way to the most genteel ready-made clothes' establishment in the city of Cologne, and finding it was kept in the Minoriten Strasse, by an ancestor of the celebrated Moses of London, the noble Childe hied him towards the emporium ; but you may be sure did not neglect to perform his religious duties by the way. Entering the cathedral, he made straight for the shrine of St. Buffo, and, hiding himself behind a pillar there (fearing he might be recognised by the Archbishop, or any· of his father's numerous friends in Cologne), he proceeded with his devotions, as was the practice of the young nobles of the age.

But though exceedingly intent upon the service, yet his eye could not refrain from wandering a *little* round about him, and he remarked with surprise that the whole church was filled with archers ; and he remembered, too, that he had seen in the streets numerous other bands of men similarly attired in green. On asking at the cathedral porch the cause of this assemblage, one of the green ones said (in a jape), "Marry, youngster, *you* must be *green*, not to know that we are all bound to the castle of his Grace Duke Adolf of Cleves, who gives an archery meeting once a year, and prizes for which we toxophilites muster strong."

Otto, whose course hitherto had been undetermined, now immediately settled what to do. He straightway repaired to the ready-made emporium of Herr Moses, and bidding that gentleman furnish him with an archer's complete dress, Moses speedily selected a suit from his vast stock, which fitted the youth to a *t*, and we need not say was sold at an exceedingly moderate price. So attired (and bidding Herr Moses a cordial farewell), young Otto was a gorgeous, a noble, a soul-inspiring boy to gaze on. A coat and breeches of the most brilliant pea-green, ornamented with a profusion of brass buttons, and fitting him with exquisite tightness, showed off a figure unrivalled for slim symmetry. His feet were covered with peaked buskins of buff leather, and a belt round his slender waist, of the same material, held his knife, his tobacco-pipe and pouch, and his long shining dirk; which, though the adventurous youth had as yet only employed it to fashion wicket-bails, or to cut bread-and-cheese, he was now quite ready to use against the enemy. His personal attractions were enhanced by a neat white hat, flung carelessly and fearlessly on one side of his open smiling countenance; and his lovely hair, curling in ten thousand yellow ringlets, fell over his shoulder like golden epaulettes, and down his back as far as the waist-buttons of his coat. I warrant me, many a lovely Cölnerinn looked after the handsome Childe with anxiety, and dreamed that night of Cupid under the guise of "a bonny boy in green."

So accoutred, the youth's next thought was, that he must supply himself with a bow. This he speedily purchased at the most fashionable bowyer's, and of the best material and make. It was of ivory, trimmed with pink ribbon, and the cord of silk. An elegant quiver, beautifully painted and embroidered, was slung across his back, with a dozen of the finest arrows, tipped with steel of Damascus, formed of the branches of the famous Upas tree of Java, and feathered with the wings of the ortolan. These purchases being completed (together with that of a knapsack, dressing-case, change, &c.), our young adventurer asked where was the hostel at which the archers were wont to assemble? and being informed that it was at the sign of the "Golden Stag," hied him to that house of entertainment, where, by calling for quantities of liquor and beer, he speedily made the acquaintance and acquired the goodwill of a company of his future comrades who happened to be sitting in the coffee-room.

After they had eaten and drunken for all, Otto said, addressing them, "When go ye forth, gentles? I am a stranger here, bound as you to the archery meeting of Duke Adolf. An ye will admit a youth into your company, 'twill gladden me upon my lonely way?"

The archers replied, "You seem so young and jolly, and you spend your gold so very like a gentleman, that we'll receive you in our band with pleasure. Be ready, for we start at half-past two!" At that hour accordingly the whole joyous company prepared to move, and Otto not a little increased his popularity among them by stepping out and having a conference with the landlord, which caused the latter to come into the room where the archers were assembled previous to departure, and to say, "Gentlemen, the bill is settled!"—words never ungrateful to an archer yet: no, marry, nor to a man of any other calling that I wot of.

They marched joyously for several leagues, singing and joking, and telling of a thousand feats of love and chase and war. While thus engaged, some one remarked to Otto, that he was not dressed in the regular uniform, having no feathers in his hat.

"I dare say I will find a feather," said the lad, smiling.

Then another gibed because his bow was new.

"See that you can use your old one as well, Master Wolfgang," said the undisturbed youth. His answers, his bearing, his generosity, his beauty, and his wit, inspired all his new toxophilite friends with interest and curiosity, and they longed to see whether his skill with the bow corresponded with their secret sympathies for him.

An occasion for manifesting this skill did not fail to present itself soon—as indeed it seldom does to such a hero of romance as young Otto was. Fate seems to watch over such : events occur to them just in the nick of time ; they rescue virgins just as ogres are on the point of devouring them ; they manage to be present at Court and interesting ceremonies, and to see the most interesting people at the most interesting moment ; directly an adventure is necessary for them, that adventure occurs : and I, for my part, have often wondered with delight (and never could penetrate the mystery of the subject) at the way in which that humblest of romance heroes, Signor Clown, when he wants anything in the Pantomime, straightway finds it to his hand. How is it that—suppose he wishes to dress himself up like a woman for instance, that minute a coalheaver walks in with a shovel-hat that answers for a bonnet : at the very next instant a butcher's lad passing with a string of sausages and a bundle of bladders unconsciously helps Master Clown to a necklace and a *tournure,* and so on through the whole toilet ? Depend upon it there is something we do not wot of in that mysterious overcoming of circumstances by great individuals : that apt and wondrous conjuncture of the *the Hour and the Man ;* and so, for my part, when I heard the above remark of one of the archers, that Otto had never a feather in his bonnet, I felt sure that a heron would spring up in the next sentence to supply him with an *aigrette.*

And such indeed was the fact : rising out of a morass by which the archers were passing, a gallant heron, arching his neck, swelling his crest, placing his legs behind him, and his beak and red eyes against the wind, rose slowly, and offered the fairest mark in the world.

"Shoot, Otto," said one of the archers. "You would not shoot just now at a crow because it was a foul bird, nor at a hawk because it was a noble bird ; bring us down yon heron : it flies slowly."

But Otto was busy that moment tying his shoestring, and Rudolf, the third best of the archers, shot at the bird and missed it.

"Shoot, Otto," said Wolfgang, a youth who had taken a liking to the young archer: "the bird is getting further and further."

But Otto was busy that moment whittling a willow-twig he had just cut. Max, the second best archer, shot and missed.

"Then," said Wolfgang, "I must try myself: a plague on you, young springald, you have lost a noble chance!"

Wolfgang prepared himself with all his care, and shot at the bird. "It is out of distance," said he, "and a murrain on the bird!"

Otto, who by this time had done whittling his willow-stick (having carved a capital caricature of Wolfgang upon it), flung the twig down and said carelessly, "Out of distance! Pshaw! We have two minutes yet," and fell to asking riddles and cutting jokes; to the which none of the archers listened, as they were all engaged, their noses in air, watching the retreating bird.

"Where shall I hit him?" said Otto.

"Go to," said Rudolf, "thou canst see no limb of him: he is no bigger than a flea."

"Here goes for his right eye!" said Otto; and stepping forward in the English manner (which his godfather having learnt in Palestine, had taught him), he brought his bowstring to his ear, took a good aim, allowing for the wind, and calculating the parabola to a nicety. Whizz! his arrow went off.

He took up the willow-twig again and began carving a head of Rudolf at the other end, chatting and laughing, and singing a ballad the while.

The archers, after standing a long time looking skywards with their noses in the air, at last brought them down from the perpendicular to the horizontal position, and said, "Pooh, this lad is a humbug! The arrow's lost; let's go!"

"*Heads!*" cried Otto, laughing. A speck was seen rapidly descending from the heavens; it grew to be as big as a crown-piece, then as a partridge, then as a tea-kettle, and flop! down fell a magnificent heron to the ground, flooring poor Max in its fall.

"Take the arrow out of his eye, Wolfgang," said Otto, without looking at the bird: "wipe it and put it back into my quiver."

The arrow indeed was there, having penetrated right through the pupil.

"Are you in league with Der Freischütz?" said Rudolf, quite amazed.

Otto laughing whistled the "Huntsman's Chorus," and said, "No, my friend. It was a lucky shot: only a lucky shot. I was taught shooting, look you, in the fashion of merry England, where the archers are archers indeed."

And so he cut off the heron's wing for a plume for his hat; and the archers walked on, much amazed, and saying, "What a wonderful country that merry England must be!"

Far from feeling any envy at their comrade's success, the jolly archers recognised his superiority with pleasure; and Wolfgang and Rudolf especially held out their hands to the younker, and besought the honour of his friendship. They continued their walk all day, and when night fell made choice of a good hostel you may be sure, where over beer, punch, champagne, and every luxury, they drank to the health of the Duke of Cleves, and indeed each other's healths all round. Next day they resumed their march, and continued it without interruption, except to take in a supply of victuals here and there (and it was found on these occasions that Otto, young as he was, could eat four times as much as the oldest archer present, and drink to correspond); and these continued refreshments having given them more than ordinary strength, they determined on making rather a long march of it, and did not halt till after nightfall at the gates of the little town of Windeck.

What was to be done? the town gates were shut. "Is there no hostel, no castle where we can sleep?" asked Otto of the sentinel at the gate. "I am so hungry that in lack of better food I think I could eat my grandmamma."

The sentinel laughed at this hyperbolical expression of hunger, and said, "You had best go sleep at the Castle of Windeck yonder;" adding, with a peculiarly knowing look, "Nobody will disturb you there."

At that moment the moon broke out from a cloud, and showed on a hill hard by a castle indeed—but the skeleton of a castle. The roof was gone, the windows were dismantled, the towers were tumbling, and the cold moonlight pierced it through and through. One end of the building was, however, still covered in, and stood looking still more frowning, vast, and gloomy, even than the other part of the edifice.

"There is a lodging, certainly," said Otto to the sentinel, who pointed towards the castle with his bartizan; "but tell me, good fellow, what are we to do for a supper?"

"Oh, the castellan of Windeck will entertain you," said the man-at-arms with a grin, and marched up the embrasure; the while the archers, taking counsel among themselves, debated whether or not they should take up their quarters in the gloomy and deserted edifice.

"We shall get nothing but an owl for supper there," said young Otto. "Marry, lads, let us storm the town; we are thirty gallant fellows, and I have heard the garrison is not more than three hundred."

But the rest of the party thought such a way of getting supper was not a very cheap one, and, grovelling knaves, preferred rather to sleep ignobly and without victuals, than dare the assault with Otto, and die, or conquer something comfortable.

One and all then made their way towards the castle. They entered its vast and silent halls, frightening the owls and bats that fled before them with hideous hootings and flappings of wings, and passing by a multiplicity of mouldy stairs, dank reeking roofs, and rickety corridors, at last came to an apartment which, dismal and dismantled as it was, appeared to be in rather better condition than the neighbouring chambers, and they therefore selected it as their place of rest for the night. They then tossed up which should mount guard. The first two hours of watch fell to Otto, who was to be succeeded by his young though humble friend Wolfgang; and, accordingly, the Childe of Godesberg, drawing his dirk, began to pace upon his weary round; while his comrades, by various gradations of snoring, told how profoundly they slept, spite of their lack of supper.

'Tis needless to say what were the thoughts of the noble Childe as he performed his two hours' watch; what gushing memories poured into his full soul; what "sweet and bitter" recollections of home inspired his throbbing heart; and what manly aspirations after fame buoyed him up. "Youth is ever confident," says the bard. Happy, happy season! The moonlit hours passed by on silver wings, the twinkling stars looked friendly down upon him. Confiding in their youthful sentinel, sound slept the valorous toxophilites, as up and down, and there and back again, marched on the noble Childe. At length his repeater told him, much to his satisfaction, that it was half-past eleven, the hour when his watch was to cease; and so, giving a playful kick to the slumbering Wolfgang, that good-humoured fellow sprung up from his lair, and, drawing his sword, proceeded to relieve Otto.

The latter laid him down for warmth's sake on the very spot which his comrade had left, and for some time could not sleep. Realities and visions then began to mingle in his mind, till he scarce knew which was which. He dozed for a minute; then he woke with a start; then he went off again; then woke up again. In one of these half-sleeping moments he thought he saw a figure, as of a woman in white, gliding into the room, and beckoning Wolfgang from it. He looked again. Wolfgang was gone. At that moment twelve o'clock clanged from the town, and Otto started up.

CHAPTER IX

THE LADY OF WINDECK

AS the bell with iron tongue called midnight, Wolfgang the Archer, pacing on his watch, beheld before him a pale female figure. He did not know whence she came: but there suddenly she stood close to him. Her blue, clear, glassy eyes were fixed upon him. Her form was of faultless beauty; her face pale as the marble of the fairy statue, ere yet the sculptor's love had given it life. A smile played upon her features, but it was no warmer than the reflection of a moonbeam on a lake; and yet it was wondrous beautiful. A fascination stole over the senses of young Wolfgang. He stared at the lovely apparition with fixed eyes and distended jaws. She looked at him with ineffable archness. She lifted one beautifully rounded alabaster arm, and made a sign as if to beckon him towards her. Did Wolfgang—the young and lusty Wolfgang—follow? Ask the iron whether it follows the magnet?—ask the pointer whether it pursues the partridge through the stubble?—ask the youth whether the lollypop-shop does not attract him? Wolfgang *did* follow. An antique door opened, as if by magic. There was no light, and yet they saw quite plain; they passed through the innumerable ancient chambers, and yet they did not wake any of the owls and bats roosting there. We know not through how many apartments the young couple passed; but at last they came to one where a feast was prepared; and on an antique table, covered with massive silver, covers were laid for two. The lady took her place at one end of the table, and with her sweetest nod beckoned Wolfgang to the other seat. He took it. The table was small, and their knees met. He felt as cold in his legs as if he were kneeling against an ice-well.

"Gallant archer," said she, "you must be hungry after your day's march. What supper will you have? Shall it be a delicate lobster salad? or a dish of elegant tripe and onions? or a slice of boar's-head and truffles? or a Welsh rabbit *à la cave au cidre?* or a beefsteak and shallot? or a couple of *rognons à la brochette?* Speak, brave bowyer: you have but to order."

As there was nothing on the table but a covered silver dish,

30

Wolfgang thought that the lady who proposed such a multiplicity of delicacies to him was only laughing at him; so he determined to try her with something extremely rare.

"Fair princess," he said, "I should like very much a pork-chop and some mashed potatoes."

She lifted the cover: there was such a pork-chop as Simpson never served, with a dish of mashed potatoes that would have formed at least six portions in our degenerate days in Rupert Street.

When he had helped himself to these delicacies, the lady put the cover on the dish again, and watched him eating with interest. He was for some time too much occupied with his own food to remark that his companion did not eat a morsel; but big as it was, his chop was soon gone; the shining silver of his plate was scraped quite clean with his knife, and heaving a great sigh, he confessed a humble desire for something to drink.

"Call for what you like, sweet sir," said the lady, lifting up a silver filigree bottle, with an india-rubber cork, ornamented with gold.

"Then," said Master Wolfgang—for the fellow's tastes were, in sooth, very humble—"I call for half-and-half." According to his wish, a pint of that delicious beverage was poured from the bottle, foaming, into his beaker.

Having emptied this at a draught, and declared that on his conscience it was the best tap he ever knew in his life, the young man felt his appetite renewed; and it is impossible to say how many different dishes he called for. Only enchantment, he was afterwards heard to declare (though none of his friends believed him), could have given him the appetite he possessed on that extraordinary night. He called for another pork-chop and potatoes, then for pickled salmon; then he thought he would try a devilled turkey wing. "I adore the devil," said he.

"So do I," said the pale lady, with unwonted animation; and the dish was served straightway. It was succeeded by black-puddings, tripe, toasted cheese, and—what was most remarkable—every one of the dishes which he desired came from under the same silver cover: which circumstance, when he had partaken of about fourteen different articles, he began to find rather mysterious.

"Oh," said the pale lady, with a smile, "the mystery is easily accounted for: the servants hear you, and the kitchen is *below*." But this did not account for the manner in which more half-and-half, bitter ale, punch (both gin and rum), and even oil and vinegar, which he took with cucumber to his salmon, came out of the self-same bottle from which the lady had first poured out his pint of half-and-half.

"There are more things in heaven and earth, Voracio," said his arch entertainer, when he put this question to her, "than are dreamt of in your philosophy : " and, sooth to say, the archer was by this time in such a state, that he did not find anything wonderful more.

"Are you happy, dear youth ?" said the lady, as, after his collation, he sank back in his chair.

"Oh, miss, ain't I !" was his interrogative and yet affirmative reply.

"Should you like such a supper every night, Wolfgang ?" continued the pale one.

"Why, no," said he ; "no, not exactly ; not *every* night : *some* nights I should like oysters."

"Dear youth," said she, "be but mine, and you may have them all the year round !" The unhappy boy was too far gone to suspect anything, otherwise this extraordinary speech would have told him that he was in suspicious company. A person who can offer oysters all the year round can live to no good purpose.

"Shall I sing you a song, dear archer ?" said the lady.

"Sweet love !" said he, now much excited, "strike up and I will join the chorus."

She took down her mandolin, and commenced a ditty. 'Twas a sweet and wild one. It told how a lady of high lineage cast her eyes on a peasant page ; it told how nought could her love assuage, her suitor's wealth and her father's rage ! it told how the youth did his foes engage ; and at length they went off in the Gretna stage, the high-born dame and the peasant page. Wolfgang beat time, waggled his head, sung woefully out of tune as the song proceeded ; and if he had not been too intoxicated with love and other excitement, he would have remarked how the pictures on the wall, as the lady sang, began to waggle their heads too, and nod and grin to the music. The song ended. "I am the lady of high lineage : Archer, will you be the peasant page ?"

"I'll follow you to the devil !" said Wolfgang.

"Come," replied the lady, glaring wildly on him, "come to the chapel ; we'll be married this minute !"

She held out her hand—Wolfgang took it. It was cold, damp, —deadly cold ; and on they went to the chapel.

As they passed out, the two pictures over the wall, of a gentleman and lady, tripped lightly out of their frames, skipped noiselessly down to the ground, and making the retreating couple a profound curtsey and bow, took the places which they had left at the table.

Meanwhile the young couple passed on towards the chapel,

threading innumerable passages, and passing through chambers of great extent. As they came along, all the portraits on the wall stepped out of their frames to follow them. One ancestor, of whom there was only a bust, frowned in the greatest rage, because, having no legs, his pedestal would not move; and several sticking-plaster profiles of the former Lords of Windeck looked quite black at being, for similar reasons, compelled to keep their places. However, there was a goodly procession formed behind Wolfgang and his bride; and by the time they reached the church, they had near a hundred followers.

The church was splendidly illuminated; the old banners of the old knights glittered as they do at Drury Lane. The organ set up of itself to play the "Bridesmaids' Chorus." The choir-chairs were filled with people in black.

"Come, love," said the pale lady.

"I don't see the parson," exclaimed Wolfgang, spite of himself rather alarmed.

"Oh, the parson! that's the easiest thing in the world! I say, bishop!" said the lady, stooping down.

Stooping down — and to what? Why, upon my word and honour, to a great brass plate on the floor, over which they were passing, and on which was engraven the figure of a bishop—and a very ugly bishop, too—with crosier and mitre, and lifted finger, on which sparkled the episcopal ring. "Do, my dear lord, come and marry us," said the lady, with a levity which shocked the feelings of her bridegroom.

The bishop got up; and directly he rose, a dean, who was sleeping under a large slate near him, came bowing and cringing up to him; while a canon of the cathedral (whose name was Schidnischmidt) began grinning and making fun at the pair. The ceremony was begun, and

.   .   .   .   .   .

As the clock struck twelve, young Otto bounded up, and remarked the absence of his companion Wolfgang. The idea he had had, that his friend disappeared in company with a white-robed female, struck him more and more. "I will follow them," said he; and, calling to the next on the watch (old Snozo, who was right unwilling to forego his sleep), he rushed away by the door through which he had seen Wolfgang and his temptress take their way.

That he did not find them was not his fault. The castle was vast, the chamber dark. There were a thousand doors, and what wonder that, after he had once lost sight of them, the intrepid Childe should not be able to follow in their steps? As might be expected, he took the wrong door, and wandered for at least three hours about the dark enormous solitary castle, calling out Wolfgang's name to the careless and indifferent echoes, knocking his young shins against the ruins scattered in the darkness, but still with a spirit entirely undaunted, and a firm resolution to aid his absent comrade. Brave Otto! thy exertions were rewarded at last!

For he lighted at length upon the very apartment where Wolfgang had partaken of supper, and where the old couple who had been in the picture-frames, and turned out to be the lady's father and mother, were now sitting at the table.

"Well, Bertha has got a husband at last," said the lady.

"After waiting four hundred and fifty-three years for one, it was quite time," said the gentleman. (He was dressed in powder and a pigtail, quite in the old fashion.)

"The husband is no great things," continued the lady, taking snuff. "A low fellow, my dear; a butcher's son, I believe. Did you see how the wretch ate at supper? To think my daughter should have to marry an archer!"

"There are archers and archers," said the old man. "Some archers are snobs, as your Ladyship states; some, on the contrary, are gentlemen by birth, at least, though not by breeding. Witness young Otto, the Landgrave of Godesberg's son, who is listening at the door like a lacquey, and whom I intend to run through the——"

"Law, Baron!" said the lady.

"I will, though," replied the Baron, drawing an immense sword, and glaring round at Otto; but though at the sight of that sword and that scowl a less valorous youth would have taken to his heels, the undaunted Childe advanced at once into the apartment. He wore round his neck a relic of Saint Buffo (the tip of the saint's ear, which had been cut off at Constantinople). "Fiends! I command you to retreat!" said he, holding up this sacred charm, which his mamma had fastened on him; and at the sight of it, with an unearthly yell the ghosts of the Baron and the Baroness sprang back into their picture-frames, as clown goes through a clock in a pantomime.

He rushed through the open door by which the unlucky Wolfgang had passed with his demoniacal bride, and went on and on through the vast gloomy chambers lighted by the ghastly moonshine: the noise of the organ in the chapel, the lights in the kaleidoscopic windows, directed him towards that edifice. He rushed to the door: 'twas barred! He knocked: the beadles were deaf. He applied his inestimable relic to the lock, and—whizz! crash! clang! bang! whang!—the gate flew open! the organ went off in a fugue—the lights quivered over the tapers, and then went off towards the ceiling—the ghosts assembled rushed away with a skurry and a scream—the bride howled, and vanished—the fat bishop waddled back under his brass plate—the dean flounced down into his family vault—and the canon Schidnischmidt, who was making a joke, as usual, on the bishop, was obliged to stop at the very point of his epigram, and to disappear into the void whence he came.

Otto fell fainting at the porch, while Wolfgang tumbled lifeless down at the altar-steps; and in this situation the archers, when they arrived, found the two youths. They were resuscitated, as we scarce need say; but when, in incoherent accents, they came to tell their wondrous tale, some sceptics among the archers said—" Pooh! they were intoxicated!" while others, nodding their older heads, exclaimed—" *They have seen the Lady of Windeck!*" and recalled the stories of many other young men, who, inveigled by her devilish arts, had not been so lucky as Wolfgang, and had disappeared—for ever!

This adventure bound Wolfgang heart and soul to his gallant preserver; and the archers—it being now morning, and the cocks crowing lustily round about—pursued their way without further delay to the castle of the noble patron of toxophilites, the gallant Duke of Cleves.

CHAPTER X

THE BATTLE OF THE BOWMEN

ALTHOUGH there lay an immense number of castles and abbeys between Windeck and Cleves, for every one of which the guide-books have a legend and a ghost, who might, with the commonest stretch of ingenuity, be made to waylay our adventurers on the road; yet, as the journey would be thus almost interminable, let us cut it short by saying that the travellers reached Cleves without any further accident, and found the place thronged with visitors for the meeting next day.

And here it would be easy to describe the company which arrived, and make display of antiquarian lore. Now we would represent a cavalcade of knights arriving, with their pages carrying their shining helms of gold, and the stout esquires, bearers of lance and banner. Anon would arrive a fat abbot on his ambling pad, surrounded by the white-robed companions of his convent. Here should come the glee-men and jongleurs, the minstrels, the mountebanks, the particoloured gipsies, the dark-eyed, nut-brown Zigeunerinnen; then a troop of peasants chanting Rhine-songs, and leading in their ox-drawn carts the peach-cheeked girls from the vine-lands. Next we would depict the litters blazoned with armorial bearings, from between the broidered curtains of which peeped out the swan-like necks and the haughty faces of the blonde ladies of the castles. But for these descriptions we have not space; and the reader is referred to the account of the tournament in the ingenious novel of "Ivanhoe," where the above phenomena are described at length. Suffice it to say, that Otto and his companions arrived at the town of Cleves, and, hastening to a hostel, reposed themselves after the day's march, and prepared them for the encounter of the morrow.

That morrow came: and as the sports were to begin early, Otto and his comrades hastened to the field, armed with their best bows and arrows, you may be sure, and eager to distinguish themselves; as were the multitude of other archers assembled. They were from all neighbouring countries—crowds of English, as you may fancy, armed with Murray's guide-books, troops of chattering Frenchmen, Frankfort Jews with roulette-tables, and Tyrolese with gloves and trinkets—all hied towards the field where the butts were set up, and the archery practice was to be held. The Childe and his brother archers were, it need not be said, early on the ground.

But what words of mine can describe the young gentleman's emotion when, preceded by a band of trumpets, bagpipes, ophicleides, and other wind instruments, the Prince of Cleves appeared with the Princess Helen, his daughter? And ah! what expressions of my humble pen can do justice to the beauty of that young lady? Fancy every charm which decorates the person, every virtue which ornaments the mind, every accomplishment which renders charming mind and charming person doubly charming, and then you will have but a faint and feeble idea of the beauties of Her Highness the Princess Helen. Fancy a complexion such as they say (I know not with what justice) Rowland's Kalydor imparts to the users of that cosmetic; fancy teeth to which orient pearls are like Wallsend coals; eyes, which were so blue, tender, and bright, that while they ran you through with their lustre, they healed you with their kindness; a neck and waist, so ravishingly slender and graceful, that the least that is said about them the better; a foot which fell upon the flowers no heavier than a dewdrop—and this charming person set off by the most elegant toilet that ever milliner devised! The lovely Helen's hair (which was as black as the finest varnish for boots) was so long, that it was borne on a cushion several yards behind her by the maidens of her train; and a hat, set off with moss-roses, sunflowers, bugles, birds-of-paradise, gold lace, and pink ribbon, gave her a *distingué* air, which would have set the editor of the *Morniny Post* mad with love.

It had exactly the same effect upon the noble Childe of Godesberg, as leaning on his ivory bow, with his legs crossed, he stood and gazed on her, as Cupid gazed on Psyche. Their eyes met: it was all over with both of them. A blush came at one and the same minute budding to the cheek of either. A simultaneous throb beat in those young hearts! They loved each other for ever from that instant. Otto still stood, cross-legged, enraptured, leaning on his ivory bow; but Helen, calling to a maiden for her pocket-handkerchief, blew her beautiful Grecian nose in order to hide her agitation. Bless ye, bless ye, pretty ones! I am old now; but not so old but that I kindle at the tale of love. Theresa MacWhirter too has lived and loved. Heigho!

Who is yon chief that stands behind the truck whereon are seated the Princess and the stout old lord her father? Who is he whose hair is of the carroty hue—whose eyes, across a snubby bunch of a nose, are perpetually scowling at each other; who has a humpback, and a hideous mouth, surrounded with bristles, and crammed full of jutting yellow odious teeth? Although he wears a sky-blue doublet laced with silver, it only serves to render his vulgar punchy figure doubly ridiculous; although his nether garment is of salmon-coloured velvet, it only draws the more attention to his legs, which are disgustingly crooked and bandy. A rose-coloured hat, with towering pea-green ostrich-plumes, looks absurd on his bull-head; and though it is time of peace, the wretch is armed with a multiplicity of daggers, knives, yataghans, dirks, sabres, and scimitars, which testify his truculent and bloody disposition. 'Tis the terrible Rowski de Donnerblitz, Margrave of Eulenschreckenstein. Report says he is a suitor for the hand of the lovely Helen. He addresses various speeches of gallantry to her, and grins hideously as he thrusts his disgusting head over her lily shoulder. But she turns away from him! turns and shudders—ay, as she would at a black dose!

Otto stands gazing still, and leaning on his bow. "What is the prize?" asks one archer of another. There are two prizes—a velvet cap, embroidered by the hand of the Princess, and a chain of massive gold, of enormous value. Both lie on cushions before her.

"I know which I shall choose, when I win the first prize," says a swarthy, savage, and bandy-legged archer, who bears the owl gules on a black shield, the cognisance of the Lord Rowski de Donnerblitz.

"Which, fellow?" says Otto, turning fiercely upon him.

"The chain, to be sure!" says the leering archer. "You do not suppose I am such a flat as to choose that velvet gimcrack there?" Otto laughed in scorn, and began to prepare his bow. The trumpets sounding proclaimed that the sports were about to commence.

Is it necessary to describe them? No: that has already been done in the novel of "Ivanhoe" before mentioned. Fancy the archers clad in Lincoln green, all coming forward in turn, and firing at the targets. Some hit, some missed; those that missed were fain to retire amidst the jeers of the multitudinous spectators. Those that hit began new trials of skill; but it was easy to see, from the first, that the battle lay between Squintoff (the Rowski archer) and the young hero with the golden hair and the ivory bow. Squintoff's fame as a marksman was known throughout Europe; but who was his young competitor? Ah! there was *one* heart in the assembly that beat most anxiously to know. 'Twas Helen's.

The crowning trial arrived. The bull's-eye of the target, set up at three-quarters of a mile distance from the archers, was so small, that it required a very clever man indeed to see, much more to hit it; and as Squintoff was selecting his arrow for the final trial, the Rowski flung a purse of gold towards his archer, saying—"Squintoff, an ye win the prize, the purse is thine." "I may as well pocket it at once, your honour," said the bowman, with a sneer at Otto. "This young chick, who has been lucky as yet, will hardly hit such a mark as that." And, taking his aim, Squintoff discharged his arrow right into the very middle of the bull's-eye.

"Can you mend that, young springald?" said he, as a shout rent the air at his success, as Helen turned pale to think that the champion of her secret heart was likely to be overcome, and as Squintoff, pocketing the Rowski's money, turned to the noble boy of Godesberg.

"Has anybody got a pea?" asked the lad. Everybody laughed at his droll request; and an old woman, who was selling porridge in the crowd, handed him the vegetable which he demanded. It was a dry and yellow pea. Otto, stepping up to the target, caused Squintoff to extract his arrow from the bull's-eye, and placed in the orifice made by the steel point of the shaft, the pea which he had received from the old woman. He then came back to his place. As he prepared to shoot, Helen was so overcome by emotion, that 'twas thought she would have fainted. Never, never had she seen a being so beautiful as the young hero now before her.

He looked almost divine. He flung back his long clusters of hair from his bright eyes and tall forehead; the blush of health mantled on his cheek, from which the barber's weapon had never shorn the down. He took his bow, and one of his most elegant arrows, and poising himself lightly on his right leg, he flung himself forward, raising his left leg on a level with his ear. He looked like Apollo, as he stood balancing himself there. He discharged his dart from the thrumming bowstring: it clove the blue air—whizz!

"*He has split the pea!*" said the Princess, and fainted. The Rowski, with one eye, hurled an indignant look at the boy, while with the other he levelled (if aught so crooked can be said to level anything) a furious glance at his archer.

The archer swore a sulky oath. "He is the better man!" said he. "I suppose, young chap, you take the gold chain?"

"The gold chain!" said Otto. "Prefer a gold chain to a cap worked by that august hand? Never!" And advancing to the balcony where the Princess, who now came to herself, was sitting, he kneeled down before her, and received the velvet cap; which, blushing as scarlet as the cap itself, the Princess Helen placed on his golden ringlets. Once more their eyes met—their hearts thrilled. They had never spoken, but they knew they loved each other for ever.

"Wilt thou take service with the Rowski of Donnerblitz?" said that individual to the youth. "Thou shalt be captain of my archers in place of yon blundering nincompoop, whom thou hast overcome."

"Yon blundering nincompoop is a skilful and gallant archer," replied Otto haughtily; "and I will *not* take service with the Rowski of Donnerblitz."

"Wilt thou enter the household of the Prince of Cleves?" said the father of Helen, laughing, and not a little amused at the haughtiness of the humble archer.

"I would die for the Duke of Cleves and *his family*," said Otto, bowing low. He laid a particular and a tender emphasis on the word family. Helen knew what he meant. *She* was the family. In fact, her mother was no more, and her papa had no other offspring.

"What is thy name, good fellow," said the Prince, "that my steward may enrol thee?"

"Sir," said Otto, again blushing, "I am OTTO THE ARCHER."

CHAPTER XI

THE MARTYR OF LOVE

THE archers who had travelled in company with young Otto, gave a handsome dinner in compliment to the success of our hero; at which his friend distinguished himself as usual in the eating and drinking department. Squintoff, the Rowski bowman, declined to attend; so great was the envy of the brute at the youthful hero's superiority. As for Otto himself, he sat on the right hand of the chairman; but it was remarked that he could not eat. Gentle reader of my page! thou knowest why full well. He was too much in love to have any appetite; for though I myself, when labouring under that passion, never found my consumption of victuals diminish, yet remember our Otto was a hero of romance, and they *never* are hungry when they're in love.

The next day, the young gentleman proceeded to enrol himself in the corps of Archers of the Prince of Cleves, and with him came his attached squire, who vowed he never would leave him. As Otto threw aside his own elegant dress, and donned the livery of the House of Cleves, the noble Childe sighed not a little. 'Twas a splendid uniform, 'tis true, but still it *was* a livery, and one of his proud spirit ill bears another's cognisances. " They are the colours of the Princess, however," said he, consoling himself; "and what suffering would I not undergo for *her?*" As for Wolfgang, the squire, it may well be supposed that the good-natured low-born fellow had no such scruples; but he was glad enough to exchange for the pink hose, the yellow jacket, the pea-green cloak, and orange-tawny hat, with which the Duke's steward supplied him, the homely patched doublet of green which he had worn for years past.

" Look at yon two archers," said the Prince of Cleves to his guest the Rowski of Donnerblitz, as they were strolling on the battlements after dinner, smoking their cigars as usual. His Highness pointed to our two young friends, who were mounting guard for the first time. " See yon two bowmen—mark their bearing! One is the youth who beat thy Squintoff, and t'other, an I mistake not, won the third prize at the butts. Both wear the same uniform

—the colours of my house—yet, wouldst not swear that the one was but a churl, and the other a noble gentleman?"

"Which looks like the nobleman?" said the Rowski, as black as thunder.

"*Which?* why, young Otto, to be sure," said the Princess Helen eagerly. The young lady was following the pair; but under pretence of disliking the odour of the cigar, she had refused the Rowski's proffered arm, and was loitering behind with her parasol.

Her interposition in favour of her young *protégé* only made the black and jealous Rowski more ill-humoured. "How long is it, Sir Prince of Cleves," said he, "that the churls who wear your livery permit themselves to wear the ornaments of noble knights? Who but a noble dare wear ringlets such as yon springald's? Ho, archer!" roared he, "come hither, fellow." And Otto stood before him. As he came, and presenting arms stood respectfully before the Prince and his savage guest, he looked for one moment at the lovely Helen— their eyes met, their hearts beat simultaneously: and, quick, two little blushes appeared in the cheek of either. I have seen one ship at sea answering another's signal so.

While they are so regarding each other, let us just remind our readers of the great estimation in which the hair was held in the North. Only nobles were permitted to wear it long. When a man disgraced himself, a shaving was sure to follow. Penalties were inflicted upon villains or vassals who sported ringlets. See the works of Aurelius Tonsor; Hirsutus de Nobilitate Capillari; Rolandus de Oleo Macassari; Schnurrbart; Frisirische Alterthumskunde, &c.

"We must have those ringlets of thine cut, good fellow," said the Duke of Cleves good-naturedly, but wishing to spare the feelings of his gallant recruit. "'Tis against the regulation cut of my archer guard."

"Cut off my hair!" cried Otto, agonised.

"Ay, and thine ears with it, yokel," roared Donnerblitz.

"Peace, noble Eulenschreckenstein," said the Duke with dignity: "let the Duke of Cleves deal as he will with his own men-at-arms. And you, young sir, unloose the grip of thy dagger."

Otto, indeed, had convulsively grasped his snickersnee, with intent to plunge it into the heart of the Rowski; but his politer feelings overcame him. "The Count need not fear, my Lord," said he: "a lady is present." And he took off his orange-tawny cap and bowed low. Ah! what a pang shot through the heart of Helen, as she thought that those lovely ringlets must be shorn from that beautiful head!

Otto's mind was, too, in commotion. His feelings as a gentleman—let us add, his pride as a man—for who is not, let us ask, proud of a good head of hair?—waged war within his soul. He expostulated with the Prince. "It was never in my contemplation," he said, "on taking service, to undergo the operation of hair-cutting."

"Thou art free to go or stay, Sir Archer," said the Prince pettishly. "I will have no churls imitating noblemen in my service: I will bandy no conditions with archers of my guard."

"My resolve is taken," said Otto, irritated too in his turn. "I will——"

"What?" cried Helen, breathless with intense agitation.

"I will *stay*," answered Otto. The poor girl almost fainted with joy. The Rowski frowned with demoniac fury, and grinding his teeth and cursing in the horrible German jargon, stalked away. "So be it," said the Prince of Cleves, taking his daughter's arm— "and here comes Snipwitz, my barber, who shall do the business for you." With this the Prince too moved on, feeling in his heart not a little compassion for the lad ; for Adolf of Cleves had been handsome in his youth, and distinguished for the ornament of which he was now depriving his archer.

Snipwitz led the poor lad into a side-room, and there—in a word—operated upon him. The golden curls—fair curls that his mother had so often played with!—fell under the shears and round the lad's knees, until he looked as if he was sitting in a bath of sunbeams.

When the frightful act had been performed, Otto, who entered the little chamber in the tower ringleted like Apollo, issued from it as cropped as a charity-boy.

See how melancholy he looks, now that the operation is over! —And no wonder. He was thinking what would be Helen's opinion of him, now that one of his chief personal ornaments was gone. "Will she know me?" thought he ; "will she love me after this hideous mutilation?"

Yielding to these gloomy thoughts, and, indeed, rather unwilling to be seen by his comrades, now that he was so disfigured, the young gentleman had hidden himself behind one of the buttresses of the wall, a prey to natural despondency ; when he saw something which instantly restored him to good spirits. He saw the lovely Helen coming towards the chamber where the odious barber had performed upon him—coming forward timidly, looking round her anxiously, blushing with delightful agitation,—and presently seeing, as she thought, the coast clear, she entered the apartment. She stooped down, and ah! what was Otto's joy when he saw her pick up a beautiful golden lock of his hair, press it to her lips, and then hide it in her bosom! No carnation ever blushed so redly as Helen did when she came out after performing this feat. Then she hurried straightway to her own apartments in the castle, and Otto, whose first impulse was to come out from his hiding-place, and, falling at her feet, call heaven and earth to witness to his passion, with difficulty restrained his feelings and let her pass: but the love-stricken young hero was so delighted with this evident proof of reciprocated attachment, that all regret at losing his ringlets at once left him, and he vowed he would sacrifice not only his hair, but his head, if need were, to do her service.

That very afternoon, no small bustle and conversation took place in the castle, on account of the sudden departure of the Rowski of Eulenschreckenstein, with all his train and equipage. He went away in the greatest wrath, it was said, after a long and loud conversation with the Prince. As that potentate conducted his guest to the gate, walking rather demurely and shamefacedly by his side, as he gathered his attendants in the court, and there mounted his charger, the Rowski ordered his trumpets to sound, and scornfully flung a largesse of gold among the servitors and men-at-arms of the House of Cleves, who were marshalled in the court. "Farewell, Sir Prince," said he to his host: "I quit you now suddenly; but remember, it is not my last visit to the Castle of Cleves." And ordering his band to play "See the Conquering Hero comes," he clattered away through the drawbridge. The Princess Helen was not present at his departure; and the venerable Prince of Cleves looked rather moody and chapfallen when his guest left him. He visited all the castle defences pretty accurately that night, and inquired of his officers the state of the ammunition, provisions, &c. He said nothing; but the Princess Helen's maid did: and everybody knew that the Rowski had made his proposals, had been rejected, and, getting up in a violent fury, had called for his people, and sworn by his great gods that he would not enter the castle again until he rode over the breach, lance in hand, the conqueror of Cleves and all belonging to it.

No little consternation was spread through the garrison at the news: for everybody knew the Rowski to be one of the most intrepid and powerful soldiers in all Germany—one of the most skilful generals. Generous to extravagance to his own followers, he was ruthless to the enemy: a hundred stories were told of the dreadful barbarities exercised by him in several towns and castles which he had captured and sacked. And poor Helen had the pain of thinking, that in consequence of her refusal she was dooming all the men, women, and children of the principality to indiscriminate and horrible slaughter.

The dreadful surmises regarding a war received in a few days dreadful confirmation. It was noon, and the worthy Prince of Cleves was taking his dinner (though the honest warrior had had little appetite for that meal for some time past), when trumpets were heard at the gate ; and presently the herald of the Rowski of Donnerblitz, clad in a tabard on which the arms of the Count were blazoned, entered the dining-hall. A page bore a steel gauntlet on a cushion ; Bleu Sanglier had his hat on his head. The Prince of Cleves put on his own, as the herald came up to the chair of state where the sovereign sat.

"Silence for Bleu Sanglier," cried the Prince gravely. "Say your say, Sir Herald."

"In the name of the high and mighty Rowski, Prince of Donnerblitz, Margrave of Eulenschreckenstein, Count of Krötenwald, Schnauzestadt, and Galgenhügel, Hereditary Grand Corkscrew of the Holy Roman Empire—to you, Adolf the Twenty-third, Prince of Cleves, I, Bleu Sanglier, bring war and defiance. Alone, and lance to lance, or twenty to twenty in field or in fort, on plain or on mountain, the noble Rowski defies you. Here, or wherever he shall meet you, he proclaims war to the death between you and him. In token whereof, here is his glove." And taking the steel glove from the page, Blue Boar flung it clanging on the marble floor.

The Princess Helen turned deadly pale : but the Prince, with a good assurance, flung down his own glove, calling upon some one to raise the Rowski's : which Otto accordingly took up and presented, to him, on his knee.

"Boteler, fill my goblet," said the Prince to that functionary, who, clothed in tight black hose, with a white kerchief, and a napkin on his dexter arm stood obsequiously by his master's chair. The goblet was filled with Malvoisie : it held about three quarts ; a precious golden hanap carved by the cunning artificer, Benvenuto the Florentine.

"Drink, Bleu Sanglier," said the Prince, "and put the goblet in thy bosom. Wear this chain, furthermore, for my sake." And so saying, Prince Adolf flung a precious chain of emeralds round the herald's neck. "An invitation to battle was ever a welcome call to Adolf of Cleves." So saying, and bidding his people take good care of Bleu Sanglier's retinue, the Prince left the hall with his daughter. All were marvelling at his dignity, courage, and generosity.

But, though affecting unconcern, the mind of Prince Adolf was far from tranquil. He was no longer the stalwart knight who, in the reign of Stanislaus Augustus, had, with his naked fist, beaten a lion to death in three minutes : and alone had kept the postern of Peterwaradin for two hours against seven hundred Turkish janissaries, who were assailing it. Those deeds which had made the heir of Cleves famous were done thirty years syne. A free liver since he had come into his principality, and of a lazy turn, he had neglected the athletic exercises which had made him in youth so famous a champion, and indolence had borne its usual fruits. He tried his old battle-sword—that famous blade with which, in Palestine, he had cut an elephant-driver in two pieces, and split asunder the skull of the elephant which he rode. Adolf of Cleves could scarcely now lift the weapon over his head. He tried his armour. It was too tight for him. And the old soldier burst into tears when he found he could not buckle it. Such a man was not fit to encounter the terrible Rowski in single combat.

Nor could he hope to make head against him for any time in the field. The Prince's territories were small; his vassals proverbially lazy and peaceable; his treasury empty. The dismallest prospects were before him : and he passed a sleepless night writing to his friends for succour, and calculating with his secretary the small amount of the resources which he could bring to aid him against his advancing and powerful enemy.

Helen's pillow that evening was also unvisited by slumber. She lay awake thinking of Otto,—thinking of the danger and the ruin her refusal to marry had brought upon her dear papa. Otto, too, slept not : but *his* waking thoughts were brilliant and heroic : the noble Childe thought how he should defend the Princess, and win *los* and honour in the ensuing combat.

31

CHAPTER XII

AND now the noble Cleves began in good earnest to prepare his castle for the threatened siege. He gathered in all the available cattle round the property, and the pigs round many miles ; and a dreadful slaughter of horned and snouted animals took place,—the whole castle resounding with the lowing of the oxen and the squeaks of the gruntlings, destined to provide food for the garrison. These, when slain (her gentle spirit, of course, would not allow of her witnessing that disagreeable operation), the lovely Helen, with the assistance of her maidens, carefully salted and pickled. Corn was brought in in great quantities, the Prince paying for the same when he had money, giving bills when he could get credit, or occasionally, marry, sending out a few stout men-at-arms to forage, who brought in wheat without money or credit either. The charming Princess, amidst the intervals of her labours, went about encouraging the garrison, who vowed to a man they would die for a single sweet smile of hers ; and in order to make their inevitable sufferings as easy as possible to the gallant fellows, she and the apothecaries got ready a plenty of efficacious simples, and scraped a vast quantity of lint to bind their warriors' wounds withal. All the fortifications were strengthened ; the fosses carefully filled with spikes and water ; large stones placed over the gates, convenient to tumble on the heads of the assaulting parties ; and caldrons prepared, with furnaces to melt up pitch, brimstone, boiling oil, &c., wherewith hospitably to receive them. Having the keenest eye in the whole garrison, young Otto was placed on the topmost tower, to watch for the expected coming of the beleaguering host.

They were seen only too soon. Long ranks of shining spears were seen glittering in the distance, and the army of the Rowski soon made its appearance in battle's magnificently stern array. The tents of the renowned chief and his numerous warriors were pitched out of arrow-shot of the castle, but in fearful proximity ; and when his army had taken up its position, an officer with a flag of truce and a trumpet was seen advancing to the castle gate. It was the same herald who had previously borne his master's defiance to the Prince of Cleves. He came once more to the castle gate, and there proclaimed that the noble Count of Eulenschreckenstein was in arms without, ready to do battle with the Prince of Cleves, or his champion; that he would remain in arms for three days, ready for combat. If no man met him at the end of that period, he would deliver an assault, and would give quarter to no single soul in the garrison. So saying, the herald nailed his lord's gauntlet on the castle gate. As before, the Prince flung him over another glove from the wall; though how he was to defend himself from such a warrior, or get a champion, or resist the pitiless assault that must follow, the troubled old nobleman knew not in the least.

The Princess Helen passed the night in the chapel, vowing tons of wax candles to all the patron saints of the House of Cleves, if they would raise her up a defender.

But how did the noble girl's heart sink—how were her notions of the purity of man shaken within her gentle bosom, by the dread intelligence which reached her the next morning, after the defiance of the Rowski! At roll-call it was discovered that he on whom she principally relied—he whom her fond heart had singled out as her champion, had proved faithless!

Otto, the degenerate Otto, had fled! His comrade, Wolfgang, had gone with him. A rope was found dangling from the casement of their chamber, and they must have swum the moat and passed over to the enemy in the darkness of the previous night. "A pretty lad was this fair-spoken archer of thine!" said the Prince her father to her; "and a pretty kettle of fish hast thou cooked for the fondest of fathers." She retired weeping to her apartment. Never before had that young heart felt so wretched.

That morning, at nine o'clock, as they were going to breakfast, the Rowski's trumpets sounded. Clad in complete armour, and mounted on his enormous piebald charger, he came out of his pavilion, and rode slowly up and down in front of the castle. He was ready there to meet a champion.

Three times each day did the odious trumpet sound the same notes of defiance. Thrice daily did the steel-clad Rowski come forth challenging the combat. The first day passed, and there was no answer to his summons. The second day came and went, but no champion had risen to defend. The taunt of his shrill clarion remained without answer; and the sun went down upon the wretchedest father and daughter in all the land of Christendom.

The trumpets sounded an hour after sunrise, an hour after noon, and an hour before sunset. The third day came, but with it brought no hope. The first and second summons met no response. At five o'clock the old Prince called his daughter and blessed her. "I go to meet this Rowski," said he. "It may be we shall meet no more, my Helen—my child—the innocent cause of all this grief. If I shall fall to-night the Rowski's victim, 'twill be that life is nothing without honour." And so saying, he put into her hands a dagger, and bade her sheathe it in her own breast so soon as the terrible champion had carried the castle by storm.

This Helen most faithfully promised to do ; and her aged father retired to his armoury, and donned his ancient war-worn corselet. It had borne the shock of a thousand lances ere this, but it was now so tight as almost to choke the knightly wearer.

The last trumpet sounded—tantara ! tantara !—its shrill call rang over the wide plains, and the wide plains gave back no answer. Again !—but when its notes died away, there was only a mournful, an awful silence. "Farewell, my child," said the Prince, bulkily lifting himself into his battle-saddle. "Remember the dagger. Hark ! the trumpet sounds for the third time. Open, warders ! Sound, trumpeters ! and good Saint Bendigo guard the right."

But Puffendorff, the trumpeter, had not leisure to lift the trumpet to his lips : when, hark ! from without there came another note of another clarion !—a distant note at first, then swelling fuller. Presently, in brilliant variations, the full rich notes of the "Huntsman's Chorus" came clearly over the breeze ; and a thousand voices of the crowd gazing over the gate exclaimed, "A champion ! a champion ! "

And, indeed, a champion *had* come. Issuing from the forest came a knight and squire : the knight gracefully cantering an elegant cream-coloured Arabian of prodigious power—the squire mounted on an unpretending grey cob ; which, nevertheless, was an animal of considerable strength and sinew. It was the squire who blew the trumpet, through the bars of his helmet ; the knight's visor was completely down. A small prince's coronet of gold, from which rose three pink ostrich-feathers, marked the warrior's rank : his blank shield bore no cognisance. As gracefully poising his lance he rode into the green space where the Rowski's tents were pitched, the hearts of all present beat with anxiety, and the poor Prince of Cleves, especially, had considerable doubts about his new champion. "So slim a figure as that can never compete with Donnerblitz," said he, moodily, to his daughter ; "but whoever he be, the fellow puts a good face on it, and rides like a man. See, he has touched the Rowski's shield with the point of his lance ! By Saint Bendigo, a perilous venture ! "

The unknown knight had indeed defied the Rowski to the death, as the Prince of Cleves remarked from the battlement where he and his daughter stood to witness the combat; and so, having defied his enemy, the Incognito galloped round under the castle wall, bowing elegantly to the lovely Princess there, and then took his ground and waited for the foe. His armour blazed in the sunshine as he sat there, motionless, on his cream-coloured steed. He looked like one of those fairy knights one has read of—one of those celestial champions who decided so many victories before the invention of gunpowder.

The Rowski's horse was speedily brought to the door of his pavilion; and that redoubted warrior, blazing in a suit of magnificent brass armour, clattered into his saddle. Long waves of blood-red feathers bristled over his helmet, which was further ornamented by two huge horns of the aurochs. His lance was painted white and red, and he whirled the prodigious beam in the air and caught it with savage glee. He laughed when he saw the slim form of his antagonist; and his soul rejoiced to meet the coming battle. He dug his spurs into the enormous horse he rode: the enormous horse snorted, and squealed, too, with fierce pleasure. He jerked and curvetted him with a brutal playfulness, and after a few minutes turning and wheeling, during which everybody had leisure to admire the perfection of his equitation, he cantered round to a point exactly opposite his enemy, and pulled up his impatient charger.

The old Prince on the battlement was so eager for the combat, that he seemed quite to forget the danger which menaced himself, should his slim champion be discomfited by the tremendous Knight of Donnerblitz. "Go it!" said he, flinging his truncheon into the ditch; and at the word, the two warriors rushed with whirling rapidity at each other.

And now ensued a combat so terrible, that a weak female hand, like that of her who pens this tale of chivalry, can never hope to do justice to the terrific theme. You have seen two engines on the Great Western line rush past each other with a pealing scream? So rapidly did the two warriors gallop towards one another; the feathers of either streamed yards behind their backs as they converged. Their shock as they met was as that of two cannon-balls; the mighty horses trembled and reeled with the concussion; the lance aimed at the Rowski's helmet bore off the coronet, the horns, the helmet itself, and hurled them to an incredible distance: a piece of the Rowski's left ear was carried off on the point of the nameless warrior's weapon. How had he fared? His adversary's weapon had glanced harmless along the blank surface of his polished buckler: and the victory so far was with him.

The expression of the Rowski's face, as, bareheaded, he glared on his enemy with fierce bloodshot eyeballs, was one worthy of a demon. The imprecatory expressions which he made use of can never be copied by a feminine pen.

His opponent magnanimously declined to take advantage of the opportunity thus offered him of finishing the combat by splitting his opponent's skull with his curtal-axe, and, riding back to his starting-place, bent his lance's point to the ground, in token that he would wait until the Count of Eulenschreckenstein was helmeted afresh.

" Blessed Bendigo ! " cried the Prince, " thou art a gallant lance : but why didst not rap the Schelm's brain out ? "

" Bring me a fresh helmet ! " yelled the Rowski.   Another casque was brought to him by his trembling squire.

As soon as he had braced it, he drew his great flashing sword from his side, and rushed at his enemy, roaring hoarsely his cry of battle.   The unknown knight's sword was unsheathed in a moment, and at the next the two blades were clanking together the dreadful music of the combat !

The Donnerblitz wielded his with his usual savageness and activity.   It whirled round his adversary's head with frightful rapidity.   Now it carried away a feather of his plume ; now it shore off a leaf of his coronet.   The flail of the thresher does not fall more swiftly upon the corn.   For many minutes it was the Unknown's only task to defend himself from the tremendous activity of the enemy.

But even the Rowski's strength would slacken after exertion. The blows began to fall less thick anon, and the point of the unknown knight began to make dreadful play.   It found and pene-trated every joint of the Donnerblitz armour.   Now it nicked him in the shoulder, where the vambrace was buckled to the corselet ; now it bored a shrewd hole under the light brassart, and blood followed ; now, with fatal dexterity, it darted through the visor, and came back to the recover deeply tinged with blood.   A scream of rage followed the last thrust ; and no wonder :—it had penetrated the Rowski's left eye.

His blood was trickling through a dozen orifices ; he was almost choking in his helmet with loss of breath, and loss of blood, and rage.   Gasping with fury, he drew back his horse, flung his great sword at his opponent's head, and once more plunged at him, wielding his curtal-axe.

Then you should have seen the unknown knight employing the same dreadful weapon !   Hitherto he had been on his defence ; now he began the attack ; and the gleaming axe whirred in his hand like a reed, but descended like a thunderbolt !   " Yield ! yield ! Sir Rowski," shouted he in a calm clear voice.

A blow dealt madly at his head was the reply.   'Twas the last blow that the Count of Eulenschreckenstein ever struck in battle! The curse was on his lips as the crushing steel descended into his brain, and split it in two. He rolled like a log from his horse : his enemy's knee was in a moment on his chest, and the dagger of mercy at his throat, as the knight once more called upon him to yield.

But there was no answer from within the helmet. When it was withdrawn, the teeth were crunched together ; the mouth that should have spoken, grinned a ghastly silence : one eye still glared with hate and fury, but it was glazed with the film of death !

The red orb of the sun was just then dipping into the Rhine. The unknown knight, vaulting once more into his saddle, made a graceful obeisance to the Prince of Cleves and his daughter, without a word, and galloped back into the forest, whence he had issued an hour before sunset.

CHAPTER XIII

THE MARRIAGE

THE consternation which ensued on the death of the Rowski speedily sent all his camp-followers, army, &c., to the right-about. They struck their tents at the first news of his discomfiture; and each man laying hold of what he could, the whole of the gallant force which had marched under his banner in the morning had disappeared ere the sun rose.

On that night, as it may be imagined, the gates of the Castle of Cleves were not shut. Everybody was free to come in. Wine-butts were broached in all the courts; the pickled meat prepared in such lots for the siege was distributed among the people, who crowded to congratulate their beloved sovereign on his victory; and the Prince, as was customary with that good man, who never lost an opportunity of giving a dinner-party, had a splendid entertainment made ready for the upper classes, the whole concluding with a tasteful display of fireworks.

In the midst of these entertainments, our old friend the Count of Hombourg arrived at the castle. The stalwart old warrior swore by Saint Bugo that he was grieved the killing of the Rowski had been taken out of his hand. The laughing Cleves vowed by Saint Bendigo, Hombourg could never have finished off his enemy so satisfactorily as the unknown knight had just done.

But who was he? was the question which now agitated the bosom of these two old nobles. How to find him—how to reward the champion and restorer of the honour and happiness of Cleves? They agreed over supper that he should be sought for everywhere. Beadles were sent round the principal cities within fifty miles, and the description of the knight advertised in the *Journal de Francfort* and the *Allgemeine Zeitung*. The hand of the Princess Helen was solemnly offered to him in these advertisements, with the reversion of the Prince of Cleves's splendid though somewhat dilapidated property.

"But we don't know him, my dear papa," faintly ejaculated that young lady. "Some impostor may come in a suit of plain armour, and pretend that he was the champion who overcame the

Rowski (a prince who had his faults certainly, but whose attachment for me I can never forget) ; and how are you to say whether he is the real knight or not? There are so many deceivers in this world," added the Princess, in tears, "that one can't be too cautious now." The fact is, that she was thinking of the desertion of Otto in the morning ; by which instance of faithlessness her heart was well-nigh broken.

As for that youth and his comrade Wolfgang, to the astonishment of everybody at their impudence, they came to the archers' mess that night, as if nothing had happened ; got their supper, partaking both of meat and drink most plentifully ; fell asleep when their comrades began to describe the events of the day, and the admirable achievements of the unknown warrior ; and, turning into their hammocks, did not appear on parade in the morning until twenty minutes after the names were called.

When the Prince of Cleves heard of the return of these deserters, he was in a towering passion. "Where were you, fellows," shouted he, "during the time my castle was at its utmost need?"

Otto replied, "We were out on particular business."

"Does a soldier leave his post on the day of battle, sir?" exclaimed the Prince. "You know the reward of such—Death ! and death you merit. But you are a soldier only of yesterday, and yesterday's victory has made me merciful. Hanged you shall not be, as you merit—only flogged, both of you. Parade the men, Colonel Tickelstern, after breakfast, and give these scoundrels five hundred apiece."

You should have seen how young Otto bounded, when this information was thus abruptly conveyed to him. "Flog *me !*" cried he. "Flog Otto of——"

"Not so, my father," said the Princess Helen, who had been standing by during the conversation, and who had looked at Otto all the while with the most ineffable scorn. "Not so : although these *persons* have forgotten their duty" (she laid a particularly sarcastic emphasis on the word persons), "we have had no need of their services, and have luckily found *others* more faithful. You promised your daughter a boon, papa : it is the pardon of these two *persons*. Let them go, and quit a service they have disgraced : a mistress—that is, a master—they have deceived."

"Drum 'em out of the castle, Tickelstern ; strip their uniforms from their backs, and never let me hear of the scoundrels again." So saying, the old Prince angrily turned on his heel to breakfast, leaving the two young men to the fun and derision of their surrounding comrades.

The noble Count of Hombourg, who was taking his usual airing on the ramparts before breakfast, came up at this juncture, and asked what was the row? Otto blushed when he saw him, and turned away rapidly; but the Count, too, catching a glimpse of him, with a hundred exclamations of joyful surprise seized upon the lad, hugged him to his manly breast, kissed him most affectionately, and almost burst into tears as he embraced him. For, in sooth, the good Count had thought his godson long ere this at the bottom of the silver Rhine.

The Prince of Cleves, who had come to the breakfast-parlour window (to invite his guest to enter, as the tea was made), beheld this strange scene from the window, as did the lovely tea-maker likewise, with breathless and beautiful agitation. The old Count and the archer strolled up and down the battlements in deep conversation. By the gestures of surprise and delight exhibited by the former, 'twas easy to see the young archer was conveying some very strange and pleasing news to him; though the nature of the conversation was not allowed to transpire.

"A godson of mine," said the noble Count, when interrogated over his muffins. "I know his family; worthy people; sad scapegrace; ran away; parents longing for him; glad you did not flog him; devil to pay," and so forth. The Count was a man of few words, and told his tale in this brief artless manner. But why, at its conclusion, did the gentle Helen leave the room, her eyes filled with tears? She left the room once more to kiss a certain lock of yellow hair she had pilfered. A dazzling delicious thought, a strange wild hope, arose in her soul!

When she appeared again, she made some side-handed inquiries regarding Otto (with that gentle artifice oft employed by women); but he was gone. He and his companion were gone. The Count of Hombourg had likewise taken his departure, under pretext of particular business. How lonely the vast castle seemed to Helen, now that *he* was no longer there. The transactions of the last few days; the beautiful archer-boy; the offer from the Rowski (always an event in a young lady's life); the siege of the castle; the death of her truculent admirer: all seemed like a fevered dream to her: all was passed away, and had left no trace behind. No trace?— yes! one: a little insignificant lock of golden hair, over which the young creature wept so much that she put it out of curl; passing hours and hours in the summer-house where the operation had been performed.

On the second day (it is my belief she would have gone into a consumption and died of languor, if the event had been delayed a day longer) a messenger, with a trumpet, brought a letter in haste to the Prince of Cleves, who was, as usual, taking refreshment.

"To the High and Mighty Prince," &c., the letter ran. "The Champion who had the honour of engaging on Wednesday last with his late Excellency the Rowski of Donnerblitz, presents his compliments to H.S.H. the Prince of Cleves. Through the medium of the public prints the C. has been made acquainted with the flattering proposal of His Serene Highness relative to a union between himself (the Champion) and Her Serene Highness the Princess Helen of Cleves. The Champion accepts with pleasure that polite invitation, and will have the honour of waiting upon the Prince and Princess of Cleves about half-an-hour after the receipt of this letter."

"Tol lol de rol, girl," shouted the Prince with heartfelt joy. (Have you not remarked, dear friend, how often in novel-books, and on the stage, joy is announced by the above burst of insensate monosyllables?) "Tol lol de rol. Don thy best kirtle, child; thy husband will be here anon." And Helen retired to arrange her toilet for this awful event in the life of a young woman. When she returned, attired to welcome her defender, her young cheek was as pale as the white satin slip and orange sprigs she wore.

She was scarce seated on the daïs by her father's side, when a huge flourish of trumpets from without proclaimed the arrival of *the Champion.* Helen felt quite sick: a draught of ether was necessary to restore her tranquillity.

The great door was flung open. He entered,—the same tall warrior, slim and beautiful, blazing in shining steel. He approached the Prince's throne, supported on each side by a friend likewise in armour. He knelt gracefully on one knee.

"I come," said he, in a voice trembling with emotion, "to claim, as per advertisement, the hand of the lovely Lady Helen." And he held out a copy of the *Allgemeine Zeitung* as he spoke.

"Art thou noble, Sir Knight?" asked the Prince of Cleves.

"As noble as yourself," answered the kneeling steel.

"Who answers for thee?"

"I, Karl, Margrave of Godesberg, his father!" said the knight on the right hand, lifting up his visor.

"And I—Ludwig, Count of Hombourg, his godfather!" said the knight on the left, doing likewise.

The kneeling knight lifted up his visor now, and looked on Helen.

"*I knew it was,*" said she, and fainted as she saw Otto the Archer.

But she was soon brought to, gentles, as I have small need to tell ye. In a very few days after, a great marriage took place at Cleves, under the patronage of Saint Bugo, Saint Buffo, and Saint Bendigo. After the marriage ceremony, the happiest and handsomest pair in the world drove off in a chaise-and-four, to pass the honeymoon at Kissingen. The Lady Theodora, whom we left locked up in her convent a long while since, was prevailed upon to come back to Godesberg, where she was reconciled to her husband. Jealous of her daughter-in-law, she idolised her son, and spoiled all her little grandchildren. And so all are happy, and my simple tale is done.

I read it in an old old book, in a mouldy old circulating library. 'Twas written in the French tongue, by the noble Alexandre Dumas; but 'tis probable that he stole it from some other, and that the other had filched it from a former tale-teller. For nothing is new under the sun. Things die and are reproduced only. And so it is that the forgotten tale of the great Dumas reappears under the signature of   THERESA MACWHIRTER.

WHISTLEBINKIE, N.B. : *December 1.*

CHARACTER SKETCHES

CHARACTER SKETCHES

CAPTAIN ROOK AND MR. PIGEON

THE statistic-mongers and dealers in geography have calculated to a nicety how many quartern loaves, bars of iron, pigs of lead, sacks of wool, Turks, Quakers, Methodists, Jews, Catholics, and Church-of-England men are consumed or produced in the different countries of this wicked world : I should like to see an accurate table showing the rogues and dupes of each nation ; the calculation would form a pretty matter for a philosopher to speculate upon. The mind loves to repose and broods benevolently over this expanded theme. What thieves are there in Paris, O heavens ! and what a power of rogues with pigtails and mandarin buttons at Pekin ! What crowds of swindlers are there at this very moment pursuing their trade at St. Petersburg ! how many scoundrels are saying their prayers alongside of Don Carlos ! how many scores are jobbing under the pretty nose of Queen Christina ! what an inordinate number of rascals is there, to be sure, puffing tobacco and drinking flat small-beer in all the capitals of Germany ; or else, without a rag to their ebony backs, swigging quass out of calabashes, and smeared over with palm-oil, lolling at the doors of clay huts in the sunny city of Timbuctoo ! It is not necessary to make any more topographical allusions, or, for illustrating the above position, to go through the whole Gazetteer ; but he is a bad philosopher who has not all these things in mind, and does not in his speculations or his estimate of mankind duly consider and weigh them. And it is fine and consolatory to think that thoughtful Nature, which has provided sweet flowers for the humming bee; fair running streams for glittering fish ; store of kids, deer, goats, and other fresh meat for roaring lions ; for active cats, mice ; for mice, cheese, and so on ; establishing throughout the whole of her realm the great doctrine that where a demand is, there will be a supply (see the romances of Adam Smith, Malthus, and Ricardo, and the philosophical works of Miss Martineau) : I say it is consolatory to think that, as Nature has provided flies for the food of fishes, and flowers for bees, so she has created fools for rogues ; and thus the scheme is consistent throughout. Yes, observation, with extensive view, will discover Captain Rooks all over the world, and Mr. Pigeons made for their benefit. Wherever shines the sun, you are sure to find Folly basking in it ; and knavery is the shadow at Folly's heels.

It is not, however, necessary to go to St. Petersburg or Pekin for rogues (and in truth I don't know whether the Timbuctoo Captain Rooks prefer cribbage or billiards). "We are not birds," as the Irishman says, "to be in half-a-dozen places at once ; " so let us pretermit all considerations of rogues in other countries, examining only those who flourish under our very noses. I have travelled much, and seen many men and cities ; and, in truth, I think that our country of England produces the best soldiers, sailors, razors, tailors, brewers, hatters, and rogues of all. Especially there is no cheat like an English cheat. Our society produces them in the greatest numbers as well as of the greatest excellence. We supply all Europe with them. I defy you to point out a great city of the Continent where half-a-dozen of them are not to be found : proofs of our enterprise and samples of our home manufacture. Try Rome, Cheltenham, Baden, Toeplitz, Madrid, or Tzarskoselo : I have been in every one of them, and give you my honour that the Englishman is the best rascal to be found in all : better than your eager Frenchman ; your swaggering Irishman, with a red velvet waistcoat and red whiskers ; your grave Spaniard, with horrid goggle eyes and profuse diamond shirt-pins ; your tallow-faced German baron, with white moustache and double chin, fat, pudgy, dirty fingers, and great gold thumb-ring ; better even than your nondescript Russian—swindler and spy as he is by loyalty and education—the most dangerous antagonist we have. Who has the best coat even at Vienna ? who has the neatest britzska at Baden ? who drinks the best champagne at Paris? Captain Rook, to be sure, of Her Britannic Majesty's service :—he *has* been of the service, that is to say, but often finds it convenient to sell out.

The life of a blackleg, which is the name contemptuously applied to Captain Rook in his own country, is such an easy, comfortable, careless, merry one, that I can't conceive why all the world do not turn Captain Rooks ; unless, maybe, there are some mysteries and difficulties in it which the vulgar know nothing of, and which only men of real genius can overcome. Call on Captain Rook in the day (in London, he lives about St. James's ; abroad, he has the very best rooms in the very best hotels), and you will find him at one o'clock dressed in the very finest *robe-de-chambre,* before a breakfast-table covered with the prettiest patties and delicacies possible; smoking, perhaps, one of the biggest meerschaum pipes you ever saw; reading, possibly, the *Morning Post*, or a novel (he has only one volume in his whole room, and that from a circulating library); or having his hair dressed; or talking to a tailor about waistcoat patterns; or drinking soda-water with a glass of sherry; all this he does every morning, and it does not seem very difficult, and lasts until three. At three, he goes to a horse-dealer's, and lounges there for half-an-hour; at four he is to be seen at the window of his Club; at five, he is cantering and curvetting in Hyde Park with one or two more (he does not know any ladies, but has many male acquaintances: some, stout old gentlemen riding cobs, who knew his family, and give him a surly grunt of recognition; some, very young lads with pale dissolute faces, little moustaches perhaps, or at least little tufts on their chin, who hail him eagerly as a man of fashion): at seven, he has a dinner at "Long's" or at the "Clarendon"; and so to bed very likely at five in the morning, after a quiet game of whist, broiled bones, and punch.

Perhaps he dines early at a tavern in Covent Garden; after which, you will see him at the theatre in a private box (Captain Rook affects the Olympic a good deal). In the box, besides himself, you will remark a young man—very young—one of the lads who spoke to him in the Park this morning, and a couple of ladies: one shabby, melancholy, raw-boned, with numberless small white ringlets, large hands and feet, and a faded light-blue silk gown; she has a large cap, trimmed with yellow, and all sorts of crumpled flowers and greasy blonde lace; she wears large gilt earrings, and sits back, and nobody speaks to her, and she to nobody, except to say, "Law, Maria, how well you *do* look to-night; there's a man opposite has been staring at you this three hours; I'm blest if it isn't him as we saw in the Park, dear!"

"I wish, Hanna, you'd 'old your tongue, and not bother me about the men. You don't believe Miss 'Ickman, Freddy, do you?" says Maria, smiling fondly on Freddy. Maria is sitting in front: she says she is twenty-three, though Miss Hickman knows very well she is thirty-one (Freddy is just of age). She wears a purple velvet gown, three different gold bracelets on each arm, as many rings on each finger of each hand; to one is hooked a gold smelling-bottle: she has an enormous fan, a laced pocket-handkerchief, a Cashmere shawl, which is continually falling off, and exposing, very unnecessarily, a pair of very white shoulders: she talks loud, always lets her playbill drop into the pit, and smells most pungently of Mr. Delcroix's shop. After this description it is not at all necessary to say who Maria is: Miss Hickman is her companion, and they live

32

together in a very snug little house in Mayfair, which has just been new-furnished *à la Louis Quatorze* by Freddy, as we are positively informed. It is even said that the little carriage, with two little white ponies, which Maria drives herself in such a fascinating way through the Park, was purchased for her by Freddy too; ay, and that Captain Rook got it for him—a great bargain, of course.

Such is Captain Rook's life. Can anything be more easy? Suppose Maria says, " Come home, Rook, and heat a cold chicken with us, and a glass of hiced champagne ; " and suppose he goes, and after chicken—just for fun—Maria proposes a little chicken-hazard ;—she only plays for shillings, while Freddy, a little bolder, won't mind half-pound stakes himself. Is there any great harm in all this ? Well, after half-an-hour Maria grows tired, and Miss Hickman has been nodding asleep in the corner long ago ; so off the two ladies set, candle in hand.

" D—n it, Fred," says Captain Rook, pouring out for that young gentleman his fifteenth glass of champagne, " what luck you are in, if you did but know how to back it ! "

What more natural, and even kind, of Rook than to say this? Fred is evidently an inexperienced player ; and every experienced player knows that there is nothing like backing your luck. Freddy does. Well, fortune is proverbially variable ; and it is not at all surprising that Freddy, after having had so much luck at the commencement of the evening, should have the tables turned on him at some time or other.—Freddy loses.

It is deuced unlucky, to be sure, that he should have won all the little *coups* and lost all the great ones ; but there is a plan which the commonest play-man knows, an infallible means of retrieving yourself at play : it is simply doubling your stake. Say, you lose a guinea : you bet two guineas, which, if you win, you win a guinea and your original stake : if you lose, you have but to bet four guineas on the third stake, eight on the fourth, sixteen on the fifth, thirty-two on the sixth, and so on. It stands to reason that you cannot lose *always ;* and the very first time you win, all your losings are made up to you. There is but one drawback to this infallible process : if you begin at a guinea, double every time you lose, and lose fifteen times, you will have lost exactly sixteen thousand three hundred and eighty-four guineas ; a sum which probably exceeds the amount of your yearly income :—mine is considerably under that figure.

Freddy does not play this game then, yet; but being a poor-spirited creature, as we have seen he must be by being afraid to win, he is equally poor-spirited when he begins to lose : he is frightened ; that is, increases his stakes, and backs his ill-luck : when a man does this, it is all over with him.

When Captain Rook goes home (the sun is peering through the shutters of the little drawing-room in Curzon Street, and the ghastly footboy—oh, how bleared his eyes look as he opens the door !)— when Captain Rook goes home, he has Freddy's I.O.U.'s in his pocket to the amount, say, of three hundred pounds. Some people say that Maria has half of the money when it is paid ; but this I don't believe : is Captain Rook the kind of fellow to give up a purse when his hand has once clawed hold of it ?

Be this, however, true or not, it concerns us very little. The Captain goes home to King Street, plunges into bed much too tired to say his prayers, and wakes the next morning at twelve to go over such another day as we have just chalked out for him. As for Freddy, not poppy, nor mandragora, nor all the soda-water at the chemist's can ever medicine him to that sweet sleep which he might have had but for his loss. "*If* I had but played my king of hearts," sighed Fred, "and kept back my trump ; but there's no standing against a fellow who turns up a king seven times running : if I *had* even but pulled up when Thomas (curse him !) brought up that infernal Curaçoa punch, I should have saved a couple of hundred," and so on go Freddy's lamentations. O luckless Freddy ! dismal Freddy ! silly *gaby* of a Freddy ! you are hit now, and there is no cure for you but bleeding you almost to death's door. The homœo-pathic maxim of *similia similibus*—which means, I believe, that you are to be cured "by a hair of the dog that bit you"—must be put in practice with regard to Freddy—only not in homœopathic infini-tesimal doses : no hair of the dog that bit him : but *vice versá*, the dog of the hair that tickled him. Freddy has begun to play—a mere trifle at first, but he must play it out ; he must go the whole dog now, or there is no chance for him. He must play until he can play no more ; he *will* play until he has not a shilling left to play with, when, perhaps, he may turn out an honest man, though the odds are against him : the betting is in favour of his being a swindler always ; a rich or a poor one, as the case may be. I need not tell Freddy's name, I think, now ; it stands on his card :—

Mr. FREDERICK PIGEON,

LONG'S HOTEL.

I have said the chances are that Frederick Pigeon, Esquire, will become a rich or a poor swindler, though the first chance, it must be confessed, is very remote. I once heard an actor, who could not write, speak, or even read English ; who was not fit for any trade in the world, and had not the " nous " to keep an apple-stall, and scarcely even enough sense to make a Member of Parliament ; I once, I say, heard an actor,—whose only qualifications were a large pair of legs, a large voice, and a very large neck,—curse his fate and his profession, by which, do what he would, he could only make eight guineas a week. " No men," said he, with a great deal of justice, " were so ill paid as ' dramatic artists ' ; they laboured for nothing all their youth, and had no provision for old age." With this, he sighed, and called for (it was on a Saturday night, the forty-ninth glass of brandy-and-water which he had drunk in the course of the week.

The excitement of his profession, I make no doubt, caused my friend Claptrap to consume this quantity of spirit-and-water, besides beer in the morning, after rehearsal ; and I could not help musing over his fate. It is a hard one. To eat, drink, work a little, and be jolly ; to be paid twice as much as you are worth, and then to go to ruin ; to drop off the tree when you are swelled out, seedy, and over-ripe ; and to lie rotting in the mud underneath, until at last you mingle with it.

Now, badly as the actor is paid (and the reader will the more readily pardon the above episode, because, in reality, it has nothing to do with the subject in hand), and luckless as his fate is, the lot of the poor blackleg is cast lower still. You never hear of a rich gambler ; or of one who wins in the end. Where does all the money go to which is lost among them ? Did you ever play a game at loo for sixpences ? At the end of the night a great many of those small coins have been lost, and in consequence, won. But ask the table all round : one man has won three shillings ; two have neither lost nor won ; one rather thinks he has lost ; and the three others have lost two pounds each. Is not this the fact, known to every-body who indulges in round games, and especially the noble game of loo ? I often think that the devil's books, as cards are called, are let out to us from Old Nick's circulating library, and that he lays his paw upon a certain part of the winnings, and carries it off privily : else, what becomes of all the money ?

For instance, there is the gentleman whom the newspapers call " a noble earl of sporting celebrity " ;—if he has lost a shilling, according to the newspaper accounts, he has lost fifty millions : he drops fifty thousand pounds at the Derby, just as you and I would lay down twopence-halfpenny for half an ounce of Macabaw. Who has won these millions ? Is it Mr. Crockford, or Mr. Bond, or Mr. Salon-des-Étrangers ? (I do not call these latter gentlemen gamblers, for their speculation is a certainty); but who wins his money, and everybody else's money who plays and loses? Much money is staked in the absence of Mr. Crockford; many notes are given without the interference of the Bonds; there are hundreds of thousands of gamblers who are *étrangers* even to the Salon-des-Étrangers.

No, my dear sir, it is not in the public gambling-houses that the money is lost; it is not in them that your virtue is chiefly in danger. Better by half lose your income, your fortune, or your master's money, in a decent public hell, than in the private society of such men as my friend Captain Rook. But we are again and again digressing: the point is, is the Captain's trade a good one, and does it yield tolerably good interest for outlay and capital?

To the latter question first:—at this very season of May, when the Rooks are very young, have you not, my dear friend, often tasted them in pies?—they are then so tender that you cannot tell the difference between them and pigeons. So, in like manner, our Rook has been in his youth undistinguishable from a pigeon. He does as he has been done by: yea, he has been plucked as even now he plucks his friend Mr. Frederick Pigeon. Say that he began the world with ten thousand pounds: every maravedi of this is gone; and may be considered as the capital, which he has sacrificed to learn his trade. Having spent £10,000, then, on an annuity o £650, he must look to a larger interest for his money—say fifteen hundred, two thousand, or three thousand pounds, decently to repay his risk and labour. Besides the money sunk in the first place, his profession requires continual annual outlays, as thus—

Horses, carriages (including Epsom, Goodwood, Ascot, &c.)	£500	0	0
Lodgings, servants, and board	350	0	0
Watering-places, and touring	300	0	0
Dinners to give	150	0	0
Pocket-money	150	0	0
Gloves, handkerchiefs, perfumery, and tobacco (very moderate)	150	0	0
Tailor's bills (£100 say, never paid) . . .	0	0	0
TOTAL . . .	£1,600	0	0

I defy any man to carry on the profession in a decent way under the above sum: ten thousand sunk, and sixteen hundred annual expenses; no, it is *not* a good profession: it is *not* good interest for one's money; it is *not* a fair remuneration for a gentleman of birth industry, and genius; and my friend Claptrap, who growls about *his* pay, may bless his eyes that he was not born a gentleman and bred up to such an unprofitable calling as this. Considering his trouble, his outlay, his birth, and breeding, the Captain is most wickedly and basely rewarded. And when he is obliged to retreat, when his hand trembles, his credit is fallen, his bills laughed at by every money-lender in Europe, his tailors rampant and inexorable —in fact, when the *coupe* of life will *sauter* for him no more— who will help the play-worn veteran? As Mitchel sings after Aristophanes—

> " In glory he was seen, when his years as yet *were green;*
> But now when his dotage is on him,
> God help him ;—for no eye of those who pass him by
> Throws a look of compassion upon him."

Who indeed will help him?—not his family, for he has bled his father, his uncle, his old grandmother; he has had slices out of his sisters' portions, and quarrelled with his brothers-in-law; the old people are dead; the young ones hate him, and will give him nothing. Who will help him?—not his friends: in the first place, my dear sir, a man's friends very seldom do: in the second place, it is Captain Rook's business not to keep, but to give up his friends. His acquaintances do not last more than a year: the time, namely, during which he is employed in plucking them; then they part. Pigeon has not a single feather left to his tail, and how should he help Rook, whom, *au reste*, he has learned to detest most cordially, and has found out to be a rascal? When Rook's ill day comes, it is simply because he has no more friends; he has exhausted them all, plucked every one as clean as the palm of your hand. And to arrive at this conclusion, Rook has been spending sixteen hundred a year, and the prime of his life, and has moreover sunk ten thousand pounds! *Is* this a proper reward for a gentleman? I say it is a sin and a shame that an English gentleman should be allowed thus to drop down the stream without a single hand to help him.

The moral of the above remarks I take to be this: that black-legging is as bad a trade as can be; and so let parents and guardians look to it, and not apprentice their children to such a villainous scurvy way of living.

It must be confessed, however, that there are some individuals who have for the profession such a natural genius, that no entreaties or example of parents will keep them from it, and no restraint or occupation occasioned by another calling. They do what Christians do not do: they leave all to follow their master the Devil; they cut friends, families, and good, thriving, profitable trades, to put

up with this one, that is both unthrifty and unprofitable. They
are in regiments: ugly whispers about certain midnight games at
blind-hookey, and a few odd bargains in horseflesh, are borne
abroad, and Cornet Rook receives the gentlest hint in the world
that he had better sell out. They are in counting-houses with a
promise of partnership, for which papa is to lay down a handsome
premium; but the firm of Hobbs, Bobbs & Higgory can never
admit a young gentleman who is a notorious gambler, is much
oftener at the races than at his desk, and has bills daily falling
due at his private banker's. The father, that excellent old man,
Sam Rook, so well known on 'Change in the war-time, discovers,
at the end of five years, that his son has spent rather more
than the four thousand pounds intended for his partnership, and
cannot, in common justice to his other thirteen children, give him
a shilling more. A pretty pass for flash young Tom Rook, with
four horses in stable, a protemporaneous Mrs. Rook, very likely,
in an establishment near the Regent's Park, and a bill for three
hundred and seventy-five pounds coming due on the fifth of next
month.

Sometimes young Rook is destined to the bar: and I am glad
to introduce one of these gentlemen and his history to the notice
of the reader. He was the son of an amiable gentleman, the
Reverend Athanasius Rook, who took high honours at Cambridge in
the year '1: was a fellow of Trinity in the year '2: and so continued a fellow and tutor of the College until a living fell vacant,
on which he seized. It was only two hundred and fifty pounds a
year; but the fact is, Athanasius was in love. Miss Gregory, a
pretty, demure, simple governess at Miss Mickle's establishment for
young ladies in Cambridge (where the reverend gentleman used often
of late to take his tea), had caught the eye of the honest College
tutor: and in Trinity walks, and up and down the Trumpington
Road, he walked with her (and another young lady, of course),
talked with her, and told his love.

Miss Gregory had not a rap, as might be imagined; but she
loved Athanasius with her whole soul and strength, and was the
most orderly, cheerful, tender, smiling, bustling little wife that ever a
country parson was blest withal. Athanasius took a couple of pupils
at a couple of hundred guineas each, and so made out a snug income;
ay, and laid by for a rainy day—a little portion for Harriet, when
she should grow up and marry, and a help for Tom at college and
at the bar. For you must know there were two little Rooks now
growing in the rookery; and very happy were father and mother
I can tell you, to put meat down their tender little throats. Oh,
if ever a man was good and happy, it was Athanasius; if ever a

woman was happy and good, it was his wife : not the whole parish, not the whole county, not the whole kingdom, could produce such a snug rectory, or such a pleasant *ménage*.

Athanasius's fame as a scholar, too, was great; and as his charges were very high, and as he received but two pupils, there was, of course, much anxiety among wealthy parents to place their children under his care. Future squires, bankers, yea, lords and dukes, came to profit by his instructions, and were led by him gracefully over the "Asses' bridge" into the sublime regions of mathematics, or through the syntax into the pleasant paths of classic lore.

In the midst of these companions, Tom Rook grew up; more fondled and petted, of course, than they; cleverer than they; as handsome, dashing, well instructed a lad for his years as ever went to College to be a senior wrangler, and went down without any such honour.

Fancy, then, our young gentleman installed at College, whither his father has taken him, and with fond veteran recollections has surveyed hall and grass-plots, and the old porter, and the old fountain, and the old rooms in which he used to live. Fancy the sobs of good little Mrs. Rook, as she parted with her boy; and the tears of sweet pale Harriet, as she clung round his neck, and brought him (in a silver paper, slobbered with many tears) a little crimson silk purse (with two guineas of her own in it, poor thing !). Fancy all this, and fancy young Tom, sorry too, but yet restless and glad, panting for the new life opening upon him; the freedom, the joy of the manly struggle for fame, which he vows he will win. Tom Rook, in other words, is installed at Trinity College, attends lectures, reads at home, goes to chapel, uses wine-parties moderately, and bids fair to be one of the topmost men of his year.

Tom goes down for the Christmas vacation. (What a man he is grown, and how his sister and mother quarrel which shall walk with him down the village; and what stories the old gentleman lugs out with his old port, and how he quotes Æschylus, to be sure !) The pupils are away too, and the three have Tom in quiet. Alas ! I fear the place has grown a little too quiet for Tom : how-ever, he reads very stoutly of mornings; and sister Harriet peeps with a great deal of wonder into huge books of scribbling-paper, containing many strange diagrams, and complicated arrangements of x's and y's.

May comes, and the College examinations; the delighted parent receives at breakfast, on the 10th of that month, two letters, as follows :—

From the Rev. Solomon Snorter to the Rev. Athanasius Rook.

"TRINITY, *May* 10.

"DEAR CREDO,*—I wish you joy. Your lad is the best man of his year, and I hope in four more to see him at our table. In classics he is, my dear friend, *facile princeps ;* in mathematics he was run hard (*entre nous*) by a lad of the name of Snick, a Westmoreland man and a sizer. We must keep up Thomas to his mathematics, and I have no doubt we shall make a fellow and a wrangler of him.

"I send you his college bill, £105, 10s. : rather heavy, but this is the first term, and that you know is expensive : I shall be glad to give you a receipt for it. By the way, the young man is *rather* too fond of amusement, and lives with a very expensive set. Give him a lecture on this score.—Yours,   SOL. SNORTER."

Next comes Mr. Tom Rook's own letter : it is long, modest ; we only give the postscript :—

"*P.S.*—Dear Father, I forgot to say that, as I live in the very best set in the University (Lord Bagwig, the Duke's eldest son you know, vows he will give me a living), I have been led into one or two expenses which will frighten you : I lost £30 to the Honourable Mr. Deuceace (a son of Lord Crabs) at Bagwig's, the other day, at dinner ; and owe £54 more for desserts and hiring horses, which I can't send into Snorter's bill.† Hiring horses is so deuced expensive ; next term I must have a nag of my own, that's positive."

The Reverend Athanasius read the postscript with much less gusto than the letter : however, Tom has done his duty, and the old gentleman won't balk his pleasure ; so he sends him £100, with a "God bless you !" and Mamma adds, in a postscript, that "he must always keep well with his aristocratic friends, for he was made only for the best society."

A year or two passes on : Tom comes home for the vacations ; but Tom has sadly changed ; he has grown haggard and pale. At the second year's examination (owing to an unlucky illness) Tom was not classed at all ; and Snick, the Westmoreland man, has carried everything before him. Tom drinks more after dinner than his father likes ; he is always riding about and dining in the

* This is most probably a joke on the Christian name of Mr. Rook.

† It is, or was, the custom for young gentlemen at Cambridge to have unlimited credit with tradesmen, whom the College tutors paid, and then sent the bills to the parents of the young men.

neighbourhood, and coming home, quite odd, his mother says—ill-humoured, unsteady on his feet, and husky in his talk.　The Reverend Athanasius begins to grow very very grave : they have high words, even the father and son ; and oh ! how Harriet and her mother tremble and listen at the study-door when these disputes are going on !

The last term of Tom's undergraduateship arrives : he is in ill health, but he will make a mighty effort to retrieve himself for his degree ; and early in the cold winter's morning,—late, late at night —he toils over his books : and the end is that, a month before the examination, Thomas Rook, Esquire, has a brain fever, and Mrs. Rook, and Miss Rook, and the Reverend Athanasius Rook, are all lodging at the "Hoop," an inn in Cambridge town, and day and night round the couch of poor Tom.

．　　．　　．　　．　　．　　．　　．

O sin, woe, repentance !　O touching reconciliation and burst of tears on the part of son and father, when one morning at the parsonage, after Tom's recovery, the old gentleman produces a bundle of receipts, and says, with a broken voice, "There, boy, don't be vexed about your debts.　Boys will be boys, I know, and I have paid all demands."　Everybody cries in the house at this news ; the mother and daughter most profusely, even Mrs. Stokes the old housekeeper, who shakes master's hand, and actually kisses Mr. Tom.

Well, Tom begins to read a little for his fellowship, but in vain ; he is beaten by Mr. Snick, the Westmoreland man.　He has no hopes of a living ; Lord Bagwig's promises were all moonshine.　Tom must go to the bar ; and his father, who has long left off taking pupils, must take them again, to support his son in London.

Why tell you what happens when there ?　Tom lives at the West End of the town, and never goes near the Temple ; Tom goes to Ascot and Epsom along with his great friends ; Tom has a long bill with Mr. Rymell, another long bill with Mr. Nugee ; he gets into the hands of the Jews—and his father rushes up to London on the outside of the coach to find Tom in a spunging-house in Cursitor Street—the nearest approach he has made to the Temple during his three years' residence in London.

I don't like to tell you the rest of the history.　The Reverend Athanasius was not immortal, and he died a year after his visit to the spunging-house, leaving his son exactly one farthing, and his wife one hundred pounds a year, with remainder to his daughter.　But, Heaven bless you ! the poor things would never allow Tom to want while they had plenty, and they sold out and sold out the three thousand pounds, until, at the end of three years, there did not remain one single stiver of them ; and now Miss Harriet is a governess, with sixty pounds a year, supporting her mother, who lives upon fifty.

As for Tom, he is a regular *leg* now—leading the life already described. When I met him last it was at Baden, where he was on a professional tour, with a carriage, a courier, a valet, a confederate, and a case of pistols. He has been in five duels, he has killed a man who spoke lightly about his honour ; and at French or English hazard, at billiards, at whist, at loo, écarté, blind hookey, drawing straws, or beggar-my-neighbour, he will cheat you—cheat you for a hundred pounds or for a guinea, and murder you afterwards if you like.

Abroad, our friend takes military rank, and calls himself Captain Rook ; when asked of what service, he says he was with Don Carlos or Queen Christina ; and certain it is that he was absent for a couple of years nobody knows where : he may have been with General Evans, or he may have been at the Sainte-Pélagie in Paris, as some people vow he was.

We must wind up this paper with some remarks concerning poor little Pigeon. Vanity has been little Pigeon's failing through life. He is a linendraper's son, and has been left with money : and the silly fashionable works that he has read, and the silly female relatives that he has—(N.B. All young men with money have silly flattering she-relatives)—and the silly trips that he has made to watering-places, where he has scraped acquaintance with the Honourable Tom Mountcoffee-house, Lord Ballyhooly, the celebrated German Prince, Sweller Mobskau, and their like (all Captain Rooks in their way), have been the ruin of him.

I have not the slightest pity in the world for little Pigeon. Look at him ! See in what absurd finery the little prig is dressed. Wine makes his poor little head ache, but he will drink because it is manly. In mortal fear he puts himself behind a curvetting camelopard of a cab-horse ; or perched on the top of a prancing dromedary, is borne through Rotten Row, when he would give the world to be on his own sofa, or with his own mamma and sisters, over a quiet pool of commerce and a cup of tea. How riding does scarify his poor little legs, and shake his poor little sides ! Smoking, how it does turn his little stomach inside out ; and yet smoke he will : Sweller Mobskau smokes ; Mountcoffee-house don't mind a cigar ; and as for Ballyhooly, he will puff you a dozen in a day, and says very truly that Pontet won't supply *him* with near such good ones as he sells Pigeon. The fact is, that Pontet vowed seven years ago not to give his Lordship a sixpence more credit ; and so the good-natured nobleman always helps himself out of Pigeon's box.

On the shoulders of these aristocratic individuals, Mr. Pigeon is carried into certain clubs, or perhaps we should say he walks into them by the aid of these "legs." But they keep him always to themselves. Captain Rooks must rob in companies; but of course, the greater the profits, the fewer the partners must be. Three are positively requisite, however, as every reader must know who has played a game at whist: Number One to be Pigeon's partner, and curse his stars at losing, and propose higher play, and "settle" with Number Two; Number Three to transact business with Pigeon, and drive him down to the City to sell out. We have known an instance where, after a very good night's work, Number Three has bolted with the winnings altogether, but the practice is dangerous; not only disgraceful to the profession, but it cuts up your own chance afterwards, as no one will act with you. There is only one occasion on which such a manœuvre is allowable. Many are sick of the profession, and desirous to turn honest men: in this case, when you can get a good *coup*, five thousand say, bolt without scruple. One thing is clear, the other men *must* be mum, and you can live at Vienna comfortably on the interest of five thousand pounds.

Well, then, in the society of these amiable confederates little Pigeon goes through that period of time which is necessary for the purpose of plucking him. To do this you must not, in most cases, tug at the feathers so as to hurt him, else he may be frightened, and hop away to somebody else: nor, generally speaking, will the feathers come out so easily at first as they will when he is used to it, and then they drop in handfuls. Nor need you have the least scruple in so causing the little creature to moult artificially: if you don't, somebody else will: a Pigeon goes into the world fated, as Chateaubriand says—

"Pigeon, il va subir le sort de tout pigeon."

He *must* be plucked, it is the purpose for which nature has formed him: if you, Captain Rook, do not perform the operation on a green table lighted by two wax-candles, and with two packs of cards to operate with, some other Rook will: are there not railroads, and Spanish bonds, and bituminous companies, and Cornish tin mines, and old dowagers with daughters to marry? If you leave him, Rook of Birchin Lane will have him as sure as fate: if Rook of Birchin Lane don't hit him, Rook of the Stock Exchange will blaze away both barrels at him, which, if the poor trembling flutterer escape, he will fly over and drop into the rookery, where dear old swindling Lady Rook and her daughters will find him and nestle him in their bosoms, and in that soft place pluck him until he turns out as naked as a cannon-ball.

Be not thou scrupulous, O Captain! Seize on Pigeon; pluck him gently but boldly; but, above all, never let him go. If he is a stout cautious bird, of course *you* must be more cautious; if he is excessively silly and scared, perhaps the best way is just to take him round the neck at once, and strip the whole stock of plumage from his back.

The feathers of the human pigeon being thus violently abstracted from him, no others supply their place : and yet I do not pity him. He is now only undergoing the destiny of pigeons, and is, I do believe, as happy in his plucked as in his feathered state. He cannot purse out his breast, and bury his head, and fan his tail, and strut in the sun as if he were a turkey-cock. Under all those fine airs and feathers, he was but what he is now, a poor little meek, silly, cowardly bird, and his state of pride is not a whit more natural to him than his fallen condition. He soon grows used to it. He is too great a coward to despair; much too mean to be frightened because he must live by doing meanness. He is sure, if he cannot fly, to fall somehow or other on his little miserable legs : on these he hops about, and manages to live somewhere in his own mean way. He has but a small stomach, and doesn't mind what food he puts into it. He spunges on his relatives; or else just before his utter ruin he marries and has nine children (and such a family *always* lives); he turns bully most likely, takes to drinking, and beats his wife, who supports him, or takes to drinking too ; or he gets a little place, a very little place : you hear he has some tide-waitership, or is clerk to some new milk company, or is lurking about a newspaper. He dies, and a subscription is raised for the Widow Pigeon, and we look no more to find a likeness of him in his children, who are as a new race. Blessed are ye little ones, for ye are born in poverty and may bear it, or surmount it and die rich. But woe to the pigeons of this earth, for they are born rich that they may die poor.

The end of Captain Rook—for we must bring both him and the paper to an end—is not more agreeable, but somewhat more manly and majestic than the conclusion of Mr. Pigeon. If you walk over to the Queen's Bench Prison, I would lay a wager that a dozen such are to be found there in a moment. They have a kind of Lucifer look with them, and stare at you with fierce, twinkling, crow-footed eyes ; or grin from under huge grizzly moustaches, as they walk up and down in their tattered brocades. What a dreadful activity is that of a madhouse, or a prison !—a dreary flagged courtyard, a long dark room, and the inmates of it, like the inmates of the menagerie cages, ceaselessly walking up and down ! Mary Queen of Scots says very touchingly :—

> " Pour mon mal estranger
> Je ne m'arreste en place ;
> Mais, j'en ay beau changer
> Si ma douleur n'efface ! "

Up and down, up and down—the inward woe seems to spur the body onwards; and I think in both madhouse and prison you will find plenty of specimens of our Captain Rook. It is fine to mark him under the pressure of this woe, and see how fierce he looks when stirred up by the long pole of memory. In these asylums the Rooks end their lives ; or, more happy, they die miserably in a miserable provincial town abroad, and for the benefit of coming Rooks they commonly die early ; you as seldom hear of an old Rook (practising his trade) as of a rich one. It is a short-lived trade : not merry, for the gains are most precarious, and perpetual doubt and dread are not pleasant accompaniments of a profession :— not agreeable either, for though Captain Rook does not mind *being* a scoundrel, no man likes to be considered as such, and as such, he knows very well, does the world consider Captain Rook : not profitable, for the expenses of the trade swallow up all the profits of it, and in addition leave the bankrupt with certain habits that have become as nature to him, and which, to live, he must gratify. I know no more miserable wretch than our Rook in his autumn days, at dismal Calais or Boulogne, or at the Bench yonder, with a whole load of diseases and wants, that have come to him in the course of his profession : the diseases and wants of sensuality, always pampered, and now agonising for lack of its unnatural food ; the mind, which *must* think now, and has only bitter recollections, mortified ambitions, and unavailing scoundrelisms to con over ! Oh, Captain Rook ! what nice "chums" do you take with you into prison ! what pleasant companions of exile follow you over the *fines patriæ*, or attend, the only watchers, round your miserable death-bed !

My son, be not a Pigeon in thy dealings with the world :—but it is better to be a Pigeon than a Rook.

THE FASHIONABLE AUTHORESS

PAYING a visit the other day to my friend Timson, who, I need not tell the public, is editor of that famous evening paper, the **** (and let it be said that there is no more profitable acquaintance than a gentleman in Timson's situation, in whose office, at three o'clock daily, you are sure to find new books, lunch, magazines, and innumerable tickets for concerts and plays) : going, I say, into Timson's office, I saw on the table an immense paper cone or funnel, containing a bouquet of such a size, that it might be called a bosquet, wherein all sorts of rare geraniums, luscious magnolias, stately dahlias, and other floral produce were gathered together—a regular flower-stack.

Timson was for a brief space invisible, and I was left alone in the room with the odours of this tremendous bow-pot, which filled the whole of the inky, smutty, dingy apartment with an agreeable incense. "O rus ! quando te aspiciam ?" exclaimed I, out of the Latin Grammar, for imagination had carried me away to the country, and I was about to make another excellent and useful quotation (from the 14th book of the *Iliad*, madam), concerning "ruddy lotuses, and crocuses, and hyacinths," when all of a sudden Timson appeared. His head and shoulders had, in fact, been engulfed in the flowers, among which he might be compared to any Cupid, butterfly, or bee. His little face was screwed up into such an expression of comical delight and triumph, that a Methodist parson would have laughed at it in the midst of a funeral sermon.

"What are you giggling at ?" said Mr. Timson, assuming a high aristocratic air.

"Has the goddess Flora made you a present of that bower, wrapped up in white paper ; or did it come by the vulgar hands of yonder gorgeous footman, at whom all the little printer's devils are staring in the passage ?"

"Stuff!" said Timson, picking to pieces some rare exotic, worth at the very least fifteenpence ; "a friend, who knows that Mrs. Timson and I are fond of these things, has sent us a nosegay, that's all."

I saw how it was. "Augustus Timson," exclaimed I sternly,

"the Pimlicoes have been with you; if that footman did not wear the Pimlico plush, ring the bell and order me out; if that three-cornered billet lying in your snuff-box has not the Pimlico seal to it, never ask me to dinner again."

"Well, if it *does*," says Mr. Timson, who flushed as red as a peony, "what is the harm? Lady Fanny Flummery may send flowers to her friends, I suppose? The conservatories at Pimlico House are famous all the world over, and the Countess promised me a nosegay the very last time I dined there."

"Was that the day when she gave you a box of bonbons for your darling little Ferdinand?"

"No, another day."

"Or the day when she promised you her carriage for Epsom Races?"

"No."

"Or the day when she hoped that her Lucy and your Barbara-Jane might be acquainted, and sent to the latter from the former a new French doll and tea-things?"

"Fiddlestick!" roared out Augustus Timson, Esquire: "I wish you wouldn't come bothering here. I tell you that Lady Pimlico is my friend—my friend, mark you, and I will allow no man to abuse her in my presence; I say again *no man!*" wherewith Mr. Timson plunged both his hands violently into his breeches-pockets, looked me in the face sternly, and began jingling his keys and shillings about.

At this juncture (it being about half-past three o'clock in the afternoon), a one-horse chaise drove up to the **** office (Timson lives at Clapham, and comes in and out in this machine), a one-horse chaise drove up; and amidst a scuffling and crying of small voices, good-humoured Mrs. Timson bounced into the room.

"Here we are, deary," said she: "we'll walk to the Mery-weathers; and I've told Sam to be in Charles Street at twelve with the chaise: it wouldn't do, you know, to come out of the Pimlico box and have the people cry, 'Mrs. Timson's carriage!' for old Sam and the chaise."

Timson, to this loving and voluble address of his lady, gave a peevish puzzled look towards the stranger, as much as to say, "*He's* here."

"La, Mr. Smith! and how *do* you do?—So rude—I didn't see you: but the fact is, we are all in *such* a bustle! Augustus has got Lady Pimlico's box for the 'Puritani' to-night, and I vowed I'd take the children."

Those young persons were evidently from their costume prepared for some extraordinary festival. Miss Barbara-Jane, a young lady of six years old, in a pretty pink slip and white muslin, her dear little poll bristling over with papers, to be removed previous to the play; while Master Ferdinand had a pair of nankeens (I can recollect Timson in them in the year 1825—a great buck), and white silk stockings, which belonged to his mamma. His frill was very large and very clean, and he was fumbling perpetually at a pair of white kid gloves, which his mamma forbade him to assume before the opera.

And "Look here!" and "Oh, precious!" and "Oh, my!" were uttered by these worthy people as they severally beheld the vast bouquet, into which Mrs. Timson's head flounced, just as her husband's had done before.

"I must have a greenhouse at the Snuggery, that's positive, Timson, for I'm passionately fond of flowers—and how kind of Lady Fanny! Do you know her Ladyship, Mr. Smith?"

"Indeed, madam, I don't remember having ever spoken to a lord or a lady in my life."

Timson smiled in a supercilious way. Mrs. Timson exclaimed, "La, how odd! Augustus knows ever so many. Let's see, there's the Countess of Pimlico and Lady Fanny Flummery; Lord Doldrum (Timson touched up his Travels, you know); Lord Gasterton, Lord Guttlebury's eldest son; Lady Pawpaw (they say she ought not to be visited, though); Baron Strum—Strom—Strumpf——"

What the baron's name was I have never been able to learn; for here Timson burst out with a "Hold your tongue, Bessy!" which stopped honest Mrs. Timson's harmless prattle altogether, and obliged that worthy woman to say meekly, "Well, Gus, I did not think there was any harm in mentioning your acquaintance." Good soul! it was only because she took pride in her Timson that she loved to enumerate the great names of the persons who did him honour. My friend the editor was, in fact, in a cruel position, looking foolish before his old acquaintance, stricken in that unfortunate sore point in his honest good-humoured character. The man adored the aristocracy, and had that wonderful respect for a lord which, perhaps the observant reader may have remarked, especially characterises men of Timson's way of thinking.

In old days at the club (we held it in a small public-house near the Coburg Theatre, some of us having free admissions to that place of amusement, and some of us living for convenience in the immediate neighbourhood of one of His Majesty's prisons in that quarter) —in old days, I say, at our spouting and toasted-cheese club, called "The Forum," Timson was called Brutus Timson, and not Augustus, in consequence of the ferocious republicanism which characterised him, and his utter scorn and hatred of a bloated do-nothing aristoc-

33

racy. His letters in the *Weekly Sentinel*, signed "Lictor," must be remembered by all our readers : he advocated the repeal of the Corn Laws, the burning of machines, the rights of labour, &c. &c., wrote some pretty defences of Robespierre, and used seriously to avow, when at all in liquor, that in consequence of those "Lictor" letters, Lord Castlereagh had tried to have him murdered, and thrown over Blackfriars Bridge.

By what means Augustus Timson rose to his present exalted position it is needless here to state ; suffice it, that in two years he was completely bound over neck-and-heels to the bloodthirsty aristocrats, hereditary tyrants, &c. One evening he was asked to dine with a Secretary of the Treasury (the **** is Ministerial, and has been so these forty-nine years) ; at the house of that Secretary of the Treasury he met a lord's son : walking with Mrs. Timson in the Park next Sunday, that lord's son saluted him. Timson was from that moment a slave, had his coats made at the West End, cut his wife's relations (they are dealers in marine stores, and live at Wapping), and had his name put down at two Clubs.

Who was the lord's son ? Lord Pimlico's son, to be sure, the Honourable Frederick Flummery, who married Lady Fanny Foxy, daughter of Pitt Castlereagh, second Earl of Reynard, Kilbrush Castle, county Kildare. The Earl had been Ambassador in '14 : Mr. Flummery, attaché : he was twenty-one at that time, with the sweetest tuft on his chin in the world. Lady Fanny was only four-and-twenty, just jilted by Prince Scoronconcolo, the horrid man who had married Miss Solomonson with a plum. Fanny had nothing—Frederick had about seven thousand pounds less. What better could the young things do than marry ? Marry they did, and in the most delicious secrecy. Old Reynard was charmed to have an opportunity of breaking with one of his daughters for ever, and only longed for an occasion never to forgive the other nine.

A wit of the Prince's time, who inherited and transmitted to his children a vast fortune of genius, was cautioned on his marriage to be very economical. "Economical!" said he ; "my wife has nothing, and I have nothing : I suppose a man can't live under *that!*" Our interesting pair, by judiciously employing the same capital, managed, year after year, to live very comfortably, until, at last, they were received into Pimlico House by the dowager (who has it for her life), where they live very magnificently. Lady Fanny gives the most magnificent entertainment in London, has the most magnificent equipage, and a very fine husband ; who has his equipage as fine as her Ladyship's ; his seat in the omnibus, while her Ladyship is in the second tier. They say he plays a good deal—ay, and pays, too, when he loses.

And how, pr'ythee? Her Ladyship is a FASHIONABLE AUTHO-
RESS. She has been at this game for fifteen years; during which
period she has published forty-five novels, edited twenty-seven new
magazines, and I don't know how many annuals, besides publishing
poems, plays, desultory thoughts, memoirs, recollections of travel,
and pamphlets without number. Going one day to church, a lady,
whom I knew by her Leghorn bonnet and red ribbons, *ruche* with
poppies and marigolds, brass ferronnière, great red hands, black silk
gown, thick shoes, and black silk stockings; a lady, whom I knew,
I say, to be a devotional cook, made a bob to me just as the psalm
struck up, and offered me a share of her hymn-book. It was—

"HEAVENLY CHORDS;

A COLLECTION OF

Sacred Strains,

SELECTED, COMPOSED, AND EDITED, BY THE

LADY FRANCES JULIANA FLUMMERY."

—Being simply a collection of heavenly chords robbed from the
lyres of Watts, Wesley, Brady and Tate, &c.; and of sacred strains
from the rare collection of Sternhold and Hopkins. Out of this,
cook and I sang; and it is amazing how much our fervour was
increased by thinking that our devotions were directed by a lady
whose name was in the Red Book.

The thousands of pages that Lady Fanny Flummery has covered
with ink exceed all belief. You must have remarked, madam, in
respect of this literary fecundity, that your amiable sex possesses
vastly greater capabilities than we do; and that while a man is
painfully labouring over a letter of two sides, a lady will produce a
dozen pages, crossed, dashed, and so beautifully neat and close, as
to be well-nigh invisible. The readiest of ready pens has Lady
Fanny; her Pegasus gallops over hot-pressed satin so as to distance
all gentlemen riders; like Camilla, it scours the plain—of Bath,
and never seems punished or fatigued; only it runs so fast that it
often leaves all sense behind it; and there it goes on, on, scribble,
scribble, scribble, never flagging until it arrives at that fair winning-
post on which is written "FINIS," or "THE END"; and shows that
the course, whether it be of novel, annual, poem, or what not, is
complete.

Now, the author of these pages doth not pretend to describe
the inward thoughts, ways, and manner of being of my Lady

Fanny, having made before that humiliating confession, that lords and ladies are personally unknown to him; so that all milliners, butchers' ladies, dashing young clerks, and apprentices, or other persons who are anxious to cultivate a knowledge of the aristocracy, had better skip over this article altogether.   But he hath heard it whispered, from pretty good authority, that the manners and customs of these men and women resemble, in no inconsiderable degree, the habits and usages of other men and women whose names are unrecorded by Debrett.   Granting this, and that Lady Fanny is a woman pretty much like another, the philosophical reader will be content that we rather consider her Ladyship in her public capacity, and examine her influence upon mankind in general.

Her person, then, being thus put out of the way, her works, too, need not be very carefully sifted and criticised ; for what is the use of peering into a millstone, or making calculations about the figure 0 ? The woman has not, in fact, the slightest influence upon literature for good or for evil : there are a certain number of fools whom she catches in her flimsy traps ; and why not ? They are made to be humbugged, or how should we live ? Lady Fanny writes everything : that is, nothing. Her poetry is mere wind ; her novels, stark nought ; her philosophy, sheer vacancy : how should she do any better than she does ? how could she succeed if she *did* do any better ? If she did write well, she would not be Lady Fanny ; she would not be praised by Timson and the critics, because she would be an honest woman, and would not bribe them. Nay, she would probably be written down by Timson & Co., because, being an honest woman, she utterly despised them and their craft.

We have said what she writes for the most part.   Individually, she will throw off any number of novels that Messrs. Soap and Diddle will pay for ; and collectively, by the aid of self and friends, scores of " Lyrics of Loveliness," " Beams of Beauty," " Pearls of Purity," &c.   Who does not recollect the success which her " Pearls of the Peerage " had ? She is going to do the " Beauties of the Baronetage " ; then we shall have the " Daughters of the Dustmen," or some such other collection of portraits.   Lady Fanny has around her a score of literary gentlemen, who are bound to her, body and soul : give them a dinner, a smile from an opera-box, a wave of the hand in Rotten Row, and they are hers, neck and heels.   *Vides, mi fili*, &c.   See, my son, with what a very small dose of humbug men are to be bought.   I know many of these individuals : there is my friend M'Lather, an immense pudgy man : I saw him one day walking through Bond Street in company with an enormous ruby breast-pin. "Mac!" shouted your humble servant, "that is a Flummery ruby;" and Mac hated and cursed us ever after. Presently came little Fitch, the artist: he was rigged out in an illuminated velvet waistcoat—Flummery again—"There's only one like it in town," whispered Fitch to me confidentially, "and Flummery has that." To be sure, Fitch had given, in return, half-a-dozen of the prettiest drawings in the world. "I wouldn't charge for them, you know," he says: "for hang it, Lady Fanny is my friend." Oh, Fitch, Fitch!

Fifty more instances could be adduced of her Ladyship's ways of bribery. She bribes the critics to praise her, and the writers to write for her; and the public flocks to her as it will to any other tradesman who is properly puffed. Out comes the book: as for its merits, we may allow, cheerfully, that Lady Fanny has no lack of that natural *esprit* which every woman possesses; but here praise stops. For the style, she does not know her own language; but, in revenge, has a smattering of half-a-dozen others. She interlards her works with fearful quotations from the French, fiddle-faddle extracts from Italian operas, German phrases fiercely mutilated, and a scrap or two of bad Spanish; and upon the strength of these murders, she calls herself an authoress. To be sure there is no such word as authoress. If any young nobleman or gentleman of Eton College, when called upon to indite a copy of verses in praise of Sappho, or the Countess of Dash, or Lady Charlotte What-d'ye-call-'em, or the Honourable Mrs. Somebody, should fondly imagine that he might apply to those fair creatures the title of *auctrix*—I pity that young nobleman's or gentleman's case. Doctor Wordsworth and assistants would swish that error out of him in a way that need not here be mentioned. Remember it henceforth, ye writeresses—there is no such word as authoress. *Auctor*, madam, is the word. "Optima tu proprii nominis auctor eris;" which, of course, means that you are, by your proper name, an author, not an authoress. The line is in Ainsworth's Dictionary, where anybody may see it.

This point is settled then: there is no such word as authoress. But what of that? Are authoresses to be bound by the rules of grammar? The supposition is absurd. We don't expect them to know their own language; we prefer rather the little graceful pranks and liberties they take with it. When, for instance, a celebrated authoress, who wrote a Diaress, calls somebody the prototype of his own father, we feel an obligation to her Ladyship; the language feels an obligation; it has a charm and a privilege with which it was never before endowed: and it is manifest, that if we call ourselves ante-types of our grandmothers—can prophesy what we had for dinner yesterday, and so on, we get into a new range of thought, and discover sweet regions of fancy and poetry, of which the mind hath never even had a notion until now.

It may be then considered as certain that an authoress *ought* not to know her own tongue. Literature and politics have this privilege in common, that any ignoramus may excel in both. No apprenticeship is required, that is certain; and if any gentleman doubts, let us refer him to the popular works of the present day, where, if he find a particle of scholarship, or any acquaintance with any books in any language, or if he be disgusted by any absurd, stiff, old-fashioned notions of grammatical propriety, we are ready to qualify our assertion. A friend of ours came to us the other day in great trouble. His dear little boy, who had been for some months attaché to the stables of Mr. Tilbury's establishment, took a fancy to the corduroy breeches of some other gentleman employed in the same emporium—appropriated them, and afterwards disposed of them for a trifling sum to a relation—I believe his uncle. For this harmless freak, poor Sam was absolutely seized, tried at Clerkenwell Sessions, and condemned to six months' useless rotatory labour at the House of Correction. "The poor fellow was bad enough before, sir," said his father, confiding in our philanthropy; "he picked up such a deal of slang among the stable-boys; but if you could hear him since he came from the mill! he knocks you down with it, sir. I am afraid, sir, of his becoming a regular prig: for though he's a 'cute chap, can read and write, and is mighty smart and handy, yet no one will take him into service, on account of that business of the breeches!"

"What, sir!" exclaimed we, amazed at the man's simplicity: "*such* a son, and you don't know what to do with him! a 'cute fellow, who can write, who has been educated in a stable-yard, and has had six months' polish in a university—I mean a prison—and you don't know what to do with him? Make a *fashionable novelist* of him, and be hanged to you!" And proud am I to say that that young man, every evening, after he comes home from his work (he has taken to street-sweeping in the day, and I don't advise him to relinquish a certainty)—proud am I to say that he devotes every evening to literary composition, and is coming out with a novel, in numbers, of the most fashionable kind.

This little episode is only given for the sake of example : *par exemple*, as our authoress would say, who delights in French of the very worst kind. The public likes only the extremes of society, and votes mediocrity vulgar. From the Author they will take nothing but Fleet Ditch; from the Authoress, only the very finest of rose-water. I have read so many of her Ladyship's novels, that, egad! now I don't care for anything under a marquis. Why the deuce should we listen to the intrigues, the misfortunes, the virtues, and conversations of a couple of countesses, for instance, when we can have duchesses for our money? What's a baronet? pish! pish! that great coarse red fist in his scutcheon turns me sick! What's a baron? a fellow with only one more ball than a pawnbroker; and, upon my conscience, just as common. Dear Lady Fanny, in your next novel, give us no more of these low people; nothing under strawberry leaves, for the mercy of Heaven! Suppose, now, you write us

"ALBERT;

OR,

WHISPERINGS AT WINDSOR.

BY THE LADY FRANCES FLUMMERY."

There is a subject—fashionable circles, curious revelations, exclusive excitement, &c. To be sure, you *must* here introduce a viscount, and that is sadly vulgar; but we will pass him for the sake of the ministerial *portefeuille*, which is genteel. Then you might do "Leopold; or, the Bride of Neuilly"; "The Victim of Würtemberg"; "Olga; or, the Autocrat's Daughter" (a capital title); "Henri! or, Rome in the Nineteenth Century"; we can fancy the book, and a sweet paragraph about it in Timson's paper.

"Henri, by Lady Frances Flummery.—Henri! Who can he be? a little bird whispers in our ear, that the gifted and talented Sappho of our hemisphere has discovered some curious particulars in the life of *a certain young chevalier*, whose appearance at Rome had so frightened the Court of the Tu–l–ries. Henri de B–rd—ux is of an age when the *young god* can shoot his darts into the bosom with fatal accuracy; and if the Marchesina degli Spinachi (whose portrait our lovely authoress has sung with a *kindred hand*) be as beauteous as she is represented (and as all who have visited in the exclusive circles of the Eternal City say she is), no wonder at her effect upon the Pr–nce. *Verbum sap.* We hear that a few copies are still remaining. The enterprising publishers, Messrs. Soap and Diddle, have announced, we see, several other works by the same accomplished pen."

This paragraph makes its appearance, in small type, in the ****, by the side, perhaps, of a disinterested recommendations of bear's-grease, or some remarks on the extraordinary cheapness of plate in Cornhill. Well, two or three days after, my dear

Timson, who has been asked to dinner, writes in his own hand, and causes to be printed in the largest type, an article to the following effect :—

"HENRI.

"BY LADY F. FLUMMERY.

"This is another of the graceful evergreens which the fair fingers of Lady Fanny Flummery are continually strewing upon our path. At once profound and caustic, truthful and passionate, we are at a loss whether most to admire the manly grandeur of her Ladyship's mind, or the exquisite nymph-like delicacy of it. Strange power of fancy! Sweet enchantress, that rules the mind at will: stirring up the utmost depths of it into passion and storm, or wreathing and dimpling its calm surface with countless summer smiles. As a great Bard of old Time has expressed it, what do we not owe to woman?

"What do we not owe her? More love, more happiness, more calm of vexed spirit, more truthful aid, and pleasant counsel; in joy, more delicate sympathy; in sorrow, more kind companionship. We look into her cheery eyes, and in those wells of love, care drowns; we listen to her siren voice, and, in that balmy music, banished hopes come winging to the breast again."

This goes on for about three-quarters of a column: I don't pretend to understand it; but with flowers, angels, Wordsworth's poems, and the old dramatists, one can never be wrong, I think: and though I have written the above paragraphs myself, and don't understand a word of them, I can't, upon my conscience, help thinking that they are mighty pretty writing. After, then, this has gone on for about three-quarters of a column (Timson does it in spare minutes, and fits it to any book that Lady Fanny brings out), he proceeds to particularise, thus :—

"The griding excitement which thrills through every fibre of the soul as we peruse these passionate pages, is almost too painful to bear. Nevertheless, one drains the draughts of poesy to the dregs, so deliciously intoxicating is its nature. We defy any man who begins these volumes to quit them ere he has perused each line. The plot may be briefly told as thus :—Henri, an exiled Prince of Franconia (it is easy to understand the flimsy allegory), arrives at Rome, and is presented to the sovereign Pontiff. At a feast given in his honour at the Vatican, a dancing girl (the loveliest creation that ever issued from poet's brain) is introduced, and exhibits some specimens of her art. The young Prince is instantaneously smitten with the charms of the Saltatrice; he breathes into her ear the accents of his love, and is listened to with favour. He has, however, a rival, and a powerful one. The POPE has already cast his eye upon the Apulian maid, and burns with lawless passion. One of the grandest scenes ever writ, occurs between the rivals. The Pope offers to Castanetta every temptation; he will even resign his crown and marry her: but she refuses. The Prince can make no such offers; he cannot wed her: 'The blood of Borbone,' he says, 'may not be thus misallied.' He determines to avoid her. In despair, she throws herself off the Tarpeian rock; and the Pope becomes a maniac. Such is an outline of this tragic tale.

"Besides this fabulous and melancholy part of the narrative, which is unsurpassed, much is written in the gay and sparkling style for which our lovely author is unrivalled. The sketch of the Marchesina degli Spinachi and her lover, the Duca di Gammoni, is delicious; and the intrigue between the beautiful Princess Kalbsbraten and Count Bouterbrod is exquisitely painted: everybody, of course, knows who these characters are. The discovery of the manner in which Kartoffeln, the Saxon envoy, poisons the Princess's dishes, is only a graceful and real repetition of a story which was agitated throughout all the diplomatic circles last year. Schinken, the Westphalian, must not be forgotten; nor Olla, the Spanish spy. How does Lady Fanny Flummery, poet as she is, possess a sense of the ridiculous and a keenness of perception which would do honour to a Rabelais or a Rochefoucauld? To those who ask this question, we have one reply, and that an example:—Not among women 'tis true; for till the Lady Fanny came among us, woman never soared so high. Not among women, indeed!—but in comparing her to that great spirit for whom our veneration is highest and holiest, we offer no dishonour to his shrine:—in saying that he who wrote of Romeo and Desdemona might have drawn Castanetta and Enrico, we utter but the truthful expressions of our hearts; in asserting that so long as SHAKSPEARE lives, so long will FLUMMERY endure; in declaring that he who rules in all hearts, and over all spirits and all climes, has found a congenial spirit, we do but justice to Lady Fanny—justice to him who sleeps by Avon!'"

With which we had better, perhaps, conclude. Our object has been, in descanting upon the Fashionable Authoress, to point out the influence which her writing possesses over society, rather than to criticise her life. The former is quite harmless: and we don't pretend to be curious about the latter. The woman herself is not so blamable; it is the silly people who cringe at her feet that do the mischief, and, gulled themselves, gull the most gullible of publics. Think you, O Timson, that her Ladyship asks you for your *beaux yeux* or your wit? Fool! you do think so, or try and think so; and yet you know she loves not you, but the **** newspaper. Think, little Fitch, in your fine waistcoat, how dearly you have paid for it! Think, M'Lather, how many smirks, and lies, and columns of good three-halfpence-a-line matter that big garnet pin has cost you! The woman laughs at you, man—you, who fancy that she is smitten with you—laughs at your absurd pretensions, your way of eating fish at dinner, your great hands, your eyes, your whiskers, your coat, and your strange north-country twang. Down with this Delilah! Avaunt, O Circe! giver of poisonous feeds. To your natural haunts, ye gentlemen of the press! if bachelors, frequent your taverns, and be content. Better is Sally the waiter and the first cut of the joint, than a dinner of four courses and humbug therewith. Ye who are married, go to your homes; dine not with those persons who scorn your wives. Go not forth to parties, that ye may act Tom Fool for the amusement of my Lord and my Lady; but play your natural follies among your natural friends. Do this for a few years, and the Fashionable Authoress is extinct. O Jove, what a prospect! She, too, has retreated to her own natural calling, being as much out of place in a book as you, my dear M'Lather, in a drawing-room. Let milliners look up to her; let Howell and James swear by her; let simpering dandies caper about her car; let her write poetry if she likes, but only for the most exclusive circles; let mantua-makers puff her—but not men: let such things be, and the Fashionable Authoress is no more! Blessed, blessed thought! No more fiddle-faddle novels! no more namby-pamby poetry! no more fribble "Blossoms of Loveliness"! When will you arrive, O happy Golden Age?

THE ARTISTS

IT is confidently stated that there was once a time when the quarter of Soho was thronged by the fashion of London. Many wide streets are there in the neighbourhood, stretching cheerfully towards Middlesex Hospital in the north, bounded by Dean Street in the west, where the Lords and Ladies of William's time used to dwell,—till in Queen Anne's time, Bloomsbury put Soho out of fashion, and Great Russell Street became the pink of the mode.

Both these quarters of the town have submitted to the awful rule of Nature, and are now to be seen undergoing the dire process of decay. Fashion has deserted Soho, and left her in her gaunt lonely old age. The houses have a vast, dingy, mouldy, dowager look. No more beaux, in mighty periwigs, ride by in gilded clattering coaches; no more lacqueys accompany them, bearing torches, and shouting for precedence. A solitary policeman paces these solitary streets, the only dandy in the neighbourhood. You hear the milkman yelling his milk with a startling distinctness, and the clack of a servant-girl's pattens sets people a-staring from the windows.

With Bloomsbury we have here nothing to do; but as genteel stockbrokers inhabit the neighbourhood of Regent's Park,—as lawyers have taken possession of Russell Square,—so Artists have seized upon the desolate quarter of Soho. They are to be found in great numbers in Berners Street. Up to the present time naturalists have never been able to account for this mystery of their residence. What has a painter to do with Middlesex Hospital? He is to be found in Charlotte Street, Fitzroy Square. And why? Philosophy cannot tell, any more than why milk is found in a cocoa-nut.

Look at Newman Street. Has earth, in any dismal corner of her great round face, a spot more desperately gloomy? The windows are spotted with wafers, holding up ghastly bills, that tell you the house is "To Let." Nobody walks there—not even an old-clothesman; the first inhabited house has bars to the windows, and bears the name of "Ahasuerus, officer to the Sheriff of Middlesex"; and here, above all places, must painters take up their quarters,—day by day must these reckless people pass Ahasuerus's treble gate. There was my poor friend Tom Tickner (who did those sweet things for "The Book of Beauty"). Tom, who could not pay his washer-woman, lived opposite the bailiff's; and could see every miserable debtor or greasy Jew writ-bearer that went in or out of his door. The street begins with a bailiff's, and ends with a hospital. I wonder how men live in it, and are decently cheerful, with this gloomy double-barrelled moral pushed perpetually into their faces. Here, however, they persist in living, no one knows why; owls may still be found roosting in Netley Abbey, and a few Arabs are to be seen at the present minute in Palmyra.

The ground-floors of the houses where painters live are mostly make-believe shops, black empty warehouses, containing fabulous goods. There is a sedan-chair opposite a house in Rathbone Place, that I have myself seen every day for forty-three years. The house has commonly a huge india-rubber-coloured door, with a couple of glistening brass-plates and bells. A portrait-painter lives on the first-floor; a great historical genius inhabits the second. Remark the first-floor's middle drawing-room window; it is four feet higher than its two companions, and has taken a fancy to peep into the second-floor front. So much for the outward appearance of their habitations, and for the quarters in which they commonly dwell. They seem to love solitude, and their mighty spirits rejoice in vastness and gloomy ruin.

I don't say a word here about those geniuses who frequent the thoroughfares of the town, and have picture-frames containing a little gallery of miniature peers, beauties, and general officers, in the Quadrant, the passages about St. Martin's Lane, the Strand, and Cheapside. Lord Lyndhurst is to be seen in many of these gratis exhibitions—Lord Lyndhurst cribbed from Chalon; Lady Peel from Sir Thomas; Miss Croker from the same; the Duke, from ditto; an original officer in the Spanish Legion; a colonel or so, of the Bunhill Row Fencibles; a lady on a yellow sofa, with four children in little caps and blue ribands. We have all of us seen these pretty pictures, and are aware that our own features may be "done in this style." Then there is the man on the chain-pier at Brighton, who pares out your likeness in sticking-plaster; there is Miss Croke,' or Miss Runt, who gives lessons in Poonah-painting, japanning, or mezzotinting; Miss Stump, who attends ladies' schools with large chalk heads from Le Brun or the Cartoons; Rubbery, who instructs young gentlemen's establishments in pencil; and Sepio, of the Water-Colour Society, who paints before eight pupils daily, at a guinea an hour, keeping his own drawings for himself.

All these persons, as the most indifferent reader must see, equally belong to the tribe of Artists (the last not more than the first), and in an article like this should be mentioned properly. But though this paper has been extended from eight pages to sixteen, not a volume would suffice to do justice to the biographies of the persons above mentioned. Think of the superb Sepio, in a light-blue satin cravat, and a light-brown coat, and yellow kids, tripping daintily from Grosvenor Square to Gloucester Place, a small sugar-loaf boy following, who carries his morocco portfolio. Sepio scents his handkerchief, curls his hair, and wears, on a great coarse fist, a large emerald ring that one of his pupils gave him. He would not smoke a cigar for the world; he is always to be found at the opera; and, gods! how he grins, and waggles his head about, as Lady Fanny nods to him from her box.

He goes to at least six great parties in the season. At the houses where he teaches, he has a faint hope that he is received as an equal, and propitiates scornful footmen by absurd donations of sovereigns. The rogue has plenty of them. He has a stock-broker, and a power of guinea-lessons stowed away in the Consols. There are a number of young ladies of genius in the aristocracy, who admire him hugely; he begs you to contradict the report about him and Lady Smigsmag; every now and then he gets a present of game from a marquis; the City ladies die to have lessons of him; he prances about the park on a high-bred cocktail, with lacquered boots and enormous high heels; and he has a mother and sisters somewhere—washerwomen, it is said, in Pimlico.

How different is his fate to that of poor Rubbery, the school drawing-master! Highgate, Homerton, Putney, Hackney, Hornsey, Turnham Green, are his resorts; he has a select seminary to attend at every one of these places; and if, from all these nurseries of youth, he obtains a sufficient number of half-crowns to pay his week's bills, what a happy man is he!

He lives most likely in a third floor in Howland Street, and has commonly five children, who have all a marvellous talent for drawing—all save one, perhaps, that is an idiot, which a poor sick mother is ever carefully tending. Sepio's great aim and battle in life is to be considered one of the aristocracy; honest Rubbery would fain be thought a gentleman, too; but, indeed, he does not know whether he is so or not. Why be a gentleman?—A gentle-man Artist does not obtain the wages of a tailor; Rubbery's butcher looks down upon him with a royal scorn; and his wife, poor gentle soul (a clergyman's daughter, who married him in the firm belief that her John would be knighted and make an immense fortune),— his wife, I say, has many fierce looks to suffer from Mrs. Butcher, and many meek excuses or prayers to proffer, when she cannot pay her bill,—or when, worst of all, she has humbly to beg for a little scrap of meat upon credit, against John's coming home. He has five-and-twenty miles to walk that day, and must have something nourishing when he comes in—he is killing himself, poor fellow, she knows he is ; and Miss Crick has promised to pay him his quarter's charge on the very next Saturday. "Gentlefolks, indeed," says Mrs. Butcher ; "pretty gentlefolks these, as can't pay for half a pound of steak ! " Let us thank Heaven that the Artist's wife has her meat, however,—there is good in that shrill, fat, mottled-faced Mrs. Brisket, after all.

Think of the labours of that poor Rubbery. He was up at four in the morning, and toiled till nine upon a huge damp icy lithographic stone,—on which he has drawn the "Star of the Wave," or the "Queen of the Tourney," or, "She met at Almack's," for Lady Flummery's last new song. This done, at half-past nine he is to be seen striding across Kensington Gardens, to wait upon the before-named Miss Crick, at Lamont House. Transport yourself in imagination to the Misses Kittle's seminary, Potzdam Villa, Upper Homerton, four miles from Shoreditch ; and at half-past two, Professor Rubbery is to be seen swinging along towards the gate. Somebody is on the look-out for him : indeed it is his eldest daughter Marianne, who has been pacing the shrubbery, and peering over the green railings this half-hour past. She is with the Misses Kittle on the "mutual system," a thousand times more despised than the butchers' and the grocers' daughters, who are educated on the same terms, and whose papas are warm men in Aldgate. Wednesday is the happiest day of Marianne's week : and this the happiest hour of Wednesday ! Behold ! Professor Rubbery wipes his hot brows and kisses the poor thing, and they go in together out of the rain, and he tells her that the twins are well out of the measles, thank God ! and that Tom has just done the Antinous, in a way that must make him sure of the Academy prize, and that mother is better of her rheumatism now. He has brought her a letter, in large round-hand, from Polly ; a famous soldier, drawn by little Frank ; and when, after his two hours' lesson, Rubbery is off again, our dear Marianne cons over the letter and picture a hundred times with soft tearful smiles, and stows them away in an old writing-desk, amidst a heap more of precious home relics, wretched trumpery scraps and baubles, that you and I, madam, would sneer at ; but that in the poor child's eyes (and, I think, in the eyes of One who knows how to value widows' mites and humble sinners' offerings) are better than banknotes and Pitt diamonds. O kind Heaven, that has given these treasures to the poor ! Many and many an hour does Marianne lie awake with full eyes, and yearn for that wretched old lodging in Howland Street, where mother and brothers lie sleeping ; and, gods ! what a fête it is, when twice or thrice in the year she comes home !

I forget how many hundred millions of miles, for how many billions of centuries, how many thousands of decillions of angels, peris, houris, demons, afreets, and the like, Mahomet travelled, lived, and counted, during the time that some water was falling from a bucket to the ground ; but have we not been wandering most egregiously away from Rubbery, during the minute in which his daughter is changing his shoes, and taking off his reeking macintosh, in the hall of Potzdam Villa ? She thinks him the finest artist that ever cut an H. B. ; that's positive : and as a drawing-master, his merits are wonderful : for at the Misses Kittle's annual vacation festival, when the young ladies' drawings are exhibited to their mammas and relatives (Rubbery attending in a clean shirt, with his wife's large brooch stuck in it, and drinking negus along with the very best) ;—at the annual festival, I say, it will be found that the sixty-four drawings exhibited—"Tintern Abbey," "Kenilworth Castle," "Horse—from Carl Vernet," "Head—from West," or what not (say sixteen of each sort)—are the one exactly as good as the other ; so that, although Miss Slamcoe gets the prize, there is really no reason why Miss Timson, who is only four years old, should not have it ; her design being accurately stroke for stroke, tree for tree, curl for curl, the same as Miss Slamcoe's, who is eighteen. The fact is, that of these drawings, Rubbery, in the course of the year, has done every single stroke, although the girls and their parents are ready to take their affidavits (or, as I heard once a great female grammarian say, their *affies davit*) that the drawing-master has never been near the sketches. This is the way with them ; but mark !—when young ladies come home, are settled in life, and mammas of families,—can they design so much as a horse, or a dog, or a "moo-cow," for little Jack who bawls out for them ? Not they ! Rubbery's pupils have no more notion of drawing, any more than Sepio's of painting, when that eminent artist is away.

Between these two gentlemen, lie a whole class of teachers of drawing, who resemble them more or less. I am ashamed to say that Rubbery takes his pipe in the parlour of an hotel, of which the largest room is devoted to the convenience of poor people, amateurs of British gin : whilst Sepio trips down to the Club, and has a pint of the smallest claret : but of course the tastes of men vary ; and you find them simple or presuming, careless or prudent, natural and vulgar, or false and atrociously genteel, in all ranks and stations of life.

As for the other persons mentioned at the beginning of this discourse, viz. the cheap portrait-painter, the portrait-cutter in sticking-plaster, and Miss Croke, the teacher of mezzotint and

Poonah-painting,—nothing need be said of them in this place, as we have to speak of matters more important. Only about Miss Croke, or about other professors of cheap art, let the reader most sedulously avoid them. Mezzotinto is a take-in, Poonah-painting a rank, villainous deception. So is "Grecian art without brush or pencils." These are only small mechanical contrivances, over which young ladies are made to lose time. And now, having disposed of these small skirmishers who hover round the great body of Artists, we are arrived in presence of the main force, that we must begin to attack in form. In the "partition of the earth," as it has been described by Schiller, the reader will remember that the poet, finding himself at the end of the general scramble without a single morsel of plunder, applied passionately to Jove, who pitied the poor fellow's condition, and complimented him with a seat in the Empyrean. "The strong and the cunning," says Jupiter, "have seized upon the inheritance of the world, whilst thou wert star-gazing and rhyming: not one single acre remains wherewith I can endow thee; but, in revenge, if thou art disposed to visit me in my own heaven, come when thou wilt, it is always open to thee."

The cunning and strong have scrambled and struggled more on our own little native spot of earth than in any other place on the world's surface; and the English poet (whether he handles a pen or a pencil) has little other refuge than that windy unsubstantial one which Jove has vouchsafed to him. Such airy board and lodging is, however, distasteful to many; who prefer, therefore, to give up their poetical calling, and, in a vulgar beef-eating world, to feed upon and fight for vulgar beef.

For such persons (among the class of painters), it may be asserted that portrait-painting was invented. It is the Artist's compromise with heaven; "the light of common day," in which, after a certain quantity of "travel from the East," the genius fades at last. Abbé Barthélemy (who sent Le Jeune Anacharsis travelling through Greece in the time of Plato,—travelling through ancient Greece in lace ruffles, red heels, and a pigtail),—Abbé Barthélemy, I say, declares that somebody was once standing against a wall in the sun, and that somebody else traced the outline of somebody's shadow; and so painting was "invented." Angelica Kauffmann has made a neat picture of this neat subject; and very well worthy she was of handling it. Her painting *might* grow out of a wall and a piece of charcoal; and honest Barthélemy might be satisfied that he had here traced the true origin of the art. What a base pedigree have these abominable Greek, French, and High-Dutch heathens invented for that which is divine!—a wall, ye gods, to be represented as the father of that which came down radiant from you ! The man who invented such a blasphemy ought to be impaled upon broken bottles, or shot off pitilessly by spring-guns, nailed to the bricks like a dead owl or a weasel, or tied up—a kind of vulgar Prometheus—and baited for ever by the house-dog.

But let not our indignation carry us too far. Lack of genius in some, of bread in others, of patronage in a shop-keeping world, that thinks only of the useful, and is little inclined to study the sublime, has turned thousands of persons calling themselves, and wishing to be, Artists, into so many common face-painters, who must look out for the "kalon" in the fat features of a red-gilled Alderman, or, at best, in a pretty, simpering, white-necked beauty from "Almack's." The dangerous charms of these latter, especially, have seduced away many painters ; and we often think that this very physical superi-ority which English ladies possess, this tempting brilliancy of health and complexion, which belongs to them more than to any others, has operated upon our Artists as a serious disadvantage, and kept them from better things. The French call such beauty "La beauté du Diable" ; and a devilish power it has truly ; before our Armidas and Helens how many Rinaldos and Parises have fallen, who are con-tent to forget their glorious calling, and slumber away their energies in the laps of these soft tempters. O ye British enchantresses ! I never see a gilded annual book without likening it to a small island near Cape Pelorus, in Sicily, whither, by twanging of harps, singing of ravishing melodies, glancing of voluptuous eyes, and the most beautiful fashionable undress in the world, the naughty sirens lured the passing seaman. Steer clear of them, ye Artists ! pull, pull for your lives, ye crews of Suffolk Street and the Water-Colour Gallery ! stop your ears, bury your eyes, tie yourselves to the mast, and away with you from the gaudy smiling "Books of Beauty." Land, and you are ruined ! Look well among the flowers on yonder beach—it is whitened with the bones of painters.

For my part, I never have a model under seventy, and her with several shawls and a cloak on. By these means the imagination gets fair play, and the morals remain unendangered.

Personalities are odious ; but let the British public look at the pictures of the celebrated Mr. Shalloon—the moral British public—and say whether our grandchildren (or the grandchildren of the exalted personages whom Mr. Shalloon paints) will not have a queer idea of the manners of their grandmammas, as they are represented in the most beautiful, dexterous, captivating water-colour drawings that ever were ? Heavenly powers, how they simper and ogle ! with what gimcracks of lace, ribbons, ferronnières, smelling-bottles, and what not, is every one of them overloaded. What shoulders, what ringlets, what funny little pug-dogs do they most of them exhibit to

34

us! The days of Lancret and Watteau are lived over again, and the Court ladies of the time of Queen Victoria look as moral as the immaculate countesses of the days of Louis Quinze. The last President of the Royal Academy * is answerable for many sins, and many imitators; especially for that gay, simpering, meretricious look which he managed to give to every lady who sat to him for her portrait; and I do not know a more curious contrast than that which may be perceived by any one who will examine a collection of his portraits by the side of some by Sir Joshua Reynolds. They seem to have painted different races of people; and when one hears very old gentlemen talking of the superior beauty that existed in their early days (as very old gentlemen, from Nestor downwards, have and will), one is inclined to believe that there is some truth in what they say; at least, that the men and women under George the Third were far superior to their descendants in the time of George the Fourth. Whither has it fled—that calm matronly grace, or beautiful virgin innocence, which belonged to the happy women who sat to Sir Joshua? Sir Thomas's ladies are ogling out of their gilt frames, and asking us for admiration; Sir Joshua's sit quiet, in maiden meditation fancy free, not anxious for applause, but sure to command it; a thousand times more lovely in their sedate serenity than Sir Thomas's ladies in their smiles, and their satin ball-dresses.

But this is not the general notion, and the ladies prefer the manner of the modern Artist. Of course, such being the case, the painters must follow the fashion. One could point out half-a-dozen Artists who, at Sir Thomas's death, have seized upon a shred of his somewhat tawdry mantle. There is Carmine, for instance, a man of no small repute, who will stand as the representative of his class.

Carmine has had the usual education of a painter in this country: he can read and write—that is, has spent years drawing the figure—and has made his foreign tour. It may be that he had original talent once, but he has learned to forget this, as the great bar to his success; and must imitate, in order to live. He is among Artists what a dentist is among surgeons—a man who is employed to decorate the human head, and who is paid enormously for so doing. You know one of Carmine's beauties at any exhibition, and see the process by which they are manufactured. He lengthens the noses, widens the foreheads, opens the eyes, and gives them the proper languishing leer; diminishes the mouth, and infallibly tips the ends of it with a pretty smile of his favourite colour.

* Sir Thomas Lawrence.

He is a personable, white-handed, bald-headed, middle-aged man now, with that grave blandness of look which one sees in so many prosperous empty-headed people. He has a collection of little stories and Court gossip about Lady This, and "my particular friend, Lord So-and So," which he lets off in succession to every sitter : indeed, a most bland, irreproachable, gentlemanlike man. He gives most patronising advice to young Artists, and makes a point of praising all—not certainly too much, but in a gentleman-like, indifferent, simpering way. This should be the maxim with prosperous persons, who have had to make their way, and wish to keep what they have made. They praise everybody, and are called good-natured benevolent men. Surely no benevolence is so easy ; it simply consists in lying, and smiling, and wishing everybody well. You will get to do so quite naturally at last, and at no expense of truth. At first, when a man has feelings of his own—feelings of love or of anger—this perpetual grin and good-humour is hard to maintain. I used to imagine, when I first knew Carmine, that there were some particular springs in his wig (that glossy, oily, curly crop of chestnut hair) that pulled up his features into a smile, and kept the muscles so fixed for the day. I don't think so now, and should say he grinned, even when he was asleep and his teeth were out ; the smile does not lie in the manufacture of the wig, but in the construction of the brain. Claude Carmine has the organ of *don't care-a-damn-ativeness* wonderfully developed ; not that reckless don't-care-a-damn-ativeness which leads a man to disregard all the world, and himself into the bargain. Claude stops before he comes to himself ; but beyond that individual member of the Royal Academy, has not a single sympathy for a single human creature. The account of his friends' deaths, woes, misfortunes, or good-luck, he receives with equal good-nature ; he gives three splendid dinners per annum,—Gunter, Dukes, Fortnum and Mason, everything ; he dines out the other three hundred and sixty-two days in the year, and was never known to give away a shilling, or to advance, for one half-hour, the forty pounds per quarter wages that he gives to Mr. Scumble, who works the backgrounds, limbs, and draperies of his portraits.

He is not a good painter : how should he be whose painting as it were never goes beyond a whisper, and who would make a general simpering as he looked at an advancing cannon-ball ?—but he is not a bad painter, being a keen respectable man of the world, who has a cool head, and knows what is what. In France, where tigerism used to be the fashion among the painters, I make no doubt Carmine would have let his beard and wig grow, and looked the fiercest of the fierce ; but with us a man must be genteel ; the perfection of style (in writing and in drawing-rooms) being "*de ne pas en avoir*," Carmine of course is agreeably vapid. His conversation has accordingly the flavour and briskness of a clear, brilliant, stale bottle of soda-water,—once in five minutes or so, you see rising up to the surface a little bubble—a little tiny shining point of wit—it rises and explodes feebly, and then dies. With regard to wit, people of fashion (as we are given to understand) are satisfied with a mere *soupçon* of it. Anything more were indecorous ; a genteel stomach could not bear it : Carmine knows the exact proportions of the dose, and would not venture to administer to his sitters anything beyond the requisite quantity.

There is a great deal more said here about Carmine—the man, than Carmine—the Artist ; but what can be written about the latter ? New ladies in white satin, new Generals in red, new Peers in scarlet and ermine, and stout Members of Parliament pointing to inkstands and sheets of letter-paper, with a Turkey-carpet beneath them, a red curtain above them, a Doric pillar supporting them, and a tremendous storm of thunder and lightning lowering and flashing in the background, spring up every year, and take their due positions "upon the line" in the Academy, and send their complements of hundreds to swell Carmine's heap of Consols. If he paints Lady Flummery for the tenth time, in the character of the tenth Muse, what need have we to say anything about it ? The man is a good workman, and will manufacture a decent article at the best price ; but we should no more think of noticing each, than of writing fresh critiques upon every new coat that Nugee or Stultz turned out. The papers say, in reference to his picture "No. 591. 'Full-length portrait of her Grace the Duchess of Doldrum. Carmine, R.A.' Mr. Carmine never fails ; this work, like all others by the same artist, is excellent."—Or, "No. 591, &c. The lovely Duchess of Doldrum has received from Mr. Carmine's pencil ample justice ; the *chiar' oscuro* of the picture is perfect ; the likeness admirable ; the keeping and colouring have the true Titianesque gusto ; if we might hint a fault, it has the left ear of the lapdog a 'little' out of drawing."

Then, perhaps, comes a criticism which says : "The Duchess of Doldrum's picture by Mr. Carmine is neither better nor worse than five hundred other performances of the same artist. It would be very unjust to say that these portraits are bad, for they have really a considerable cleverness ; but to say that they were good, would be quite as false ; nothing in our eyes was ever further from being so. Every ten years Mr. Carmine exhibits what is called an original picture of three inches square, but beyond this, nothing original is to be found in him : as a lad, he copied Reynolds, then

Opie, then Lawrence; then having made a sort of style of his own, he has copied himself ever since," &c.

And then the critic goes on to consider the various parts of Carmine's pictures. In speaking of critics, their peculiar relationship with painters ought not to be forgotten; and as in a former paper we have seen how a fashionable authoress has her critical toadies, in like manner has the painter his enemies and friends in the press; with this difference, probably, that the writer can bear a fair quantity of abuse without wincing, while the artist not uncommonly grows mad at such strictures, considers them as personal matters, inspired by a private feeling of hostility, and hates the critic for life who has ventured to question his judgment in any way. We have said before, poor Academicians, for how many conspiracies are you made to answer! We may add now, poor critics, what black personal animosities are discovered for you, when you happen (right or wrong, but according to your best ideas) to speak the truth! Say that Snooks's picture is badly coloured,—" O heavens!" shrieks Snooks, "what can I have done to offend this fellow?" Hint that such a figure is badly drawn—and Snooks instantly declares you to be his personal enemy, actuated only by envy and vile pique. My friend Pebbler, himself a famous Artist, is of opinion that the critic should *never* abuse the painter's performances, because, says he, the painter knows much better than any one else what his own faults are, and because you never do him any good. Are men of the brush so obstinate?—very likely; but the public —the public? are we not to do our duty by it too? and, aided by our superior knowledge and genius for the fine arts, point out to it the way it should go? Yes, surely; and as by the efforts of dull or interested critics many bad painters have been palmed off upon the nation as geniuses of the first degree; in like manner, the sagacious and disinterested (like some we could name) have endeavoured to provide this British nation with pure principles of taste,—or at least, to prevent them from adopting such as are impure.

Carmine, to be sure, comes in for very little abuse; and, indeed, he deserves but little. He is a fashionable painter, and preserves the golden mediocrity which is necessary for the fashion. Let us bid him good-bye. He lives in a house all to himself, most likely, —has a footman, sometimes a carriage; is apt to belong to the "Athenæum"; and dies universally respected: that is, not one single soul cares for him dead, as he, living, did not care for one single soul.

Then, perhaps, we should mention M'Gilp, or Blather, rising young men, who will fill Carmine's place one of these days, and occupy his house in ——, when the fulness of time shall come, and (he borne to a narrow grave in the Harrow Road by the whole mourning Royal Academy) they shall leave their present first-floor in Newman Street, and step into his very house and shoes.

There is little difference between the juniors and the seniors : they grin when they are talking of him together, and express a perfect confidence that they can paint a head against Carmine any day—as very likely they can. But until his demise, they are occupied with painting people about the Regent's Park and Russell Square ; are very glad to have the chance of a popular clergyman, or a college tutor, or a mayor of Stoke Poges after the Reform Bill. Such characters are commonly mezzotinted afterwards ; and the portrait of our esteemed townsman So-and-So, by that talented artist Mr. M'Gilp, of London, is favourably noticed by the provincial press, and is to be found over the sideboards of many country gentlemen. If they come up to town, to whom do they go ? To M'Gilp, to be sure ; and thus, slowly, his practice and his prices increase.

The Academy student is a personage that should not be omitted here ; he resembles very much, outwardly, the medical student, and has many of the latter's habits and pleasures. He very often wears a broad-brimmed hat and a fine dirty crimson velvet waistcoat, his hair commonly grows long, and he has braiding to his pantaloons. He works leisurely at the Academy, he loves theatres, billiards, and novels, and has his house-of-call somewhere in the neighbourhood of St. Martin's Lane, where he and his brethren meet and sneer at Royal Academicians. If you ask him what line of art he pursues, he answers with a smile exceedingly supercilious, " Sir, I am an historical painter ; " meaning that he will only condescend to take subjects from Hume, or Robertson, or from the classics—which he knows nothing about. This stage of an historical painter is only preparatory, lasting perhaps from eighteen to five-and-twenty, when the gentleman's madness begins to disappear, and he comes to look at life sternly in the face, and to learn that man shall not live by historical painting alone. Then our friend falls to portrait-painting or animal-painting, or makes some other such sad compromise with necessity.

He has probably a small patrimony, which defrays the charge of his studies and cheap pleasures during his period of apprenticeship. He makes the *obligé* tour to France and Italy, and returns from those countries with a multitude of spoiled canvases, and a large pair of moustaches, with which he establishes himself in one of the dingy streets of Soho before mentioned. There is poor Pipson, a man of indomitable patience, and undying enthusiasm for his profession. He could paper Exeter Hall with his studies from the life, and with portraits in chalk and oil of French *sapeurs* and Italian brigands, that kindly descend from their mountain-caverns, and quit their murderous occupations, in order to sit to young gentlemen at Rome, at the rate of tenpence an hour. Pipson returns from abroad, establishes himself, has his cards printed, and waits and waits for commissions for great historical pictures. Meanwhile, night after night, he is to be found at his old place in the Academy, copying the old life-guardsman—working, working away —and never advancing one jot. At eighteen, Pipson copied statues and life-guardsmen to admiration ; at five-and-thirty he can make admirable drawings of life-guardsmen and statues. Beyond this he never goes ; year after year his historical picture is returned to him by the envious Academicians, and he grows old, and his little patrimony is long since spent ; and he earns nothing himself. How does he support hope and life ?—that is the wonder. No one knows until he tries (which God forbid he should !) upon what a small matter hope and life can be supported. Our poor fellow lives on from year to year in a miraculous way ; tolerably cheerful in the midst of his semi-starvation, and wonderfully confident about next year, in spite of the failures of the last twenty-five. Let us thank God for imparting to us, poor weak mortals, the inestimable blessing of *vanity*. How many half-witted votaries of the arts—poets, painters, actors, musicians—live upon this food, and scarcely any other ! If the delusion were to drop from Pipson's eyes, and he should see himself as he is,—if some malevolent genius were to mingle with his feeble brains one fatal particle of common sense,— he would just walk off Waterloo Bridge, and abjure poverty, in-capacity, cold lodgings, unpaid baker's bills, ragged elbows, and deferred hopes, at once and for ever.

We do not mean to depreciate the profession of historical painting, but simply to warn youth against it as dangerous and unprofitable. It is as if a young fellow should say, " I will be a Raffaelle or a Titian,—a Milton or a Shakespeare," and if he will count up how many people have lived since the world began, and how many there have been of the Raffaelle or Shakespeare sort, he can calculate to a nicety what are the chances in his favour. Even successful his-torical painters, what are they ?—in a worldly point of view, they mostly inhabit the second-floor, or have great desolate studios in back premises, whither life-guardsmen, old-clothesmen, blackamoors, and other " properties " are conducted, to figure at full length as Roman conquerors, Jewish high-priests, or Othellos on canvas. Then there are gay smart water-colour painters,—a flourishing and pleasant trade. Then there are shabby, fierce-looking geniuses, in ringlets, and all but rags, who paint, and whose pictures are never sold, and who vow they are the objects of some general and scoundrelly conspiracy. There are landscape-painters, who travel to the uttermost ends of the earth and brave heat and cold, to bring to the greedy British public views of Cairo, Calcutta, St. Petersburg, Timbuctoo. You see English artists under the shadow of the Pyramids, making sketches of the Copts, perched on the backs of dromedaries, accompanying a caravan across the desert, or getting materials for an annual in Iceland or Siberia. What genius and what energy do not they all exhibit— these men, whose profession, in this wise country of ours, is scarcely considered as liberal!

If we read the works of the Reverend Doctor Lemprière, Monsieur Winckelmann, Professor Plato, and others who have written concerning the musty old Grecians, we shall find that the Artists of those barbarous times meddled with all sorts of trades besides their own, and dabbled in fighting, philosophy, metaphysics, both Scotch and German, politics, music, and the deuce knows what. A rambling sculptor, who used to go about giving lectures in those days, Socrates by name, declared that the wisest of men in his time were Artists. This Plato, before mentioned, went through a regular course of drawing, figure and landscape, black-lead, chalk, with or without stump, sepia, water-colour, and oils. Was there ever such absurdity known? Among these benighted heathens, painters were the most accomplished gentlemen,—and the most accomplished gentlemen were painters: the former would make you a speech, or read you a dissertation on Kant, or lead you a regiment,—with the very best statesman, philosopher, or soldier in Athens. And they had the folly to say, that by thus busying and accomplishing themselves in all manly studies, they were advancing eminently in their own peculiar one. What was the consequence? Why, that fellow Socrates not only made a miserable fifth-rate sculptor, but was actually hanged for treason.

And serve him right. Do *our* young artists study anything beyond the proper way of cutting a pencil, or drawing a model? Do you hear of *them* hard at work over books, and bothering their brains with musty learning? Not they, forsooth: we understand the doctrine of division of labour, and each man sticks to his trade. Artists do not meddle with the pursuits of the rest of the world; and, in revenge, the rest of the world does not meddle with Artists. Fancy an Artist being a senior wrangler or a politician; and, on the other hand, fancy a real gentleman turned painter! No, no; ranks are defined. A real gentleman may get money by the law, or by wearing a red coat and fighting, or a black one and preaching; but that he should sell himself to *Art*—forbid it, Heaven! And do not let your Ladyship on reading this cry "Stuff!—stupid envy, rank republicanism,—an artist *is* a gentleman." Madam, would you like to see your son, the Honourable Fitzroy Plantagenet, a painter? You would die sooner; the escutcheon of the Smigsmags would be blotted for ever, if Plantagenet ever ventured to make a mercantile use of a bladder of paint.

Time was—some hundred years back—when writers lived in Grub Street, and poor ragged Johnson shrank behind a screen in Cave's parlour—that the author's trade was considered a very mean one, which a gentleman of family could not take up but as an amateur. This absurdity is pretty nearly worn out now, and I do humbly hope and pray for the day when the other shall likewise disappear. If there be any nobleman with a talent that way, why —why don't we see him among the R.A.'s?

501. The Schoolmaster. Sketch taken abroad . .	Brum, Henry, Lord, *R.A., F.R.S. S.A., of the National Institute of France.*
502. View of the Artist's Residence at Windsor .	Maconkey, Right Honourable T. B.
503. Murder of the Babes in the Tower . . .	Rustle, Lord J. Pill, Right Honourable Sir Robert.
504. A Little Agitation . .	O'Carrol, Daniel, M.R.I.A.

Fancy, I say, such names as these figuring in the Catalogue of the Academy: and why should they not? The real glorious days of the art (which wants equality and not patronage) will revive then. Patronage—a plague on the word!—it implies inferiority; and in the name of all that is sensible, why is a respectable country gentleman, or a city attorney's lady, or any person of any rank, however exalted, to "patronise" an Artist?

There are some who sigh for the past times, when magnificent swaggering Peter Paul Rubens (who himself patronised a queen) rode abroad with a score of gentlemen in his train, and a purse-bearer to scatter ducats; and who love to think how he was made an English knight and a Spanish grandee, and went of embassies as if he had been a born marquis. Sweet it is to remember, too, that Sir Antony Vandyck, K.B., actually married out of the peerage: and that when Titian dropped his mahlstick, the Emperor Charles V. picked it up (O gods! what heroic self-devotion)—picked it up, saying, "I can make fifty dukes, but not one Titian." Nay, was not the Pope of Rome going to make Raffaelle a Cardinal,—and were not these golden days?

Let us say at once, "No." The very fuss made about certain painters in the sixteenth and seventeenth centuries shows that the body of Artists had no rank or position in the world. They hung upon single patrons : and every man who holds his place by such a tenure must feel himself an inferior, more or less. The times are changing now, and as authors are no longer compelled to send their works abroad under the guardianship of a great man and a slavish dedication, painters, too, are beginning to deal directly with the public. Who are the great picture-buyers now?—the engravers and their employers, the people,—"the only source of legitimate power," as they say after dinner. A fig then for Cardinals' hats ! Were Mr. O'Connell in power to-morrow, let us hope he would not give one, not even a paltry bishopric *in partibus*, to the best painter in the Academy. What need have they of honours out of the profession? Why are they to be be-knighted like a parcel of aldermen?—for my part, I solemnly declare, that I will take nothing under a peerage, after the exhibition of my great picture, and don't see, if painters *must* have titles conferred upon them for eminent services, why the Marquis of Mulready or the Earl of Landseer should not sit in the House as well as any law or soldier lord.

The truth to be elicited from this little digressive dissertation is this painful one,—that young Artists are not generally as well instructed as they should be ; and let the Royal Academy look to it, and give some sound courses of lectures to their pupils on literature and history, as well as on anatomy, or light and shade.

THE FATAL BOOTS

THE FATAL BOOTS

JANUARY—THE BIRTH OF THE YEAR

SOME poet has observed, that if any man would write down what has really happened to him in this mortal life he would be sure to make a good book, though he never had met with a single adventure from his birth to his burial. How much more, then, must I, who *have* had adventures, most singular, pathetic, and unparalleled, be able to compile an instructive and entertaining volume for the use of the public.

I don't mean to say that I have killed lions, or seen the wonders of travel in the deserts of Arabia or Persia; or that I have been a very fashionable character, living with dukes and peeresses, and writing my recollections of them, as the way now is. I never left this my native isle, nor spoke to a lord (except an Irish one, who had rooms in our house, and forgot to pay three weeks' lodging and extras); but, as our immortal bard observes, I have in the course of my existence been so eaten up by the slugs and harrows of out-rageous fortune, and have been the object of such continual and extraordinary ill-luck, that I believe it would melt the heart of a milestone to read of it—that is, if a milestone had a heart of any-thing but stone.

Twelve of my adventures, suitable for meditation and perusal during the twelve months of the year, have been arranged by me for this work. They contain a part of the history of a great, and, confidently I may say, a *good* man. I was not a spendthrift like other men. I never wronged any man of a shilling, though I am as sharp a fellow at a bargain as any in Europe. I never injured a fellow-creature; on the contrary, on several occasions, when injured myself, have shown the most wonderful forbearance. I come of a tolerably good family; and yet, born to wealth—of an inoffensive disposition, careful of the money that I had, and eager to get more,—I have been going down hill ever since my journey of life began, and have been pursued by a complication of misfortunes such as surely never happened to any man but the unhappy Bob Stubbs.

Bob Stubbs is my name; and I haven't got a shilling: I have borne the commission of lieutenant in the service of King George, and am *now*—but never mind what I am now, for the public will know in a few pages more.   My father was of the Suffolk Stubbses —a well-to-do gentleman of Bungay.   My grandfather had been a respected attorney in that town, and left my papa a pretty little fortune.   I was thus the inheritor of competence, and ought to be at this moment a gentleman.

My misfortunes may be said to have commenced about a year before my birth, when my papa, a young fellow pretending to study the law in London, fell madly in love with Miss Smith, the daughter of a tradesman, who did not give her a sixpence, and afterwards became bankrupt.   My papa married this Miss Smith, and carried her off to the country, where I was born, in an evil hour for me.

Were I to attempt to describe my early years, you would laugh at me as an impostor; but the following letter from mamma to a friend, after her marriage, will pretty well show you what a poor foolish creature she was; and what a reckless extravagant fellow was my other unfortunate parent :—

To Miss Eliza Kicks, in Gracechurch Street, London.

"OH, Eliza! your Susan is the happiest girl under heaven! My Thomas is an angel! not a tall grenadier-like looking fellow, such as I always vowed I would marry :—on the contrary, he is what the world would call dumpy, and I hesitate not to confess that his eyes have a cast in them.   But what then? when one of his eyes is fixed on me, and one on my babe, they are lighted up with an affection which my pen cannot describe, and which, cer- tainly, was never bestowed upon any woman so strongly as upon your happy Susan Stubbs.

"When he comes home from shooting, or the farm, if you *could* see dear Thomas with me and our dear little Bob! as I sit on one knee, and baby on the other, and as he dances us both about.   I often wish that we had Sir Joshua, or some great painter, to depict the group; for sure it is the prettiest picture in the whole world, to see three such loving merry people.

"Dear baby is the most lovely little creature that *can possibly be*—the very *image* of papa; he is cutting his teeth, and the delight of *everybody*.   Nurse says that, when he is older, he will get rid of his squint, and his hair will get a *great deal* less red.   Doctor Bates is as kind, and skilful, and attentive as we could desire.

Think what a blessing to have had him! Ever since poor baby's birth, it has never had a day of quiet; and he has been obliged to give it from three to four doses every week;—how thankful ought we to be that the *dear thing* is as well as it is! It got through the measles wonderfully; then it had a little rash; and then a nasty hooping-cough; and then a fever, and continual pains in its poor little stomach, crying, poor dear child, from morning till night.

"But dear Tom is an excellent nurse; and many and many a night has he had no sleep, dear man! in consequence of the poor little baby. He walks up and down with it *for hours*, singing a kind of song (dear fellow, he has no more voice than a tea-kettle), and bobbing his head backwards and forwards, and looking, in his nightcap and dressing-gown, *so droll*. Oh, Eliza! how you would laugh to see him.

"We have one of the best nursemaids *in the world*, an Irish-woman, who is as fond of baby almost as his mother (but that can *never be*). She takes it to walk in the park for hours together, and I really don't know why Thomas dislikes her. He says she is tipsy, very often, and slovenly, which I cannot conceive;—to be sure, the nurse is sadly dirty, and sometimes smells very strong of gin.

"But what of that?—these little drawbacks only make home more pleasant. When one thinks how many mothers have *no* nursemaids: how many poor dear children have no doctors: ought we not to be thankful for Mary Malowney, and that Doctor Bates's bill is forty-seven pounds? How ill must dear baby have been, to require so much physic!

"But they are a sad expense, these dear babies, after all. Fancy, Eliza, how much this Mary Malowney costs us. Ten shillings every week; a glass of brandy or gin at dinner; three pint-bottles of Mr. Thrale's best porter every day—making twenty-one in a week, and nine hundred and ninety in the eleven months she has been with us. Then, for baby, there is Doctor Bates's bill of forty-five guineas, two guineas for christening, twenty for a grand christening supper and ball (rich Uncle John mortally offended because he was made godfather, and had to give baby a silver cup: he has struck Thomas out of his will: and old Mr. Firkin quite as much hurt because he was *not* asked: he will not speak to me or Thomas in consequence); twenty guineas for flannels, laces, little gowns, caps, napkins, and such baby's ware: and all this out of three hundred pounds a year! But Thomas expects to make *a great deal* by his farm.

"We have got the most charming country-house *you can imagine:* it is *quite shut in* by trees, and so retired that, though only thirty miles from London, the post comes to us but once a week. The roads, it must be confessed, are execrable ; it is winter now, and we are up to our knees in mud and snow.   But oh, Eliza ! how happy we are : with Thomas (he has had a sad attack of rheumatism, dear man !) and little Bobby, and our kind friend Doctor Bates, who comes so far to see us, I leave you to fancy that we have a charming merry party, and do not care for all the gaieties of Ranelagh.

"Adieu ! dear baby is crying for his mamma.   A thousand kisses from your affectionate   SUSAN STUBBS."

There it is !   Doctor's bills, gentleman-farming, twenty-one pints of porter a week.   In this way my unnatural parents were already robbing me of my property.

FEBRUARY—CUTTING WEATHER

I HAVE called this chapter "cutting weather," partly in compliment to the month of February, and partly in respect of my own misfortunes, which you are going to read about. For I have often thought that January (which is mostly twelfth-cake and holiday-time) is like the first four or five years of a little boy's life; then comes dismal February, and the working-days with it, when chaps begin to look out for themselves, after the Christmas and the New Year's heyday and merry-making are over, which our infancy may well be said to be. Well can I recollect that bitter first of February, when I first launched out into the world and appeared at Doctor Swishtail's academy.

I began at school that life of prudence and economy which I have carried on ever since. My mother gave me eighteenpence on setting out (poor soul! I thought her heart would break as she kissed me, and bade God bless me); and, besides, I had a small capital of my own, which I had amassed for a year previous. I'll tell you what I used to do. Wherever I saw six halfpence I took one. If it was asked for, I said I had taken it, and gave it back; —if it was not missed, I said nothing about it, as why should I?— those who don't miss their money, don't lose their money. So I had a little private fortune of three shillings, besides mother's eighteen-pence. At school they called me the Copper-Merchant, I had such lots of it.

Now, even at a preparatory school, a well-regulated boy may better himself; and I can tell you I did. I never was in any quarrels ; I never was very high in the class or very low; but there was no chap so much respected :—and why? *I'd always money.* The other boys spent all theirs in the first day or two, and they gave me plenty of cakes and barley-sugar then, I can tell you. I'd no need to spend my own money, for they would insist upon treating me. Well, in a week, when theirs was gone, and they had but their threepence a week to look to for the rest of the half-year, what did I do? Why, I am proud to say that three-halfpence out of the threepence a week of almost all the young gentlemen at Doctor Swishtail's, came into my pocket. Suppose, for instance, Tom

Hicks wanted a slice of gingerbread, who had the money? Little
Bob Stubbs, to be sure. "Hicks," I used to say, "*I'll* buy you
three-halfp'orth of gingerbread, if you'll give me threepence next
Saturday." And he agreed; and next Saturday came, and he very
often could not pay me more than three-halfpence. Then there was
the threepence I was to have *the next* Saturday. I'll tell you what
I did for a whole half-year: I lent a chap, by the name of Dick
Bunting, three-halfpence the first Saturday for threepence the next:
he could not pay me more than half when Saturday came, and I'm
blest if I did not make him pay me three-halfpence *for three-and-
twenty weeks running,* making two shillings and tenpence-halfpenny.
But he was a sad dishonourable fellow, Dick Bunting; for, after I'd
been so kind to him, and let him off for three-and-twenty weeks the
money he owed me, holidays came, and threepence he owed me still.
Well, according to the common principles of practice, after six weeks'
holidays, he ought to have paid me exactly sixteen shillings which
was my due. For the

First week the 3d. would be 6d.			Fourth week	.	.	. 4s.
Second week	.	. 1s.	Fifth week	.	.	. 8s.
Third week .	.	. 2s.	Sixth week	.	.	. 16s.

Nothing could be more just; and yet—will it be believed?—when
Bunting came back he offered me *three-halfpence!* the mean dishonest scoundrel.

However, I was even with him, I can tell you.—He spent all
his money in a fortnight, and *then* I screwed him down! I made
him, besides giving me a penny for a penny, pay me a quarter of
his bread-and-butter at breakfast and a quarter of his cheese at
supper; and before the half-year was out, I got from him a silver
fruit-knife, a box of compasses, and a very pretty silver-laced waistcoat, in which I went home as proud as a king: and, what's more,
I had no less than three golden guineas in the pocket of it, besides
fifteen shillings, the knife, and a brass bottle-screw, which I got from
another chap. It wasn't bad interest for twelve shillings—which
was all the money I'd had in the year—was it? Heigho! I've
often wished that I could get such a chance again in this wicked
world; but men are more avaricious now than they used to be in
those dear early days.

Well, I went home in my new waistcoat as fine as a peacock;
and when I gave the bottle-screw to my father, begging him to take
it as a token of my affection for him, my dear mother burst into
such a fit of tears as I never saw, and kissed and hugged me fit
to smother me   "Bless him, bless him!" says she, "to think of

FEBRUARY—CUTTING WEATHER.

his old father. And where did you purchase it, Bob?"—"Why, mother," says I, "I purchased it out of my savings" (which was as true as the gospel).—When I said this, mother looked round to father, smiling, although she had tears in her eyes, and she took his hand, and with her other hand drew me to her. "Is he not a noble boy?" says she to my father: "and only nine years old!" —"Faith," says my father, "he *is* a good lad, Susan. Thank thee, my boy; and here is a crown-piece in return for thy bottle-screw:— it shall open us a bottle of the very best too," says my father. And he kept his word. I always was fond of good wine (though never, from a motive of proper self-denial, having any in my cellar); and, by Jupiter! on this night I had my little skinful,—for there was no stinting,—so pleased were my dear parents with the bottle-screw. The best of it was, it only cost me threepence originally, which a chap could not pay me.

Seeing this game was such a good one, I became very generous towards my parents; and a capital way it is to encourage liberality in children. I gave mamma a very neat brass thimble, and she gave me a half-guinea piece. Then I gave her a very pretty needle-book, which I made myself with an ace of spades from a new pack of cards we had, and I got Sally, our maid, to cover it with a bit of pink satin her mistress had given her; and I made the leaves of the book, which I vandyked very nicely, out of a piece of flannel I had had round my neck for a sore throat. It smelt a little of hartshorn, but it was a beautiful needlebook; and mamma was so delighted with it, that she went into town and bought me a gold-laced hat. Then I bought papa a pretty china tobacco-stopper: but I am sorry to say of my dear father that he was not so generous as my mamma or myself, for he only burst out laughing, and did not give me so much as a half-crown piece, which was the least I expected from him. "I shan't give you anything, Bob, this time, says he; "and I wish, my boy, you would not make any more such presents,—for, really, they are too expensive." Expensive indeed! I hate meanness,—even in a father.

I must tell you about the silver-edged waistcoat which Bunting gave me. Mamma asked me about it, and I told her the truth, that it was a present from one of the boys for my kindness to him. Well, what does she do but writes back to Doctor Swishtail, when I went to school, thanking him for his attention to her dear son, and sending a shilling to the good and grateful little boy who had given me the waistcoat!

"What waistcoat is it," says the Doctor to me, "and who gave it to you?"

"Bunting gave it me, sir," says I.

"Call Bunting!" And up the little ungrateful chap came. Would you believe it, he burst into tears,—told that the waistcoat had been given him by his mother, and that he had been forced to give it for a debt to Copper-Merchant, as the nasty little blackguard called me? He then said how, for three-halfpence, he had been compelled to pay me three shillings (the sneak! as if he had been *obliged* to borrow the three-halfpence!)—how all the other boys had been swindled (swindled!) by me in like manner,—and how, with only twelve shillings, I had managed to scrape together four guineas. . . .

My courage almost fails me as I describe the shameful scene that followed. The boys were called in, my own little account-book was dragged out of my cupboard, to prove how much I had received from each, and every farthing of my money was paid back to them. The tyrant took the thirty shillings that my dear parents had given me, and said he should put them into the poor-box at church; and, after having made a long discourse to the boys about meanness and usury, he said, "Take off your coat, Mr. Stubbs, and restore Bunting his waistcoat." I did, and stood without coat and waistcoat in the midst of the nasty grinning boys. I was going to put on my coat,—

"Stop!" says he. "TAKE DOWN HIS BREECHES!"

Ruthless brutal villain! Sam Hopkins, the biggest boy, took them down—horsed me—and *I was flogged, sir:* yes, flogged! O revenge! I, Robert Stubbs, who had done nothing but what was right, was brutally flogged at ten years of age!—Though February was the shortest month, I remembered it long.

MARCH—SHOWERY

WHEN my mamma heard of the treatment of her darling she was for bringing an action against the schoolmaster, or else for tearing his eyes out (when, dear soul! she would not have torn the eyes out of a flea, had it been her own injury), and, at the very least, for having me removed from the school where I had been so shamefully treated. But papa was stern for once, and vowed that I had been served quite right, declared that I should not be removed from the school, and sent old Swishtail a brace of pheasants for what he called his kindness to me. Of these the old gentleman invited me to partake, and made a very queer speech at dinner, as he was cutting them up, about the excellence of my parents, and his own determination to be *kinder still* to me if ever I ventured on such practices again. So I was obliged to give up my old trade of lending : for the Doctor declared that any boy who borrowed should be flogged, and any one who *paid* should be flogged twice as much. There was no standing against such a prohibition as this, and my little commerce was ruined.

I was not very high in the school : not having been able to get farther than that dreadful *Propria quæ maribus* in the Latin grammar, of which, though I have it by heart even now, I never could understand a syllable : but, on account of my size, my age, and the prayers of my mother, was allowed to have the privilege of the bigger boys, and on holidays to walk about in the town. Great dandies we were, too, when we thus went out. I recollect my costume very well : a thunder-and-lightning coat, a white waist-coat embroidered neatly at the pockets, a lace frill, a pair of knee-breeches, and elegant white cotton or silk stockings. This did very well, but still I was dissatisfied : I wanted *a pair of boots*. Three boys in the school had boots—I was mad to have them too.

But my papa, when I wrote to him, would not hear of it ; and three pounds, the price of a pair, was too large a sum for my mother to take from the housekeeping, or for me to pay, in the present impoverished state of my exchequer ; but the desire for the boots was so strong, that have them I must at any rate.

There was a German bootmaker who had just set up in *our* town in those days, who afterwards made his fortune in London. I determined to have the boots from him, and did not despair, before the end of a year or two, either to leave the school, when I should not mind his dunning me, or to screw the money from mamma, and so pay him.

So I called upon this man—Stiffelkind was his name—and he took my measure for a pair.

"You are a vary yong gentleman to wear dop-boots," said the shoemaker.

"I suppose, fellow," says I, "that is my business and not yours. Either make the boots or not—but when you speak to a man of my rank, speak respectfully!" And I poured out a number of oaths, in order to impress him with a notion of my respectability.

They had the desired effect. "Stay, sir," says he. "I have a nice littel pair of dop-boots dat I tink will jost do for you." And he produced, sure enough, the most elegant things I ever saw. "Dey were made," said he, "for de Honourable Mr. Stiffney, of de Gards, but were too small."

"Ah, indeed!" said I. "Stiffney is a relation of mine. And what, you scoundrel, will you have the impudence to ask for these things?" He replied, "Three pounds."

"Well," said I, "they are confoundedly dear; but, as you will have a long time to wait for your money, why, I shall have my revenge, you see." The man looked alarmed, and began a speech: "Sare,—I cannot let dem go vidout——" but a bright thought struck me, and I interrupted—"Sir! don't sir me. Take off the boots, fellow, and, hark ye, when you speak to a nobleman, don't say Sir."

"A hundert tousand pardons, my Lort," says he: "if I had known you were a lort, I vood never have called you Sir. Vat name shall I put down in my books?"

"Name?—Oh! why, Lord Cornwallis, to be sure," said I, as I walked off in the boots.

"And vat shall I do vid my Lort's shoes?"

"Keep them until I send for them," said I. And giving him a patronising bow, I walked out of the shop, as the German tied up my shoes in paper.

.   .   .   .   .   .

This story I would not have told, but that my whole life turned upon these accursed boots. I walked back to school as proud as a peacock, and easily succeeded in satisfying the boys as to the manner in which I came by my new ornaments.

MARCH—SHOWERY.

Well, one fatal Monday morning—the blackest of all black
Mondays that ever I knew—as we were all of us playing between
school-hours, I saw a posse of boys round a stranger, who seemed to
be looking out for one of us. A sudden trembling seized me—I
knew it was Stiffelkind. What had brought him here? He talked
loud and seemed angry. So I rushed into the schoolroom, and,
burying my head between my hands, began reading for dear life.

"I vant Lort Cornvallis," said the horrid bootmaker. "His
Lortship belongs, I know, to dis honourable school, for I saw him
vid de boys at chorch yesterday."

"Lord who?"

"Vy, Lort Cornvallis to be sure—a very fat yong nobleman,
vid red hair : he squints a little, and svears dreadfully."

"There's no Lord Cornvallis here," said one ; and there was
a pause.

"Stop! I have it," says that odious Bunting. "*It must be
Stubbs !* " And "Stubbs! Stubbs!" every one cried out, while I
was so busy at my book as not to hear a word.

At last, two of the biggest chaps rushed into the schoolroom,
and, seizing each an arm, ran me into the playground—bolt up
against the shoemaker.

"Dis is my man. I beg your Lortship's pardon," says he, "I
have brought your Lortship's shoes, vich you left. See, dey have
been in dis parcel ever since you vent avay in my boots."

"Shoes, fellow!" says I. "I never saw your face before."
For I knew there was nothing for it but brazening it out. "Upon
the honour of a gentleman!" said I, turning round to the boys.
They hesitated ; and if the trick had turned in my favour, fifty of
them would have seized hold of Stiffelkind and drubbed him soundly.

"Stop!" says Bunting (hang him!). "Let's see the shoes.
If they fit him, why then the cobbler's right." They did fit me ;
and not only that, but the name of STUBBS was written in them at
full length.

"Vat!" said Stiffelkind. "Is he not a lort? So help me
Himmel, I never did vonce tink of looking at de shoes, which have
been lying ever since in dis piece of brown paper." And then,
gathering anger as he went on, he thundered out so much of his
abuse of me, in his German-English, that the boys roared with
laughter. Swishtail came out in the midst of the disturbance, and
asked what the noise meant.

"It's only Lord Cornwallis, sir," said the boys, "battling with
his shoemaker about the price of a pair of top-boots."

"Oh, sir," said I, "it was only in fun that I called myself
Lord Cornwallis."

APRIL—FOOLING

AFTER this, as you may fancy, I left this disgusting establishment, and lived for some time along with pa and mamma at
home. My education was finished, at least mamma and I
agreed that it was ; and from boyhood until hobbadyhoyhood (which
I take to be about the sixteenth year of the life of a young man,
and may be likened to the month of April when spring begins to
bloom)—from fourteen until seventeen, I say, I remained at home,
doing nothing—for which I have ever since had a great taste—the
idol of my mamma, who took part in all my quarrels with father,
and used regularly to rob the weekly expenses in order to find me
in pocket-money. Poor soul! many and many is the guinea I have
had from her in that way; and so she enabled me to cut a very
pretty figure.

Papa was for having me at this time articled to a merchant, or
put to some profession : but mamma and I agreed that I was born
to be a gentleman and not a tradesman, and the army was the only
place for me. Everybody was a soldier in those times, for the
French war had just begun, and the whole country was swarming
with militia regiments. " We'll get him a commission in a marching
regiment," said my father. " As we have no money to purchase
him up, he'll *fight* his way, I make no doubt." And papa looked
at me with a kind of air of contempt, as much as to say he doubted
whether I should be very eager for such a dangerous way of bettering myself.

I wish you could have heard mamma's screech when he talked
so coolly of my going out to fight! " What, send him abroad,
across the horrid, horrid sea—to be wrecked and perhaps drowned,
and only to land for the purpose of fighting the wicked Frenchmen,
—to be wounded and perhaps kick—kick—killed! Oh, Thomas,
Thomas! would you murder me and your boy?" There was a
regular scene. However, it ended—as it always did—in mother's
getting the better, and it was settled that I should go into the
militia. And why not? The uniform is just as handsome, and
the danger not half so great. I don't think in the course of my
whole military experience I ever fought anything, except an old

woman, who had the impudence to hollo out, " Heads up, lobster ! "
—Well, I joined the North Bungays, and was fairly launched into
the world.

I was not a handsome man, I know ; but there was *something*
about me—that's very evident—for the girls always laughed when
they talked to me, and the men, though they affected to call me a
poor little creature, squint-eyes, knock-knees, red-head, and so on,
were evidently annoyed by my success, for they hated me so confoundedly. Even at the present time they go on, though I have
given up gallivanting, as I call it. But in the April of my existence,
—that is, in anno Domini 1791, or so—it was a different case ;
and having nothing else to do, and being bent upon bettering my
condition, I did some very pretty things in that way. But I was
not hot-headed and imprudent, like most young fellows. Don't
fancy I looked for beauty ! Pish !—I wasn't such a fool. Nor for
temper ; I don't care about a bad temper : I could break any woman's
heart in two years. What I wanted was to get on in the world.
Of course I didn't *prefer* an ugly woman, or a shrew ; and when
the choice offered, would certainly put up with a handsome good-
humoured girl, with plenty of money, as any honest man would.

Now there were two tolerably rich girls in our parts : Miss
Magdalen Crutty, with twelve thousand pounds (and, to do her
justice, as plain a girl as ever I saw), and Miss Mary Waters, a fine,
tall, plump, smiling, peach-cheeked, golden-haired, white-skinned
lass, with only ten. Mary Waters lived with her uncle, the Doctor,
who had helped me into the world, and who was trusted with this
little orphan charge very soon after. My mother, as you have
heard, was so fond of Bates, and Bates so fond of little Mary, that
both, at first, were almost always in our house ; and I used to call
her my little wife as soon as I could speak, and before she could
walk almost. It was beautiful to see us, the neighbours said.

Well, when her brother, the lieutenant of an India ship, came
to be captain, and actually gave Mary five thousand pounds when
she was about ten years old, and promised her five thousand more,
there was a great talking, and bobbing, and smiling between the
Doctor and my parents, and Mary and I were left together more
than ever, and she was told to call me her little husband. And she
did ; and it was considered a settled thing from that day. She was
really amazingly fond of me.

Can any one call me mercenary after that ? Though Miss Crutty
had twelve thousand, and Mary only ten (five in hand, and five in
the bush), I stuck faithfully to Mary. As a matter of course, Miss
Crutty hated Miss Waters. The fact was, Mary had all the country
dangling after her, and not a soul would come to Magdalen, for all

APRIL—FOOLING.

her twelve thousand pounds. I used to be attentive to her though (as it's always useful to be); and Mary would sometimes laugh and sometimes cry at my flirting with Magdalen. This I thought proper very quickly to check. "Mary," said I, "you know that my love for you is disinterested,—for I am faithful to you, though Miss Crutty is richer than you. Don't fly into a rage, then, because I pay her attentions, when you know that my heart and my promise are engaged to you."

The fact is, to tell a little bit of a secret, there is nothing like the having two strings to your bow. "Who knows?" thought I. "Mary may die: and then where are my ten thousand pounds?" So I used to be very kind indeed to Miss Crutty; and well it was that I was so: for when I was twenty and Mary eighteen, I'm blest if news did not arrive that Captain Waters, who was coming home to England with all his money in rupees, had been taken—ship, rupees, self and all—by a French privateer; and Mary, instead of ten thousand pounds, had only five thousand, making a difference of no less than three hundred and fifty pounds per annum betwixt her and Miss Crutty.

I had just joined my regiment (the famous North Bungay Fencibles, Colonel Craw commanding) when this news reached me; and you may fancy how a young man, in an expensive regiment and mess, having uniforms and what not to pay for, and a figure to cut in the world, felt at hearing such news! "My dearest Robert," wrote Miss Waters, "will deplore my dear brother's loss: but not, I am sure, the money which that kind and generous soul had promised me. I have still five thousand pounds, and with this and your own little fortune (I had one thousand pounds in the Five per Cents.) we shall be as happy and contented as possible."

Happy and contented indeed! Didn't I know how my father got on with his three hundred pounds a year, and how it was all he could do out of it to add a hundred a year to my narrow income, and live himself? My mind was made up. I instantly mounted the coach and flew to our village,—to Mr. Crutty's, of course. It was next door to Doctor Bates's; but I had no business *there*.

I found Magdalen in the garden. "Heavens, Mr. Stubbs!" said she, as in my new uniform I appeared before her, "I really did never—such a handsome officer—expect to see you." And she made as if she would blush, and began to tremble violently. I led her to a garden-seat. I seized her hand—it was not withdrawn. I pressed it;—I thought the pressure was returned. I flung myself on my knees, and then I poured into her ear a little speech which I had made on the top of the coach. "Divine Miss Crutty," said I; "idol of my soul! It was but to catch one glimpse of you that I passed through this garden. I never intended to breathe the secret passion " (oh no ; of course not) " which was wearing my life away. You know my unfortunate pre-engagement—it is broken, and *for ever !* I am free ;—free, but to be your slave,—your humblest, fondest, truest slave ! " And so on. , . .

"Oh, Mr. Stubbs," said she, as I imprinted a kiss upon her cheek, "I can't refuse you; but I fear you are a sad naughty man. . . ."

Absorbed in the delicious reverie which was caused by the dear creature's confusion, we were both silent for a while, and should have remained so for hours perhaps, so lost were we in happiness, had I not been suddenly roused by a voice exclaiming from behind us—

"*Don't cry, Mary ! He is a swindling sneaking scoundrel, and you are well rid of him !* "

I turned round. O Heaven, there stood Mary, weeping on Doctor Bates's arm, while that miserable apothecary was looking at me with the utmost scorn. The gardener, who had let me in, had told them of my arrival, and now stood grinning behind them. " Imperence ! " was my Magdalen's only exclamation, as she flounced by with the utmost self-possession, while I, glancing daggers at *the spies,* followed her. We retired to the parlour, where she repeated to me the strongest assurances of her love.

I thought I was a made man. Alas ! I was only an APRIL FOOL !

MAY—RESTORATION DAY

AS the month of May is considered, by poets and other philo-
sophers, to be devoted by nature to the great purpose of
love-making, I may as well take advantage of that season
and acquaint you with the result of *my* amours.

Young, gay, fascinating, and an ensign—I had completely won
the heart of my Magdalen; and as for Miss Waters and her nasty
uncle the Doctor, there was a complete split between us, as you
may fancy; Miss pretending, forsooth, that she was glad I had
broken off the match, though she would have given her eyes, the
little minx, to have had it on again. But this was out of the
question. My father, who had all sorts of queer notions, said I had
acted like a rascal in the business; my mother took my part, of
course, and declared I acted rightly, as I always did: and I got
leave of absence from the regiment in order to press my beloved
Magdalen to marry me out of hand—knowing, from reading and
experience, the extraordinary mutability of human affairs.

Besides, as the dear girl was seventeen years older than myself,
and as bad in health as she was in temper, how was I to know
that the grim king of terrors might not carry her off before she
became mine? With the tenderest warmth, then, and most delicate
ardour, I continued to press my suit. The happy day was fixed—
the ever-memorable 10th of May 1792. The wedding-clothes were
ordered; and, to make things secure, I penned a little paragraph
for the county paper to this effect: "Marriage in High Life. We
understand that Ensign Stubbs, of the North Bungay Fencibles,
and son of Thomas Stubbs, of Sloffemsquiggle, Esquire, is about to
lead to the hymeneal altar the lovely and accomplished daughter of
Solomon Crutty, Esquire, of the same place. A fortune of twenty
thousand pounds is, we hear, the lady's portion. 'None but the
brave deserve the fair.'

. . . .

"Have you informed your relatives, my beloved?" said I to
Magdalen one day after sending the above notice; "will any of
them attend at your marriage?"

"Uncle Sam will, I dare say," said Miss Crutty, "dear mamma's brother."

"And who *was* your dear mamma ?" said I : for Miss Crutty's respected parent had been long since dead, and I never heard her name mentioned in the family.

Magdalen blushed, and cast down her eyes to the ground. "Mamma was a foreigner," at last she said.

"And of what country ? "

"A German. Papa married her when she was very young :— she was not of a very good family," said Miss Crutty, hesitating.

"And what care I for family, my love ! " said I, tenderly kissing the knuckles of the hand which I held. "She must have been an angel who gave birth to you."

"She was a shoemaker's daughter."

"*A German shoemaker !* Hang 'em ! " thought I, " I have had enough of them ; " and so broke up this conversation, which did not somehow please me.

.   .   .   .

Well, the day was drawing near : the clothes were ordered ; the banns were read. My dear mamma had built a cake about the size of a washing-tub ; and I was only waiting for a week to pass to put me in possession of twelve thousand pounds in the *Five* per Cents., as they were in those days, Heaven bless 'em. Little did I know the storm that was brewing, and the disappointment which was to fall upon a young man who really did his best to get a fortune.

.   .   .   .

"Oh, Robert ! " said my Magdalen to me, two days before the match was to come off, " I have *such* a kind letter from Uncle Sam in London. I wrote to him as you wished. He says that he is coming down to-morrow ; that he has heard of you often, and knows your character very well ; and that he has got a *very handsome present* for us ! What can it be, I wonder ? "

"Is he rich, my soul's adored ? " says I.

"He is a bachelor, with a fine trade, and nobody to leave his money to."

"His present can't be less than a thousand pounds ? " says I.

"Or, perhaps, a silver tea-set, and some corner-dishes," says she.

But we could not agree to this : it was too little—too mean for a man of her uncle's wealth ; and we both determined it must be the thousand pounds.

"Dear good uncle ! he's to be here by the coach," says Magdalen. "Let us ask a little party to meet him." And so we did, and so

MAY—RESTORATION DAY.

they came : my father and mother, old Crutty in his best wig, and the parson who was to marry us the next day. The coach was to come in at six. And there was the tea-table, and there was the punch-bowl, and everybody ready and smiling to receive our dear uncle from London.

Six o'clock came, and the coach, and the man from the " Green Dragon " with a portmanteau, and a fat old gentleman walking behind, of whom I just caught a glimpse—a venerable old gentleman : I thought I'd seen him before.

.   .   .   .   .   .

Then there was a ring at the bell ; then a scuffling and bumping in the passage ; then old Crutty rushed out, and a great laughing and talking, and " How are you ? " and so on, was heard at the door ; and then the parlour-door was flung open, and Crutty cried out with a loud voice—

" Good people all ! my brother-in-law, Mr. STIFFELKIND ! "

Mr. Stiffelkind !—I trembled as I heard the name !

Miss Crutty kissed him ; mamma made him a curtsey, and papa made him a bow ; and Doctor Snorter, the parson, seized his hand, and shook it most warmly : then came my turn !

" Vat ! " says he. " It is my dear goot yong frend from Doctor Schvischentail's ! is dis de yong gentleman's honorable moder " (mamma smiled and made a curtsey), " and dis his fader ? Sare and madam, you should be broud of soch a sonn. And you my niece, if you have him for a husband you vill be locky, dat is all. Vat dink you, broder Croty, and Madame Stobbs, I 'ave made your sonn's boots ! Ha—ha ! "

My mamma laughed, and said, " I did not know it, but I am sure, sir, he has as pretty a leg for a boot as any in the whole county."

Old Stiffelkind roared louder. " A very nice leg, ma'am, and a very *sheap* boot too. Vat ! did you not know I make his boots ? Perhaps you did not know something else too—p'raps you did not know " (and here the monster clapped his hand on the table and made the punch-ladle tremble in the bowl)—" p'raps you did not know as dat yong man, dat Stobbs, that sneaking, baltry, squinting fellow, is as vicked as he is ogly. He bot a pair of boots from me and never paid for dem. Dat is noting, nobody never pays ; but he bought a pair of boots, and called himself Lord Cornvallis. And I was fool enough to believe him vonce. But look you, niece Magdalen, I 'ave got five tousand pounds : if you marry him I vill not give you a benny. But look you what I will gif you : I bromised you a bresent, and I will give you DESE ! "

And the old monster produced THOSE VERY BOOTS which Swish-tail had made him take back.

. . . . . .

I *didn't* marry Miss Crutty: I am not sorry for it though. She was a nasty, ugly, ill-tempered wretch, and I've always said so ever since.

And all this arose from those infernal boots, and that unlucky paragraph in the county paper—I'll tell you how.

In the first place, it was taken up as a quiz by one of the wicked, profligate, unprincipled organs of the London press, who chose to be very facetious about the "Marriage in High Life," and made all sorts of jokes about me and my dear Miss Crutty.

Secondly, it was read in this London paper by my mortal enemy, Bunting, who had been introduced to old Stiffelkind's acquaintance by my adventure with him, and had his shoes made regularly by that foreign upstart.

Thirdly, he happened to want a pair of shoes made at this particular period, and as he was measured by the disgusting old High-Dutch cobbler, he told him his old friend Stubbs was going to be married.

"And to whom?" said old Stiffelkind. "To a voman wit geld, I vill take my oath."

"Yes," says Bunting, "a country girl—a Miss Magdalen Carotty or Crotty, at a place called Sloffemsquiggle."

"*Schloffemschwiegel!*" bursts out the dreadful bootmaker. "Mein Gott, mein Gott! das geht nicht! I tell you, sare, it is no go. Miss Crotty is my niece. I vill go down myself. I vill never let her marry dat goot-for-nothing schwindler and tief." *Such* was the language that the scoundrel ventured to use regarding me!

JUNE—MARROWBONES AND CLEAVERS

WAS there ever such confounded ill-luck? My whole life has been a tissue of ill-luck: although I have laboured perhaps harder than any man to make a fortune, something always tumbled it down. In love and in war I was not like others. In my marriages, I had an eye to the main chance; and you see how some unlucky blow would come and throw them over. In the army I was just as prudent, and just as unfortunate. What with judicious betting, and horse-swapping, good luck at billiards, and economy, I do believe I put up my pay every year,—and that is what few can say who have but an allowance of a hundred a year.

I'll tell you how it was. I used to be very kind to the young men: I chose their horses for them, and their wine; and showed them how to play billiards, or écarté, of long mornings, when there was nothing better to do. I didn't cheat: I'd rather die than cheat;—but if fellows *will* play, I wasn't the man to say no—why should I? There was one young chap in our regiment off whom I really think I cleared three hundred a year.

His name was Dobble. He was a tailor's son, and wanted to be a gentleman. A poor weak young creature; easy to be made tipsy; easy to be cheated; and easy to be frightened. It was a blessing for him that I found him; for if anybody else had, they would have plucked him of every shilling.

Ensign Dobble and I were sworn friends. I rode his horses for him, and chose his champagne, and did everything, in fact, that a superior mind does for an inferior,—when the inferior has got the money. We were inseparables,—hunting everywhere in couples. We even managed to fall in love with two sisters, as young soldiers will do, you know; for the dogs fall in love with every change of quarters.

Well, once, in the year 1793 (it was just when the French had chopped poor Louis's head off), Dobble and I, gay young chaps as ever wore sword by side, had cast our eyes upon two young ladies by the name of Brisket, daughters of a butcher in the town where we were quartered. The dear girls fell in love with us, of course.

And many a pleasant walk in the country, many a treat to a tea-garden, many a smart riband and brooch used Dobble and I (for his father allowed him six hundred pounds, and our purses were in common) to present to these young ladies. One day, fancy our pleasure at receiving a note couched thus :—

"Deer Capting Stubbs and Dobble,—Miss Briskets presents their compliments, and as it is probble that our papa will be till twelve at the corprayshun dinner, we request the pleasure of their company to tea."

Didn't we go! Punctually at six we were in the little back-parlour; we quaffed more Bohea, and made more love than half-a-dozen ordinary men could. At nine, a little punch-bowl succeeded to the little teapot; and, bless the girls! a nice fresh steak was frizzling on the gridiron for our supper. Butchers were butchers then, and their parlour was their kitchen too; at least old Brisket's was—one door leading into the shop, and one into the yard, on the other side of which was the slaughter-house.

Fancy, then, our horror when, just at this critical time, we heard the shop-door open, a heavy staggering step on the flags, and a loud husky voice from the shop, shouting, "Hallo, Susan; hallo, Betsy! show a light!" Dobble turned as white as a sheet; the two girls each as red as a lobster; I alone preserved my presence of mind. "The back-door," says I.—"The dog's in the court," say they. "He's not so bad as the man," said I. "Stop!" cries Susan, flinging open the door and rushing to the fire. "Take *this*, and perhaps it will quiet him."

What do you think "this" was? I'm blest if it was not the *steak!*

She pushed us out, patted and hushed the dog, and was in again in a minute. The moon was shining on the court, and on the slaughter-house, where there hung the white ghastly looking carcasses of a couple of sheep; a great gutter ran down the court—a gutter of *blood!* The dog was devouring his beef-steak (*our* beef-steak) in silence; and we could see through the little window the girls bustling about to pack up the supper-things, and presently the shop-door being opened, old Brisket entering, staggering, angry, and drunk. What's more, we could see, perched on a high stool, and nodding politely, as if to salute old Brisket, the *feather of Dobble's cocked hat!* When Dobble saw it, he turned white, and deadly sick; and the poor fellow, in an agony of fright, sank shivering down upon one of the butcher's cutting-blocks, which was in the yard.

We saw old Brisket look steadily (as steadily as he could) at

JUNE—MARROWBONES AND CLEAVERS.

the confounded, impudent, pert, waggling feather ; and then an idea
began to dawn upon his mind, that there was a head to the hat ;
and then he slowly rose up—he was a man of six feet, and fifteen
stone—he rose up, put on his apron and sleeves, and *took down his
cleaver.*

Betsy," says he, "open the yard door." But the poor girls
screamed, and flung on their knees, and begged, and wept, and did
their very best to prevent him. " OPEN THE YARD DOOR ! " says
he, with a thundering loud voice ; and the great bulldog, hearing it,
started up and uttered a yell which sent me flying to the other end
of the court.—Dobble couldn't move ; he was sitting on the block,
blubbering like a baby.

The door opened, and out Mr. Brisket came.

" *To him, Jowler !* " says he. " *Keep him, Jowler!* "—and the
horrid dog flew at me, and I flew back into the corner, and drew
my sword, determining to sell my life dearly.

" That's it," says Brisket. " Keep him there,—good dog,—
good dog ! And now, sir," says he, turning round to Dobble, " is
this your hat ? "

" Yes," says Dobble, fit to choke with fright.

" Well, then," says Brisket, " it's my—(hic)—my painful duty
to—(hic)—to tell you, that as I've got your hat, I must have your
head ;—it's painful, but it must be done. You'd better—(hic)—
settle yourself com—comfumarably against that—(hic)—that block,
and I'll chop it off before you can say Jack—(hic)—no, I mean
Jack Robinson."

Dobble went down on his knees and shrieked out, " I'm an only
son, Mr. Brisket ! I'll marry her, sir ; I will, upon my honour,
sir.—Consider my mother, sir ; consider my mother."

" That's it, sir," says Brisket—" that's a good—(hic)—a good
boy ;—just put your head down quietly—and I'll have it off—yes,
off—as if you were Louis the Six—the Sixtix—the Siktickleteenth.
—I'll chop the other *chap afterwards.*"

When I heard this, I made a sudden bound back, and gave such
a cry as any man might who was in such a way. The ferocious
Jowler, thinking I was going to escape, flew at my throat ;
screaming furious ; I flung out my arms in a kind of desperation,
—and, to my wonder, down fell the dog, dead, and run through
the body !

.   .   .   .   .   .

At this moment a posse of people rushed in upon old Brisket,—
one of his daughters had had the sense to summon them,—and
Dobble's head was saved. And when they saw the dog lying dead
at my feet, my ghastly look, my bloody sword, they gave me no

small credit for my bravery. "A terrible fellow that Stubbs," said they ; and so the mess said, the next day.

I didn't tell them that the dog had committed *suicide*—why should I ? And I didn't say a word about Dobble's cowardice. I said he was a brave fellow, and fought like a tiger ; and this prevented *him* from telling tales. I had the dogskin made into a pair of pistol-holsters, and looked so fierce, and got such a name for courage in our regiment, that when we had to meet the regulars, Bob Stubbs was always the man put forward to support the honour of the corps. The women, you know, adore courage ; and such was my reputation at this time, that I might have had my pick out of half-a-dozen, with three, four, or five thousand pounds apiece, who were dying for love of me and my red coat. But I wasn't such a fool. I had been twice on the point of marriage, and twice disappointed ; and I vowed by all the Saints to have a wife, and a rich one. Depend upon this, as an infallible maxim to guide you through life : *It's as easy to get a rich wife as a poor one ;*—the same bait that will hook a trout will hook a salmon.

DOBBLE'S reputation for courage was not increased by the butcher's-dog adventure; but mine stood very high : little Stubbs was voted the boldest chap of all the bold North Bungays. And though I must confess, what was proved by subsequent circumstances, that nature has *not* endowed me with a large, or even, I may say, an average share of bravery, yet a man is very willing to flatter himself to the contrary ; and, after a little time, I got to believe that my killing the dog was an action of undaunted courage, and that I was as gallant as any of the one hundred thousand heroes of our army. I always had a military taste—it's only the brutal part of the profession, the horrid fighting and blood, that I don't like.

I suppose the regiment was not very brave itself—being only militia ; but certain it was, that Stubbs was considered a most terrible fellow, and I swore so much, and looked so fierce, that you would have fancied I had made half a hundred campaigns. I was second in several duels : the umpire in all disputes ; and such a crack shot myself, that fellows were shy of insulting me. As for Dobble, I took him under my protection ; and he became so attached to me, that we ate, drank, and rode together every day ; his father didn't care for money, so long as his son was in good company—and what so good as that of the celebrated Stubbs ? Heigho ! I *was* good company in those days, and a brave fellow too, as I should have remained, but for—what I shall tell the public immediately.

It happened, in the fatal year ninety-six, that the brave North Bungays were quartered at Portsmouth, a maritime place, which I need not describe, and which I wish I had never seen. I might have been a General now, or, at least, a rich man.

The red-coats carried everything before them in those days ; and I, such a crack character as I was in my regiment, was very well received by the townspeople : many dinners I had ; many tea-parties ; many lovely young ladies did I lead down the pleasant country-dances.

Well, although I had had the two former rebuffs in love which I have described, my heart was still young ; and the fact was, knowing that a girl with a fortune was my only chance, I made love here as furiously as ever. I shan't describe the lovely creatures on whom I fixed, whilst at Portsmouth. I tried more than—several—and it is a singular fact, which I never have been able to account for, that, successful as I was with ladies of maturer age, by the young ones I was refused regular.

But "faint heart never won fair lady;" and so I went on, and on, until I had got a Miss Clopper, a tolerably rich navy-contractor's daughter, into such a way, that I really don't think she could have refused me. Her brother, Captain Clopper, was in a line regiment, and helped me as much as ever he could; he swore I was such a brave fellow.

As I had received a number of attentions from Clopper, I determined to invite him to dinner; which I could do without any sacrifice of my principle upon this point : for the fact is, Dobble lived at an inn, and as he sent all his bills to his father, I made no scruple to use his table. We dined in the coffee-room, Dobble bringing *his* friend; and so we made a party *carry*, as the French say. Some naval officers were occupied in a similar way at a table next to ours.

Well—I didn't spare the bottle, either for myself or for my friends; and we grew very talkative, and very affectionate as the drinking went on. Each man told stories of his gallantry in the field, or amongst the ladies, as officers will, after dinner. Clopper confided to the company his wish that I should marry his sister, and vowed that he thought me the best fellow in Christendom.

Ensign Dobble assented to this. "But let Miss Clopper beware," says he, "for Stubbs is a sad fellow : he has had I don't know how many *liaisons* already; and he has been engaged to I don't know how many women."

"Indeed!" says Clopper. "Come, Stubbs, tell us your adventures."

"Psha!" said I modestly, "there is nothing indeed to tell. I have been in love, my dear boy—who has not?—and I have been jilted—who has not?"

Clopper swore that he would blow his sister's brains out if ever *she* served me so.

"Tell him about Miss Crutty," said Dobble. "He! he! Stubbs served *that* woman out, anyhow; she didn't jilt *him*, I'll be sworn."

"Really, Dobble, you are too bad, and should not mention names. The fact is, the girl was desperately in love with me, and had money —sixty thousand pounds, upon my reputation. Well, everything was arranged, when who should come down from London but a relation."

"Well, and did he prevent the match?"

JULY—SUMMARY PROCEEDINGS.

"Prevent it—yes, sir, I believe you he did; though not in the sense that *you* mean. He would have given his eyes—ay, and ten thousand pounds more—if I would have accepted the girl, but I would not."

"Why, in the name of goodness?"

"Sir, her uncle was a *shoemaker*. I never would debase myself by marrying into such a family."

"Of course not," said Dobble; "he couldn't, you know. Well, now—tell him about the other girl, Mary Waters, you know."

"Hush, Dobble, hush! don't you see one of those naval officers has turned round and heard you? My dear Clopper, it was a mere childish bagatelle."

"Well, but let's have it," said Clopper—"let's have it. I won't tell my sister, you know." And he put his hand to his nose and looked monstrous wise.

"Nothing of that sort, Clopper—no, no—'pon honour—little Bob Stubbs is no *libertine*; and the story is very simple. You see that my father has a small place, merely a few hundred acres, at Sloffemsquiggle. Isn't it a funny name? Hang it, there's the naval gentleman staring again"—(I looked terribly fierce as I returned this officer's stare, and continued in a loud careless voice). "Well, at this Sloffemsquiggle there lived a girl, a Miss Waters, the niece of some blackguard apothecary in the neighbourhood; but my mother took a fancy to the girl, and had her up to the park and petted her. We were both young—and—and—the girl fell in love with me, that's the fact. I was obliged to repel some rather warm advances that she made me; and here, upon my honour as a gentleman, you have all the story about which that silly Dobble makes such a noise."

Just as I finished this sentence, I found myself suddenly taken by the nose, and a voice shouting out,—

"Mr. Stubbs, you are a LIAR AND A SCOUNDREL! Take this, sir,—and this, for daring to meddle with the name of an innocent lady."

I turned round as well as I could—for the ruffian had pulled me out of my chair—and beheld a great marine monster, six feet high, who was occupied in beating and kicking me, in the most ungentlemanly manner, on my cheeks, my ribs, and between the tails of my coat. "He is a liar, gentlemen, and a scoundrel! The bootmaker had detected him in swindling, and so his niece refused him. Miss Waters was engaged to him from childhood, and he deserted her for the bootmaker's niece, who was richer."—And then sticking a card between my stock and my coat-collar, in what is called the scruff of my neck, the disgusting brute gave me another blow behind my back, and left the coffee-room with his friends

Dobble raised me up ; and taking the card from my neck, read, CAPTAIN WATERS. Clopper poured me out a glass of water, and said in my ear, " If this is true, you are an infernal scoundrel, Stubbs ; and must fight me, after Captain Waters ; " and he flounced out of the room.

I had but one course to pursue. I sent the Captain a short and contemptuous note, saying that he was beneath my anger. As for Clopper, I did not condescend to notice his remark ; but in order to get rid of the troublesome society of these low blackguards, I determined to gratify an inclination I had long entertained, and make a little tour. I applied for leave of absence, and set off *that very night*. I can fancy the disappointment of the brutal Waters, on coming, as he did, the next morning to my quarters and finding me *gone*. Ha ! ha !

After this adventure I became sick of a military life—at least the life of my own regiment, where the officers, such was their unaccountable meanness and prejudice against me, absolutely refused to see me at mess. Colonel Craw sent me a letter to this effect, which I treated as it deserved.—I never once alluded to it in any way, and have since never spoken a single word to any man in the North Bungays.

AUGUST—DOGS HAVE THEIR DAYS

SEE, now, what life is! I have had ill-luck on ill-luck from that day to this. I have sunk in the world, and, instead of riding my horse and drinking my wine, as a real gentleman should, have hardly enough now to buy a pint of ale; ay, and am very glad when anybody will treat me to one. Why, why was I born to undergo such unmerited misfortunes?

You must know that very soon after my adventure with Miss Crutty, and that cowardly ruffian, Captain Waters (he sailed the day after his insult to me, or I should most certainly have blown his brains out; *now* he is living in England, and is my relation; but, of course, I cut the fellow)—very soon after these painful events another happened, which ended, too, in a sad disappointment. My dear papa died, and, instead of leaving five thousand pounds, as I expected at the very least, left only his estate, which was worth but two. The land and house were left to me; to mamma and my sisters he left, to be sure, a sum of two thousand pounds in the hands of that eminent firm Messrs. Pump, Aldgate & Co., which failed within six months after his demise, and paid in five years about one shilling and ninepence in the pound; which really was all my dear mother and sisters had to live upon.

The poor creatures were quite unused to money matters; and, would you believe it? when the news came of Pump and Aldgate's failure, mamma only smiled, and threw her eyes up to heaven, and said, "Blessed be God, that we have still wherewithal to live. There are tens of thousands in this world, dear children, who would count our poverty riches." And with this she kissed my two sisters, who began to blubber, as girls always will do, and threw their arms round her neck, and then round my neck, until I was half stifled with their embraces, and slobbered all over with their tears.

"Dearest mamma," said I, "I am very glad to see the noble manner in which you bear your loss; and more still to know that you are so rich as to be able to put up with it." The fact was, I really thought the old lady had got a private hoard of her own, as many of them have—a thousand pounds or so in a stocking. Had she put by thirty pounds a year, as well she might, for the thirty years of her marriage, there would have been nine hundred pounds clear, and no mistake. But still I was angry to think that any such paltry concealment had been practised—concealment too of *my* money ; so I turned on her pretty sharply, and continued my speech. "You say, ma'am, that you are rich, and that Pump and Aldgate's failure has no effect upon you. I am very happy to hear you say so, ma'am—very happy that you *are* rich ; and I should like to know where your property, my father's property, for you had none of your own,—I should like to know where this money lies—*where you have concealed it*, ma'am ; and permit me to say, that when I agreed to board you and my two sisters for eighty pounds a year, I did not know that you had *other* resources than those mentioned in my blessed father's will."

This I said to her because I hated the meanness of concealment, not because I lost by the bargain of boarding them : for the three poor things did not eat much more than sparrows ; and I've often since calculated that I had a clear twenty pounds a year profit out of them.

Mamma and the girls looked quite astonished when I made the speech. "What does he mean ? " said Lucy to Eliza.

Mamma repeated the question. "My beloved Robert, what concealment are you talking of ? "

"I am talking of concealed property, ma'am," says I sternly.

"And do you—what—can you—do you really suppose that I have concealed—any of that blessed sa-a-a-aint's prop-op-op-operty ?" screams out mamma. "Robert," says she—"Bob, my own darling boy—my fondest, best beloved, now *he* is gone " (meaning my late governor—more tears)—"you don't, you cannot fancy that your own mother, who bore you, and nursed you, and wept for you, and would give her all to save you from a moment's harm—you don't suppose that she would che-e-e-eat you ! " And here she gave a louder screech than ever, and flung back on the sofa ; and one of my sisters went and tumbled into her arms, and t'other went round, and the kissing and slobbering scene went on again, only I was left out, thank goodness. I hate such sentimentality.

"*Che-e-e-eat me,*" says I, mocking her. "What do you mean, then, by saying you're so rich ? Say, have you got money, or have you not ? " (And I rapped out a good number of oaths, too, which I don't put in here ; but I was in a dreadful fury, that's the fact.)

"So help me Heaven," says mamma, in answer, going down on her knees and smacking her two hands, "I have but a Queen Anne's guinea in the whole of this wicked world."

"Then what, madam, induces you to tell these absurd stories to

AUGUST—DOGS HAVE THEIR DAYS.

me, and to talk about your riches, when you know that you and your daughters are beggars, ma'am—*beggars ?*"

"My dearest boy, have we not got the house, and the furniture, and a hundred a year still; and have you not great talents, which will make all our fortunes?" says Mrs. Stubbs, getting up off her knees, and making believe to smile as she clawed hold of my hand and kissed it.

This was *too* cool. "*You* have got a hundred a year, ma'am?" says I—"*you* have got a house? Upon my soul and honour this is the first I ever heard of it; and I'll tell you what, ma'am," says I (and it cut her *pretty sharply* too) : "As you've got it, *you'd better go and live in it.* I've got quite enough to do with my own house, and every penny of my own income."

Upon this speech the old lady said nothing, but she gave a screech loud enough to be heard from here to York, and down she fell—kicking and struggling in a regular fit.

. . . .

I did not see Mrs. Stubbs for some days after this, and the girls used to come down to meals, and never speak ; going up again and stopping with their mother. At last, one day, both of them came in very solemn to my study, and Eliza, the eldest, said, "Robert, mamma has paid you our board up to Michaelmas."

"She has," says I ; for I always took precious good care to have it in advance.

"She says, Robert, that on Michaelmas Day—we'll—we'll go away, Robert."

"Oh, she's going to her own house, is she, Lizzy? Very good. She'll want the furniture, I suppose, and that she may have too, for I'm going to sell the place myself." And so *that* matter was settled.

. . . .

On Michaelmas Day—and during these two months I hadn't, I do believe, seen my mother twice (once, about two o'clock in the morning, I woke and found her sobbing over my bed)—on Michaelmas-Day morning, Eliza comes to me and says, "*Robert, they will come and fetch us at six this evening.*" Well, as this was the last day, I went and got the best goose I could find (I don't think I ever saw a primer, or ate more hearty myself), and had it roasted at three, with a good pudding afterwards ; and a glorious bowl of punch. "Here's a health to you, dear girls," says I, "and you, Ma, and good luck to all three ; and as you've not eaten a morsel, I hope you won't object to a glass of punch. It's the old stuff, you know, ma'am, that that Waters sent to my father fifteen years ago."

Six o'clock came, and with it came a fine barouche. As I live, Captain Waters was on the box (it was his coach); that old thief, Bates, jumped out, entered my house, and before I could say Jack Robinson, whipped off mamma to the carriage : the girls followed, just giving me a hasty shake of the hand ; and as mamma was helped in, Mary Waters, who was sitting inside, flung her arms round her, and then round the girls ; and the Doctor, who acted footman, jumped on the box, and off they went ; taking no more notice of *me* than if I'd been a nonentity.

Here's a picture of the whole business :—Mamma and Miss Waters are sitting kissing each other in the carriage, with the two girls in the back seat ; Waters is driving (a precious bad driver he is too) ; and I'm standing at the garden door, and whistling. That old fool Mary Malowney is crying behind the garden gate : she went off next day along with the furniture ; and I to get into that precious scrape which I shall mention next.

SEPTEMBER—PLUCKING A GOOSE

AFTER my papa's death, as he left me no money, and only a little land, I put my estate into an auctioneer's hands, and determined to amuse my solitude with a trip to some of our fashionable watering-places. My house was now a desert to me. I need not say how the departure of my dear parent, and her children, left me sad and lonely.

Well, I had a little ready money, and, for the estate, expected a couple of thousand pounds. I had a good military-looking person : for though I had absolutely cut the old North Bungays (indeed, after my affair with Waters, Colonel Craw hinted to me, in the most friendly manner, that I had better resign)—though I had left the army, I still retained the rank of Captain ; knowing the advantages attendant upon that title in a watering-place tour.

Captain Stubbs became a great dandy at Cheltenham, Harrogate, Bath, Leamington, and other places. I was a good whist and billiard player ; so much so, that in many of these towns, the people used to refuse, at last, to play with me, knowing how far I was their superior. Fancy my surprise, about five years after the Portsmouth affair, when strolling one day up the High Street, in Leamington, my eyes lighted upon a young man, whom I remembered in a certain butcher's yard, and elsewhere—no other, in fact, than Dobble. He, too, was dressed *en militaire*, with a frogged coat and spurs ; and was walking with a showy-looking, Jewish-faced, black-haired lady, glittering with chains and rings, with a green bonnet and a bird-of-Paradise—a lilac shawl, a yellow gown, pink silk stockings, and light-blue shoes. Three children, and a handsome footman, were walking behind her, and the party, not seeing me, entered the "Royal Hotel" together.

I was known myself at the "Royal," and calling one of the waiters, learned the names of the lady and gentleman. He was Captain Dobble, the son of the rich army-clothier, Dobble (Dobble, Hobble & Co., of Pall Mall) ;—the lady was a Mrs. Manasseh, widow of an American Jew, living quietly at Leamington with her children, but possessed of an immense property. There's no use to give one's self out to be an absolute pauper : so the fact is, that

I myself went everywhere with the character of a man of very large means. My father had died, leaving me immense sums of money, and landed estates. Ah! I was the gentleman then, the real gentleman, and everybody was too happy to have me at table.

Well, I came the next day and left a card for Dobble, with a note. He neither returned my visit, nor answered my note. The day after, however, I met him with the widow, as before; and going up to him, very kindly seized him by the hand, and swore I was—as really was the case—charmed to see him. Dobble hung back, to my surprise, and I do believe the creature would have cut me, if he dared; but I gave him a frown, and said—

"What, Dobble my boy, don't you recollect old Stubbs, and our adventure with the butcher's daughters—ha?"

Dobble gave a sickly kind of grin, and said, "Oh! ah! yes! It is—yes! it is, I believe, Captain Stubbs."

"An old comrade, madam, of Captain Dobble's, and one who has heard so much, and seen so much of your Ladyship, that he must take the liberty of begging his friend to introduce him."

Dobble was obliged to take the hint; and Captain Stubbs was duly presented to Mrs. Manasseh. The lady was as gracious as possible; and when, at the end of the walk, we parted, she said she "hoped Captain Dobble would bring me to her apartments that evening, where she expected a few friends." Everybody, you see, knows everybody at Leamington; and I, for my part, was well known as a retired officer of the army, who, on his father's death, had come into seven thousand a year. Dobble's arrival had been subsequent to mine; but putting up as he did at the "Royal Hotel," and dining at the ordinary there with the widow, he had made her acquaintance before I had. I saw, however, that if I allowed him to talk about me, as he could, I should be compelled to give up all my hopes and pleasures at Leamington; and so I determined to be short with him. As soon as the lady had gone into the hotel, my friend Dobble was for leaving me likewise; but I stopped him, and said, "Mr. Dobble, I saw what you meant just now : you wanted to cut me, because, forsooth, I did not choose to fight a duel at Portsmouth. Now look you, Dobble, I am no hero, but I am not such a coward as you—and you know it. You are a very different man to deal with from Waters; and *I will fight* this time."

Not perhaps that I would : but after the business of the butcher, I knew Dobble to be as great a coward as ever lived; and there never was any harm in threatening, for you know you are not obliged to stick to it afterwards. My words had their effect upon Dobble, who stuttered and looked red, and then declared he never

SEPTEMBER—PLUCKING A GOOSE.

had the slightest intention of passing me by; so we became friends, and his mouth was stopped.

He was very thick with the widow, but that lady had a very capacious heart, and there were a number of other gentlemen who seemed equally smitten with her. " Look at that Mrs. Manasseh," said a gentleman (it was droll, *he* was a Jew, too) sitting at dinner by me. " She is old, ugly, and yet, because she has money, all the men are flinging themselves at her."

" She has money, has she ? "

" Eighty thousand pounds, and twenty thousand for each of her children. I know it *for a fact*," said the strange gentleman. " I am in the law, and we of our faith, you know, know pretty well what the great families amongst us are worth."

" Who was Mr. Manasseh ? " said I.

" A man of enormous wealth—a tobacco-merchant—West Indies; a fellow of no birth, however ; and who, between ourselves, married a woman that is not much better than she should be. My dear sir," whispered he, " she is always in love. Now it is with that Captain Dobble ; last week it was somebody else—and it may be you next week, if—ha ! ha ! ha !—you are disposed to enter the lists. I wouldn't, for *my* part, have the woman with twice her money."

What did it matter to me whether the woman was good or not, provided she was rich ? My course was quite clear. I told Dobble all that this gentleman had informed me, and being a pretty good hand at making a story, I made the widow appear *so* bad, that the poor fellow was quite frightened, and fairly quitted the field. Ha ! ha ! I'm dashed if I did not make him believe that Mrs. Manasseh had *murdered* her last husband.

I played my game so well, thanks to the information that my friend the lawyer had given me, that in a month I had got the widow to show a most decided partiality for me. I sat by her at dinner, I drank with her at the " Wells "—I rode with her, I danced with her, and at a picnic to Kenilworth, where we drank a good deal of champagne, I actually popped the question, and was accepted. In another month, Robert Stubbs, Esquire, led to the altar, Leah, widow of the late Z. Manasseh, Esquire, of St. Kitt's !

.   .   .   .

We drove up to London in her comfortable chariot : the children and servants following in a postchaise. I paid, of course, for everything; and until our house in Berkeley Square was painted, we stopped at " Stevens's Hotel."

.   .   .   .   .

My own estate had been sold, and the money was lying at a bank in the City. About three days after our arrival, as we took our breakfast in the hotel, previous to a visit to Mrs. Stubbs's banker, where certain little transfers were to be made, a gentleman was introduced, who, I saw at a glance, was of my wife's persuasion.

He looked at Mrs. Stubbs, and made a bow. "Perhaps it will be convenient to you to pay this little bill, one hundred and fifty-two pounds?"

"My love," says she, "will you pay this?—it is a trifle which I had really forgotten."

"My soul!" said I, "I have really not the money in the house."

"Vell, denn, Captain Shtubbsh," says he, "I must do my duty—and arrest you—here is the writ! Tom, keep the door!"—My wife fainted—the children screamed, and fancy my condition as I was obliged to march off to a spunging-house along with a horrid sheriff's officer!

OCTOBER—MARS AND VENUS IN OPPOSITION

I SHALL not describe my feelings when I found myself in a cage in Cursitor Street, instead of that fine house in Berkeley Square, which was to have been mine as the husband of Mrs. Manasseh. What a place!—in an odious dismal street leading from Chancery Lane. A hideous Jew boy opened the second of three doors, and shut it when Mr. Nabb and I (almost fainting) had entered ; then he opened the third door, and then I was introduced to a filthy place called a coffee-room, which I exchanged for the solitary comfort of a little dingy back-parlour, where I was left for a while to brood over my miserable fate. Fancy the change between this and Berkeley Square ! Was I, after all my pains, and cleverness, and perseverance, cheated at last ? Had this Mrs. Manasseh been imposing upon me, and were the words of the wretch I met at the table-d'hôte at Leamington only meant to mislead me and take me in ? I determined to send for my wife, and know the whole truth. I saw at once that I had been the victim of an infernal plot, and that the carriage, the house in town, the West India fortune, were only so many lies which I had blindly believed. It was true the debt was but a hundred and fifty pounds ; and I had two thousand at my bankers'. But was the loss of *her* eighty thousand pounds nothing ? Was the destruction of my hopes nothing ? The accursed addition to my family of a Jewish wife and three Jewish children, nothing ? And all these I was to support out of my two thousand pounds. I had better have stopped at home with my mamma and sisters, whom I really did love, and who produced me eighty pounds a year.

I had a furious interview with Mrs. Stubbs ; and when I charged her, the base wretch ! with cheating me, like a brazen serpent as she was, she flung back the cheat in my teeth, and swore I had swindled her. Why did I marry her, when she might have had twenty others ? She only took me, she said, because I had twenty thousand pounds. I *had* said I possessed that sum : but in love, you know, and war all's fair.

We parted quite as angrily as we met ; and I cordially vowed that when I had paid the debt into which I had been swindled by her, I would take my two thousand pounds and depart to some desert island; or, at the very least, to America, and never see her more, or any of her Israelitish brood. There was no use in remaining in the spunging-house (for I knew that there were such things as detainers, and that where Mrs. Stubbs owed a hundred pounds, she might owe a thousand): so I sent for Mr. Nabb, and tendering him a cheque for one hundred and fifty pounds and his costs, requested to be let out forthwith. " Here, fellow," said I, " is a cheque on Child's for your paltry sum."

" It may be a sheck on Shild's," says Mr. Nabb; " but I should be a baby to let you out on such a paper as dat."

" Well," said I, " Child's is but a step from this : you may go and get the cash,—just give me an acknowledgment."

Nabb drew out the acknowledgment with great punctuality, and set off for the bankers', whilst I prepared myself for departure from this abominable prison.

He smiled as he came in. " Well," said I, " you have touched your money; and now, I must tell you, that you are the most infernal rogue and extortioner I ever met with."

" Oh no, Mishter Shtubbsh," says he, grinning still. " Dere is som greater roag dan me,—mosh greater."

" Fellow," said I, " don't stand grinning before a gentleman; but give me my hat and cloak, and let me leave your filthy den."

" Shtop, Shtubbsh," says he, not even Mistering me this time. " Here ish a letter, vich you had better read."

I opened the letter; something fell to the ground,—it was my cheque.

The letter ran thus :—

" Messrs. Child & Co. present their compliments to Captain Stubbs, and regret that they have been obliged to refuse payment of the enclosed, having been served this day with an attachment by Messrs. Solomonson & Co., which compels them to retain Captain Stubbs's balance of £2,010, 11s. 6d. until the decision of the suit of Solomonson v. Stubbs.

" FLEET STREET."

" You see," says Mr. Nabb, as I read this dreadful letter—" you see, Shtubbsh, dere vas two debts,—a little von and a big von. So dey arrested you for de little von, and attashed your money for de big von."

Don't laugh at me for telling this story. If you knew what tears are blotting over the paper as I write it—if you knew that for weeks after I was more like a madman than a sane man,—a mad-

OCTOBER—MARS AND VENUS IN OPPOSITION.

man in the Fleet Prison, where I went instead of to the desert island! What had I done to deserve it? Hadn't I always kept an eye to the main chance? Hadn't I lived economically, and not like other young men? Had I ever been known to squander or give away a single penny? No! I can lay my hand on my heart, and, thank Heaven, say, No! Why, why was I punished so?

Let me conclude this miserable history. Seven months—my wife saw me once or twice, and then dropped me altogether—I remained in that fatal place. I wrote to my dear mamma, begging her to sell her furniture, but got no answer. All my old friends turned their backs upon me. My action went against me—I had not a penny to defend it. Solomonson proved my wife's debt, and seized my two thousand pounds. As for the detainer against me, I was obliged to go through the court for the relief of insolvent debtors. I passed through it, and came out a beggar. But fancy the malice of that wicked Stiffelkind: he appeared in court as my creditor for three pounds, with sixteen years' interest at five per cent., for a PAIR OF TOP-BOOTS. The old thief produced them in court, and told the whole story—Lord Cornwallis, the detection, the pumping and all.

Commissioner Dubobwig was very funny about it. "So Doctor Swishtail would not pay you for the boots, eh, Mr. Stiffelkind?"

"No: he said, ven I asked him for payment, dey was ordered by a yong boy, and I ought to have gone to his schoolmaster."

"What! then you came on a *bootless* errand, hey, sir?" (A laugh.)

"Bootless! no sare, I brought de boots back vid me. How de devil else could I show dem to you?" (Another laugh.)

"You've never *soled* 'em since, Mr. Tickleshins?"

"I never would sell dem; I svore I never vood, on porpus to be revenged on dat Stobbs."

"What! your wound has never been *healed*, eh?"

"Vat de you mean vid your bootless errands, and your soling and healing? I tell you I have done vat I svore to do: I have exposed him at school; I have broak off a marriage for him, ven he vould have had tventy tousand pound; and now I have showed him up in a court of justice. Dat is vat I 'ave done, and dat's enough." And then the old wretch went down, whilst everybody was giggling and staring at poor me—as if I was not miserable enough already.

"This seems the dearest pair of boots you ever had in your life, Mr. Stubbs," said Commissioner Dubobwig very archly, and then he began to inquire about the rest of my misfortunes.

In the fulness of my heart I told him the whole of them: how Mr. Solomonson the attorney had introduced me to the rich widow,

Mrs. Manasseh, who had fifty thousand pounds, and an estate in the West Indies. How I was married, and arrested on coming to town, and cast in an action for two thousand pounds brought against me by this very Solomonson for my wife's debts.

"Stop!" says a lawyer in the court. "Is this woman a showy black-haired woman with one eye? very often drunk, with three children?—Solomonson, short, with red hair?"

"Exactly so," said I, with tears in my eyes.

"That woman has married *three men* within the last two years. One in Ireland, and one at Bath. A Solomonson is, I believe, her husband, and they both are off for America ten days ago."

"But why did you not keep your two thousand pounds?" said the lawyer.

"Sir, they attached it."

"Oh, well, we may pass you. You have been unlucky, Mr. Stubbs, but it seems as if the biter had been bit in this affair."

"No," said Mr. Dubobwig. "Mr. Stubbs is the victim of a FATAL ATTACHMENT."

NOVEMBER—A GENERAL POST DELIVERY

I WAS a free man when I went out of the court; but I was a beggar—I, Captain Stubbs, of the bold North Bungays, did not know where I could get a bed, or a dinner.

As I was marching sadly down Portugal Street, I felt a hand on my shoulder and a rough voice which I knew well.

"Vell, Mr. Stobbs, have I not kept my promise? I told you dem boots would be your ruin."

I was much too miserable to reply; and only cast my eyes towards the roofs of the houses, which I could not see for the tears.

"Vat! you begin to gry and blobber like a shild? you vood marry, vood you? and noting vood do for you but a vife vid monny—ha, ha—but you vere de pigeon, and she was de grow. She has plocked you, too, pretty vell—eh? ha! ha!"

"Oh, Mr. Stiffelkind," said I, "don't laugh at my misery: she has not left me a single shilling under heaven. And I shall starve: I do believe I shall starve." And I began to cry fit to break my heart.

"Starf! stoff and nonsense! You vill never die of starfing—you vill die of *hanging*, I tink—ho! ho!—and it is moch easier vay too." I didn't say a word, but cried on; till everybody in the street turned round and stared.

"Come, come," said Stiffelkind, "do not gry, Gaptain Stobbs—it is not goot for a Gaptain to gry—ha! ha! Dere—come vid me, and you shall have a dinner, and a bregfast too,—vich shall gost you nothing, until you can bay vid your earnings."

And so this curious old man, who had persecuted me all through my prosperity, grew compassionate towards me in my ill-luck; and took me home with him as he promised. "I saw your name among de Insolvents, and I vowed, you know, to make you repent dem boots. Dere now, it is done, and forgotten, look you. Here, Betty, Bettchen, make de spare bed, and put a clean knife and fork; Lort Cornvallis is come to dine vid me."

I lived with this strange old man for six weeks. I kept his books, and did what little I could to make myself useful: carrying about boots and shoes, as if I had never borne His Majesty's commission. He gave me no money, but he fed and lodged me comfortably. The men and boys used to laugh and call me General, and Lord Cornwallis, and all sorts of nicknames; and old Stiffelkind made a thousand new ones for me.

One day I can recollect—one miserable day, as I was polishing on the trees a pair of boots of Mr. Stiffelkind's manufacture—the old gentleman came into the shop, with a lady on his arm.

"Vere is Gaptain Stobbs?" said he. "Vere is dat ornament to His Majesty's service?"

I came in from the back shop, where I was polishing the boots, with one of them in my hand.

"Look, my dear," says he, "here is an old friend of yours, his Excellency Lort Cornvallis!—Who would have thought such a nobleman vood turn shoeblack? Gaptain Stobbs, here is your former flame, my dear niece, Miss Grotty. How could you, Magdalen, ever leaf such a lof of a man? Shake hands vid her, Gaptain;—dere, never mind de blacking!" But Miss drew back.

"I never shake hands with a *shoeblack*," said she, mighty contemptuous.

"Bah! my lof, his fingers von't soil you. Don't you know he has just been *vitevashed?*"

"I wish, uncle," says she, "you would not leave me with such low people."

"Low, because he cleans boots? De Gaptain prefers *pumps* to boots, I tink—ha! ha!"

"Captain indeed; a nice Captain," says Miss Crutty, snapping her fingers in my face, and walking away: "a Captain who has had his nose pulled! ha! ha!"—And how could I help it? it wasn't by my own *choice* that that ruffian Waters took such liberties with me. Didn't I show how averse I was to all quarrels by refusing altogether his challenge?—But such is the world. And thus the people at Stiffelkind's used to tease me, until they drove me almost mad.

At last he came home one day more merry and abusive than ever. "Gaptain," says he, "I have goot news for you—a goot place. Your Lordship vill not be able to geep your garridge, but you vill be gomfortable, and serve His Majesty."

"Serve His Majesty?" says I. "Dearest Mr. Stiffelkind, have you got me a place under Government?"

"Yes, and somting better still—not only a place, but a uniform: yes, Gaptain Stobbs, a *red goat.*"

"A red coat! I hope you don't think I would demean myself by entering the ranks of the army? I am a gentleman, Mr. Stiffelkind—I can never—no, I never———"

NOVEMBER—A GENERAL POST DELIVERY.

"No, I know you will never—you are too great a goward—ha! ha!—though dis is a red coat, and a place where you must give some *hard knocks* too—ha! ha!—do you gomprehend?—and you shall be a general instead of a gaptain—ha! ha!"

"A general in a red coat, Mr. Stiffelkind?"

"Yes, a GENERAL BOSTMAN!—ha! ha! I have been vid your old friend, Bunting, and he has an uncle in the Post-Office, and he has got you de place—eighteen shillings a veek, you rogue, and your goat. You must not oben any of de letters, you know."

And so it was—I, Robert Stubbs, Esquire, became the vile thing he named—a general postman!

.   .   .   .   .   .

I was so disgusted with Stiffelkind's brutal jokes, which were now more brutal than ever, that when I got my place in the Post-Office, I never went near the fellow again; for though he had done me a favour in keeping me from starvation, he certainly had done it in a very rude disagreeable manner, and showed a low and mean spirit in *shoving* me into such a degraded place as that of postman. But what had I to do? I submitted to fate, and for three years or more, Robert Stubbs, of the North Bungay Fencibles, was——

I wonder nobody recognised me. I lived in daily fear the first year: but afterwards grew accustomed to my situation, as all great men will do, and wore my red coat as naturally as if I had been sent into the world only for the purpose of being a letter-carrier.

I was first in the Whitechapel district, where I stayed for nearly three years, when I was transferred to Jermyn Street and Duke Street—famous places for lodgings. I suppose I left a hundred letters at a house in the latter street, where lived some people who must have recognised me had they but once chanced to look at me.

You see that, when I left Sloffemsquiggle, and set out in the gay world, my mamma had written to me a dozen times at least; but I never answered her, for I knew she wanted money, and I detest writing. Well, she stopped her letters, finding she could get none from me:—but when I was in the Fleet, as I told you, I wrote repeatedly to my dear mamma, and was not a little nettled at her refusing to notice me in my distress, which is the very time one most wants notice.

Stubbs is not an uncommon name; and though I saw MRS. STUBBS on a little bright brass plate in Duke Street, and delivered so many letters to the lodgers in her house, I never thought of asking who she was, or whether she was my relation or not.

One day the young woman who took in the letters had not got change, and she called her mistress. An old lady in a poke-bonnet came out of the parlour, and put on her spectacles, and looked at the letter, and fumbled in her pocket for eightpence, and apologised to the postman for keeping him waiting. And when I said, " Never mind, ma'am, it's no trouble," the old lady gave a start, and then she pulled off her spectacles, and staggered back ; and then she began muttering, as if about to choke ; and then she gave a great screech, and flung herself into my arms, and roared out, " MY SON, MY SON ! "

" Law, mamma," said I, " is that you ? " and I sat down on the hall bench with her, and let her kiss me as much as ever she liked. Hearing the whining and crying, down comes another lady from upstairs,—it was my sister Eliza ; and down come the lodgers. And the maid gets water and what not, and I was the regular hero of the group. I could not stay long then, having my letters to deliver. But, in the evening, after mail-time, I went back to my mamma and sister ; and, over a bottle of prime old port, and a precious good leg of boiled mutton and turnips, made myself pretty comfortable, I can tell you.

DECEMBER—"THE WINTER OF OUR DISCONTENT"

MAMMA had kept the house in Duke Street for more than two years. I recollected some of the chairs and tables from dear old Sloffemsquiggle, and the bowl in which I had made that famous rum-punch, the evening she went away, which she and my sisters left untouched, and I was obliged to drink after they were gone ; but that's not to the purpose.

Think of my sister Lucy's luck ! that chap, Waters, fell in love with her, and married her; and she now keeps her carriage, and lives in state near Sloffemsquiggle. I offered to make it up with Waters; but he bears malice, and never will see or speak to me.—He had the impudence, too, to say, that he took in all letters for mamma at Sloffemsquiggle ; and that as mine were all begging-letters, he burned them, and never said a word to her concerning them. He allowed mamma fifty pounds a year, and, if she were not such a fool, she might have had three times as much ; but the old lady was high and mighty forsooth, and would not be beholden, even to her own daughter, for more than she actually wanted. Even this fifty pound she was going to refuse ; but when I came to live with her, of course I wanted pocket-money as well as board and lodging, and so I had the fifty pounds for *my* share, and eked out with it as well as I could.

Old Bates and the Captain, between them, gave mamma a hundred pounds when she left me (she had the deuce's own luck, to be sure—much more than ever fell to *me*, I know) ; and as she said she *would* try and work for her living, it was thought best to take a house and let lodgings, which she did. Our first and second floor paid us four guineas a week on an average ; and the front parlour and attic made forty pounds more. Mamma and Eliza used to have the front attic ; but *I* took that, and they slept in the servants' bed-room. Lizzy had a pretty genius for work, and earned a guinea a week that way ; so that we had got nearly two hundred a year over the rent to keep house with,—and we got on pretty well. Besides, women eat nothing: my women didn't care for meat for days together sometimes,—so that it was only necessary to dress a good steak or so for me.

Mamma would not think of my continuing in the Post-Office. She said her dear Robert, her husband's son, her gallant soldier, and all that, should remain at home and be a gentleman—which I was, certainly, though I didn't find fifty pounds a year very much to buy clothes and be a gentleman upon. To be sure, mother found me shirts and linen, so that *that* wasn't in the fifty pounds. She kicked a little at paying the washing too; but she gave in at last, for I was her dear Bob, you know; and I'm blest if I could not make her give me the gown off her back. Fancy! once she cut up a very nice rich black silk scarf, which my sister Waters sent her, and made me a waistcoat and two stocks of it. She was so *very* soft, the old lady!

.   .   .   .

I'd lived in this way for five years or more, making myself content with my fifty pounds a year (*perhaps* I'd saved a little out of it; but that's neither here nor there). From year's end to year's end I remained faithful to my dear mamma, never leaving her except for a month or so in the summer—when a bachelor may take a trip to Gravesend or Margate, which would be too expensive for a family. I say a bachelor, for the fact is, I don't know whether I am married or not—never having heard a word since of the scoundrelly Mrs. Stubbs.

I never went to the public-house before meals: for, with my beggarly fifty pounds, I could not afford to dine away from home: but there I had my regular seat, and used to come home *pretty glorious*, I can tell you. Then bed till eleven; then breakfast and the newspaper; then a stroll in Hyde Park or St. James's; then home at half-past three to dinner—when I jollied, as I call it, for the rest of the day. I was my mother's delight; and thus, with a clear conscience, I managed to live on.

.   .   .   .

How fond she was of me, to be sure! Being sociable myself and loving to have my friends about me, we often used to assemble a company of as hearty fellows as you would wish to sit down with, and keep the nights up royally. "Never mind, my boys," I used to say, "send the bottle round: mammy pays for all." As she did, sure enough: and sure enough we punished her cellar too. The good old lady used to wait upon us, as if for all the world she had been my servant, instead of a lady and my mamma. Never used she to repine, though I often, as I must confess, gave her occasion (keeping her up till four o'clock in the morning, because she never could sleep until she saw her "dear Bob" in bed, and leading her a sad anxious life). She was of such a sweet temper, the old lady, that

DECEMBER—"THE WINTER OF OUR DISCONTENT."

I think in the course of five years I never knew her in a passion, except twice : and then with sister Lizzy, who declared I was ruining the house, and driving the lodgers away, one by one. But mamma would not hear of such envious spite on my sister's part. "Her Bob" was always right, she said. At last Lizzy fairly retreated, and went to the Waters's.—I was glad of it, for her temper was dreadful, and we used to be squabbling from morning till night !

Ah, those *were* jolly times ! but ma was obliged to give up the lodging-house at last—for, somehow, things went wrong after my sister's departure—the nasty uncharitable people said, on account of *me ;* because I drove away the lodgers by smoking and drinking, and kicking up noises in the house ; and because ma gave me so much of her money :—so she did, but if she *would* give it, you know, how could I help it ? Heigho ! I wish I'd *kept* it.

No such luck. The business I thought was to last for ever ; but at the end of two years came a smash—shut up shop—sell off everything. Mamma went to the Waters's : and, will you believe it ? the ungrateful wretches would not receive me ! that Mary, you see, was so disappointed at not marrying me.

Twenty pounds a year they allow, it is true ; but what's that for a gentleman ? For twenty years I have been struggling manfully to gain an honest livelihood, and, in the course of them, have seen a deal of life, to be sure. I've sold cigars and pocket-handkerchiefs at the corners of streets ; I've been a billiard-marker ; I've been a director (in the panic year) of the Imperial British Consolidated Mangle and Drying Ground Company. I've been on the stage (for two years as an actor, and about a month as a cad, when I was very low) ; I've been the means of giving to the police of this empire some very valuable information (about licensed victuallers, gentlemen's carts, and pawnbrokers' names) ; I've been very nearly an officer again—that is, an assistant to an officer of the Sheriff of Middlesex : it was my last place.

On the last day of the year 1837, even *that* game was up. It's a thing that very seldom happened to a gentleman, to be kicked out of a spunging-house ; but such was my case. Young Nabb (who succeeded his father) drove me ignominiously from his door, because I had charged a gentleman in the coffee-room seven-and-sixpence for a glass of ale and bread and cheese, the charge of the house being only six shillings. He had the meanness to deduct the eighteen-pence from my wages, and because I blustered a bit, he took me by the shoulders and turned me out—me, a gentleman, and, what is more, a poor orphan !

How I did rage and swear at him when I got out into the street ! There stood he, the hideous Jew monster, at the double door, writh-

ing under the effect of my language.   I had my revenge !   Heads
were thrust out of every bar of his windows, laughing at him.   A
crowd gathered round me, as I stood pounding him with my satire,
and they evidently enjoyed his discomfiture.   I think the mob would
have pelted the ruffian to death (one or two of their missiles hit *me*,
I can tell you), when a policeman came up, and in reply to a gentleman, who was asking what was the disturbance, said, " Bless you,
sir, it's Lord Cornwallis."   " Move on, *Boots*," said the fellow to
me ; for the fact is, my misfortunes and early life are pretty well
known—and so the crowd dispersed.

" What could have made that policeman call you Lord Cornwallis
and Boots ? " said the gentleman, who seemed mightily amused, and
had followed me.   " Sir," says I, " I am an unfortunate officer of
the North Bungay Fencibles, and I'll tell you willingly for a pint
of beer. "   He told me to follow him to his chambers in the Temple,
which I did (a five-pair back), and there, sure enough, I had the
beer ; and told him this very story you've been reading.   You see
he is what is called a literary man—and sold my adventures for me
to the booksellers : he's a strange chap ; and says they're *moral*.

.   .   .   .

I'm blest if *I* can see anything moral in them.   I'm sure I
ought to have been more lucky through life, being so very wide
awake.   And yet here I am, without a place, or even a friend,
starving upon a beggarly twenty pounds a year—not a single sixpence more, upon *my honour*.

THE BEDFORD-ROW CONSPIRACY

THE

BEDFORD-ROW CONSPIRACY *

CHAPTER I

OF THE LOVES OF MR. PERKINS AND MISS GORGON, AND OF THE TWO GREAT FACTIONS IN THE TOWN OF OLDBOROUGH

"MY dear John," cried Lucy, with a very wise look indeed, "it must and shall be so. As for Doughty Street, with our means, a house is out of the question. We must keep three servants, and Aunt Biggs says the taxes are one-and-twenty pounds a year."

"I have seen a sweet place at Chelsea," remarked John: "Paradise Row, No. 17,—garden—greenhouse—fifty pounds a year —omnibus to town within a mile."

"What! that I may be left alone all day, and you spend a fortune in driving backward and forward in those horrid breakneck cabs? My darling, I should die there—die of fright, I know I should. Did you not say yourself that the road was not as yet lighted, and that the place swarmed with public-houses and dreadful tipsy Irish bricklayers? Would you kill me, John?"

"My da—arling," said John, with tremendous fondness, clutching Miss Lucy suddenly round the waist, and rapping the hand of that young person violently against his waistcoat,—"My da—arling, don't say such things, even in a joke. If I objected to the chambers, it is only because you, my love, with your birth and connections, ought to have a house of your own. The chambers are quite large enough, and certainly quite good enough for me." And so, after some more sweet parley on the part of these young people, it was agreed that they should take up their abode, when married, in a part of the House number One hundred and something, Bedford Row.

* A story of Charles de Bernard furnished the plot of "The Bedford-Row Conspiracy."

It will be necessary to explain to the reader that John was no other than John Perkins, Esquire, of the Middle Temple, barrister-at-law, and that Miss Lucy was the daughter of the late Captain Gorgon, and Marianne Biggs, his wife. The Captain being of noble connections, younger son of a baronet, cousin to Lord X——, and related to the Y—— family, had angered all his relatives by marrying a very silly pretty young woman, who kept a ladies'-school at Canterbury. She had six hundred pounds to her fortune, which the Captain laid out in the purchase of a sweet travelling-carriage and dressing-case for himself; and going abroad with his lady, spent several years in the principal prisons of Europe, in one of which he died. His wife and daughter were meantime supported by the contributions of Mrs. Jemima Biggs, who still kept the ladies'-school.

At last a dear old relative—such a one as one reads of in romances—died and left seven thousand pounds apiece to the two sisters, whereupon the elder gave up schooling and retired to London; and the younger managed to live with some comfort and decency at Brussels, upon two hundred and ten pounds per annum. Mrs. Gorgon never touched a shilling of her capital, for the very good reason that it was placed entirely out of her reach; so that when she died, her daughter found herself in possession of a sum of money that is not always to be met with in this world.

Her aunt the baronet's lady, and her aunt the ex-schoolmistress, both wrote very pressing invitations to her, and she resided with each for six months after her arrival in England. Now, for a second time, she had come to Mrs. Biggs, Caroline Place, Mecklenburgh Square. It was under the roof of that respectable old lady that John Perkins, Esquire, being invited to take tea, wooed and won Miss Gorgon.

Having thus described the circumstances of Miss Gorgon's life, let us pass for a moment from that young lady, and lift up the veil of mystery which envelops the deeds and character of Perkins.

Perkins, too, was an orphan; and he and his Lucy, of summer evenings, when Sol descending lingered fondly yet about the minarets of the Foundling, and gilded the grassplots of Mecklenburgh Square —Perkins, I say, and Lucy would often sit together in the summer-house of that pleasure-ground, and muse upon the strange coincidences of their life. Lucy was motherless and fatherless; so too was Perkins. If Perkins was brotherless and sisterless, was not Lucy likewise an only child? Perkins was twenty-three: his age and Lucy's united, amounted to forty-six; and it was to be remarked, as a fact still more extraordinary, that while Lucy's relatives were *aunts*, John's were *uncles*. Mysterious spirit of love! let us treat thee with respect and whisper not too many of thy secrets. The fact is, John and Lucy were a pair of fools (as every young couple *ought* to be who have hearts that are worth a farthing), and were ready to find coincidences, sympathies, hidden gushes of feeling, mystic unions of the soul, and what not, in every single circumstance that occurred from the rising of the sun to the going down thereof, and in the intervals. Bedford Row, where Perkins lived, is not very far from Mecklenburgh Square ; and John used to say that he felt a comfort that his house and Lucy's were served by the same muffin-man.

Further comment is needless. A more honest, simple, clever, warm-hearted, soft, whimsical, romantical, high-spirited young fellow than John Perkins did not exist. When his father, Doctor Perkins, died, this, his only son, was placed under the care of John Perkins, Esquire, of the house of Perkins, Scully, and Perkins, those celebrated attorneys in the trading town of Oldborough, which the second partner, William Pitt Scully, Esquire, represented in Parliament and in London.

All John's fortune was the house in Bedford Row, which, at his father's death, was let out into chambers, and brought in a clear hundred a year. Under his uncle's roof at Oldborough, where he lived with thirteen red-haired male and female cousins, he was only charged fifty pounds for board, clothes, and pocket-money, and the remainder of his rents was carefully put by for him until his majority. When he approached that period—when he came to belong to two spouting-clubs at Oldborough, among the young merchants and lawyers' clerks—to blow the flute nicely, and play a good game at billiards—to have written one or two smart things in the *Oldborough Sentinel*—to be fond of smoking (in which act he was discovered by his fainting aunt at three o'clock one morning)—in one word, when John Perkins arrived at manhood, he discovered that he was quite unfit to be an attorney, that he detested all the ways of his uncle's stern, dull, vulgar, regular, red-headed family, and he vowed that he would go to London and make his fortune. Thither he went, his aunt and cousins, who were all " serious," vowing that he was a lost boy ; and when his history opens, John had been two years in the metropolis, inhabiting his own garrets ; and a very nice compact set of apartments, looking into the back-garden, at this moment falling vacant, the prudent Lucy Gorgon had visited them, and vowed that she and her John should there commence housekeeping.

All these explanations are tedious, but necessary ; and furthermore, it must be said, that as John's uncle's partner was the Liberal member for Oldborough, so Lucy's uncle was its Ministerial representative.

38

This gentleman, the brother of the deceased Captain Gorgon, lived at the paternal mansion of Gorgon Castle, and rejoiced in the name and title of Sir George Grimsby Gorgon. He, too, like his younger brother, had married a lady beneath his own rank in life ; having espoused the daughter and heiress of Mr. Hicks, the great brewer at Oldborough, who held numerous mortgages on the Gorgon property, all of which he yielded up, together with his daughter Juliana, to the care of the baronet.

What Lady Gorgon was in character, this history will show. In person, if she may be compared to any vulgar animal, one of her father's heavy, healthy, broad-flanked, Roman-nosed white dray-horses might, to the poetic mind, appear to resemble her. At twenty she was a splendid creature, and though not at her full growth, yet remarkable for strength and sinew ; at forty-five she was as fine a woman as any in His Majesty's dominions. Five feet seven in height, thirteen stone, her own teeth and hair, she looked as if she were the mother of a regiment of Grenadier Guards. She had three daughters of her own size, and at length, ten years after the birth of the last of the young ladies, a son—one son—George Augustus Frederick Grimsby Gorgon, the godson of a royal duke, whose steady officer in waiting Sir George had been for many years.

It is needless to say, after entering so largely into a description of Lady Gorgon, that her husband was a little shrivelled wizen-faced creature, eight inches shorter than her Ladyship. This is the way of the world, as every single reader of this book must have remarked ; for frolic love delights to join giants and pigmies of different sexes in the bonds of matrimony. When you saw her Ladyship, in flame-coloured satin and gorgeous toque and feathers, entering the drawing-room, as footmen along the stairs shouted melodiously, " Sir George and Lady Gorgon," you beheld in her company a small withered old gentleman, with powder and large royal household buttons, who tripped at her elbow as a little weak-legged colt does at the side of a stout mare.

The little General had been present at about a hundred and twenty pitched battles on Hounslow Heath and Wormwood Scrubs, but had never drawn his sword against an enemy. As might be expected, therefore, his talk and *tenue* were outrageously military. He had the whole Army List by heart—that is, as far as the field-officers : all below them he scorned. A bugle at Gorgon Castle always sounded at breakfast and dinner : a gun announced sunset. He clung to his pigtail for many years after the army had forsaken that ornament, and could never be brought to think much of the Peninsular men for giving it up. When he spoke of the Duke, he used to call him " *My Lord Wellington—I recollect him as*

Captain Wellesley." He swore fearfully in conversation, was most regular at church, and regularly read to his family and domestics the morning and evening prayer; he bullied his daughters, *seemed* to bully his wife, who led him whither she chose; gave grand entertainments, and never asked a friend by chance; had splendid liveries, and starved his people; and was as dull, stingy, pompous, insolent, cringing, ill-tempered a little creature as ever was known.

With such qualities you may fancy that he was generally admired in society and by his country. So he was: and I never knew a man so endowed whose way through life was not safe—who had fewer pangs of conscience—more positive enjoyments—more respect shown to him—more favours granted to him, than such a one as my friend the General.

Her Ladyship was just suited to him, and they did in reality admire each other hugely. Previously to her marriage with the baronet, many love-passages had passed between her and William Pitt Scully, Esquire, the attorney; and there was especially one story, *à propos* of certain syllabubs and Sally-Lunn cakes, which seemed to show that matters had gone very far. Be this as it may, no sooner did the General (Major Gorgon he was then) cast an eye on her, than Scully's five years' fabric of love was instantly dashed to the ground. She cut him pitilessly, cut Sally Scully, his sister, her dearest friend and confidante, and bestowed her big person upon the little aide-de-camp at the end of a fortnight's wooing. In the course of time their mutual fathers died; the Gorgon estates were unencumbered: patron of both the seats in the borough of Old-borough, and occupant of one, Sir George Grimsby Gorgon, Baronet, was a personage of no small importance.

He was, it scarcely need to be said, a Tory; and this was the reason why William Pitt Scully, Esquire, of the firm of Perkins and Scully, deserted those principles in which he had been bred and christened; deserted that church which he had frequented, for he could not bear to see Sir George and my Lady flaunting in their grand pew;—deserted, I say, the church, adopted the conventicle, and became one of the most zealous and eloquent supporters that Freedom has known in our time. Scully, of the house of Scully and Perkins, was a dangerous enemy. In five years from that marriage, which snatched from the jilted solicitor his heart's young affections, Sir George Gorgon found that he must actually spend seven hundred pounds to keep his two seats. At the next election, a Liberal was set up against his man, and actually ran him hard; and finally, at the end of eighteen years, the rejected Scully—the mean attorney—was actually the *first* Member for Oldborough, Sir George Grimsby Gorgon, Baronet, being only the second!

The agony of that day cannot be imagined—the dreadful curses of Sir George, who saw fifteen hundred a year robbed from under his very nose—the religious resignation of my Lady—the hideous window-smashing that took place at the "Gorgon Arms," and the discomfiture of the pelted Mayor and Corporation. The very next Sunday, Scully was reconciled to the church (or attended it in the morning, and the meeting twice in the afternoon), and as Doctor Snorter uttered the prayer for the High Court of Parliament, his eye, the eye of his whole party—turned towards Lady Gorgon and Sir George in a most unholy triumph. Sir George (who always stood during prayers, like a military man) fairly sank down among the hassocks, and Lady Gorgon was heard to sob as audibly as ever did little beadle-belaboured urchin.

Scully, when at Oldborough, came from that day forth to church. "What," said he, "was it to him? were we not all brethren?" Old Perkins, however, kept religiously to the Square-toes congregation. In fact, to tell the truth, this subject had been debated between the partners, who saw the advantage of courting both the Establishment and the Dissenters—a manœuvre which, I need not say, is repeated in almost every country town in England, where a solicitor's house has this kind of power and connection.

Three months after this election came the races at Oldborough, and the race-ball. Gorgon was so infuriated by his defeat, that he gave "the Gorgon cup and cover," a matter of fifteen pounds. Scully, "although anxious," as he wrote from town, "anxious beyond measure to preserve the breed of horses for which our beloved country has ever been famous, could attend no such sports as these, which but too often degenerated into vice." It was voted a shabby excuse. Lady Gorgon was radiant in her barouche and four, and gladly became the patroness of the ball that was to ensue ; and which all the gentry and townspeople, Tory and Whig, were in the custom of attending. The ball took place on the last day of the races. On that day, the walls of the market-house, the principal public buildings, and the "Gorgon Arms Hotel" itself, were plastered with the following—

" Letter from our distinguished representative, William P. Scully, Esquire, etc., etc.

"HOUSE OF COMMONS : *June* 1, 18—.

"MY DEAR HEELTAP,—You know my opinion about horse racing, and though I blame neither you nor any brother English man who enjoys that manly sport, you will, I am sure, appreciate the conscientious motives which induce me not to appear among my friends and constituents on the festival of the 3rd, 4th, and 5th instant.   If *I*, however, cannot allow my name to appear among your list of stewards, *one* at least of the representatives of Old-borough has no such scruples.   Sir George Gorgon is among you : and though I differ from that honourable Baronet on more than *one vital point*, I am glad to think that he is with you.   A gentleman, a soldier, a man of property in the county, how can he be better employed than in forwarding the county's amuse-ments, and in forwarding the happiness of all?

"Had I no such scruples as those to which I have just alluded, I must still have refrained from coming among you.   Your great Oldborough common-drainage and enclosure bill comes on to-morrow, and I shall be *at my post*.   I am sure, if Sir George Gorgon were here, he and I should on this occasion vote side by side, and that party strife would be forgotten in the object of our common interest —*our dear native town*.

"There is, however, another occasion at hand, in which I shall be proud to meet him.   Your ball is on the night of the 6th. Party forgotten—brotherly union—innocent mirth—beauty, *our dear town's beauty*, our daughters in the joy of their expanding loveliness, our matrons in the exquisite contemplation of their children's bliss—can you, can I, can any Whig or Tory, can any Briton be indifferent to a scene like this, or refuse to join in this heart-stirring festival?   If there *be* such let them pardon me—I, for one, my dear Heeltap, will be among you on Friday night—ay, and hereby invite all pretty Tory Misses, who are in want of a partner.

"I am here in the very midst of good things, you know, and we old folks like *a supper* after a dance.   Please to accept a brace of bucks and a turtle, which come herewith.   My worthy colleague, who was so liberal last year of his soup to the poor, will not, I trust, refuse to taste a little of Alderman Birch's—'tis offered on my part with hearty goodwill.   Hey for the 6th, and *vive la joie!* —Ever, my dear Heeltap, your faithful   W. PITT SCULLY.

"*P.S.*—Of course this letter is *strictly private*.   Say that the venison, &c., came from a *well-wisher to Oldborough*."

This amazing letter was published, in defiance of Mr. Scully's injunctions, by the enthusiastic Heeltap, who said bluntly, in a preface, "that he saw no reason why Mr. Scully should be ashamed of his action, and he, for his part, was glad to let all friends at Oldborough know of it."

The allusion about the Gorgon soup was killing: thirteen

paupers in Oldborough had, it was confidently asserted, died of it. Lady Gorgon, on the reading of this letter, was struck completely dumb ; Sir George Gorgon was wild.   Ten dozen of champagne was he obliged to send down to the "Gorgon Arms," to be added to the festival.   He would have stayed away if he could, but he dared not.

At nine o'clock, he in general's uniform ; his wife in blue satin and diamonds ; his daughters in blue crape and white roses ; his niece, Lucy Gorgon, in white muslin ; his son, George Augustus Frederick Grimsby Gorgon, in a blue velvet jacket, sugar-loaf buttons, and nankeens, entered the north door of the ballroom, to much cheering, and the sound of "God save the King ! "

At that very same moment, and from the south door, issued William Pitt Scully, Esquire, M.P., and his staff.   Mr. Scully had a brand-new blue coat and brass buttons, buff waistcoat, white kersey-mere tights, pumps with large rosettes, and pink silk stockings.

" This wool," said he to a friend, " was grown on Oldborough sheep, this cloth was spun in Oldborough looms, these buttons were cast in an Oldborough manufactory, these shoes were made by an Oldborough tradesman, this *heart* first beat in Oldborough town, and pray Heaven may be buried there ! "

Could anything resist a man like this ?   John Perkins, who had come down as one of Scully's aides-de-camp, in a fit of generous enthusiasm, leaped on a whist-table, flung up a pocket-handkerchief, and shrieked—" Scully for ever ! "

Heeltap, who was generally drunk, fairly burst into tears, and the grave tradesmen and Whig gentry, who had dined with the Member at his inn, and accompanied him thence to the "Gorgon Arms," lifted their deep voices and shouted, " Hear ! " " Good ! " " Bravo ! " " Noble ! " " Scully for ever ! " " God bless him ! " and " Hurrah ! "

The scene was tumultuously affecting ; and when young Perkins sprang down from the table and came blushing up to the Member, that gentleman said, " Thank you, Jack ! *thank* you, my boy ! THANK you," in a way which made Perkins think that his supreme cup of bliss was quaffed ; that he had but to die : for that life had no other such joy in store for him.   Scully was Perkins's Napoleon —he yielded himself up to the attorney, body and soul.

Whilst this scene was going on under one chandelier of the ball-room, beneath the other scarlet little General Gorgon, sumptuous Lady Gorgon, the daughters and niece Gorgons, were standing surrounded by their Tory court, who affected to sneer and titter at the Whig demonstrations which were taking place.

" What a howwid thmell of whithkey ! " lisped Cornet Fitch, of the Dragoons, to Miss Lucy, confidentially.   "And thethe are what they call Whigth, are they?   He ! he ! "

"They are drunk, —— me—drunk, by —— ! " said the General to the Mayor.

"*Which* is Scully ? " said Lady Gorgon, lifting her glass gravely (she was at that very moment thinking of the syllabubs).   "Is it that tipsy man in the green coat, or that vulgar creature in the blue one ? "

"Law, my Lady," said the Mayoress, "have you forgotten him ? Why, that's him in blue and buff."

"And a monthous fine man, too," said Cornet Fitch.   "I wish we had him in our twoop—he'th thix feet thwee, if he'th an inch ; ain't he, Genewal ? "

No reply.

"And heavens ! mamma," shrieked the three Gorgons in a breath, "see, one creature is on the whist-table.   Oh, the wretch ! "

"I'm sure he's very good-looking," said Lucy simply.

Lady Gorgon darted at her an angry look, and was about to say something very contemptuous, when, at that instant, John Perkins's shout taking effect, Master George Augustus Frederick Grimsby Gorgon, not knowing better, incontinently raised a small shout on his side.

"Hear ! good ! bravo ! " exclaimed he ; "Scully for ever ! Hurra-a-a-ay ! " and fell skipping about like the Whigs opposite.

"Silence, you brute you ! " groaned Lady Gorgon ; and seizing him by the shirt-frill and coat-collar, carried him away to his nurse, who, with many other maids of the Whig and Tory parties, stood giggling and peeping at the landing-place.

Fancy how all these small incidents augmented the heap of Lady Gorgon's anger and injuries !   She was a dull phlegmatic woman for the most part, and contented herself generally with merely despising her neighbours ; but oh ! what a fine active hatred raged in her bosom for victorious Scully !   At this moment Mr. Perkins had finished shaking hands with his Napoleon—Napoleon seemed bent upon some tremendous enterprise.   He was looking at Lady Gorgon very hard.

"She's a fine woman," said Scully thoughtfully ; he was still holding the hand of Perkins.   And then, after a pause, "Gad ! I think I'll try.'

"Try what, sir ? "

"She's a *deuced* fine woman ! " burst out again the tender solicitor.   "I *will* go.   Springer, tell the fiddlers to strike up."

Springer scuttled across the room, and gave the leader of the band a knowing nod.   Suddenly, "God save the King" ceased, and

"Sir Roger de Coverley" began.   The rival forces eyed each other;
Mr. Scully, accompanied by his friend, came forward, looking very
red, and fumbling two large kid gloves.

"*He's going to ask me to dance,*" hissed out Lady Gorgon, with
a dreadful intuition, and she drew back behind her lord.

"D—— it, madam, *then dance* with him!" said the General.
"Don't you see that the scoundrel is carrying it all his own way!
—— him! and —— him! and —— him!" (All of which dashes
the reader may fill up with oaths of such strength as may be
requisite.)

"General!" cried Lady Gorgon, but could say no more.   Scully
was before her.

"Madam!" exclaimed the Liberal Member for Oldborough, "in
a moment like this—I say—that is—that on the present occasion—
your Ladyship—unaccustomed as I am—pooh, psha—*will* your
Ladyship give me the distinguished honour and pleasure of going
down the country-dance with your Ladyship?"

An immense heave of her Ladyship's ample chest was per-
ceptible.   Yards of blond lace, which might be compared to a
foam of the sea, were agitated at the same moment, and by the
same mighty emotion.   The river of diamonds which flowed round
her Ladyship's neck, seemed to swell and to shine more than ever.
The tall plumes on her ambrosial head bowed down beneath the
storm.   In other words, Lady Gorgon, in a furious rage, which
she was compelled to restrain, trembled, drew up, and bowing
majestically, said—

"Sir, I shall have much pleasure."   With this, she extended
her hand.   Scully, trembling, thrust forward one of his huge kid-
gloves, and led her to the head of the country-dance.   John Perkins
—who I presume had been drinking pretty freely, so as to have
forgotten his ordinary bashfulness—looked at the three Gorgons in
blue, then at the pretty smiling one in white, and stepping up to
her, without the smallest hesitation, asked her if she would dance
with him.   The young lady smilingly agreed.   The great example
of Scully and Lady Gorgon was followed by all dancing men and
women.   Political enmities were forgotten.   Whig voters invited
Tory voters' wives to the dance.   The daughters of Reform accepted
the hands of the sons of Conservatism.   The reconciliation of the
Romans and Sabines was not more touching than this sweet fusion.
Whack—whack!   Mr. Springer clapped his hands; and the fiddlers
adroitly obeying the cheerful signal, began playing "Sir Roger de
Coverley" louder than ever.

I do not know by what extraordinary charm (*nescio quâ præter
solitum,* &c.), but young Perkins, who all his life had hated country-

dances, was delighted with this one, and skipped and laughed, pous-
setting, crossing, down-the-middling, with his merry little partner,
till every one of the bettermost sort of the thirty-nine couples had
dropped panting away, and till the youngest Miss Gorgon, coming
up to his partner, said in a loud hissing scornful whisper, "Lucy,
mamma thinks you have danced quite enough with this — this
person." And Lucy, blushing, starting back, and looking at Perkins
in a very melancholy way, made him a little curtsey, and went off
to the Gorgonian party with her cousin. Perkins was too frightened
to lead her back to her place—too frightened at first, and then too
angry. "Person!" said he: his soul swelled with a desperate republicanism : he went back to his patron more of a Radical than
ever.

He found that gentleman in the solitary tea-room, pacing up
and down before the observant landlady and handmaidens of the
"Gorgon Arms," wiping his brows, gnawing his fingers—his ears
looming over his stiff white shirt-collar as red as fire. Once more
the great man seized John Perkins's hand as the latter came up.

"D—— the aristocrats!" roared the ex-follower of Squaretoes.

"And so say I! but what's the matter, sir?"

"What's the matter? — Why, that woman — that infernal,
haughty, straitlaced, cold-blooded brewer's daughter! I loved that
woman, sir—I *kissed* that woman, sir, twenty years ago : we were
all but engaged, sir : we've walked for hours and hours, sir—us
and the governess—I've got a lock of her hair, sir, among my papers
now ; and to-night, would you believe it?—as soon as she got to
the bottom of the set, away she went—not one word would she
speak to me all the way down : and when I wanted to lead her
to her place, and asked her if she would have a glass of negus, 'Sir,'
says she, 'I have done my duty ; I bear no malice : but I consider
you a traitor to Sir George Gorgon's family — a traitor and an
upstart! I consider your speaking to me as a piece of insolent
vulgarity, and beg you will leave me to myself!' There's her
speech, sir. Twenty people heard it, and all of her Tory set too.
I'll tell you what, Jack : at the next election I'll put *you* up. Oh
that woman! that woman!—and to think that I love her still!"
Here Mr. Scully paused, and fiercely consoled himself by swallow-
ing three cups of Mrs. Rincer's green tea.

The act is, that Lady Gorgon's passion had completely got the
better of her reason. Her Ladyship was naturally cold, and
artificially extremely squeamish ; and when this great red-faced
enemy of hers looked tenderly at her through his red little eyes,
and squeezed her hand and attempted to renew old acquaintance,
she felt such an intolerable disgust at his triumph, at his familiarity,

and at the remembrance of her own former liking for him, that she gave utterance to the speech above correctly reported. The Tories were delighted with her spirit, and Cornet Fitch, with much glee, told the story to the General; but that officer, who was at whist with some of his friends, flung down his cards, and coming up to his lady, said briefly—

"Madam, you are a fool!"

"I will *not* stay here to be bearded by that disgusting man!—Mr. Fitch, call my people.—Henrietta, bring Miss Lucy from that linendraper with whom she is dancing. I will not stay, General, once for all."

Henrietta ran—she hated her cousin: Cornet Fitch was departing. "Stop, Fitch," said Sir George, seizing him by the arm. "You are a fool, Lady Gorgon," said he, "and I repeat it—a —— fool! This fellow Scully is carrying all before him: he has talked with everybody, laughed with everybody—and you, with your infernal airs—a brewer's daughter, by ——, must sit like a queen and not speak to a soul! You've lost me one seat of my borough, with your .infernal pride—fifteen hundred a year, by Jove!—and you think you will bully me out of another. No, madam, you *shall* stay, and stay supper too;—and the girls shall dance with every cursed chimney-sweep and butcher in the room: they shall—confound me!"

Her Ladyship saw that it was necessary to submit; and Mr. Springer, the master of the ceremonies, was called, and requested to point out some eligible partners for the young ladies. One went off with a Whig auctioneer; another figured in a quadrille with a very Liberal apothecary; and the third, Miss Henrietta, remained.

"Hallo you, sir!" roared the little General to John Perkins, who was passing by. John turned round and faced him.

"You were dancing with my niece just now—show us your skill now, and dance with one of my daughters. Stand up, Miss Henrietta Gorgon—Mr. What's-your-name?"

"My name," said John, with marked and majestic emphasis, "is PERKINS." And he looked towards Lucy, who dared not look again.

"Miss Gorgon—Mr. Perkins. There, now go and dance."

"Mr. Perkins regrets, madam," said John, making a bow to Miss Henrietta, "that he is not able to dance this evening. I am this moment obliged to look to the supper; but you will find, no doubt, some other PERSON who will have much pleasure."

"Go to ——, sir!" screamed the General, starting up, and shaking his cane.

"Calm yourself, dearest George," said Lady Gorgon, clinging

fondly to him. Fitch twiddled his moustaches. Miss Henrietta Gorgon stared with open mouth. The silks of the surrounding dowagers rustled—the countenances of all looked grave.

"I will follow you, sir, wherever you please; and you may hear of me whenever you like," said Mr. Perkins, bowing and retiring. He heard little Lucy sobbing in a corner. He was lost at once—lost in love; he felt as if he could combat fifty generals ! he never was so happy in his life.

The supper came; but as that meal cost five shillings a head, General Gorgon dismissed the four spinsters of his family homewards in the carriage, and so saved himself a pound. This added to Jack Perkins's wrath; he had hoped to have seen Miss Lucy once more. He was a steward, and, in the General's teeth, would have done his duty. He was thinking how he would have helped her to the most delicate chicken-wings and blancmanges, how he *would* have made her take champagne. Under the noses of indignant aunt and uncle, what glorious fun it would have been !

Out of place as Mr. Scully's present was, and though Lady Gorgon and her party sneered at the vulgar notion of venison and turtle for supper, all the world at Oldborough ate very greedily of those two substantial dishes; and the Mayor's wife became from that day forth a mortal enemy of the Gorgons : for, sitting near her Ladyship, who refused the proffered soup and meat, the Mayoress thought herself obliged to follow this disagreeable example. She sent away the plate of turtle with a sigh, saying, however, to the baronet's lady, "I thought, mem, that the *Lord Mayor of London* always had turtle to his supper ?"

"And what if he didn't, Biddy ?" said his Honour the Mayor; "a good thing's a good thing, and here goes !" wherewith he plunged his spoon into the savoury mess. The Mayoress, as we have said, dared not; but she hated Lady Gorgon, and remembered it at the next election.

The pride, in fact, and insolence of the Gorgon party rendered every person in the room hostile to them; so soon as, gorged with meat, they began to find that courage which Britons invariably derive from their victuals. The show of the Gorgon plate seemed to offend the people. The Gorgon champagne was a long time, too, in making its appearance. Arrive, however, it did. The people were waiting for it; the young ladies, not accustomed to that drink, declined pledging their admirers until it was produced; the men, too, despised the bucellas and sherry, and were looking continually towards the door. At last, Mr. Rincer, the landlord, Mr. Hock, Sir George's butler, and sundry others entered the room. Bang ! went the corks—fizz the foamy liquor sparkled into all sorts of

glasses that were held out for its reception.   Mr. Hock helped Sir
George and his party, who drank with great gusto; the wine which
was administered to the persons immediately around Mr. Scully
was likewise pronounced to be good.   But Mr. Perkins, who had
taken his seat among the humbler individuals, and in the very
middle of the table, observed that all these persons, after drinking,
made to each other very wry and ominous faces, and whispered
much.   He tasted his wine: it was a villainous compound of sugar,
vitriol, soda-water, and green gooseberries.   At this moment a great
clatter of forks was made by the president's and vice-president's
party.   Silence for a toast—'twas silence all.

"Landlord," said Mr. Perkins, starting up (the rogue, where
did his impudence come from?) "have you any champagne of
your own ?"

"Silence! down!" roared the Tories, the ladies looking aghast.
"Silence, sit down you!" shrieked the well-known voice of the
General.

"I beg your pardon, General," said young John Perkins; "but
where *could* you have bought this champagne?   My worthy friend
I know is going to propose the ladies; let us at any rate drink such
a toast in good wine."   ("Hear, hear!")   "Drink her Ladyship's
health in *this* stuff?   I declare to goodness I would sooner drink it
in beer!"

No pen can describe the uproar which arose: the anguish of
the Gorgonites—the shrieks, jeers, cheers, ironic cries of "Swipes!"
&c., which proceeded from the less genteel but more enthusiastic
Scullyites.

"This vulgarity is too much," said Lady Gorgon, rising; and
Mrs. Mayoress and the ladies of the party did so too.

The General, two squires, the clergyman, the Gorgon apothecary
and attorney, with their respective ladies, followed her: they were
plainly beaten from the field.   Such of the Tories as dared remained,
and in inglorious compromise shared the jovial Whig feast.

"Gentlemen and ladies," hiccoughed Mr. Heeltap, "I'll give
you a toast.   'Champagne to our real—hic—friends,' no, 'Real
champagne to our friends,' and—hic—pooh!   'Champagne to our
friends, and real pain to our enemies,'—huzzay!"

The Scully faction on this day bore the victory away, and if the
polite reader has been shocked by certain vulgarities on the part
of Mr. Scully, he must remember *imprimis* that
Oldborough was an inconsiderable place—that the inhabitants thereof
were chiefly tradespeople, not of refined habits—that Mr. Scully
himself had only for three months mingled among the aristocracy—
that his young friend Perkins was violently angry—and finally, and

to conclude, that the proud vulgarity of the great Sir George Gorgon and his family was infinitely more odious and contemptible than the mean vulgarity of the Scullyites and their leader.

Immediately after this event, Mr. Scully and his young friend Perkins returned to town; the latter to his garrets in Bedford Row —the former to his apartments on the first floor of the same house. He lived here to superintend his legal business: his London agents, Messrs. Higgs, Biggs, and Blatherwick, occupying the ground floor; the junior partner, Mr. Gustavus Blatherwick, the second flat of the house. Scully made no secret of his profession or residence: he was an attorney, and proud of it; he was the grandson of a labourer, and thanked God for it; he had made his fortune by his own honest labour, and why should he be ashamed of it?

And now, having explained at full length who the several heroes and heroines of this history were, and how they conducted themselves in the country, let us describe their behaviour in London, and the great events which occurred there.

You must know that Mr. Perkins bore away the tenderest recollections of the young lady with whom he had danced at the Oldborough ball, and, having taken particular care to find out where she dwelt when in the metropolis, managed soon to become acquainted with Aunt Biggs, and made himself so amiable to that lady, that she begged he would pass all his disengaged evenings at her lodgings in Caroline Place. Mrs. Biggs was perfectly aware that the young gentleman did not come for her bohea and muffins, so much as for the sweeter conversation of her niece, Miss Gorgon; but seeing that these two young people were of an age when ideas of love and marriage will spring up, do what you will; seeing that her niece had a fortune, and Mr. Perkins had the prospect of a place, and was moreover a very amiable and well-disposed young fellow, she thought her niece could not do better than marry him; and Miss Gorgon thought so too. Now the public will be able to understand the meaning of that important conversation which is recorded at the very commencement of this history.

Lady Gorgon and her family were likewise in town; but, when in the metropolis, they never took notice of their relative, Miss Lucy: the idea of acknowledging an ex-schoolmistress living in Mecklenburgh Square being much too preposterous for a person of my Lady Gorgon's breeding and fashion. She did not, therefore, know of the progress which sly Perkins was making all this while; for Lucy Gorgon did not think it was at all necessary to inform her Ladyship how deeply she was smitten by the wicked young gentleman who had made all the disturbance at the Oldborough ball.

The intimacy of these young persons had, in fact, become so

close, that on a certain sunshiny Sunday in December, after having accompanied Aunt Biggs to church, they had pursued their walk as far as that rendezvous of lovers, the Regent's Park, and were talking of their coming marriage, with much confidential tenderness, before the bears in the Zoological Gardens.

Miss Lucy was ever and anon feeding those interesting animals with buns, to perform which act of charity she had clambered up on the parapet which surrounds their den.   Mr. Perkins was below; and Miss Lucy, having distributed her buns, was on the point of following,—but whether from timidity, or whether from a desire to do young Perkins an essential service, I know not: however, she found herself quite unwilling to jump down unaided.

"My dearest John," said she, "I never can jump that."

Whereupon John stepped up, put one hand round Lucy's waist; and as one of hers gently fell upon his shoulder, Mr. Perkins took the other and said—

"Now jump."

Hoop ! jump she did, and so excessively active and clever was Mr. John Perkins, that he jumped Miss Lucy plump into the middle of a group formed of—

Lady Gorgon ;

The Misses Gorgon ;

Master George Augustus Frederick Grimsby Gorgon ;

And a footman, poodle, and French governess; who had all been for two or three minutes listening to the billings and cooings of these imprudent young lovers.

CHAPTER II

SHOWS HOW THE PLOT BEGAN TO THICKEN IN OR
ABOUT BEDFORD ROW

"M ISS Lucy!"
  "Upon my word!"
  "I'm hanged if it aren't Lucy! How do, Lucy," uttered Lady, the Misses, and Master Gorgon in a breath.

Lucy came. forward, bending down her ambrosial curls, and blushing, as a modest young woman should: for, in truth, the scrape was very awkward. And as for John Perkins, he made a start, and then a step forwards, and then two backwards, and then began laying hands upon his black satin stock—in short, the sun did not shine at that moment upon a man who looked so exquisitely foolish.

"Miss Lucy Gorgon, is your aunt—is Mrs. Briggs here?" said Lady Gorgon, drawing herself up with much state.

"Mrs. Biggs, aunt?" said Lucy demurely.

"Biggs or Briggs, madam, it is not of the slightest consequence. I presume that persons in my rank of life are not expected to know everybody's name in Magdeburg Square?" (Lady Gorgon had a house in Baker Street, and a dismal house it was.) "*Not* here," continued she, rightly interpreting Lucy's silence, "NOT here?—and may I ask how long is it that young ladies have been allowed to walk abroad without chaperons, and to—to take a part in such scenes as that which we have just seen acted?"

To this question—and indeed it was rather difficult to answer— Miss Gorgon had no reply. There were the six grey eyes of her cousins glowering at her; there was George Augustus Frederick examining her with an air of extreme wonder, Mademoiselle the governess turning her looks demurely away, and awful Lady Gorgon glancing fiercely at her in front. Not mentioning the footman and poodle, what could a poor modest timid girl plead before such an inquisition, especially when she was clearly guilty? Add to this, that as Lady Gorgon, that majestic woman, always remarkable for her size and insolence of demeanour, had planted herself in the middle of the path, and spoke at the extreme pitch of her voice, many persons walking in the neighbourhood had heard her Lady-ship's speech and stopped, and seemed disposed to await the rejoinder.

"For Heaven's sake, aunt, don't draw a crowd around us," said Lucy, who, indeed, was glad of the only escape that lay in her power. "I will tell you of the—of the circumstances of—of my engagement with this gentleman—with Mr. Perkins," added she, in a softer tone—so soft that the 'erkins was quite inaudible.

"A Mr. What? An engagement without consulting your guardians!" screamed her Ladyship. "This must be looked to! Jerningham, call round my carriage. Mademoiselle, you will have the goodness to walk home with Master Gorgon, and carry him, if you please, where there is wet; and, girls, as the day is fine, you will do likewise. Jerningham, you will attend the young ladies. Miss Gorgon, I will thank you to follow me immediately." And so saying, and looking at the crowd with ineffable scorn, and at Mr. Perkins not at all, the lady bustled away forwards, the files of Gorgon daughters and governess closing round and enveloping poor Lucy, who found herself carried forward against her will, and in a minute seated in her aunt's coach, along with that tremendous person.

Her case was bad enough, but what was it to Perkins's? Fancy his blank surprise and rage at having his love thus suddenly ravished from him, and his delicious tête-à-tête interrupted. He managed, in an inconceivably short space of time, to conjure up half-a-million obstacles to his union. What should he do? he would rush on to Baker Street, and wait there until his Lucy left Lady Gorgon's house.

He could find no vehicle in the Regent's Park, and was in consequence obliged to make his journey on foot. Of course, he nearly killed himself with running, and ran so quick, that he was just in time to see the two ladies step out of Lady Gorgon's carriage at her own house, and to hear Jerningham's fellow-footman roar to the Gorgonian coachman, "Half-past seven!" at which hour, we are, to this day, convinced that Lady Gorgon was going out to dine. Mr. Jerningham's associate having banged to the door, with an insolent look towards Perkins, who was prying in with the most suspicious and indecent curiosity, retired, exclaiming, "That chap has a hi to our greatcoats, I reckon!" and left John Perkins to pace the street and be miserable.

John Perkins then walked resolutely up and down dismal Baker Street, determined on an éclaircissement. He was for some time occupied in thinking how it was that the Gorgons were not at church, they who made such a parade of piety; and John Perkins smiled as he passed the chapel, and saw that two *charity sermons* were to be preached that day—and therefore it was that General Gorgon read prayers to his family at home in the morning.

Perkins, at last, saw that little General, in blue frock-coat and spotless buff gloves, saunter scowling home; and half-an-hour before his arrival had witnessed the entrance of Jerningham, and the three gaunt Miss Gorgons, poodle, son-and-heir, and French governess, protected by him, into Sir George's mansion.

"Can she be going to stay all night?" mused poor John, after being on the watch for three hours: "that footman is the only person who has left the house:" when presently, to his inexpressible delight, he saw a very dirty hackney-coach clatter up to the Gorgon door, out of which first issued the ruby plush breeches and stalwart calves of Mr. Jerningham; these were followed by his body, and then the gentleman, ringing modestly, was admitted.

Again the door opened: a lady came out, nor was she followed by the footman, who crossed his legs at the door-post and allowed her to mount the jingling vehicle as best she might. Mr. Jerningham had witnessed the scene in the Park Gardens, had listened to the altercation through the library keyhole, and had been mighty sulky at being ordered to call a coach for this young woman. He did not therefore deign to assist her to mount.

But there was *one* who did! Perkins was by the side of his Lucy: he had seen her start back and cry, "La, John!"—had felt her squeeze his arm—had mounted with her into the coach, and then shouted with a voice of thunder to the coachman, "Caroline Place, Mecklenburgh Square."

But Mr. Jerningham would have been much more surprised and puzzled if he had waited one minute longer, and seen this Mr. Perkins, who had so gallantly escaladed the hackney-coach, step out of it with the most mortified, miserable, chapfallen countenance possible.

The fact is, he had found poor Lucy sobbing fit to break her heart, and instead of consoling her, as he expected, he only seemed to irritate her further: for she said, "Mr. Perkins—I beg—I insist, that you leave the carriage." And when Perkins made some movement (which, not being in the vehicle at the time, we have never been able to comprehend), she suddenly sprang from the back-seat and began pulling at a large piece of cord which communicated with the wrist of the gentleman driving; and, screaming to him at the top of her voice, bade him immediately stop.

This Mr. Coachman did, with a curious, puzzled, grinning air.

Perkins descended, and on being asked, "Vere ham I to drive the young 'oman, sir?" I am sorry to say muttered something like an oath, and uttered the above-mentioned words, "Caroline Place, Mecklenburgh Square," in a tone which I should be inclined to describe as both dogged and sheepish—very different from that cheery voice which he had used when he first gave the order.

Poor Lucy, in the course of those fatal three hours which had passed while Mr. Perkins was pacing up and down Baker Street, had received a lecture which lasted exactly one hundred and eighty minutes—from her aunt first, then from her uncle, whom we have seen marching homewards, and often from both together.

Sir George Gorgon and his lady poured out such a flood of advice and abuse against the poor girl, that she came away from the interview quite timid and cowering; and when she saw John Perkins (the sly rogue! how well he thought he had managed the trick!) she shrank from him as if he had been a demon of wickedness, ordered him out of the carriage, and went home by herself, convinced that she had committed some tremendous sin.

While, then, her coach jingled away to Caroline Place, Perkins, once more alone, bent his steps in the same direction.   A desperate, heart-stricken man, he passed by the beloved's door, saw lights in the front drawing-room, felt probably that she was there; but he could not go in.   Moodily he paced down Doughty Street, and turning abruptly into Bedford Row, rushed into his own chambers, where Mrs. Snooks, the laundress, had prepared his humble Sabbath meal.

A cheerful fire blazed in his garret, and Mrs. Snooks had prepared for him the favourite blade-bone he loved (blest four-days' dinner for a bachelor—roast, cold, hashed, grilled blade-bone, the fourth being better than the first); but although he usually did rejoice in this meal—ordinarily, indeed, grumbling that there was not enough to satisfy him—he, on this occasion, after two mouthfuls, flung down his knife and fork, and buried his two claws in his hair.

"Snooks," said he at last, very moodily, "remove this d—— mutton, give me my writing things, and some hot brandy-and-water."

This was done without much alarm : for you must know that Perkins used to dabble in poetry, and ordinarily prepared himself for composition by this kind of stimulus.

He wrote hastily a few lines.

"Snooks, put on your bonnet," said he, "and carry this—*you know where !* " he added, in a hollow, heart-breaking tone of voice, that affected poor Snooks almost to tears.   She went, however, with the note, which was to this purpose :—

"LUCY ! Lucy ! my soul's love—what, what has happened ?   I am writing this "—(*a gulp of brandy-and-water*)—"in a state bordering on distraction—madness—insanity " (*another*). "Why did you send me out of the coach in that cruel, cruel way? Write to me a word, a line—tell me, tell me, I may come to you—and leave me not in this agonising condition; your faithful " (*glog—glog —glog the whole glass*)—— J. P."

He never signed John Perkins in full—he couldn't, it was so unromantic.

Well, this missive was despatched by Mrs. Snooks, and Perkins, in a fearful state of excitement, haggard, wild, and with more brandy-and-water, awaited the return of his messenger.

When at length, after about an absence of forty years, as it seemed to him, the old lady returned with a large packet, Perkins seized it with a trembling hand, and was yet more frightened to see the handwriting of Mrs. or Miss Biggs.

"MY DEAR MR. PERKINS," she began—" Although I am not your soul's adored, I performed her part for once, since I have read your letter, as I told her. You need not be very much alarmed, although Lucy is at this moment in bed and unwell: for the poor girl has had a sad scene at her grand uncle's house in Baker Street, and came home very much affected. Rest, however, will restore her, for she is not one of your nervous sort; and I hope when you come in the morning, you will see her as blooming as she was when you went out to-day on that unlucky walk.

"See what Sir George Gorgon says of us all! You won't challenge him, I know, as he is to be your uncle, and so I may show you his letter.

"Good-night, my dear John. Do not go *quite* distracted before morning; and believe me your loving aunt, JEMIMA BIGGS."

"BAKER STREET: 11*th December.*

"MAJOR-GENERAL SIR GEORGE GORGON has heard with the utmost disgust and surprise of the engagement which Miss Lucy Gorgon has thought fit to form.

"The Major-General cannot conceal his indignation at the share which Miss Biggs has taken in this disgraceful transaction.

"Sir George Gorgon puts an absolute veto upon all further communication between his niece and the low-born adventurer who had been admitted into her society, and begs to say that Lieutenant Fitch, of the Lifeguards, is the gentleman who he intends shall marry Miss Gorgon.

"It is the Major-General's wish, that on the 28th Miss Gorgon should be ready to come to his house, in Baker Street, where she will be more safe from impertinent intrusions than she has been in Mucklebury Square.

"Mrs. Biggs,
    "Caroline Place,
        "Mecklenburgh Square.'

When poor John Perkins read this epistle, blank rage and wonder filled his soul, at the audacity of the little General, who thus, without the smallest title in the world, pretended to dispose of the hand and fortune of his niece.   The fact is, that Sir George had such a transcendent notion of his own dignity and station, that it never for a moment entered his head that his niece, or anybody else connected with him, should take a single step in life without previously receiving his orders; and Mr. Fitch, a baronet's son, having expressed an admiration of Lucy, Sir George had determined that his suit should be accepted, and really considered Lucy's preference of another as downright treason.

John Perkins determined on the death of Fitch as the very least reparation that should satisfy him; and vowed too that some of the General's blood should be shed for the words which he had dared to utter.

We have said that William Pitt Scully, Esquire, M.P., occupied the first floor of Mr. Perkins's house in Bedford Row: and the reader is further to be informed that an immense friendship had sprung up between these two gentlemen.   The fact is, that poor John was very much flattered by Scully's notice, and began in a very short time to fancy himself a political personage; for he had made several of Scully's speeches, written more than one letter from him to his constituents, and, in a word, acted as his gratis clerk. At least a guinea a week did Mr. Perkins save to the pockets of Mr. Scully, and with hearty goodwill too, for he adored the great William Pitt, and believed every word that dropped from the pompous lips of that gentleman.

Well, after having discussed Sir George Gorgon's letter, poor Perkins, in the utmost fury of mind that his darling should be slandered so, feeling a desire for fresh air, determined to descend to the garden and smoke a cigar in that rural quiet spot.   The night was very calm.   The moonbeams slept softly upon the herbage of Gray's Inn gardens, and bathed with silver splendour Theobald's Row.   A million of little frisky twinkling stars attended their queen, who looked with bland round face upon their gambols, as they peeped in and out from the azure heavens.   Along Gray's Inn wall a lazy row of cabs stood listlessly, for who would call a cab on such a night? Meanwhile their drivers, at the alehouse near, smoked the short pipe or quaffed the foaming beer. Perhaps from Gray's Inn Lane some broken sounds of Irish revelry might rise. Issuing perhaps from Raymond Buildings gate, six lawyers' clerks might whoop a tipsy song—or the loud watchman yell the passing hour; but beyond this all was silence; and young Perkins, as he sat in the summer-house at the bottom of the garden, and contemplated the peaceful heaven, felt some influences of it entering into his soul, and almost forgetting revenge, thought but of peace and love.

Presently, he was aware there was some one else pacing the garden. Who could it be?—Not Blatherwick, for he passed the Sabbath with his grandmamma at Clapham; not Scully surely, for he always went to Bethesda Chapel, and to a select prayer-meeting afterwards. Alas! it *was* Scully; for though that gentleman *said* that he went to chapel, we have it for a fact that he did not always keep his promise, and was at this moment employed in rehearsing an extempore speech, which he proposed to deliver at St. Stephen's.

"Had I, sir," spouted he, with folded arms, slowly pacing to and fro—"Had I, sir, entertained the smallest possible intention of addressing the House on the present occasion—hum, on the present occasion—I would have endeavoured to prepare myself in a way that should have at least shown my sense of the greatness of the subject before the House's consideration, and the nature of the distinguished audience I have the honour to address. I am, sir, a plain man—born of the people—myself one of the people, having won, thank Heaven, an honourable fortune and position by my own honest labour; and standing here as I do——"

.   .   .   .

Here Mr. Scully (it may be said that he never made a speech without bragging about himself: and an excellent plan it is, for people cannot help believing you at last)—here, I say, Mr. Scully, who had one arm raised, felt himself suddenly tipped on the shoulder, and heard a voice saying, "Your money or your life!"

The honourable gentleman twirled round as if he had been shot; the papers on which a great part of this impromptu was written dropped from his lifted hand, and some of them were actually borne on the air into neighbouring gardens. The man was, in fact, in the direst fright.

"It's only I," said Perkins, with rather a forced laugh, when he saw the effect that his wit had produced.

"Only you! And pray what the dev—— what right have you to—to come upon a man of my rank in that way, and disturb

me in the midst of very important meditations ? " asked Mr. Scully,
beginning to grow fierce.

" I want your advice," said Perkins, " on a matter of the very
greatest importance to me.   You know my idea of marrying ? "

" Marry ! " said Scully ; " I thought you had given up that silly
scheme.   And how, pray, do you intend to live ? "

" Why, my intended has a couple of hundreds a year, and my
clerkship in the Tape and Sealing-Wax Office will be as much
more."

" Clerkship—Tape and Sealing-Wax Office—Government sinecure !—Why, good heavens ! John Perkins, you don't tell *me* that
you are going to accept any such thing ? "

" It *is* a very small salary, certainly," said John, who had a
decent notion of his own merits ; " but consider, six months' vacation, two hours in the day, and those spent over the newspapers.
After all, it's——"

" After all, it's a swindle," roared out Mr. Scully—" a swindle
upon the country ; an infamous tax upon the people, who starve that
you may fatten in idleness.   But take this clerkship in the Tape
and Sealing-Wax Office," continued the patriot, his bosom heaving
with noble indignation, and his eye flashing the purest fire,—" *Take*
this clerkship, John Perkins, and sanction tyranny, by becoming
one of its agents ; sanction dishonesty by sharing in its plunder—
do this, BUT never more be friend of mine.   Had I a child," said
the patriot, clasping his hands and raising his eyes to heaven, " I
would rather see him dead, sir—dead, dead at my feet, than the
servant of a Government which all honest men despise."   And here,
giving a searching glance at Perkins, Mr. Scully began tramping up
and down the garden in a perfect fury.

" Good heavens ! " exclaimed the timid John Perkins—" don't
say *so*.   My dear Mr. Scully, I'm not the dishonest character you
suppose me to be—I never looked at the matter in this light.   I'll
—I'll consider of it.   I'll tell Crampton that I will give up the
place ; but for Heaven's sake, don't let me forfeit *your* friendship,
which is dearer to me than any place in the world."

Mr. Scully pressed his hand, and said nothing ; and though their
interview lasted a full half-hour longer, during which they paced up
and down the gravel walk, we shall not breathe a single syllable of
their conversation, as it has nothing to do with our tale.

The next morning, after an interview with Miss Lucy, John
Perkins, Esquire, was seen to issue from Mrs. Biggs's house, looking
particularly pale, melancholy, and thoughtful ; and he did not stop
until he reached a certain door in Downing Street, where was the

office of a certain great Minister, and the offices of the clerks in his Lordship's department.

The head of them was Mr. Josiah Crampton, who has now to be introduced to the public. He was a little old gentleman, some sixty years of age, maternal uncle to John Perkins ; a bachelor, who had been about forty-two years employed in the department of which he was now the head.

After waiting four hours in an anteroom, where a number of Irishmen, some newspaper editors, many pompous-looking political personages asking for the "first lord," a few sauntering clerks, and numbers of swift active messengers passed to and fro ;—after waiting for four hours, making drawings on the blotting-book, and reading the *Morning Post* for that day week, Mr. Perkins was informed that he might go into his uncle's room, and did so accordingly.

He found a little hard old gentleman seated at a table covered with every variety of sealing-wax, blotting-paper, envelopes, despatch-boxes, green tapers, &c. &c. An immense fire was blazing in the grate, an immense sheet-almanack hung over that, a screen, three or four chairs, and a faded Turkey carpet, formed the rest of the furniture of this remarkable room—which I have described thus particularly, because, in the course of a long official life, I have remarked that such is the invariable decoration of political rooms.

"Well, John," said the little hard old gentleman, pointing to an arm-chair, "I'm told you've been here since eleven. Why the deuce do you come so early ?"

"I had important business," answered Mr. Perkins stoutly ; and as his uncle looked up with a comical expression of wonder, John began in a solemn tone to deliver a little speech which he had composed, and which proved him to be a very worthy, easy, silly fellow.

"Sir," said Mr. Perkins, "you have known for some time past the nature of my political opinions, and the intimacy which I have had the honour to form with one—with some of the leading members of the Liberal party." (A grin from Mr. Crampton.) "When first, by your kindness, I was promised the clerkship in the Tape and Sealing-Wax Office, my opinions were not formed as they are now ; and having taken the advice of the gentlemen with whom I act "—(an enormous grin)—" the advice, I say, of the gentlemen with whom I act, and the counsel likewise of my own conscience, I am compelled, with the deepest grief, to say, my dear uncle, that I—I——"

"That you—what, sir ? " exclaimed little Mr. Crampton, bouncing off his chair. "You don't mean to say that you are such a fool as to decline the place ? "

"I do decline the place," said Perkins, whose blood rose at the word "fool." "As a man of honour, I cannot take it."

"Not take it! and how are you to live? On the rent of that house of yours? For, by gad, sir, if you give up the clerkship, I never will give you a shilling."

"It cannot be helped," said Mr. Perkins, looking as much like a martyr as he possibly could, and thinking himself a very fine fellow. "I have talents, sir, which I hope to cultivate; and am member of a profession by which a man may hope to rise to the very highest offices of the State."

"Profession, talents, offices of the State! Are you mad, John Perkins, that you come to me with such insufferable twaddle as this? Why, do you think if you *had* been capable of rising at the bar, I would have taken so much trouble about getting you a place? No, sir; you are too fond of pleasure, and bed, and tea-parties, and small-talk, and reading novels, and playing the flute, and writing sonnets. You would no more rise at the bar than my messenger, sir. It was because I knew your disposition—that hopeless, careless, irresolute good-humour of yours—that I had determined to keep you out of danger, by placing you in a snug shelter, where the storms of the world would not come near you. You must have principles forsooth! and you must marry Miss Gorgon, of course; and by the time you have gone ten circuits, and had six children, you will have eaten up every shilling of your wife's fortune, and be as briefless as you are now. Who the deuce has put all this nonsense into your head? I think I know."

Mr. Perkins's ears tingled as these hard words saluted them; and he scarcely knew whether he ought to knock his uncle down, or fall at his feet and say, "Uncle, I have been a fool, and I know it." The fact is, that in his interview with Miss Gorgon and her aunt in the morning, when he came to tell them of the resolution he had formed to give up the place, both the ladies and John himself had agreed, with a thousand rapturous tears and exclamations, that he was one of the noblest young men that ever lived, had acted as became himself, and might with perfect propriety give up the place, his talents being so prodigious that no power on earth could hinder him from being Lord Chancellor. Indeed, John and Lucy had always thought the clerkship quite beneath him, and were not a little glad, perhaps, at finding a pretext for decently refusing it. But as Perkins was a young gentleman whose candour was such that he was always swayed by the opinions of the last speaker, he did begin to feel now the truth of his uncle's statements, however disagreeable they might be.

Mr. Crampton continued :—

"I think I know the cause of your patriotism. Has not William Pitt Scully, Esquire, had something to do with it?"

Mr. Perkins *could* not turn any redder than he was, but confessed with deep humiliation that "he *had* consulted Mr. Scully among other friends."

Mr. Crampton smiled—drew a letter from a heap before him, and tearing off the signature, handed over the document to his nephew. It contained the following paragraphs :—

"Hawksby has sounded Scully : we can have him any day we want him. He talks very big at present, and says he would not take anything under a . . . This is absurd. He has a Yorkshire nephew coming up to town, and wants a place for him. There is one vacant in the Tape Office, he says : have you not a promise of it?"

"I can't—I can't believe it," said John; "this, sir, is some weak invention of the enemy. Scully is the most honourable man breathing."

"Mr. Scully is a gentleman in a very fair way to make a fortune," answered Mr. Crampton. "Look you, John—it is just as well for your sake that I should give you the news a few weeks before the papers, for I don't want you to be ruined, if I can help it, as I don't wish to have you on my hands. We know all the particulars of Scully's history. He was a Tory attorney at Old-borough ; he was jilted by the present Lady Gorgon, turned Radical, and fought Sir George in his own borough. Sir George would have had the peerage he is dying for, had he not lost that second seat (by-the-bye, my Lady will be here in five minutes), and Scully is now quite firm there. Well, my dear lad, we have bought your incorruptible Scully. Look here,"—and Mr. Crampton produced three *Morning Posts.*

"'THE HONOURABLE HENRY HAWKSBY'S DINNER-PARTY.—Lord So-and-So—Duke of So-and-So—W. Pitt Scully, Esq., M.P.'

"Hawksby is our neutral, our dinner-giver.

"'LADY DIANA DOLDRUM'S ROUT.—W. Pitt Scully, Esq.,' again.

"'THE EARL OF MANTRAP'S GRAND DINNER.'—A Duke—four Lords—'Mr. Scully, and *Sir George Gorgon.*'"

"Well, but I don't see how you have bought him ; look at his votes."

"My dear John," said Mr. Crampton, jingling his watch-seals very complacently, "I am letting you into fearful secrets. The great common end of party is to buy your opponents—the great statesman buys them for nothing."

Here the attendant genius of Mr. Crampton made his appearance, and whispered something, to which the little gentleman said, "Show her Ladyship in,"—when the attendant disappeared.

"John," said Mr. Crampton, with a very queer smile, "you can't stay in this room while Lady Gorgon is with me; but there is a little clerk's room behind the screen there, where you can wait until I call you."

John retired, and as he closed the door of communication, strange to say, little Mr. Crampton sprang up and said, "Confound the young ninny, he has shut the door!"

Mr. Crampton then, remembering that he wanted a map in the next room, sprang into it, left the door half open in coming out, and was in time to receive her Ladyship with smiling face as she, ushered by Mr. Strongitharm, majestically sailed in.

CHAPTER III

BEHIND THE SCENES

IN issuing from and leaving open the door of the inner room, Mr. Crampton had bestowed upon Mr. Perkins a look so peculiarly arch, that even he, simple as he was, began to imagine that some mystery was about to be cleared up, or some mighty matter to be discussed. Presently he heard the well-known voice of Lady Gorgon in conversation with his uncle. What could their talk be about? Mr. Perkins was dying to know, and—shall we say it?—advanced to the door on tiptoe and listened with all his might.

Her Ladyship, that Juno of a woman, if she had not borrowed Venus's girdle to render herself irresistible, at least had adopted a tender, coaxing, wheedling, frisky tone, quite different from her ordinary dignified style of conversation. She called Mr. Crampton a naughty man, for neglecting his old friends, vowed that Sir George was quite hurt at his not coming to dine—nor fixing a day when he would come—and added, with a most engaging ogle, that she had three fine girls at home, who would perhaps make an evening pass pleasantly, even to such a gay bachelor as Mr. Crampton.

"Madam," said he, with much gravity, "the daughters of such a mother must be charming; but I, who have seen your Ladyship, am, alas! proof against even them."

Both parties here heaved tremendous sighs and affected to be wonderfully unhappy about something.

"I wish," after a pause, said Lady Gorgon—"I wish, dear Mr. Crampton, you would not use that odious title 'my Ladyship': you know it always makes me melancholy."

"Melancholy, my dear Lady Gorgon; and why?"

"Because it makes me think of another title that ought to have been mine—ours (I speak for dear Sir George's and my darling boy's sake, Heaven knows, not mine). What a sad disappointment it has been to my husband, that after all his services, all the promises he has had, they have never given him his peerage. As for me, you know——"

"For you, my dear madam, I know quite well that you care for no such bauble as a coronet, except in so far as it may confer honour upon those most dear to you—excellent wife and noble mother as you are.   Heigho ! what a happy man is Sir George ! "

Here there was another pause, and if Mr. Perkins could have seen what was taking place behind the screen, he would have beheld little Mr. Crampton looking into Lady Gorgon's face, with as love-sick a Romeo-gaze as he could possibly counterfeit ; while her Ladyship, blushing somewhat and turning her own grey gogglers up to heaven, received all his words for gospel, and sat fancying herself to be the best, most meritorious, and most beautiful creature in the three kingdoms.

" You men are terrible flatterers," continued she ; " but you say right : for myself I value not these empty distinctions.   I am grow-ing old, Mr. Crampton,—yes, indeed, I am, although you smile so incredulously,—and let me add, that *my* thoughts are fixed upon *higher* things than earthly crowns.   But tell me, you who are all in all with Lord Bagwig, are we never to have our peerage ?   His Majesty, I know, is not averse ; the services of dear Sir George to a member of His Majesty's august family, I know, have been appreciated in the highest quarter.   Ever since the peace we have had a promise. Four hundred pounds has Sir George spent at the Heralds' Office (I myself am of one of the most ancient families in the kingdom, Mr. Crampton), and the poor dear man's health is really ruined by the anxious sickening feeling of hope so long delayed."

Mr. Crampton now assumed an air of much solemnity.

" My dear Lady Gorgon," said he, " will you let me be frank with you, and will you promise solemnly that what I am going to tell you shall never be repeated to a single soul ? "

Lady Gorgon promised.

" Well, then, since the truth you must know, you yourselves have been in part the cause of the delay of which you complain. You gave us two votes five years ago : you now only give us one. If Sir George were to go up to the Peers, we should lose even that one vote ; and would it be common sense in us to incur such a loss ? Mr. Scully, the Liberal, would return another Member of his own way of thinking ; and as for the Lords, we have, you know, a majority there."

"Oh, that horrid man !" said Lady Gorgon, cursing Mr. Scully in her heart, and beginning to play a rapid tattoo with her feet, " that miscreant, that traitor, that—that attorney has been our ruin."

" Horrid man, if you please, but give me leave to tell you that the horrid man is not the sole cause of your ruin—if ruin you will call it.   I am sorry to say that I do candidly think Ministers believe that Sir George Gorgon has lost his influence in Oldborough as much through his own fault as through Mr. Scully's cleverness."

"Our own fault! Good heavens! Have we not done every-thing—everything that persons of our station in the county could do, to keep those misguided men? Have we not remonstrated, threatened, taken away our custom from the Mayor, established a Conservative apothecary—in fact, done all that gentlemen could do? But these are such times, Mr. Crampton: the spirit of revolution is abroad, and the great families of England are menaced by democratic insolence."

This was Sir George Gorgon's speech always after dinner, and was delivered by his lady with a great deal of stateliness. Some-what, perhaps, to her annoyance, Mr. Crampton only smiled, shook his head, and said—

"Nonsense, my dear Lady Gorgon—pardon the phrase, but I am a plain old man, and call things by their names. Now, will you let me whisper in your ear one word of truth? You have tried all sorts of remonstrances, and exerted yourself to maintain your in-fluence in every way, except the right one, and that is——"

"What, in Heaven's name?"

"Conciliation. We know your situation in the borough. Mr. Scully's whole history, and, pardon me for saying so (but we men in office know everything), yours——"

Lady Gorgon's ears and cheeks now assumed the hottest hue of crimson. She thought of her former passages with Scully, and of the days when—but never mind when: for she suffered her veil to fall, and buried her head in the folds of her handkerchief. Vain folds! The wily little Mr. Crampton could see all that passed behind the cambric, and continued—

"Yes, madam, we know the absurd hopes that were formed by a certain attorney twenty years since. We know how, up to this moment, he boasts of certain walks——"

"With the governess—we were always with the governess!" shrieked out Lady Gorgon, clasping her hands. "She was not the wisest of women."

"With the governess, of course," said Mr. Crampton firmly. "Do you suppose that any man dare breathe a syllable against your spotless reputation? Never, my dear madam; but what I would urge is this—you have treated your disappointed admirer too cruelly."

"What! the traitor who has robbed us of our rights?"

"He never would have robbed you of your rights if you had been more kind to him. You should be gentle, madam; you should forgive him—you should be friends with him."

"With a traitor, never!"

"Think what made him a traitor, Lady Gorgon; look in your

glass, and say if there be not some excuse for him? Think of the feelings of the man who saw beauty such as yours—I am a plain man and must speak—virtue such as yours, in the possession of a rival. By heavens, madam, I think he was *right* to hate Sir George Gorgon! Would you have him allow such a prize to be ravished from him without a pang on his part?"

"He was, I believe, very much attached to me," said Lady Gorgon, quite delighted; "but you must be aware that a young man of his station in life could not look up to a person of my rank."

"Surely not: it was monstrous pride and arrogance in Mr. Scully. But *que voulez-vous?* Such is the world's way. Scully could not help loving you—who that knows you can? I am a plain man, and say what I think. He loves you still. Why make an enemy of him, who would at a word be at your feet? Dearest Lady Gorgon, listen to me. Sir George Gorgon and Mr. Scully have already met—their meeting was our contrivance. It is for our interest, for yours, that they should be friends. If there were two Ministerial Members for Oldborough, do you think your husband's peerage would be less secure? I am not at liberty to tell you all I know on this subject; but do, I entreat you, be reconciled to him."

And after a little more conversation, which was carried on by Mr. Crampton in the same tender way, this important interview closed, and Lady Gorgon, folding her shawl round her, threaded certain mysterious passages and found her way to her carriage in Whitehall.

"I hope you have not been listening, you rogue?" said Mr. Crampton to his nephew, who blushed most absurdly by way of answer. "You would have heard great State secrets, if you had dared to do so. That woman is perpetually here, and if peerages are to be had for the asking, she ought to have been a duchess by this time. I would not have admitted her but for a reason that I have. Go you now and ponder upon what you have heard and seen. Be on good terms with Scully, and, above all, speak not a word concerning our interview—no, not a word even to your mistress. By the way, I presume, sir, you will recall your resignation?"

The bewildered Perkins was about to stammer out a speech, when his uncle, cutting it short, pushed him gently out of the door.

. . . .

At the period when the important events occurred which have been recorded here, parties ran very high, and a mighty struggle for the vacant Speakership was about to come on. The Right Honourable Robert Pincher was the Ministerial candidate, and Sir Charles Macabaw was patronised by the Opposition. The two

Members for Oldborough of course took different sides, the baronet
being of the Pincher faction, while Mr. William Pitt Scully strongly
supported the Macabaw party.

It was Mr. Scully's intention to deliver an impromptu speech
upon the occasion of the election, and he and his faithful Perkins
prepared it between them : for the latter gentleman had wisely kept
his uncle's counsel and his own, and Mr. Scully was quite ignorant
of the conspiracy that was brooding.   Indeed, so artfully had that
young Machiavel of a Perkins conducted himself, that when asked
by his patron whether he had given up his place in the Tape and
Sealing-Wax Office, he replied that "he *had* tendered his resignation," but did not say one word about having recalled it.

"You were right, my boy, quite right," said Mr. Scully.   "A
man of uncompromising principles should make no compromise."
And herewith he sat down and wrote off a couple of letters, one
to Mr. Hawksby, telling him that the place in the Sealing-Wax
Office was, as he had reason to know, vacant ; and the other to
his nephew, stating that it was to be his.   "Under the rose, my
dear Bob," added Mr. Scully, "it will cost you five hundred pounds ;
but you cannot invest your money better."

It is needless to state that the affair was to be conducted "with
the strictest secrecy and honour," and that the money was to pass
through Mr. Scully's hands.

While, however, the great Pincher and Macabaw question was
yet undecided, an event occurred to Mr. Scully, which had a great
influence upon his after-life.   A second grand banquet was given
at the Earl of Mantrap's : Lady Mantrap requested him to conduct
Lady Gorgon to dinner ; and the latter, with a charming timidity,
and a gracious melancholy look into his face (after which her veined
eyelids veiled her azure eyes), put her hand into the trembling one
of Mr. Scully and said, as much as looks could say, "Forgive and
forget."

Down went Scully to dinner.   There were dukes on his right
hand and earls on his left ; there were but two persons without title
in the midst of that glittering assemblage ; the very servants looked
like noblemen.   The cook had done wonders ; the wines were cool
and rich, and Lady Gorgon was splendid !   What attention did
everybody pay to her and to him !   Why *would* she go on gazing
into his face with that tender imploring look ?   In other words,
Scully, after partaking of soup and fish (he, during their discus-
sion, had been thinking over all the former love-and-hate passages
between himself and Lady Gorgon), turned very red, and began
talking to her.

"Were you not at the opera on Tuesday ?" began he, assuming

at once the airs of a man of fashion. " I thought I caught a glimpse of you in the Duchess of Diddlebury's box."

" Opera, Mr. Scully?" (pronouncing the word " Scully" with the utmost softness). " Ah, no ! we seldom go, and yet too often. For serious persons the enchantments of that place are too dangerous. I am so nervous—so delicate ; the smallest trifle so agitates, depresses, or irritates me, that I dare not yield myself up to the excitement of music. I am too passionately attached to it ; and, shall I tell you? it has such a strange influence upon me, that the smallest false note almost drives me to distraction, and for that very reason I hardly ever go to a concert or a ball."

" Egad," thought Scully, " I recollect when she would dance down a matter of five-and-forty couple, and jingle away at the ' Battle of Prague' all day."

She continued : " Don't you recollect, I do, with—oh, what regret !—that day at Oldborough race-ball, when I behaved with such sad rudeness to you? You will scarcely believe me, and yet I assure you 'tis the fact, the music had made me almost mad. Do let me ask your pardon for my conduct. I was not myself. Oh, Mr. Scully ! I am no worldly woman ; I know my duties, and I feel my wrongs. Nights and days have I lain awake weeping and thinking of that unhappy day—that I should ever speak so to an old friend ; for we *were* old friends, were we not ? "

Scully did not speak ; but his eyes were bursting out of his head, and his face was the exact colour of a deputy-lieutenant's uniform.

" That I should ever forget myself and you so ! How I have been longing for this opportunity to ask you to forgive me ! I asked Lady Mantrap, when I heard you were to be here, to invite me to her party. Come, I know you will forgive me—your eyes say you will. You used to look so in old days, and forgive me my caprices *then*. Do give me a little wine—we will drink to the memory of old days."

Her eyes filled with tears ; and poor Scully's hand caused such a rattling and trembling of the glass and the decanter that the Duke of Doldrum—who had been, during the course of this whispered sentimentality, describing a famous run with the Queen's hounds at the top of his voice—stopped at the jingling of the glass, and his tale was lost for ever. Scully hastily drank his wine, and Lady Gorgon turned round to her next neighbour, a little gentleman in black, between whom and herself certain conscious looks passed.

" I am glad poor Sir George is not here," said he, smiling.

Lady Gorgon said, " Pooh, for shame ! " The little gentleman was no other than Josiah Crampton, Esquire, that eminent financier, and he was now going through the curious calculation before mentioned, by which you *buy a man for nothing*. He intended to pay the very same price for Sir George Gorgon, too; but there was no need to tell the baronet so; only of this the reader must be made aware.

While Mr. Crampton was conducting this intrigue, which was to bring a new recruit to the Ministerial ranks, his mighty spirit condescended to ponder upon subjects of infinitely less importance, and to arrange plans for the welfare of his nephew and the young woman to whom he had made a present of his heart. These young persons, as we said before, had arranged to live in Mr. Perkins's own house in Bedford Row. It was of a peculiar construction, and might more properly be called a house and a half: for a snug little tenement of four chambers protruded from the back of the house into the garden. These rooms communicated with the drawing-rooms occupied by Mr. Scully; and Perkins, who acted as his friend and secretary, used frequently to sit in the one nearest the Member's study, in order that he might be close at hand to confer with that great man. The rooms had a private entrance too, were newly decorated, and in them the young couple proposed to live; the kitchen and garrets being theirs likewise. What more could they need? We are obliged to be particular in describing these apartments, for extraordinary events occurred therein.

To say the truth, until the present period Mr. Crampton had taken no great interest in his nephew's marriage, or, indeed, in the young man himself. The old gentleman was of a saturnine turn, and inclined to undervalue the qualities of Mr. Perkins, which were idleness, simplicity, enthusiasm, and easy good-nature.

"Such fellows never do anything in the world," he would say, and for such he had accordingly the most profound contempt. But when, after John Perkins's repeated entreaties, he had been induced to make the acquaintance of Miss Gorgon, he became instantly charmed with her, and warmly espoused her cause against her overbearing relations.

At his suggestion she wrote back to decline Sir George Gorgon's peremptory invitation, and hinted at the same time that she had attained an age and a position which enabled her to be the mistress of her own actions. To this letter there came an answer from Lady Gorgon which we shall not copy, but which simply stated that Miss Lucy Gorgon's conduct was unchristian, ungrateful, unladylike, and immodest; that the Gorgon family disowned her for the future, and left her at liberty to form whatever base connections she pleased.

"A pretty world this!" said Mr. Crampton, in a great rage, when the letter was shown to him. "This same fellow, Scully,

40

dissuades my nephew from taking a place, because Scully wants it for himself. This prude of a Lady Gorgon cries out shame, and disowns an innocent amiable girl: she a heartless jilt herself once, and a heartless flirt now. The Pharisees, the Pharisees! And to call mine a base family, too!"

Now, Lady Gorgon did not in the least know Mr. Crampton's connection with Mr. Perkins, or she would have been much more guarded in her language; but whether she knew it or not, the old gentleman felt a huge indignation, and determined to have his revenge.

"That's right, uncle! *Shall* I call Gorgon out?" said the impetuous young Perkins, who was all for blood.

"John, you are a fool," said his uncle. "You shall have a better revenge: you shall be married from Sir George Gorgon's house, and you shall see Mr. William Pitt Scully sold for nothing." This to the veteran diplomatist seemed to be the highest triumph which man could possibly enjoy.

It was very soon to take place: and, as has been the case ever since the world began, woman, lovely woman was to be the cause of Scully's fall. The tender scene at Lord Mantrap's was followed by many others equally sentimental. Sir George Gorgon called upon his colleague the very next day, and brought with him a card from Lady Gorgon inviting Mr. Scully to dinner. The attorney eagerly accepted the invitation, was received in Baker Street by the whole amiable family with much respectful cordiality, and was pressed to repeat his visits as country neighbours should. More than once did he call, and somehow always at the hour when Sir George was away at his club, or riding in the Park, or elsewhere engaged. Sir George Gorgon was very old, very feeble, very much shattered in constitution. Lady Gorgon used to impart her fears to Mr. Scully every time he called there, and the sympathising attorney used to console her as best he might. Sir George's country agent neglected the property—his lady consulted Mr. Scully concerning it. He knew to a fraction how large her jointure was; how she was to have Gorgon Castle for her life; and how, in the event of the young baronet's death (he, too, was a sickly poor boy), the chief part of the estates, bought by her money, would be at her absolute disposal.

"What a pity these odious politics prevent me from having you for our agent!" would Lady Gorgon say; and indeed Scully thought it was a pity too. Ambitious Scully! what wild notions filled his brain. He used to take leave of Lady Gorgon and ruminate upon these things; and when he was gone, Sir George and her Ladyship used to laugh.

"If we can but commit him—if we can but make him vote for

Pincher," said the General, "my peerage is secure. Hawksby and Crampton as good as told me so."

The point had been urged upon Mr. Scully repeatedly and adroitly. "Is not Pincher a more experienced man than Macabaw?" would Sir George say to his guest over their wine. Scully allowed it. "Can't you vote for him on personal grounds, and say so in the House?" Scully wished he could—how he wished he could! Every time the General coughed, Scully saw his friend's desperate situation more and more, and thought how pleasant it would be to be lord of Gorgon Castle. "Knowing my property," cried Sir George, "as you do, and with your talents and integrity, what a comfort it would be could I leave you as guardian to my boy! But these cursed politics prevent it, my dear fellow. Why *will* you be a Radical?" And Scully cursed politics too. "Hang the low-bred rogue," added Sir George, when William Pitt Scully left the house : " he will do everything but promise."

"My dear General," said Lady Gorgon, sidling up to him and patting him on his old yellow cheek—"My dear Georgy, tell me one thing,—are you jealous?"

"Jealous, my dear! and jealous of *that* fellow—pshaw!"

"Well, then, give me leave, and you shall have the promise to-morrow."

. . . .

To-morrow arrived. It was a remarkably fine day, and in the forenoon Mr. Perkins gave his accustomed knock at Scully's study, which was only separated from his own sitting-room by a double door. John had wisely followed his uncle's advice, and was on the best terms with the honourable Member.

"Here are a few sentences," said he, "which I think may suit your purpose. Great public services—undeniable merit—years of integrity—cause of Reform, and Macabaw for ever!" He put down the paper. It was, in fact, a speech in favour of Mr. Macabaw.

"Hush," said Scully, rather surlily ; for he was thinking how disagreeable it was to support Macabaw ; and besides, there were clerks in the room, whom the thoughtless Perkins had not at first perceived. As soon as that gentleman saw them, "You are busy, I see," continued he in a lower tone. "I came to say that I must be off duty to-day, for I am engaged to take a walk with some ladies of my acquaintance."

So saying, the light-hearted young man placed his hat unceremoniously on his head, and went off through his own door, humming a song. He was in such high spirits that he did not even think of closing the doors of communication, and Scully looked after him with a sneer.

"Ladies, forsooth!" thought he; "I know who they are. This precious girl that he is fooling with, for one, I suppose." He was right: Perkins was off on the wings of love, to see Miss Lucy; and she and Aunt Biggs and Uncle Crampton had promised this very day to come and look at the apartments which Mrs. John Perkins was to occupy with her happy husband.

"Poor devil!" so continued Mr. Scully's meditations, "it is almost too bad to do him out of his place; but my Bob wants it, and John's girl has, I hear, seven thousand pounds. His uncle will get him another place before all that money is spent." And herewith Mr. Scully began conning the speech which Perkins had made for him.

He had not read it more than six times,—in truth, he was getting it by heart,—when his head clerk came to him from the front room, bearing a card: a footman had brought it, who said his lady was waiting below. Lady Gorgon's name was on the card! To seize his hat and rush downstairs was, with Mr. Scully, the work of an infinitesimal portion of time.

It was indeed Lady Gorgon in her Gorgonian chariot.

"Mr. Scully," said she, popping her head out of window and smiling in a most engaging way, "I want to speak to you on something very particular *indeed*"—and she held him out her hand. Scully pressed it most tenderly: he hoped all heads in Bedford Row were at the windows to see him. "I can't ask you into the carriage, for you see the governess is with me, and I want to talk secrets to you."

"Shall I go and make a little promenade?" said mademoiselle innocently. And her mistress hated her for that speech.

"No. Mr. Scully, I am sure, will let me come in for five minutes?"

Mr. Scully was only too happy. My Lady descended and walked upstairs, leaning on the happy solicitor's arm. But how should he manage? The front room was consecrated to clerks; there were clerks too, as ill-luck would have it, in his private room. "Perkins is out for the day," thought Scully; "I will take her into his room." And into Perkins's room he took her—ay, and he shut the double doors after him too, and trembled as he thought of his own happiness.

"What a charming little study!" said Lady Gorgon, seating herself. And indeed it was very pretty: for Perkins had furnished it beautifully, and laid out a neat tray with cakes, a cold fowl, and sherry, to entertain his party withal. "And do you bachelors always live so well?" continued she, pointing to the little cold collation.

Mr. Scully looked rather blank when he saw it, and a dreadful suspicion crossed his soul; but there was no need to trouble Lady Gorgon with explanations: therefore, at once, and with much presence of mind, he asked her to partake of his bachelor's fare (she would refuse Mr. Scully nothing that day). A pretty sight would it have been for young Perkins to see strangers so unceremoniously devouring his feast. She drank—Mr. Scully drank—and so emboldened was he by the draught that he actually seated himself by the side of Lady Gorgon on John Perkins's new sofa.

Her Ladyship had of course something to say to him. She was a pious woman, and had suddenly conceived a violent wish for building a chapel-of-ease at Oldborough, to which she entreated him to subscribe. She enlarged upon the benefits that the town would derive from it, spoke of Sunday-schools, sweet spiritual instruction, and the duty of all well-minded persons to give aid to the scheme.

"I will subscribe a hundred pounds," said Scully, at the end of her Ladyship's harangue: "would I not do anything for you?"

"Thank you, thank you, dear Mr. Scully," said the enthusiastic woman. (How the "dear" went burning through his soul!) "Ah!" added she, "if you *would* but do anything for me—if you, who are so eminently, so truly distinguished, in a religious point of view, would but see the truth in politics too; and if I could see your name among those of the true patriot party in this empire, how blest—oh! how blest should I be! Poor Sir George often says he should go to his grave happy, could he but see you the guardian of his boy; and I, your old friend (for we *were* friends, William), how have I wept to think of you as one of those who are bringing our monarchy to ruin. Do, do promise me this too!" And she took his hand and pressed it between hers.

The heart of William Pitt Scully, during this speech, was thumping up and down with a frightful velocity and strength. His old love, the agency of the Gorgon property—the dear widow—five thousand a year clear—a thousand delicious hopes rushed madly through his brain, and almost took away his reason. And there she sat—she, the loved one, pressing his hand and looking softly into his eyes.

Down, down he plumped on his knees.

"Juliana!" shrieked he, "don't take away your hand! **My love—my only love!**—speak but those blessed words again! Call me William once more, and do with me what you will."

Juliana cast down her eyes and said, in the very smallest type—

"William!"

. . . .

—when the door opened, and in walked Mr. Crampton, leading Mrs. Biggs, who could hardly contain herself for laughing, and Mr. John

Perkins, who was squeezing the arm of Miss Lucy.   They had heard every word of the two last speeches.

For at the very moment when Lady Gorgon had stopped at Mr. Scully's door, the four above-named individuals had issued from Great James Street into Bedford Row.

Lucy cried out that it was her aunt's carriage, and they all saw Mr. Scully come out, bareheaded, in the sunshine, and my Lady descend, and the pair go into the house.   They meanwhile entered by Mr. Perkins's own private door, and had been occupied in examining the delightful rooms on the ground floor, which were to be his dining-room and library—from which they ascended a stair to visit the other two rooms, which were to form Mrs. John Perkins's drawing-room and bedroom.   Now whether it was that they trod softly, or that the stairs were covered with a grand new carpet and drugget, as was the case, or that the party within were too much occupied in themselves to heed any outward disturbances, I know not ; but Lucy, who was advancing with John (he was saying something about one of the apartments, the rogue !)—Lucy suddenly started and whispered, "There is somebody in the rooms ! " and at that instant began the speech already reported, " *Thank you, thank you, dear Mr. Scully,*" &c. &c., which was delivered by Lady Gorgon in a full clear voice ; for, to do her Ladyship justice, *she* had not one single grain of love for Mr. Scully, and, during the delivery of her little oration, was as cool as the coolest cucumber.

Then began the impassioned rejoinder, to which the four listened on the landing-place ; and then the little " *William,*" as narrated above : at which juncture Mr. Crampton thought proper to rattle at the door, and, after a brief pause, to enter with his party.

"William" had had time to bounce off his knees, and was on a chair at the other end of the room.

"What, Lady Gorgon ! " said Mr. Crampton, with excellent surprise, " how delighted I am to see you !   Always, I see, employed in works of charity " (the chapel-of-ease paper was on her knees), " and on such an occasion, too,— it is really the most wonderful coincidence !   My dear madam, here is a silly fellow, a nephew of mine, who is going to marry a silly girl, a niece of your own."

" Sir, I——" began Lady Gorgon, rising.

"They heard every word," whispered Mr. Crampton eagerly. "Come forward, Mr. Perkins, and show yourself."   Mr. Perkins made a genteel bow.   " Miss Lucy, please to shake hands with your aunt ; and this, my dear madam, is Mrs. Biggs of Mecklenburgh Square, who, if she were not too old, might marry a gentleman in the Treasury, who is your very humble servant."   And with this gallant speech, old Mr. Crampton began helping everybody to sherry and cake.

As for William Pitt Scully, he had disappeared, evaporated, in the most absurd sneaking way imaginable. Lady Gorgon made good her retreat presently, with much dignity, her countenance undismayed, and her face turned resolutely to the foe.

.   .   .   .

About five days afterwards, that memorable contest took place in the House of Commons, in which the partisans of Mr. Macabaw were so very nearly getting him the Speakership. On the day that the report of the debate appeared in the *Times*, there appeared also an announcement in the Gazette as follows :—

"The King has been pleased to appoint John Perkins, Esquire, to be Deputy-Subcomptroller of His Majesty's Tape Office and Custos of the Sealing-Wax Department."

Mr. Crampton showed this to his nephew with great glee, and was chuckling to think how Mr. William Pitt Scully would be annoyed, who had expected the place, when Perkins burst out laughing and said, "By heavens, here is my own speech! Scully has spoken every word of it; he has only put in Mr. Pincher's name in the place of Mr. Macabaw's."

"He is ours now," responded his uncle, "and I told you *we would have him for nothing.* I told you, too, that you should be married from Sir George Gorgon's, and here is proof of it."

It was a letter from Lady Gorgon, in which she said that, "had she known Mr. Perkins to be a nephew of her friend Mr. Crampton, she never for a moment would have opposed his marriage with her niece, and she had written that morning to her dear Lucy, begging that the marriage breakfast should take place in Baker Street."

"It shall be in Mecklenburgh Square," said John Perkins stoutly; and in Mecklenburgh Square it was.

William Pitt Scully, Esquire, was, as Mr. Crampton said, hugely annoyed at the loss of the place for his nephew. He had still, however, his hopes to look forward to, but these were unluckily dashed by the coming in of the Whigs. As for Sir George Gorgon, when he came to ask about his peerage, Hawksby told him that they could not afford to lose him in the Commons, for a Liberal Member would infallibly fill his place.

And now that the Tories are out and the Whigs are in, strange to say a Liberal does fill his place. This Liberal is no other than Sir George Gorgon himself, who is still longing to be a lord, and his lady is still devout and intriguing. So that the Members for Oldborough have changed sides, and taunt each other with apostasy, and hate each other cordially. Mr. Crampton still chuckles over the manner in which he tricked them both, and talks of those five minutes during which he stood on the landing-place, and hatched and executed his " Bedford-Row Conspiracy."

GOING TO SEE A MAN HANGED

GOING TO SEE A MAN HANGED

July 1840

X——, who had voted with Mr. Ewart for the abolition of the punishment of death, was anxious to see the effect on the public mind of an execution, and asked me to accompany him to see Courvoisier killed. We had not the advantage of a sheriff's order, like the "six hundred noblemen and gentlemen" who were admitted within the walls of the prison; but determined to mingle with the crowd at the foot of the scaffold, and take up our positions at a very early hour.

As I was to rise at three in the morning, I went to bed at ten, thinking that five hours' sleep would be amply sufficient to brace me against the fatigues of the coming day. But, as might have been expected, the event of the morrow was perpetually before my eyes through the night, and kept them wide open. I heard all the clocks in the neighbourhood chime the hours in succession; a dog from some court hard by kept up a pitiful howling; at one o'clock, a cock set up a feeble melancholy crowing; shortly after two the daylight came peeping grey through the window-shutters; and by the time that X—— arrived, in fulfilment of his promise, I had been asleep about half-an-hour. He, more wise, had not gone to rest at all, but had remained up all night at the Club along with Dash and two or three more. Dash is one of the most eminent wits in London, and had kept up the company merry all night with appropriate jokes about the coming event. It is curious that a murder is a great inspirer of jokes. We all like to laugh and have our fling about it; there is a certain grim pleasure in the circum-stance—a perpetual jingling antithesis between life and death, that is sure of its effect.

In mansion or garret, on down or straw, surrounded by weeping friends and solemn oily doctors, or tossing unheeded upon scanty hospital beds, there were many people in this great city to whom that Sunday night was to be the last of any that they should pass on earth here.   In the course of half-a-dozen dark wakeful hours, one had leisure to think of these (and a little, too, of that certain supreme night, that shall come at one time or other, when he who writes shall be stretched upon the last bed, prostrate in the last struggle, taking the last look of dear faces that have cheered us here, and lingering—one moment more—ere we part for the tremendous journey); but, chiefly, I could not help thinking, as each clock sounded, what is *he* doing now? has *he* heard it in his little room in Newgate yonder?   Eleven o'clock.   He has been writing until now.   The gaoler says he is a pleasant man enough to be with; but he can hold out no longer, and is very weary. "Wake me at four," says he, "for I have still much to put down." From eleven to twelve the gaoler hears how he is grinding his teeth in his sleep.   At twelve he is up in his bed and asks, "Is it the time?"   He has plenty more time yet for sleep; and he sleeps, and the bell goes on tolling.   Seven hours more—five hours more. Many a carriage is clattering through the streets, bringing ladies away from evening parties; many bachelors are reeling home after a jolly night; Covent Garden is alive; and the light coming through the cell-window turns the gaoler's candle pale.   Four hours more!   "Courvoisier," says the gaoler, shaking him, "it's four o'clock now, and I've woke you as you told me; but there's no call for you *to get up yet.*"   The poor wretch leaves his bed, how-ever, and makes his last toilet; and then falls to writing, to tell the world how he did the crime for which he has suffered.   This time he will tell the truth and the whole truth.   They bring him his breakfast "from the coffee-shop opposite—tea, coffee, and thin bread and butter."   He will take nothing, however, but goes on writing.   He has to write to his mother—the pious mother far away in his own country—who reared him and loved him; and even now has sent him her forgiveness and her blessing.   He finishes his memorials and letters, and makes his will, disposing of his little miserable property of books and tracts that pious people have furnished him with.   " Ce 6 Juillet 1840.   François Benjamin Courvoisier vous donne ceci, mon ami, pour souvenir." He has a token for his dear friend the gaoler; another for his dear friend the under-sheriff.   As the day of the convict's death draws nigh, it is painful to see how he fastens upon everybody who approaches him, how pitifully he clings to them and loves them.

While these things are going on within the prison (with which we are made accurately acquainted by the copious chronicles of such events which are published subsequently), X——'s carriage has driven up to the door of my lodgings, and we have partaken of an elegant *déjeuner* that has been prepared for the occasion. A cup of coffee at half-past three in the morning is uncommonly pleasant; and X—— enlivens us with the repetition of the jokes that Dash has just been making. Admirable, certainly—they must have had a merry night of it, that's clear; and we stoutly debate whether, when one has to get up so early in the morning, it is best to have an hour or two of sleep, or wait and go to bed afterwards at the end of the day's work. That fowl is extraordinarily tough— the wing, even, is as hard as a board; a slight disappointment, for there is nothing else for breakfast. "Will any gentleman have some sherry and soda-water before he sets out? It clears the brains famously." Thus primed, the party sets out. The coachman has dropped asleep on the box, and wakes up wildly as the hall-door opens. It is just four o'clock. About this very time they are waking up poor—pshaw! who is for a cigar? X—— does not smoke himself; but vows and protests, in the kindest way in the world, that he does not care in the least for the new drab-silk linings in his carriage. Z——, who smokes, mounts, however, the box. "Drive to Snow Hill," says the owner of the chariot. The policemen, who are the only people in the street, and are standing by, look knowing—they know what it means well enough.

How cool and clean the streets look, as the carriage startles the echoes that have been asleep in the corners all night. Somebody has been sweeping the pavements clean in the night-time surely; they would not soil a lady's white satin shoes, they are so dry and neat. There is not a cloud or a breath in the air, except Z——'s cigar, which whiffs off, and soars straight upwards in volumes of white pure smoke. The trees in the squares look bright and green —as bright as leaves in the country in June. We who keep late hours don't know the beauty of London air and verdure; in the early morning they are delightful—the most fresh and lively companions possible. But they cannot bear the crowd and the bustle of mid-day. You don't know them then—they are no longer the same things. We have come to Gray's Inn; there is actually dew upon the grass in the gardens; and the windows of the stout old red houses are all in a flame.

As we enter Holborn the town grows more animated; and there are already twice as many people in the streets as you see at mid-day in a German *Residenz* or an English provincial town. The ginshop keepers have many of them taken their shutters down, and many persons are issuing from them pipe in hand. Down they go along the broad bright street, their blue shadows marching *after* them; for they are all bound the same way, and are bent like us upon seeing the hanging.

It is twenty minutes past four as we pass St. Sepulchre's : by this time many hundred people are in the street, and many more are coming up Snow Hill.   Before us lies Newgate Prison ; but something a great deal more awful to look at, which seizes the eye at once, and makes the heart beat, is

There it stands black and ready, jutting out from a little door in the prison.   As you see it, you feel a kind of dumb electric shock, which causes one to start a little, and give a sort of gasp for breath.   The shock is over in a second ; and presently you examine the object before you with a certain feeling of complacent curiosity. At least, such was the effect that the gallows produced upon the writer, who is trying to set down all his feelings as they occurred, and not to exaggerate them at all.

After the gallows-shock had subsided, we went down into the crowd, which was very numerous, but not dense as yet.   It was evident that the day's *business* had not begun.   People sauntered up, and formed groups, and talked ; the new-comers asking those who seemed *habitués* of the place about former executions ; and did the victim hang with his face towards the clock or towards Ludgate Hill ? and had he the rope round his neck when he came on the scaffold, or was it put on by Jack Ketch afterwards ? and had Lord W—— taken a window, and which was he ?   I may mention the noble Marquis's name, as he was not at the exhibition.   A pseudo W—— was pointed out in an opposite window, towards whom all the people in our neighbourhood looked eagerly, and with great respect too.   The mob seemed to have no sort of ill-will against him, but sympathy and admiration.   This noble lord's personal courage and strength have won the plebs over to him.   Perhaps his exploits against policemen have occasioned some of this popularity ; for the mob hate them, as children the schoolmaster.

Throughout the whole four hours, however, the mob was extra-ordinarily gentle and good-humoured.   At first we had leisure to talk to the people about us; and I recommend X——'s brother senators of both sides of the House to see more of this same people and to appreciate them better.   Honourable Members are battling and struggling in the House; shouting, yelling, crowing, hear-hearing, pooh-poohing, making speeches of three columns, and gaining "great Conservative triumphs," or "signal successes of the Reform cause," as the case may be.   Three hundred and ten gentlemen of good fortune, and able for the most part to quote Horace, declare solemnly that unless Sir Robert comes in, the nation is ruined. Three hundred and fifteen on the other side swear by their great gods that the safety of the empire depends upon Lord John; and to this end they quote Horace too.   I declare that I have never been in a great London crowd without thinking of what they call the two "great" parties in England with wonder.   For which of the two great leaders do these people care, I pray you?   When Lord Stanley withdrew his Irish Bill the other night, were they in transports of joy, like worthy persons who read the *Globe* and the *Chronicle?* or when he beat the Ministers, were they wild with delight, like honest gentlemen who read the *Post* and the *Times?* Ask yonder ragged fellow, who has evidently frequented debating-clubs, and speaks with good sense and shrewd good-nature.   He cares no more for Lord John than he does for Sir Robert; and, with due respect be it said, would mind very little if both of them were ushered out by Mr. Ketch, and took their places under yonder black beam.   What are the two great parties to him, and those like him?   Sheer wind, hollow humbug, absurd claptraps; a silly mummery of dividing and debating, which does not in the least, however it may turn, affect his condition.   It has been so ever since the happy days when Whigs and Tories began; and a pretty pastime no doubt it is for both.   August parties, great balances of British freedom: are not the two sides quite as active, and eager, and loud, as at their very birth, and ready to fight for place as stoutly as ever they fought before?   But lo! in the meantime, whilst you are jangling and brawling over the accounts, Populus, whose estate you have administered while he was an infant, and could not take care of himself—Populus has been growing and growing, till he is every bit as wise as his guardians.   Talk to our ragged friend.   He is not so polished, perhaps, as a member of the "Oxford and Cambridge Club;" he has not been to Eton; and never read Horace in his life; but he can think just as soundly as the best of you; he can speak quite as strongly in his own rough way; he has been reading all sorts of books of late years, and gathered together no little information.   He is as good a man as the common run of us; and there are ten million more men in the

country, as good as he—ten million, for whom we, in our infinite
superiority, are acting as guardians, and to whom, in our bounty,
we give—exactly nothing. Put yourself in their position, worthy
sir. You and a hundred others find yourselves in some lone place,
where you set up a government. You take a chief, as is natural;
he is the cheapest order-keeper in the world. You establish half-a-
dozen worthies, whose families you say shall have the privilege to
legislate for you for ever ; half-a-dozen more, who shall be appointed
by a choice of thirty of the rest : and the other sixty, who shall
have no choice, vote, place, or privilege at all. Honourable sir,
suppose that you are one of the last sixty : how will you feel, you
who have intelligence, passions, honest pride, as well as your
neighbour ; how will you feel towards your equals, in whose hands
lie all the power and all the property of the community ? Would
you love and honour them, tamely acquiesce in their superiority,
see their privileges, and go yourself disregarded without a pang ?
you are not a man if you would. I am not talking of right or
wrong, or debating questions of government. But ask my friend
there, with the ragged elbows and no shirt, what he thinks ? You
have your party, Conservative or Whig, as it may be. You believe
that an aristocracy is an institution necessary, beautiful, and
virtuous. You are a gentleman, in other words, and stick by
your party.

And our friend with the elbows (the crowd is thickening hugely
all this time) sticks by *his*. Talk to him of Whig or Tory, he grins
at them : of virtual representation, pish ! He is a *democrat*, and
will stand by his friends, as you by yours ; and they are twenty
millions, his friends, of whom a vast minority now, a majority a few
years hence, will be as good as you. In the meantime we shall
continue electing, and debating, and dividing, and having every day
new triumphs for the glorious cause of Conservatism, or the glorious
cause of Reform, until——

.   .   .   .

What is the meaning of this unconscionable republican tirade
—*à propos* of a hanging ? Such feelings, I think, must come
across any man in a vast multitude like this. What good sense
and intelligence have most of the people by whom you are surrounded ; how much sound humour does one hear bandied about
from one to another ! A great number of coarse phrases are
used, that would make ladies in drawing-rooms blush ; but the
morals of the men are good and hearty. A ragamuffin in the
crowd (a powdery baker in a white sheep's-wool cap) uses some
indecent expression to a woman near : there is an instant cry of
shame, which silences the man, and a dozen people are ready to give

the woman protection. The crowd has grown very dense by this time, it is about six o'clock, and there is great heaving, and pushing, and swaying to and fro ; but round the women the men have formed a circle, and keep them as much as possible out of the rush and trample. In one of the houses, near us, a gallery has been formed on the roof. Seats were here let, and a number of persons of various degrees were occupying them. Several tipsy dissolute-looking young men, of the Dick Swiveller cast, were in this gallery. One was lolling over the sunshiny tiles, with a fierce sodden face, out of which came a pipe, and which was shaded by long matted hair, and a hat cocked very much on one side. This gentleman was one of a party which had evidently not been to bed on Sunday night, but had passed it in some of these delectable night-houses in the neighbour- hood of Covent Garden. The debauch was not over yet, and the women of the party were giggling, drinking, and romping, as is the wont of these delicate creatures ; sprawling here and there, and falling upon the knees of one or other of the males. Their scarves were off their shoulders, and you saw the sun shining down upon the bare white flesh, and the shoulder-points glittering like burning- glasses. The people about us were very indignant at some of the proceedings of this debauched crew, and at last raised up such a yell as frightened them into shame, and they were more orderly for the remainder of the day. The windows of the shops opposite began to fill apace, and our before-mentioned friend with ragged elbows pointed out a celebrated fashionable character who occupied one of them ; and, to our surprise, knew as much about him as the *Court Journal* or the *Morning Post*. Presently he entertained us with a long and pretty accurate account of the history of Lady ——, and indulged in a judicious criticism upon her last work. I have met with many a country gentleman who had not read half as many books as this honest fellow, this shrewd *prolétaire* in a black shirt. The people about him took up and carried on the conversation very knowingly, and were very little behind him in point of information. It was just as good a company as one meets on common occasions. I was in a genteel crowd in one of the galleries at the Queen's coronation ; indeed, in point of intelligence, the democrats were quite equal to the aristocrats. How many more such groups were there in this immense multitude of nearly forty thousand, as some say ? How many more such throughout the country ? I never yet, as I said before, have been in an English mob without the same feeling for the persons who composed it, and without wonder at the vigorous orderly good sense and intelligence of the people.

The character of the crowd was as yet, however, quite festive. Jokes bandying about here and there, and jolly laughs breaking out.

Some men were endeavouring to climb up a leaden pipe on one of the houses. The landlord came out, and endeavoured with might and main to pull them down. Many thousand eyes turned upon this contest immediately. All sorts of voices issued from the crowd, and uttered choice expressions of slang. When one of the men was pulled down by the leg, the waves of this black mob-ocean laughed innumerably ; when one fellow slipped away, scrambled up the pipe, and made good his lodgment on the shelf, we were all made happy, and encouraged him by loud shouts of admiration. What is there so particularly delightful in the spectacle of a man clambering up a gas-pipe? Why were we kept for a quarter of an hour in deep interest gazing upon this remarkable scene? Indeed it is hard to say : a man does not know what a fool he is until he tries ; or, at least, what mean follies will amuse him. The other day I went to Astley's, and saw clown come in with a fool's cap and pinafore, and six small boys who represented his schoolfellows. To them enters schoolmaster ; horses clown, and flogs him hugely on the back part of his pinafore. I never read anything in Swift, Boz, Rabelais, Fielding, Paul de Kock, which delighted me so much as this sight, and caused me to laugh so profoundly. And why? What is there so ridiculous in the sight of one miserably rouged man beating another on the breech? Tell us where the fun lies in this and the before-mentioned episode of the gas-pipe? Vast, indeed, are the capacities and ingenuities of the human soul that can find, in incidents so wonderfully small, means of contemplation and amusement.

Really the time passed away with extraordinary quickness. A thousand things of the sort related here came to amuse us. First the workmen knocking and hammering at the scaffold, mysterious clattering of blows was heard within it, and a ladder painted black was carried round, and into the interior of the edifice by a small side door. We all looked at this little ladder and at each other —things began to be very interesting. Soon came a squad of policemen : stalwart rosy-looking men, saying much for City feeding ; well dressed, well limbed, and of admirable good-humour. They paced about the open space between the prison and the barriers which kept in the crowd from the scaffold. The front line, as far as I could see, was chiefly occupied by blackguards and boys— professional persons, no doubt, who saluted the policemen on their appearance with a volley of jokes and ribaldry. As far as I could judge from faces, there were more blackguards of sixteen and seventeen than of any maturer age ; stunted, sallow, ill-grown lads, in rugged fustian, scowling about. There were a considerable number of girls, too, of the same age : one that Cruikshank and Boz might have taken as a study for Nancy. The girl was a young thief's mistress evidently; if attacked, ready to reply without a particle of modesty; could give as good ribaldry as she got; made no secret (and there were several inquiries) as to her profession and means of livelihood. But with all this, there was something good about the girl; a sort of devil-may-care candour and simplicity that one could not fail to see. Her answers to some of the coarse questions put to her, were very ready and good-humoured. She had a friend with her of the same age and class, of whom she seemed to be very fond, and who looked up to her for protection. Both of these women had beautiful eyes. Devil-may-care's were extraordinarily bright and blue, an admirably fair complexion, and a large red mouth full of white teeth. *Au reste*, ugly, stunted, thick-limbed, and by no means a beauty. Her friend could not be more than fifteen. They were not in rags, but had greasy cotton shawls, and old faded rag-shop bonnets. I was curious to look at them, having, in late fashionable novels, read many accounts of such personages. Bah! what figments these novelists tell us! Boz, who knows life well, knows that his Miss Nancy is the most unreal fantastical personage possible; no more like a thief's mistress than one of Gesner's shepherdesses resembles a real country wench. He dare not tell the truth concerning such young ladies. They have, no doubt, virtues like other human creatures; nay, their position engenders virtues that are not called into exercise among other women. But on these an honest painter of human nature has no right to dwell; not being able to paint the whole portrait, he has no right to present one or two favourable points as characterising the whole; and therefore, in fact, had better leave the picture alone altogether. The new French literature is essentially false and worthless from this very error—the writers giving us favourable pictures of monsters, and (to say nothing of decency or morality) pictures quite untrue to nature.

But yonder, glittering through the crowd in Newgate Street—see, the Sheriffs' carriages are slowly making their way. We have been here three hours! Is it possible that they can have passed so soon? Close to the barriers where we are, the mob has become so dense that it is with difficulty a man can keep his feet. Each man, however, is very careful in protecting the women, and all are full of jokes and good-humour. The windows of the shops opposite are now pretty nearly filled by the persons who hired them. Many young dandies are there with moustaches and cigars; some quiet fat family-parties, of simple honest tradesmen and their wives, as we fancy, who are looking on with the greatest imaginable calmness, and sipping their tea. Yonder is the sham Lord W——, who is flinging various articles among the crowd; one of his companions, a tall, burly man, with large moustaches, has provided himself with a squirt, and is aspersing the mob with brandy-and-water. Honest gentleman! high-bred aristocrat! genuine lover of humour and wit! I would walk some miles so see thee on the treadmill, thee and thy Mohawk crew!

We tried to get up a hiss against these ruffians, but only had a trifling success; the crowd did not seem to think their offence very heinous; and our friend, the philosopher in the ragged elbows, who had remained near us all the time, was not inspired with any such savage disgust at the proceedings of certain notorious young gentlemen, as I must confess fills my own particular bosom. He only said, "So-and-so is a lord, and they'll let him off," and then discoursed about Lord Ferrers being hanged. The philosopher knew the history pretty well, and so did most of the little knot of persons about him, and it must be a gratifying thing for young gentlemen to find that their actions are made the subject of this kind of conversation.

Scarcely a word had been said about Courvoisier all this time. We were all, as far as I could judge, in just such a frame of mind as men are in when they are squeezing at the pit-door of a play, or pushing for a review or a Lord Mayor's show. We asked most of the men who were near us, whether they had seen many executions? most of them had, the philosopher especially; whether the sight of them did any good? "For the matter of that, no; people did not care about them at all; nobody ever thought of it after a bit." A countryman, who had left his drove in Smithfield, said the same thing; he had seen a man hanged at York, and spoke of the ceremony with perfect good sense, and in a quiet sagacious way.

J. S——, the famous wit, now dead, had, I recollect, a good story upon the subject of executing, and of the terror which the punishment inspires. After Thistlewood and his companions were hanged, their heads were taken off, according to the sentence, and the executioner, as he severed each, held it up to the crowd, in the proper orthodox way, saying, "Here is the head of a traitor!" At the sight of the first ghastly head the people were struck with terror, and a general expression of disgust and fear broke from them. The second head was looked at also with much interest, but the excitement regarding the third head diminished. When the executioner had come to the last of the heads, he lifted it up, but, by some clumsiness, allowed it to drop. At this the crowd yelled out, "Ah, Butter-fingers!"—the excitement had passed entirely away. The punishment had grown to be a joke—Butter-fingers was the word— a pretty commentary, indeed, upon the august nature of public executions, and the awful majesty of the law.

It was past seven now; the quarters rang and passed away; the crowd began to grow very eager and more quiet, and we turned back every now and then and looked at St. Sepulchre's clock. Half-an-hour, twenty-five minutes. What is he doing now? He has his irons off by this time. A quarter: he's in the press-room now, no doubt. Now at last we had come to think about the man we were going to see hanged. How slowly the clock crept over the last quarter! Those who were able to turn round and see (for the crowd was now extraordinarily dense) chronicled the time, eight minutes, five minutes; at last—ding, dong, dong, dong!—the bell is tolling the chimes of eight.

. . . . . .

Between the writing of this line and the last, the pen has been put down, as the reader may suppose, and the person who is addressing him has gone through a pause of no very pleasant thoughts and recollections. The whole of the sickening, ghastly, wicked scene passes before the eyes again; and, indeed, it is an awful one to see, and very hard and painful to describe.

As the clock began to strike, an immense sway and movement swept over the whole of that vast dense crowd. They were all uncovered directly, and a great murmur arose, more awful, bizarre, and indescribable than any sound I had ever before heard. Women and children began to shriek horribly. I don't know whether it was the bell I heard; but a dreadful quick feverish kind of jangling noise mingled with the noise of the people, and lasted for about two minutes. The scaffold stood before us, tenantless and black; the black chain was hanging down ready from the beam. Nobody came. "He has been respited," some one said; another said, "He has killed himself in prison."

Just then, from under the black prison-door, a pale quiet head peered out. It was shockingly bright and distinct; it rose up directly, and a man in black appeared on the scaffold, and was silently followed by about four more dark figures. The first was a tall grave man: we all knew who the second man was. "*That's he—that's he!*" you heard the people say, as the devoted man came up.

I have seen a cast of the head since, but, indeed, should never have known it. Courvoisier bore his punishment like a man, and walked very firmly. He was dressed in a new black suit, as it seemed: his shirt was open. His arms were tied in front of him. He opened his hands in a helpless kind of way, and clasped them once or twice together. He turned his head here and there, and looked about him for an instant with a wild imploring look. His mouth was contracted into a sort of pitiful smile. He went and

placed himself at once under the beam, with his face towards St.
Sepulchre's. The tall grave man in black twisted him round swiftly
in the other direction, and, drawing from his pocket a nightcap,
pulled it tight over the patient's head and face.   I am not ashamed
to say that I could look no more, but shut my eyes as the last
dreadful act was going on which sent this wretched guilty soul into
the presence of God.

If a public execution is beneficial—and beneficial it is, no doubt,
or else the wise laws would not encourage forty thousand people
to witness it—the next useful thing must be a full description
of such a ceremony, and all its *entourages*, and to this end the
above pages are offered to the reader.   How does an individual man
feel under it?   In what way does he observe it,—how does he view
all the phenomena connected with it,—what induces him, in the first
instance, to go and see it,—and how is he moved by it afterwards?
The writer has discarded the magazine "We" altogether, and spoken
face to face with the reader, recording every one of the impressions
felt by him as honestly as he could.
I must confess, then (for " I " is the shortest word, and the best
in this case), that the sight has left on my mind an extraordinary
feeling of terror and shame.   It seems to me that I have been
abetting an act of frightful wickedness and violence, performed by a
set of men against one of their fellows ; and I pray God that it may
soon be out of the power of any man in England to witness such
a hideous and degrading sight.   Forty thousand persons (say the
Sheriffs), of all ranks and degrees,—mechanics, gentlemen, pick-
pockets, members of both Houses of Parliament, street-walkers,
newspaper-writers, gather together before Newgate at a very early
hour ; the most part of them give up their natural quiet night's
rest, in order to partake of this hideous debauchery, which is more
exciting than sleep, or than wine, or the last new ballet, or any
other amusement they can have.   Pickpocket and Peer, each is
tickled by the sight alike, and has that hidden lust after blood
which influences our race.   Government, a Christian Government,
gives us a feast every now and then : it agrees—that is to say, a
majority in the two Houses agrees—that for certain crimes it is
necessary that a man should be hanged by the neck.   Government commits the criminal's soul to the mercy of God, stating that
here on earth he is to look for no mercy ; keeps him for a fortnight
to prepare, provides him with a clergyman to settle his religious
matters (if there be time enough, but Government can't wait) ; and
on a Monday morning, the bell tolling, the clergyman reading out
the word of God, " I am the resurrection and the life," " The Lord

giveth, and the Lord taketh away,"—on a Monday morning, at eight o'clock, this man is placed under a beam, with a rope connecting it and him; a plank disappears from under him, and those who have paid for good places may see the hands of the Government agent, Jack Ketch, coming up from his black hole, and seizing the prisoner's legs, and pulling them, until he is quite dead—strangled.

Many persons, and well-informed newspapers, say that it is mawkish sentiment to talk in this way, morbid humanity, cheap philanthropy, that any man can get up and preach about. There is the *Observer*, for instance, a paper conspicuous for the tremendous sarcasm which distinguishes its articles, and which falls cruelly foul of the *Morning Herald*. "Courvoisier is dead," says the *Observer*: "he died as he had lived—a villain; a lie was in his mouth. Peace be to his ashes. We war not with the dead." What a magnanimous *Observer*! From this, *Observer* turns to the *Herald*, and says, "Fiat justitia, ruat cœlum." So much for the *Herald*.

We quote from memory, and the quotation from the *Observer* possibly is,—"De mortuis nil nisi bonum;" or, "Omne ignotum pro magnifico;" or, "Sero nunquam est ad bonos mores via;" or, "Ingenuas didicisse fideliter artes emollit mores nec sinit esse feros:" all of which pithy Roman apophthegms would apply just as well.

"Peace be to his ashes. He died a villain." This is both benevolence and reason. Did he die a villain? The *Observer* does not want to destroy him body and soul, evidently, from that pious wish that his ashes should be at peace. Is the next Monday but one after the sentence the time necessary for a villain to repent in? May a man not require more leisure—a week more—six months more—before he has been able to make his repentance sure before Him who died for us all?—for all, be it remembered,—not alone for the judge and jury, or for the sheriffs, or for the executioner who is pulling down the legs of the prisoner,—but for him too, murderer and criminal as he is, whom we are killing for his crime. Do we want to kill him body and soul? Heaven forbid! My Lord in the black cap specially prays that Heaven may have mercy on him; but he must be ready by Monday morning.

Look at the documents which came from the prison of this unhappy Courvoisier during the few days which passed between his trial and execution. Were ever letters more painful to read? At first, his statements are false, contradictory, lying. He has not repented then. His last declaration seems to be honest, as far as the relation of the crime goes. But read the rest of his statement, the account of his personal history, and the crimes which he committed in his young days,—then "how the evil thought came to him to put his hand to the work,"—it is evidently the writing of a mad, distracted man. The horrid gallows is perpetually before him; he is wild with dread and remorse. Clergymen are with him ceaselessly; religious tracts are forced into his hands; night and day they ply him with the heinousness of his crime, and exhortations to repentance. Read through that last paper of his; by Heaven, it is pitiful to read it. See the Scripture phrases brought in now and anon; the peculiar terms of tract-phraseology (I do not wish to speak of these often meritorious publications with disrespect); one knows too well how such language is learned,—imitated from the priest at the bedside, eagerly seized and appropriated, and confounded by the poor prisoner.

But murder is such a monstrous crime (this is the great argument),—when a man has killed another it is natural that he should be killed. Away with your foolish sentimentalists who say no—it is *natural*. That is the word, and a fine philosophical opinion it is —philosophical and Christian. Kill a man, and you must be killed in turn: that is the unavoidable *sequitur*. You may talk to a man for a year upon the subject, and he will always reply to you, "It is natural, and therefore it must be done. Blood demands blood."

Does it? The system of compensations might be carried on *ad infinitum*,—an eye for an eye, a tooth for a tooth, as by the old Mosaic law. But (putting the fact out of the question, that we have had this statute repealed by the Highest Authority), why, because you lose your eye, is that of your opponent to be extracted likewise? Where is the reason for the practice? And yet it is just as natural as the death dictum, founded precisely upon the same show of sense. Knowing, however, that revenge is not only evil, but useless, we have given it up on all minor points. Only to the last we stick firm, contrary though it be to reason and to Christian law.

There is some talk, too, of the terror which the sight of this spectacle inspires, and of this we have endeavoured to give as good a notion as we can in the above pages. I fully confess that I came away down Snow Hill that morning with a disgust for murder, but it was for *the murder I saw done*. As we made our way through the immense crowd, we came upon two little girls of eleven and twelve years: one of them was crying bitterly, and begged, for Heaven's sake, that some one would lead her from that horrid place. This was done, and the children were carried into a place of safety. We asked the elder girl—and a very pretty one—what brought her into such a neighbourhood? The child grinned knowingly, and said, "We've koom to see the mon hanged!" Tender law, that brings out babes upon such errands, and provides them with such gratifying moral spectacles !

This is the 20th of July, and I may be permitted for my part to declare that, for the last fourteen days, so salutary has the impression of the butchery been upon me, I have had the man's face continually before my eyes ; that I can see Mr. Ketch at this moment, with an easy air, taking the rope from his pocket ; that I feel myself ashamed and degraded at the brutal curiosity which took me to that brutal sight ; and that I pray to Almighty God to cause this disgraceful sin to pass from among us, and to cleanse our land of blood.

THE END

Milton Keynes UK
Ingram Content Group UK Ltd.
UKHW031457231024
450082UK00001B/83

9 781434 414403